THE IDEA OF PAKISTAN

STEPHEN PHILIP COHEN

OXFORD
UNIVERSITY PRESS

OXFORD

UNIVERSITY PRESS

YMCA Library Building, Jai Singh Road, New Delhi 110 001

Oxford University Press is a department of the University of Oxford. It furthers the
University's objective of excellence in research, scholarship, and education
by publishing worldwide in

Oxford New York

Auckland Cape Town Dar es Salaam Hong Kong Karachi
Kuala Lumpur Madrid Melbourne Mexico City Nairobi
New Delhi Shanghai Taipei Toronto

With offices in

Argentina Austria Brazil Chile Czech Republic France Greece
Guatemala Hungary Italy Japan Poland Portugal Singapore
South Korea Switzerland Thailand Turkey Ukraine Vietnam

Oxford is a registered trademark of Oxford University Press
in the UK and in certain other countries

Published in India by Oxford University Press, New Delhi

© Brookings Institution 2004

The moral rights of the author have been asserted
Database right Oxford University Press (maker)

First published 2005
Second impression 2005

Originally published in the United States of America
by Brookings Institution Press 2004

ISBN 019 567350 6

This edition for sale only in India, Bangladesh, Nepal, Bhutan,
Sri Lanka, and Myanmar

Printed by Roopak Printers Delhi, 110 032
Published by Manzar Khan, Oxford University Press
YMCA Library Building, Jai Singh Road, New Delhi 110 001

CONTENTS

MAPS

MAPS

Pakistan in 2004   xii

The Subcontinent on the Eve of Islam,
    and Early Arab Inroads, 700–975   14

The Ghurid and Mamluk Dynasties, 1170–1290
    and the Delhi Sultanate under the Khaljis and
    Tughluqs, 1290–1390   17

The Mughal Empire, 1556–1707   19

Choudhary Ramat Ali's 1940 Plan for Pakistan   27

Pakistan in 1947   40

Pakistan in 1972   76

Languages of Pakistan, Afghanistan, and Northwest India 209

PREFACE

It has taken me forty-four years to write this book—the length of time I have been studying Pakistan (and India). My early interests were in the role of the military, but I was unable to visit Pakistan until 1978, as an earlier application for a visa had been turned down by the government of Zulfiqar Ali Bhutto.

When I did visit Pakistan for the first time I was surprised to discover that my personal "idea of Pakistan" was wildly inaccurate: not better, not worse, just different. That trip led to a book, *The Pakistan Army*. Research for that book was made possible by General Zia ul-Haq, who promptly banned it, although he eventually told an aide to "let the professor's book be published." Zia's decision was only one of the many paradoxes I encountered in studying Pakistan, and the mixture of hope and frustration reflected in *The Pakistan Army* is to be found here as well.

This book is not quite comparable to *India: Emerging Power*. It focuses primarily on internal dynamics, not strategic policy. One important difference between the two states is that Pakistan's domestic and external policies are more entwined than those of India, partly because of Pakistan's more perilous geostrategic position and partly because the dominant Pakistan army looks both inward and outward. Writing this book provided me with the opportunity to extend my knowledge of Pakistan beyond the army and to gain a fuller understanding of the country's political parties, Islamists, civilian elites, and various ethnic, linguistic, and sectarian minorities. Above all, I have learned more about the contested *idea* of Pakistan.

Many individuals and institutions have assisted me on this journey. First and foremost, I wish to thank those Pakistanis who have given their time in innumerable discussions and meetings. My Pakistani friends have always been courteous and considerate, even when we have disagreed; I hope that they will find here an accurate representation of their views. In particular, I would like to thank Moonis Ahmar, Samina Ahmed, Qazi Hussein Ahmed, Akbar Ahmed, Benazir Bhutto, Pervaiz Iqbal Cheema, Mahmud Durrani, Ejaz Haider, Husain Haqqani, Pervez Hoodbhoy, Mushahid Hussain, Rifaat Hussein, Jehangir Karamat, Shaukat Qadir, Ashraf Jehangir Qazi, Ahmed Rashid, Hasan Askari Rizvi, Najam Sethi, Aqil Shah, Mohammed Waseem, and innumerable other civilians and serving officers and officials of the Pakistan government. Some Pakistanis may disagree with the arguments and conclusions of this book; I hope that in such cases it will lead to the beginning of a dialogue and not the end of a friendship.

Many Washington friends and colleagues have generously shared their knowledge and special insights. Chief among these are Marvin G. Weinbaum, now of the Middle East Institute and a friend and colleague for forty years; Nisar A. Chaudhry; Selig Harrison; Rodney Jones; Anatol Lieven; Polly Nayak; and former ambassadors Dennis Kux, William Milam, Robert Oakley, and Howard and Teresita Schaffer (whose own Pakistan project helpfully paralleled the writing of this book).

Brookings has provided me with admirable support and a lively intellectual home for over six years, and I would like to acknowledge the special help of my two junior colleagues, Sunil Dasgupta, who provided much of the research support, and Tanvi Madan, who helped bring the book to completion. We have been assisted over the years by diligent and hardworking associates, Azeema Cheema, Meena Mallipeddi, Zaid Safdar, Taylor Sherman, and Moeed Yusuf. Strobe Talbott contributed, among other things, the book's title, and Jim Steinberg provided a meticulous critique. At the Brookings Institution Press, Vicky Macintyre very ably edited the manuscript, while Inge Lockwood handled proofreading, and Enid Zafran indexed the pages. Larry Converse and Susan Woollen were helpful in developing the cover and getting the book to print. Generous support for the research and writing of this book was provided by the Smith Richardson Foundation and the United States Institute of Peace.

As ever, I wish to thank my wife, Roberta, for her unfailing support and for being my first and best reader and critic.

Finally, I am deeply grateful to my own students, past and present, including the hundreds of young Pakistanis, Indians, and Chinese who participated in the Summer Workshops on South Asian Security issues held since 1993 in Pakistan, India, Sri Lanka, Nepal, and China. They reinforce the wisdom of the Latin, *docendo discimus* (we learn by teaching).

THE
IDEA
OF PAKISTAN

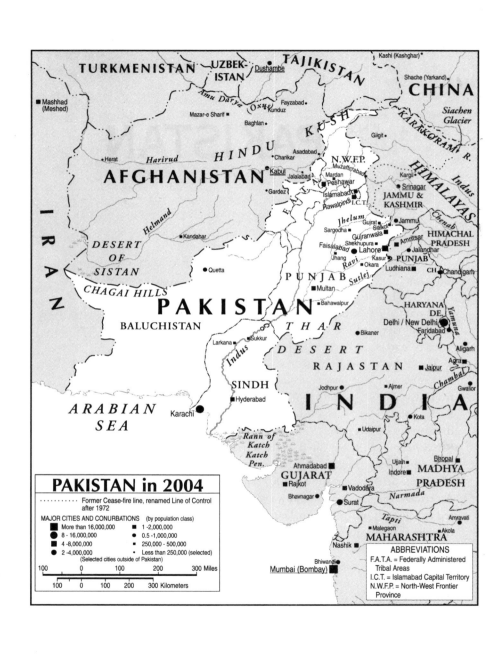

PAKISTAN in 2004

Former Cease-fire line, renamed Line of Control after 1972

MAJOR CITIES AND CONURBATIONS (by population class)

- More than 16,000,000
- 8 - 16,000,000
- 4 -8,000,000
- 2 -4,000,000
  (Selected cities outside of Pakistan)

- 1 -2,000,000
- 0.5 -1,000,000
- 250,000 - 500,000
- Less than 250,000 (selected)

100   0   100   200   300 Miles

100   0   100   200   300 Kilometers

ABBREVIATIONS
F.A.T.A. = Federally Administered Tribal Areas
I.C.T. = Islamabad Capital Territory
N.W.F.P. = North-West Frontier Province

INTRODUCTION

In recent years Pakistan has become a strategically important state, both criticized as a rogue power and praised as being on the front line in the ill-named war on terrorism. The final report of the National Commission on Terrorist Attacks upon the United States identifies Pakistan, along with Afghanistan and Saudi Arabia, as a high-priority state.

This is not a new development. In the 1950s and 1960s Pakistan was a member of two American-sponsored alliances, but then drifted away from Washington. In the 1980s Pakistan was a vital partner in evicting the Soviet Union from Afghanistan, even though its covert nuclear program drew much criticism. In 1996 it was one of three states (the others being Saudi Arabia and the United Arab Emirates, UAE) to recognize the Taliban regime, which was by then playing host to the terrorist organization al Qaeda. After September 11, 2001, Pakistan was again characterized by American officials as a vital ally, even though it was caught, and admitted to, covertly spreading nuclear technology to a number of states; further, its enthusiasm in tracking down al Qaeda and Taliban leaders was suspect.[1]

Unfortunately, the United States has only a few true Pakistan experts and knows remarkably little about this country. Much of what has been written is palpably wrong, or at best superficial.[2] Over the years, it has become difficult to conduct research in Pakistan's deteriorating security environment, and support for such work has dried up. It is little wonder, then, that views cover a wide spectrum, with "rogue state" at one extreme—some would call it a potential nuclear Yugoslavia or even the most dangerous place in the world.[3] The flamboyant French intellectual Bernard-Henri Levy called Pakistan "the most delinquent of nations."[4] According to a senior Indian diplomat, it "represents everything . . . in the forefront of U.S. concerns: religious fundamentalism, terrorism, weapons of mass destruction in possession of a failing state, a military dictatorship masquerading behind a pale democratic façade." To Jaswant Singh, former Indian minister of external affairs, Pakistan is "Taliban East."[5] Others, however, notably senior officials of the George W. Bush administration, have praised Pakistan as a misunderstood, but still effective, friend deserving of American support.[6]

To probe beyond the headlines, this book offers a double biography. One biography is that of the idea of Pakistan, the notion that India's Muslims needed a homeland for their protection and to fulfill their cultural and civilizational destiny. The second biography is that of the state of Pakistan, the largely military-dominated entity that now possesses nuclear weapons, has a hostile relationship with most of its neighbors, and is characterized by weak and uneven economic growth, political chaos, and sectarian violence.

I also try to peek into Pakistan's future, to ask whether failure is a strong possibility. If so, would Pakistan dissolve slowly or collapse in a sudden cataclysm? Or would it become an outlaw and threat to the entire world, acting as a base for international terrorism and perhaps sharing its nuclear weapons technology with other states and terrorist groups? Can Pakistan become a normal state at peace with its neighbors and itself?

In the ensuing discussion, I return to questions I addressed at length back in 1985.[7] At that time, I warned that Pakistan could again become its own worst enemy, that highly dangerous futures might be in store, including a repetition of the 1971 catastrophe when Pakistan became the first post–World War II state to break up.[8] Here, I again ask which policies—economic, political, strategic—pursued *now* might avert the worst outcomes and help steer the country in a direction compatible with its own identity and interests, as well as the key interests of the United States and Pakistan's important neighbors. A stable, prosperous, progressive Pakistan could trigger a new spurt of South Asian development, in partnership with India and Afghanistan.

Several factors bode well in this regard. Pakistan's economy was once viewed as a success story, and its governments, though often military in nature, have been relatively moderate and have maintained many political freedoms. For most of its history, Pakistan has oscillated between unstable democracy and benign authoritarianism. It has never had a popular revolution, its levels of political violence (except for the Bangladesh interregnum) have been high but not pathological, and it has always had a cohesive and well-educated political elite. This did not translate into a full-fledged democracy, but then Pakistan did not undergo the excesses of neighbors such as China or Iran, nor, despite its Islamic identity, did it veer toward religious authoritarianism. Pakistan does well in many areas and arguably can still emerge as a successful state and cohesive nation.

Hence it is necessary to take a nuanced view of "failure"—a term widely and imprecisely used to describe Pakistan. The term derives from a sparse literature on recent cases in which states were unable to deliver the most fundamental necessities to their citizens.[9] Most of these entities—Somalia, parts of sub-Saharan Africa, and Afghanistan—were hardly states to begin with and could not withstand the external and internal stresses that stripped away their capacity to provide food, shelter, and security to their citizens. However, surely the term also applies when states are unable to defend against foreign aggression, or, more spectacularly, when they commit genocide against their own citizens? Is it not a failure of the state when its leaders embark upon a ruinous quixotic policy? In short, failure is not a straightforward concept, since even the most advanced and competent states "fail" from time to time, either in relation to their own citizens or as political entities operating in a complex global environment. At least five kinds of failure can be identified:

—*The failure to live up to past expectations, one's own and those of others.* Nations seldom fulfill their high ideals and early promise. Pakistan, created as a haven for Indian Muslims, was to be a stable and prosperous Islamic state. The discrepancy between its early aspirations and contemporary reality is one of the country's more notable features.

—*Failure of vision.* Pakistan's founders expected the *idea* of Pakistan to shape the *state* of Pakistan; instead, a military bureaucracy governs the state and imposes its own vision of a Pakistani nation.

—*Economic failure.* With the loss of the very poor East Wing in 1971, Pakistan expected to gain middle-income status. But the economy did not fire up, and its per capita income today is below that of India.

—*Failure of leadership*. Pakistan has a distinct political and governing class: the "Establishment," a moderate oligarchy that has presided over many political, economic, and strategic disasters, and whose most promising leaders, notably Benazir Bhutto, have by and large disappointed their ardent supporters, creating further disillusionment with the political process.

—*Catastrophic failure*. Failing states, at one time absorbed by imperial powers or neighbors or placed under international trusteeship, today pose a highly visible and serious problem for the world, complicated by refugees and migrants, televised holocausts, and the internationalization of ethnic conflict. An additional concern in Pakistan's case is the possible spread of nuclear weapons, missiles, and Islamic radicalism: a catastrophically failed Pakistan would become a matter of grave concern to many states.

Like their neighbors, Pakistanis themselves are concerned about the country's future.[10] The internal debate intensified after the military again assumed power in 1999. Although some resigned themselves to another spell of military rule, hoping that this time the generals would "fix" the system once and for all, others grew cynical. The coup, they argued, simply represented another failure, adding to the four or five earlier ones.

Yet there is evidence that success and the high expectations of its founding fathers and friends abroad may not altogether elude Pakistan. State *resurrection* is not out of reach, as has been amply demonstrated in Eastern Europe, Latin America, and perhaps most dramatically in Russia—which had failed as the Soviet Union but was able to reinvent itself and take its place as a normal state with reasonable prospects for the future.

In laying out the evidence for this possibility in Pakistan's case, I begin with a historical overview, followed by a more detailed examination of the evolution of both the idea and the state of Pakistan (chapters 1–2), and then a survey of Pakistan's major political and social institutions, notably its military, political, Islamist, and regional elites (chapters 3–6). I also ask how they themselves diagnose Pakistan's assets and liabilities. What are their organizational or ideological imperatives? How do they establish the legitimacy of their own perspectives on Pakistan, and who are their key foreign allies? What policies would they introduce if they were to come to power? Next comes a discussion of some critical demographic, economic, and educational constraints in Pakistan (chapter 7) and the resulting range of its plausible "futures"(chapter 8). The book closes with some policy options for the United States (chapter 9).

Any study of Pakistan must be careful to see it as it is—not as an evil or blessed twin of India, to which it is often compared—but as a state with its own identity, logic, and future. My approach is to examine the way in which the idea of Pakistan intersects with the hard realities of the state and to determine what this bodes for the future. Pakistan is both interesting and alarming. It could emerge as the pariah of Asia. This is not a welcome prospect, but there are worse: a collapsing Pakistan, spewing out nuclear weapons and Islamic extremists, or even a Pakistan transformed into a truly radical and militant state.

Pakistan: A Short History

Until the arrival of Muslim traders, missionaries, and armies in the late seventh and early eighth centuries, the population of South Asia was primarily Hindu and Buddhist. By A.D. 1100 a number of Indo-Muslim states had been established, and by the sixteenth century the Mughal Empire dominated northern India. The British formally disbanded the empire in 1858, at which time about one-quarter of India's population were Muslims. They were concentrated in East Bengal, the Northwest Frontier, Punjab, Sindh, and Baluchistan, with large Muslim minorities in present-day Uttar Pradesh and Madhya Pradesh.[11]

India's Muslims slowly adapted to British rule yet maintained their identity, establishing the Aligarh Muslim University (1875) and the Muslim League (1906). The latter, dominated by wealthy landowners and Muslim professionals, was largely secular in orientation, though a basic concern was the fate of Muslims in a mainly Hindu political order. There was no suggestion of a separate Muslim state until 1930, when the Punjabi poet-politician Mohammed Iqbal raised the idea. Three years later a group of Indian students at Cambridge proposed naming it Pakistan. As the prospects for British withdrawal from South Asia increased, the Muslim League, led by the lawyer-politician Mohammed Ali Jinnah (born December 1876, died September 1948), declared its support for the idea of Pakistan at its 1940 Lahore session; one year later the most powerful of the religious—or Islamist—groups, the Jama'at-i-Islami, was founded.

Following negotiations between the British, the secular but largely Hindu Indian National Congress, and the Muslim League in 1946, the state of Pakistan was born on August 14, 1947, and India gained independence on August 15. Pakistan was carved out of five provinces of British India plus some princely states. Under the new boundaries, the provinces of Bengal and Punjab were partitioned, and millions of people had to move. The eastern part of Bengal, which was overwhelmingly Muslim (but with a 15 percent Hindu minority), became East Pakistan, or the East Wing. It was slightly more populous than West Pakistan (together their population was about a quarter of India's). Western Punjab, including the important princely state of Bahawalpur, became the Pakistani province of Punjab. The eastern area, and a number of ethnically Punjabi princely states, became the Indian state of Punjab. West Pakistan also included Baluchistan, the Northwest Frontier Province (NWFP), and Sindh.

However, India and Pakistan could not agree on the disposition of the state of Jammu and Kashmir and in October 1948 went to war over it, with former comrades now pitted against each other even though Pakistan's higher military command was still entirely British. A cease-fire brokered by the United Nations in January 1949 left about three-fourths of the state, including the prized Valley, in Indian hands. Since then Kashmir has figured in most India-Pakistan crises, including the 1965 war and the miniwar in Kargil in 1999. Obtaining justice for Muslim Kashmiris living in the Indian-administered parts of the state has been a central goal of Pakistan's foreign and security policy for five decades. Pakistan has tried diplomatic, military, and low-level military pressure on India to hold a plebiscite (as recommended in several UN resolutions) or to negotiate a change in the status quo, all to no avail. A fresh approach, featuring diplomacy rather than coercion, began in January 2004 after a summit meeting between Pakistan's president, Pervez Musharraf, and India's prime minister, Atal Behari Vajpayee. In a statement issued before the summit, Vajpayee indicated that he wanted to make a third "and last" effort to normalize relations with Pakistan. After some secret diplomacy between the two countries, President Musharraf stated that the UN resolutions on Kashmir might be set aside in the event of progress on a Kashmir settlement. Subsequently, both states began to ease travel and other restrictions, and an Indian cricket team toured Pakistan, to great popular acclaim in both countries. By July 2004 the India-Pakistan dialogue on nuclear confidence-building measures had resumed, but with little expectation of a breakthrough, or of rapid movement toward a dialogue on more contentious issues, such as Kashmir.

At independence, Jinnah was appointed Pakistan's governor-general, and his close associate, Liaquat Ali Khan, became prime minister, but neither man had deep roots in the new state. Jinnah was from Bombay and Liaquat had spent much of his career in North India. Then both suffered untimely deaths that threw the country into political chaos. Jinnah succumbed to tuberculosis on September 11, 1948, and Liaquat was assassinated at a political rally in Rawalpindi on October 17, 1951. Toward 1954 the Muslim League, whose supporters were in large part migrants from India, went into decline, losing power in both wings. Control fell to a coalition of émigré politicians, bureaucrats, and, eventually, the army. Also in 1954 the four provinces of West Pakistan were combined into a single administrative entity under a "One-Unit" scheme, to balance the more populous East Wing.

It was not until March 23, 1956, that the Constituent Assembly approved the first constitution, which renamed the state the Islamic Republic of Pakistan. A former soldier, Iskander Mirza, became president under the new constitution, which he abrogated two and a half years later, on October 7, 1958. Mirza was himself displaced in a 1958 coup by General Ayub Khan, beginning Pakistan's long experiment with military rule.

Pakistan has had four spells of direct or indirect military rule and several failed coup attempts. The successful coups were by Generals Ayub Khan (1958), Yahya Khan (1969), Zia ul-Haq (1977), and Pervez Musharraf (1999). Each was justified on the grounds of national security, with the army claiming to be Pakistan's ultimate protector, and each of the generals derided the incompetence or corruption of the politicians. Despite these claims and the variety of military governments, none left Pakistan better equipped to face its multiple domestic and foreign challenges. Of the failed coups, usually by low-level officers (the successful ones were led by the army chiefs), the first was the Rawalpindi Conspiracy of 1951, and the most recent an attempt by an Islamic-minded general and several junior officers in 1995; in 2004 several officers of lower rank were implicated in an assassination attempt on President Musharraf.

After winning 80 percent of the votes in a "yes or no" referendum, Ayub became president on February 17, 1960. He strengthened the

One-Unit scheme by appointing a powerful governor of West Pakistan and introduced a system of "basic democracies" that provided the framework for National Assembly elections in April 1962. Assisted by a tolerant attitude toward private enterprise and considerable foreign aid, Pakistan experienced rapid economic growth during Ayub's tenure. He also concluded a division of the Indus waters with India in 1960, which secured a reliable flow of water.

Pakistan's growing foreign ties had been marked by a mutual defense agreement with the United States and entry into the Southeast Asia Treaty Organization (SEATO) in 1954, as well as membership in the Baghdad Pact (later Central Treaty Organization, CENTO) in 1955. However, these counted for little during the full-scale war with India over Kashmir between September 6 and 22, 1965. American interest in the region then faded, and it fell to the Soviet Union to mediate the postwar negotiations between Ayub Khan and Prime Minister Lal Bahadur Shastri. By then Pakistan had developed a close strategic tie with China; this eventually yielded significant military assistance, including missile and nuclear technology and large quantities of technically mediocre aircraft and armor.

The 1965 war contributed to domestic unrest, as did Ayub's ill health and treatment of the East Wing (which, he remarked, was militarily expendable). On March 26, 1969, the army commander, General Yahya Khan, removed Ayub, imposed martial law, dissolved the national and provincial assemblies, and did away with the One-Unit scheme. When East Pakistan's Awami League Party won an absolute majority in the new national assembly two years later, Yahya denied its leader, Sheikh Mujibur Rahman, the prime ministership and instead allowed a military crackdown in East Pakistan. In response, Sheikh Mujibur declared Bangladesh an independent state, and an independent government was formed. Because India had militarily supported the Bangladesh movement, war again broke out between India and Pakistan on December 3, 1971.

Two weeks later, the Pakistan army was defeated in the east (there were few battles in the west), and more than 90,000 Pakistani troops surrendered. East Pakistan became the independent state of Bangladesh, and Pakistan lost over half of its population. China, which had developed a strategic and military tie with Pakistan to maintain a balance with the Soviet Union and India, declined to intervene on Pakistan's behalf, while the United States did little more than make political and military gestures, which included the dispatch of a carrier, the *Enterprise*, to the Bay of Bengal.

The loss of East Pakistan not only meant a loss of people but it changed the nature of the state. East Bengal, though Pakistan's poorest region, was home to a more moderate Islam. This region had also contributed an important and diverse Bengali element to Pakistani society and culture. The balance of political power changed too. Punjab became Pakistan's dominant province, being both more populous than Sindh, Baluchistan, or the NWFP and economically far more prosperous, as well as contributing the overwhelming number of officers and soldiers to the ruling military.

Following the loss, Yahya was forced to resign by his fellow officers. They turned to West Pakistan's most charismatic politician, Zulfiqar Ali Bhutto, to assume power in what remained of Pakistan. Bhutto first became chief martial law administrator, then president, and finally, in a new constitutional order, prime minister. The constitution, approved by parliament on April 10, 1973, though subsequently modified, still provides the overall framework for Pakistani governance.

One of Bhutto's first acts was to sign a peace treaty with Indian prime minister Indira Gandhi at Simla in July 1972, and the following year to secure the return of Pakistani prisoners of war captured by India in East Pakistan. At the same time, he ruthlessly suppressed a separatist movement in Baluchistan that was modeled after the East Pakistan breakaway. Bhutto also pursued a policy of "Islamic socialism" attempting to appease both his Islamist critics and his leftist supporters, but his autocratic style of governance (and the army's wariness) led to mass protests over delegitimized parliamentary elections and a coup on July 4, 1977. Subsequently, in a dubious trial, the Lahore High Court convicted Bhutto of conspiracy to commit murder, and he was hanged in Rawalpindi on April 4, 1979.

While in office, Bhutto had begun a Pakistani nuclear weapons program. After he was deposed in 1977 by General Zia ul-Haq, it fell under the army's direct control. Nuclear weapons were seen as a way of countering India's larger army, matching India's suspected nuclear program, and providing an umbrella under which Pakistan might launch low-level probes in the disputed Kashmir region.

General Zia ul-Haq was the first (and so far the only) Pakistani leader truly committed to a program of Islamization. The United States became

Zia's staunchest supporter since Pakistan was the channel for military aid to the Afghan mujahiddin, then engaging the Soviet Union in Afghanistan.[12] The Zia years saw the acceleration of the nuclear program, growing Islamization in the armed forces and Pakistani society at large, and a decline in spending on health, education, and social services. Under American pressure, Zia did allow nonparty elections in February 1985 and lifted martial law in the last week of that year; but he dismissed his own prime minister (Mohammad Khan Junejo) in May 1988 when the latter showed some sign of independence on foreign policy issues. After Zia died in a still-unexplained plane crash on August 17, 1988, both the press and Pakistan's political parties showed an impressive regenerative capacity, and Pakistan embarked on a ten-year experiment with democracy.

This experiment featured two prominent politicians, Benazir Bhutto (Zulfiqar Ali Bhutto's intelligent, Western-educated daughter) and Nawaz Sharif, a member of a Punjabi business family that Zia had brought into politics. Benazir had assumed the leadership of the left-centrist Pakistan People's Party (PPP), the country's only true national party, and Nawaz headed the reborn Pakistan Muslim League, a somewhat more conservative group. Benazir and Nawaz each served as prime minister for two terms—Benazir from December 1988 to August 1990 and October 1993 to November 1996, and Nawaz from November 1990 to July 1993 and February 1997 to October 1999.

For the most part, freedom was protected, other parties were allowed to function normally, and it appeared that Pakistan had evolved into a two-party democracy. However, the army, conservative members of Pakistan's powerful Establishment, the intelligence services, and the former bureaucrat Ghulam Ishaq Khan, who had succeeded Zia as president, could not resist the temptation to interfere behind the scenes. Neither Benazir nor Nawaz served a full term—both were dismissed by the president (often with the connivance of the army), and the election process was manipulated by the internal wing of the Inter-Services Intelligence Directorate (ISID) and other intelligence services. Benazir and Nawaz provided the excuse for their own dismissals as both engaged in or tolerated a degree of corruption. Furthermore, Nawaz showed signs of deep insecurity by interfering with the operations of Pakistan's judiciary and indulging in other abuses of power. The army also suspected the two of being "soft" on India and the Kashmir problem. Under their governments,

Pakistan's Varied Islam

Islam is divided into two major sects, Sunni and Shi'ia. Pakistan mirrors the global percentage of each: of the total number of Muslims, about 85 percent are Sunni and 12 percent are Shi'ia. Shiism is anchored in Iran, an almost totally Shi'ia state. The sects differ over the legitimate successor to the Prophet and are organized along different lines. By analogy, Sunnis resemble Protestants in that they believe they have a direct spiritual linkage to God; Shi'ia tend to be more formally organized, like the Catholic Church, and the clergy (many of whom trace their theological roots back to Iran and Iraq) are hierarchically structured. Sunni and Shi'ia have separate mosques in Pakistan, although in some cases—notably in the army—they pray together in a syncretic Islamic service.

Pakistan is also home to a number of other Islamic sects, including the Ismailis, the followers of the Aga Khan. The Ismailis reside in some of the urban areas, primarily Karachi, and in the far northern mountainous region; they have contributed to Pakistan's medical and charitable institutions, mostly through the renowned Aga Khan Foundation. There is no theological opposition to them, as there was to another sect, the Ahmediyyas, founded in the Punjabi town of Qadian in 1889. Its followers were declared non-Muslims by Pakistan's parliament in 1974, a move supported by Zulfiqar Ali Bhutto. They were subsequently threatened with death if they passed themselves off as Muslims, prayed in a mosque, or uttered the basic declaration of faith, the *Kalima*. While these four are the main formal sects, most Pakistanis in rural areas remain vague about their Islam, and their religion is strongly intermixed with folk practices, Sufi beliefs, and even Hinduism and Buddhism.

sectarian violence also increased, especially in Karachi and Lahore, with Sunni and Shi'ia murder squads targeting doctors and other elites.

During the democratic interregnum, as in previous decades, the army remained the true power in Pakistan, coming to the forefront again in October 1999 when Nawaz's army chief, General Pervez Musharraf, dismissed the civilian government and assumed power as "chief executive." Musharraf accused Nawaz of attempted murder after the former's aircraft was diverted on a return flight from abroad. The murder charge was dropped, but Nawaz and his immediate family were exiled to Saudi Arabia; Benazir also resides outside Pakistan, while her husband remains imprisoned back home, awaiting trial for corruption.

After a farcical national referendum in May 2001, Musharraf declared himself president on June 20, 2001. Pakistan's intelligence services were active in the subsequent October 2002 election, preventing both the PML and the PPP from effectively organizing themselves. This enabled a coalition of Islamic parties to come to power in the Northwest Frontier Province and share power in Baluchistan. A kind of parliamentary government exists in Pakistan today, with Musharraf as president, choosing and dismissing prime ministers as he sees fit—first selecting a pliable Baluch politician, Mir Zafarullah Khan Jamali, and then forcing him to resign eighteen months later, in June 2004, to be replaced by the minister of finance, Shaukat Aziz, a former Citibank official. It remains to be seen whether Aziz's technocratic credentials are sufficient for him to tackle Pakistan's sectarian and ethnic conflicts and still retain the confidence of the army.

Since 1999 Musharraf has, with Shaukat Aziz's expert guidance, succeeded to some extent in repairing the economic damage from ten years of free-spending governments. There has been some progress in the form of modest growth and an increase in available foreign exchange, but Pakistan remains an unattractive place for investment. Despite the rise of sectarian violence and the better performance of the Islamic and religious parties, there is no "green wave" washing over Pakistan; most of its citizens remain devout Muslims but are not attracted to Islamic extremism. Yet, given the increase in poverty, the still faltering economy, the lack of a real political process, and Pakistan's continuing conflicts with its neighbors—notably Afghanistan and India—few Pakistanis are optimistic about the future. Musharraf's version of military rule was far more tolerant than that of Zia, but as with previous military regimes, the army appears unable to govern Pakistan itself but will not allow anyone else the opportunity to do so either.

Furthermore, Pakistan's repeated conflicts with India continue to alarm the international community. Since 1987 there have been three major near-war crises (in 1987, 1990, and 2002) and one miniwar (in the Kargil region of Kashmir in 1999). All but the first involved two nuclear weapons states. These crises alternate with periods of détente and seeming cordiality, hence the complexity of India-Pakistan relations and the dual role played by the army in Pakistan—with one face turned inward and enforcing its version of political order and stability, the other turned toward India (and to a lesser degree, Afghanistan) and the threats lying there. Even the army is aware of India's growing strategic and economic power and Pakistan's relative decline, which may have prompted the decision to soften Pakistan's position on Kashmir in late 2003. This, plus cooperation with the United States in rounding up al Qaeda and Taliban remnants, led to a series of assassination attempts against President Musharraf, who in the waning days of 2003 pledged to give up his army post by the end of 2004, seek parliamentary legitimacy as president, and serve at least one full term in that office, through 2007. As I discuss more fully in chapter 8, Musharraf's declared course suggests one plausible future for Pakistan, but there are other, less benign ones.

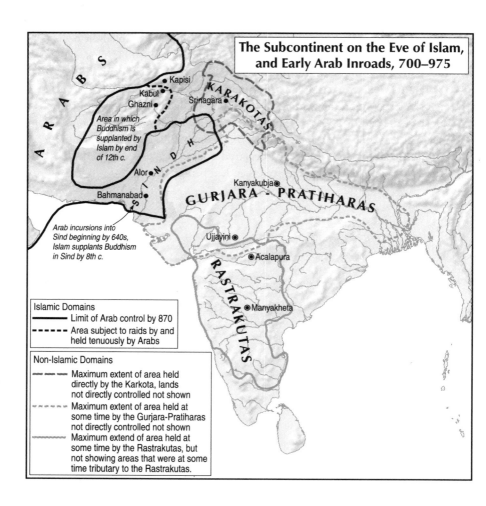

The Subcontinent on the Eve of Islam, and Early Arab Inroads, 700–975

Kapisi

Kabul
Ghazni
Srinagara

ARABS

KARAKOTAS

SINDH

Area in which
Buddhism is
supplanted by
Islam by end
of 12th c.

Alor

Bahmanabad

Kanyakubja

GURJARA - PRATIHARAS

Arab incursions into
Sind beginning by 640s,
Islam supplants Buddhism
in Sind by 8th c.

Ujjayini

Acalapura

RASTRAKUTAS

Manyakheta

Islamic Domains
———— Limit of Arab control by 870
- - - - - Area subject to raids by and
held tenuously by Arabs

Non-Islamic Domains

Maximum extent of area held
directly by the Karkota, lands
not directly controlled not shown

Maximum extent of area held at
some time by the Gurjara-Pratiharas
not directly controlled not shown

Maximum extend of area held at
some time by the Rastrakutas, but
not showing areas that were at some
time tributary to the Rastrakutas.

CHAPTER ONE

THE IDEA
OF PAKISTAN

For millennia, ideas, people, and goods moved freely between the Indian subcontinent and what is now the Middle East, with routine trade well established by the sixth century A.D. In A.D. 660 the second caliph, Umar, sent the first Arab expedition to Sindh, and in 711 the province was conquered by Mohammad ibn Qasim. Along with advanced military power came missionaries and traders, and the process of conversion to Islam began. There are still important Muslim trading communities throughout South India, Sri Lanka, and the Maldives—and farther east in Malaysia, Indonesia, and the Philippines. These traders (and minor Muslim rulers) shared their knowledge of the sea route from East Africa to India with the Portuguese explorer Vasco da Gama, the first European to make the long journey around Africa and across the Arabian Sea.[1] Parenthetically, just as Islam came to India in the seventh to eighth century, South Indian Hindu kingdoms began their exploration and domination over large parts of Southeast Asia.

Origins of the Idea of Pakistan

In the early eleventh century Muslim invaders arrived in India's northwest, with the Mongols following in the thirteenth. By then Indo-Islamic states had been established in north and northwest India. Some invaders were seasonal, based in present-day Afghanistan, and were influenced by Persian political and military models. These Central Asians came to loot and convert but eventually stayed on to rule.

By 1290 nearly all of India was under the loose domination of Muslim rulers. Two and a half centuries of internecine war among various Indo-Islamic, Hindu, and Sikh states followed, after which the Mughals established an empire in the early sixteenth century that stretched from the Northwest Frontier to Bengal and down to the Deccan (present-day Andhra Pradesh). The attempts of Mughal emperor Aurangzeb to extend his control to South India, coupled with his brutal treatment of his subjects, led to a crisis of empire.[2] The empire lasted until 1858, when it was finally eliminated by the British. A few major Muslim and Hindu principalities remained intact; these were all absorbed into India or Pakistan after the British departed India in 1947.

Islam, Conversion, and Mythology

As Islam moved eastward, it encountered Persian, Hindu, Buddhist, and eventually Chinese cultures, none of which was composed of "people of the book"—Christians and Jews. This encounter along the new Asian frontier led to considerable adaptation and change in Islam, a religion of the desert lands. In India, the caste system crept into Islam, and Hindu religious practices were incorporated in Islamic rituals. In turn, Islam had a profound impact on India, notably in transforming Sikhism from a pietistic Hindu sect into a martial faith. Further, those variants of Islam such as Sufism, which incorporated saint worship, mysticism, and piety, had a great attraction for India's Hindus and Buddhists, and today Sufism is important in a good part of Pakistan, especially Sindh and Punjab.

Because of wide regional variations, the impact of Islam on India is difficult to summarize. In the south and the east, Muslim rule was relatively benign and inclusivist. In Hyderabad-Deccan and Bengal, Muslim rulers presided over vast Hindu populations, and conversion was extensive and peaceful.[3] In some instances Hindu institutions received state patronage and there was extensive intermarriage between Muslim ruling families and their high-caste Hindu counterparts, as family ties were used to shore up political alliances. Gradually, many Muslim dynasties, especially the Mughals, became "Indianized" through the marriage of Muslim princes and Hindu princesses, with their children assuming prominent positions in the state apparatus. However, some regions experienced the militant,

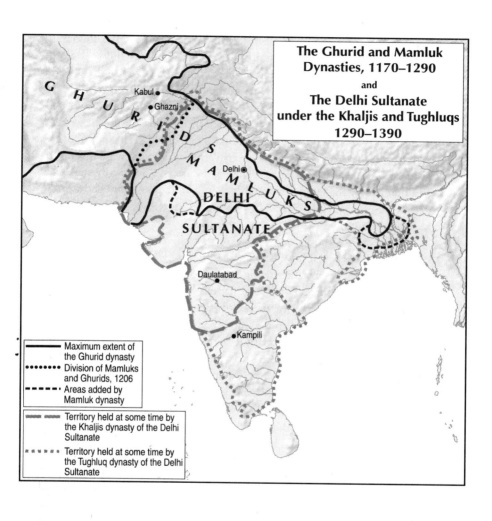

The Ghurid and Mamluk
Dynasties, 1170–1290

and

The Delhi Sultanate
under the Khaljis and Tughluqs
1290–1390

Maximum extent of
the Ghurid dynasty
Division of Mamluks
and Ghurids, 1206
Areas added by
Mamluk dynasty

Territory held at some time by
the Khaljis dynasty of the Delhi
Sultanate

Territory held at some time by
the Tughluq dynasty of the Delhi
Sultanate

Kabul
Ghazni
Delhi
DELHI
SULTANATE
GHURIDS
MAMLUKS
Daulatabad
Kampili

exclusivist side of Islam, with the destruction of Hindu temples and attacks on the Brahmin-dominated Hindu social order taking place in such renowned pilgrimage destinations as Multan (in the Pakistani province of Punjab) and Somnath (in the contemporary Indian state of Gujarat). The most vivid account of these conquests is that of the Central Asian scholar Alberuni, who wrote in the early eleventh century: "Mahmud [of Ghazni] utterly ruined the prosperity of the country, and performed there wonderful exploits, by which the Hindus became like atoms of dust scattered in all directions, and like a tale of old in the mouth of the people. Their scattered remains cherish, of course, the most inveterate aversion towards all Muslims."[4] These sites are still politically sensitive, and that is why the Hindu nationalist politician L. K. Advani chose Somnath to begin his "Rath Yatra" on September 25, 1990, in an attempt to mobilize Hindu sentiment.

No question is more contentious, or of more contemporary political relevance, than that of how Islam spread *within* South Asia.[5] The entire state of Pakistan rests on certain interpretations of that expansion, and in India conversion and reconversion to Hinduism are intensely divisive political issues. Remarkably, there is little objective scholarship on the subject, but there is an enormous amount of mythmaking and fabrication.

The fact is that Muslims constituted about one-quarter of India's population around the time the British arrived, concentrated in eastern Bengal and Sindh, Northwest Frontier Province (NWFP), and parts of Punjab. Muslims were a majority in East Bengal and parts of India's northwest, although it took the British nearly a hundred years to recognize this. Their earlier estimates were that Muslims constituted no more than 1 to 10 percent of the total population, and not until the first census, in the late nineteenth century, were accurate numbers obtained. The British were also uncertain about how many Muslims were immigrant-descended (*Ashraf*) and how many were converts; further, it took them some time before they (and Indian scholars) came to understand that conversion to Islam was still taking place, in some places at a rapid rate, even in parts of India directly governed by the British.[6]

Of the many theories about the distribution and numbers of Muslims in India, one was that Muslim power rested on superior military technology and tactics, which enabled Muslim rulers to forcefully convert Hindus to Islam.[7] Another (favored by some British writers) was that

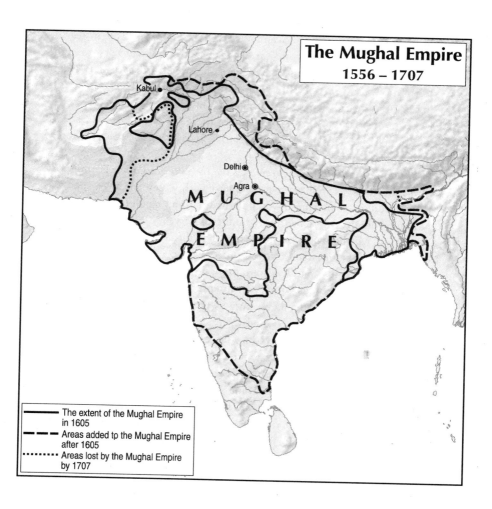

The Mughal Empire
1556 – 1707

Kabul

Lahore

Delhi

Agra

M U G H A L

E M P I R E

The extent of the Mughal Empire
in 1605

Areas added to the Mughal Empire
after 1605

Areas lost by the Mughal Empire
by 1707

Islam, like Christianity, was a monotheistic religion, and pagan Hinduism could not withstand the moral arguments of either. According to some Muslim writers, the Sufi movement played an important role in recruiting converts to Islam, as indicated by the close linkage between Hinduism, Buddhism, and Sufism, a pietistic, mystical form of Islam.[8] Islam, others point out, matched up well with the requirements of an expanding economic and demographic frontier in places like East Bengal. A large number of conversions took place there (as on the island of Java) because Islam was adaptable and effective in assisting the colonization of new lands.[9]

A significant factor in the west was the proximity to other Islamic societies and states, as well as the greater ease with which Sindh—which was more Buddhist than Hindu—could convert to an egalitarian Islam.[10] In parts of Punjab, where for many hundreds of years differences between Hindu and Muslim were less important than differences of clan and tribe, conversion to Islam often occurred for economic and social reasons.[11] As in present-day India, families commonly designated one son for conversion to facilitate dealings with a Muslim ruler. Forced conversions, which occurred in parts of India as recently as the 1920s, should also be mentioned, although these have been exaggerated by both Hindu and Muslim historians. In sum, Islam thrived in India for a variety of reasons: intermarriage, conversion, the attractiveness of Islamic egalitarianism, and social and political advantages in a context of Muslim rulers.

Until the 1920s English-speaking Muslims were not too concerned about seeing Hindus, Buddhists, and followers of folk religions convert to Islam. Rather, the presence of masses of Muslim converts was a political liability, and educated Muslims focused on rescuing the noble families who had suffered under British rule. When it became evident that numbers counted, however, the upper-class Westernized Muslims of India began welcoming the *awwam* (Urdu for lower or uneducated classes).[12] They argued that the converted Indian Muslim had a distinctive political identity, as did some earlier British writers and scholars who had identified the "Mohammedans" of India as a distinct nation.

In the 1920s more and more Muslims and Hindus engaged in myth creation, a process that continues unchecked today in both India and Pakistan. On one hand, many Muslims, including the leaders of the Pakistan movement, saw India's Islamic period as a golden age, an era of high culture and material and spiritual progress that was all but absent under the displaced "pagan" Hindu regimes.[13] To Hindu nationalists, on the other hand, the coming of the Muslims brought a new dark age, marked by the mass destruction of places of worship, forced conversions, and Muslim cultural imperialism. In fact, scholars have found little evidence of massive cruelty and cultural barbarism, or the wholesale destruction of temples, only some temple looting and capture of holy images by Muslim and Hindu rulers alike.[14] Histories of this nature are manufactured by propagandists on both sides and are periodically refreshed by such events as the demolition of the Babri Masjid in India in 1992, the communal riots in the state of Gujarat in 2002, and attacks on Hindu temples and Christian churches throughout the subcontinent.[15]

The Company and the Raj

The first great encounter between Islam and the West took place between 711 and 1492, when Christian armies expelled the Muslims from the Iberian peninsula. The second occurred when Portuguese, Dutch, French, and British traders came to South Asia and warred with each other in the subcontinent, allied with various Hindu, Muslim, and Sikh regional powers. Eventually the triumphant British stayed on to rule.

The first British "government" in India was that of the crown-chartered East India Company. The Company gradually assumed responsibility for governance from the decaying Mughal Empire and layered a Chinese-inspired bureaucracy over existing Mughal and Hindu patterns. This was a major innovation in the history of South Asia. The role of the British-Indian bureaucracy, which had originally been established as a means of collecting revenue (the title of district officials in many parts of India is still "collector"), expanded to include administering law and order, disaster relief, and development projects. Until recently the collector also served as a magistrate, but now judicial and executive functions are separated at the district level in both India and Pakistan. Building upon the early canal system created by the Mughals, the British also helped India devise the world's largest integrated irrigation system, which had to be divided between India and Pakistan in 1960, however, since it lay astride their frontier.

In addition, the British bequeathed a lasting military legacy to Pakistan. Emulating the French, the East India Company recruited Indians and trained them along Western lines. These "sepoys" (a corruption of *spahi*, the Persian-Turkic word for cavalryman) were led by British officers selected and promoted largely on merit. Two hundred years later, the professional descendants of those British officers run Pakistan.

In 1833 control of India passed from the East India Company to Whitehall, although a powerless Mughal emperor, Bahadur Shah Zafar, continued to sit on Delhi's throne. This arrangement did not prevent massive discontent in India, culminating in the uprising of 1857 one consequence of which was that the dual pretext of Company rule and Mughal sovereignty was swept away. The events of 1857 are referred to as an uprising by Pakistani historians, a mutiny by the British, and the First War of Independence by nationalist Indians.

Whereas the Company had governed the many for the benefit of the few, namely, its shareholders, the new government of India, the Raj, was responsible to London and hence developed strategic and moral justifications for its rule retroactively. Strategically, the British saw India as the jewel in the crown of the empire, although by the 1930s the jewel had become less of an asset. Morally, they envisioned their rule as a mission: to elevate the Indian people to the point where they might, eventually, become independent of British tutelage. Rubbing it in, they carved the following inscription over an entrance to the Central Secretariat Building in New Delhi: "Liberty will not descend to a people. A people must raise themselves to liberty. It is a blessing that must be earned before it can be enjoyed."[16]

In sum, the Raj's approach was to adopt Persian and Mughal practices, but to denigrate its Indo-Islamic predecessors.[17] Since the British considered themselves the tutors of India, the trustees of an empire, they sought no mass conversion or state-sponsored religion, although their cultural penetration—through the English language and Western education—was to be as deep and as lasting as that of the Muslims. The Raj endured because it was efficient and powerful, and because it appealed to higher instincts. It became the model for good government on the subcontinent, in Pakistan even more than in India.

The Loss of Power and Identity

By the mid-1800s northern India had significant numbers of Muslims, concentrated in the northwest and East Bengal, especially Awadh/Oudh, a princely state until it was absorbed into British India in 1856. Its capital, Lucknow, was a center for education and Muslim culture. After the mutiny of 1857, many elite Muslim families went to the nizamate of Hyderabad in the south (some later migrated to Pakistan when Hyderabad was taken over by India after independence), which regarded itself as the legatee of the Mughal Empire and remained outside of British India. Of the state's nearly 12 million residents, 12 percent were Muslims. Furthermore, it had not only a well-run administration but also higher levels of education and income than adjacent districts in British India. Hyderabad's Muslim elites included Persian and Arabic speakers, leaders of Turkish (Mongol) descent, and Urdu-speaking Muslims from North India.

Hyderabad was but one of the 500 or more princely states remaining after the breakup of the Mughal Empire, some others being Junagadh, Bhopal, Rampur, Bahawalpur, and Jammu and Kashmir (J & K). Unlike Hyderabad, which had a Muslim ruler but a largely Hindu population, Kashmir had a Hindu ruler but a largely Muslim population with Hindu and Buddhist minorities, the latter tucked away in the districts of Ladakh. India's subsequent forceful absorption of Junagadh, Kashmir, and Hyderabad became a major source of Pakistani grievances against New Delhi.

The dismantlement of the enfeebled Mughal court had a major impact on India's Muslims. After the mutiny and revolution of 1857, in the words of the Pakistani scholar-administrator Akbar S. Ahmed, the Muslims of India "lost their kingdom, their Mughal Empire, their emperor, their language, their culture, their capital city of Delhi, and their sense of self."[18] Even the poorest Muslim could identify with the Mughal Empire, or with the smaller but still substantial Muslim princely states that had not been incorporated into the Mughal system. All this was swept away in an instant—and the fundamental political, social, and economic structure of India was reordered in a fashion that gave the Muslims little social space and no political power. In 1835 Persian was replaced as the official language of the East India Company, and after the mutiny "the Indian establishment switched entirely to speaking English. Muslim ways—dress, style, food—were also put aside. Muslims now felt not only politically vulnerable but concerned for their very identity."[19]

There is a rich polemic literature on the response of Indian Muslims to the decline of the Mughal Empire. Indian nationalist historians tend to argue that Muslims reacted like "Indians" to the creation of the Raj—both wanted to throw the foreigners out. To them, as already mentioned, the mutiny was India's First War of Independence, and subsequent demands for a separate Pakistan arose from the machinations of the British, who were trying to divide the two communities in order to rule them.

By contrast, many Pakistani scholars and publicists see the dislocation of the Muslim community after 1857 as the *original* source of Muslim discontent, and they attribute it to malevolent anti-Muslim sentiments of the British. By favoring Hindus in education, administration, and other spheres, they tilted against Muslims culturally, economically, and politically.[20] And by promoting democratic institutions, liberal British authorities inadvertently bestowed a permanent minority status on Muslims in greater India, as they would always be outnumbered by the larger Hindu community.

Not surprisingly, the early Muslim leadership did not favor democratic elections, which from the Muslim point of view signified parliamentary democracy—where 51 percent forms the government—and thus would make Muslims a permanent minority. Another, more practical concern was the traditional relationship of dominance-subordination between the predominantly petit-aristocratic Muslim leadership and the large Muslim peasantry. Although some mass-based Muslim political organizations were present in East Bengal, there was no guarantee that they would be the chosen representatives of the Muslim population.

For all their distinctiveness, Muslims shared many interests with the other populations of India, and on the regional level their cultures were intertwined. Punjabis—whether Hindu, Muslim, or Sikh—had a similar worldview and approach to life. Likewise, many South Indian Muslim communities had more in common with their fellow Tamil or Malayalam speakers than with the Urdu or Punjabi speakers to the north. Even in Bengal, which had a huge minority Muslim population, the dominant culture was Bengali, although here the two communities were sharply divided along class and social lines. Hyderabad (Deccan) and the Vale of Kashmir (sometimes referred to as "the Valley" and site of the region's largest city, Srinagar) saw rich fusions of Hindu and Islamic cultures. Much of the Hindu-Muslim tension in British India (and in India and Bangladesh today) stemmed not from religious but from class and social differences.

Still, certain issues had a particular appeal to India's Muslims. One was the abolition of the Khilafat (see the next section) after the defeat of the Ottoman Empire. Another was the disposition of Islam's holy sites in

Arabia and Palestine. One hundred years ago these issues fomented riots throughout India, but even today, pan-Islamic concerns such as the Israel-Palestine conflict are still capable of stirring public passions throughout the subcontinent.

By the time of the Raj, India's Muslims had become a politically and culturally mixed population. They had a dispossessed court, narrow elite, and large poor peasantry. Filled with fresh memories of grandeur and glory, they grew increasingly frustrated and fearful as Hindus adapted more swiftly than Muslims to the Raj's new political and social order.

The Birth of an Idea

Though ideologues claim that Pakistan was born on the day that Muslims first set foot on Indian soil, the first person to systematically set forth the argument for what eventually became Pakistan was the jurist, author, and educator Sir Syed Ahmed Khan (1817–98).[21] He respected—even feared—the British, tirelessly arguing that the only way for India's Muslims to resist the encroachment of Christian missionaries and the larger Hindu community was to become educated to a high standard and remain loyal to the Raj. In 1875 Sir Syed laid the basis for what would become Aligarh Muslim University, which in turn produced the scholars and professionals who staffed the Pakistan movement. Although Sir Syed was dedicated to Muslim modernization, Islam's destiny, and the idea of a pan-Islamic identity, he stopped short of advocating a separate state for India's Muslims.

Nevertheless, a separate *status* for India's Muslims was in the works and became an important milestone on the road leading to Pakistan. In the late nineteenth century the British began to examine more carefully the population they now ruled. Aware of the vast social differences in Indian society, they felt an obligation to protect its vulnerable segments and adopted the principle of separate electorates and quota systems, first for deprived Hindu castes—notably the "untouchables" and non-Hindu tribals.[22] Then they acceded to Muslim demands for separate electorates.

The predominantly Hindu Congress did not oppose these seats for so-called Mohammedans and in 1916 came to an agreement with the Muslim League on the issue. The Congress and the Muslim League shared other policies as well. Mohandas Karamchand Gandhi—later known as the Mahatma—afterward supported the Khilafat movement (the 1919–24 movement that attempted to restore the Ottoman caliph).[23] This was the first time that a predominately religious issue had been introduced into Indian politics.[24] Interestingly, two of India's leading Muslims, Iqbal and Jinnah, were not involved in the Khilafat movement but were deeply impressed with Turkey's Kamal Ataturk and his regime.

Separate electorates soon became a highly contentious issue, one that remains politically significant today. India's Muslims, some reasoned, were descendants of peoples who had migrated to the subcontinent several centuries earlier and thus might be considered quite different from indigenous Indians—a separate "nation"—and as such deserving of protection and a separate electoral status. In the view of others, they were largely converts, their underlying culture, moral values, and social order not unlike those of the "sons of the soil," which meant both groups could share an "Indian" political nationality in a common electoral arrangement.[25]

Swayed by the latter argument, the Congress reversed its position on separate electorates for Muslims—although it continued to support them for disadvantaged Hindus and tribals. Troubled by this inconsistency, Indians debated whether there were valid reasons for differential treatment of religion, on the one hand, and language, ethnicity, or economic status on the other. To this day, India and Pakistan have been unable to reach a conclusive position on the question of quotas and reservations, as is the case in every state that tries to legislate political equality between economically or socially unequal groups.

As for the concept of a separate Indian Muslim political entity, it was first put forth in the 1930s by Choudhary Rahmat Ali, an Indian Muslim living in Cambridge, England. He and a group of Indian students outlined a plan for a federation of ten Muslim states, which they named Pakistan by drawing letters from the provinces that had a Muslim majority or close to it: Punjab, Afghanistan, Kashmir, and Baluchistan.[26] In Persian, *Pakistan* also means "land of the pure," an implicit gibe at the ritually "pure" high-caste Hindus who dominated the Indian National Congress. However, the name did not come into common use until 1945. Even the 1940 resolution of the Muslim League calling for a separate state for India's Muslims did not mention it.

Despite the increasing support for Pakistan—whether as a separate entity within India or as a state—many distinguished Indian Muslims rejected the idea, choosing to be loyal to the politically dominant Indian National Congress. Badr-ud-Din Tyabji, Zakir Husain, and Maulana Abul

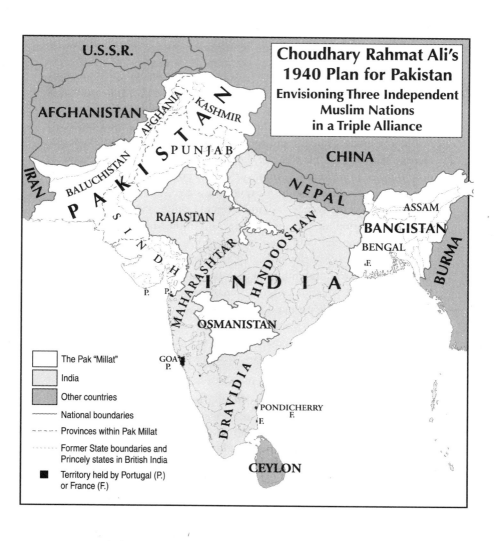

Choudhary Rahmat Ali's 1940 Plan for Pakistan
Envisioning Three Independent
Muslim Nations
in a Triple Alliance

U.S.S.R.

AFGHANISTAN

IRAN

AFGHANIA

KASHMIR

PAKISTAN

PUNJAB

BALUCHISTAN

SINDH

RAJASTAN

CHINA

NEPAL

ASSAM

BANGISTAN

BENGAL

F.

BURMA

MAHARASHTAR

HINDOOSTAN

INDIA

OSMANISTAN

P.

P.

GOA
P.

DRAVIDIA

PONDICHERRY
F.

F.

CEYLON

The Pak "Millat"

India

Other countries

National boundaries

Provinces within Pak Millat

Former State boundaries and
Princely states in British India

Territory held by Portugal (P.)
or France (F.)

Kalam Azad remained staunch members of the Congress to the end of their lives.

Jinnah of India

Mohammed Ali Jinnah, a Bombay lawyer, was the second great advocate of a distinctive Muslim Indian identity. He served as governor-general of the new state until his death in 1948. A secular lawyer-politician, he is revered in Pakistan today as the Quaid-i-Azam, or "Great Leader." A brilliant political strategist and speaker, he was Pakistan's Tom Paine and George Washington. He was not, however, a Jefferson, a theoretician or deep thinker. Jinnah was the first world-class political figure produced by Pakistan—in this case, by the idea, not the state.[27]

After joining the secular Indian National Congress in 1905, he rose to a leading position as "the ambassador of Hindu-Muslim Unity." Ironically, he became the individual most responsible for the merger of the idea of Pakistan with the state of Pakistan. He quit active politics in 1930 and went to London to practice law, but returned to India in 1934 to revitalize the Muslim League. Jinnah organized the campaign that compelled both the British and the Indian National Congress to concede to the demand for the state of Pakistan. He summarized his life's struggle in a historic address at a mass meeting in Lahore on March 23, 1940, that set forth the logic of Pakistan, echoing Alberuni's observation 900 years earlier:

> The Hindus and the Muslims belong to two different religious philosophies, social customs, and literatures. They neither intermarry, nor inter-dine together and, indeed, they belong to two different civilizations which are based mainly on conflicting ideas and conceptions. Their aspects on life and of life are different. It is quite clear that Hindus and Musalmans derive their inspiration from different sources of history. They have different epics, their heroes are different, and they have different episodes. Very often the hero of one is a foe of the other, and likewise, their victories and defeats overlap.[28]

Jinnah turned the "two-nation" theory (the idea that India's Muslims and Hindus constituted two "nations," each deserving their own state) into an effective political movement. Because he had to weld together disparate elements of the Indian Muslim community, Jinnah's arguments were deliberately vague. This vagueness brought both strength and weakness to the Pakistan movement, enabling it to muster support for independence and opposition to Hindu domination, but not to build a consensus on the kind of state Pakistan was to become. In addition, Jinnah's dominance left little room for second-tier leadership, which was to prove disastrous when he died shortly after independence.

The Two-Nation Theory and Iqbal

From 1929 onward, the Indian National Congress called for an independent state of India. The following year the Muslim League demanded not only that India become independent from Britain but that it consist of two "nations," one Hindu and one Muslim, with suitable protection for Muslims from what was envisioned as a Hindu-dominant India.

Indian Muslims were split on both questions. Some, such as the princes, had good working relations with the British and saw nothing to gain from an independent India or even a Muslim-dominated Pakistan. Many of the rulers of the princely states (Hindu, Muslim, and Sikh) opposed partition and only grudgingly gave in to British pressure to join one or the other dominions. A few, especially the nizam of Hyderabad, had sought independence. Other Indian Muslims, such as Maulana Azad, wanted a free but undivided India. Azad had arrived at this position after journeying in the opposite direction of Jinnah: he was originally a member of the Muslim League but then joined Congress in the 1920s.[29] Still others favored a separate Pakistan within India, or a confederation of India and Pakistan. Some pious Muslims (like some Jewish sects that deny Israel's legitimacy) even opposed the idea of Pakistan on the grounds that Muslims should not pay allegiance to any single state but to a larger community of believers, the *ummah*.

What percentage of Indian Muslims favored an independent Pakistan is still unclear, but there is no doubt that the most prominent community leaders wanted a separate state—or at least staked out a claim for Pakistan in the hope of winning concessions in the final round of negotiations. The third towering figure of this group was Allama Iqbal, who in his own way propelled the idea of Pakistan forward as effectively as Jinnah or Sir Syed.

An eclectic figure who was a great and influential poet from Punjab, Iqbal did not fall into any single category. Caught between cultural conservatism and political reformism, his message was complex and subtle. He, too, began as an advocate of Hindu-Muslim unity, and one of his poems, *Tarana-e-Hind* ("Indian Anthem") is still a popular song in India (it begins: "Our Hindustan is the best place in the world . . ."). At the same time, Iqbal, more than Jinnah, anticipated the rage of contemporary Pakistanis, and much of his poetry and writing is a lament for the poor condition to which India's Muslims had fallen after their glorious past. Iqbal turned the idea of a separate homeland for India's Muslims into a mass movement, drawing intellectuals, professionals, and community leaders into the fold. He heightened community pride—the community being defined as the Muslims of India—and credibly argued that this community desired and needed a separate state in which it could establish a South Asian counterpart of the great Islamic empires of Persia and Arabia. For Iqbal, this state—he did not call it Pakistan—would not only solve India's Hindu-Muslim puzzle, it would awaken and re-create Islam, freeing it from both alien Hinduism and obsolescent Islamic encrustations. At first Iqbal did not advocate a separate country, but one or more distinct components in a federated India; if that was not possible, he declared in his 1930 presidential address to the Muslim League, then Indian Muslims should seek a completely separate state via "concerted political action."

Iqbal's idea of Pakistan was not based on a European model of a nation-state, but on "an acute understanding that political power was essential to the higher ends of establishing God's law."[30] Like many of his coreligionists, including those who set the stage for today's Islamic parties, Iqbal saw territorial nationalism as a step toward a larger Islamic community, a vehicle for the perfection of Islam. By contrast, Jinnah envisioned Pakistan as a "nation" consisting of Indian Muslims.

By the late 1930s Hindus and Muslims were on a collision course. In 1940 the learned B. R. Ambedkar, leader of India's scheduled castes and chief drafter of India's constitution, anticipated the current India-Pakistan rivalry, noting the two were like hostile states in an arms race, competing in the establishment of militant groups, educational institutions, and political parties: "Both appear to be preparing for war and each is watching the 'preparations' of the other."[31] Even the idea of reform in one community threatened the other, he remarked: for Muslims, Hindu reform implied a weakening of the traditional alliance between Muslims and India's untouchable population, while Hindus viewed Islam as a proselytizing religion, like Christianity, luring Hindus away from their civilizational roots.[32] These arguments echo today, as Hindu extremists launch a major reconversion movement in India, arguing that Pakistan-sponsored terrorists are merely continuing the civilizational war waged by Muslim raiders a thousand years ago.

Pakistan and the World

If there was any concern about South Asia's security after partition, it revolved around India's status, not that of Pakistan. Very little thought was given to the strategic implications of a new state of Pakistan. There were so few Muslim officers, the British observed, that India and Pakistan would have to enter into some form of military confederation, requiring a British presence in Pakistan for many years to come. Though widely held, the assumption that both India and Pakistan would remain dependent upon Britain was tragically wrong. No proponent of the Pakistan movement dreamed that Pakistan and India would become bitter enemies, or that the armed forces of Pakistan would dominate Pakistani politics.

Before 1947 the regional security debate revolved around *India's* security in the face of an independent Pakistan, which would stand between India and Afghanistan, on the one hand, and between India and the Soviet Union, on the other. Could Pakistan maintain a viable army? Would it serve as a bulwark for India against Soviet pressure or radical Islamic movements? Jinnah and Iqbal both believed that a new Pakistan would enhance the defense of the subcontinent precisely because of its Muslim and Islamic nature, arguing that security considerations strengthened the case for Pakistan. According to Iqbal, the Muslims of Punjab and the Northwest Frontier Province would "be the best defenders of India against a foreign invasion, be that invasion the one of ideas or bayonets. The Punjab with 56 percent Muslim population supplies 54 percent of the total combatant troops in the Indian army and (if the Gurkhas are excluded) the Punjab contingent amounts to 62 percent of the whole."[33]

Iqbal disagreed that such a concentration of armed Muslims would put pressure on India, as was feared by a number of his coreligionists who supported the Congress. In a prophetic analysis of Pakistan's strategic future, a Muslim member of the Congress, Shaukatullah Ansari, argued that Pakistan would have insufficient resources to defend itself without outside help for it would face *three* conflicts involving two fronts.

In the west there was a potential threat from both Russia and Afghanistan, in the east from Japan and China, and in both the east and west from India. Further, a united India would be a great power, whereas a divided one would be as weak as Egypt, Burma, or "Siam," and the British would use an independent Pakistan to control India (this idea later resurfaced in India, with the United States replacing Britain as the potentially controlling power).[34] Ansari failed to persuade the Congress to concede a substantial degree of autonomy to the Muslims of a united India, perhaps as a confederation.

In B. R. Ambedkar's opinion, India actually stood to benefit from a separate Pakistan. For one thing, separation would leave most of the subcontinent's wealth in predominately Hindu India and make Pakistan, with its poor resource base, a weak state. For another, India's army would no longer be dominated by Muslims (the British had drawn most of their manpower from districts that would become Pakistan), and its primarily Hindu civilian government would not be vulnerable to the army. "A safe army," Ambedkar commented, "is better than a safe border."[35]

One of Pakistan's many ironies is that neither of its two greatest leaders correctly foretold its strategic future. Iqbal wrongly believed that the Islamic nature of a new Pakistan would give it inherent strength. Instead, Pakistan has had to draw power from its relationship with other states and thus lacked the capacity to prevent the breakup of 1971. Jinnah, too, was excessively optimistic in thinking that the minorities in Pakistan would be hostages to good behavior, and that natural cultural and economic linkages would strengthen relations between its various groups. As Ambedkar correctly observed, Pakistan has always lacked the industrial base to sustain a modern army, let alone the technological capacity to develop a modern air force or navy, yet historical circumstances have enabled its predominately Punjabi army to dominate Pakistani politics. Meanwhile, India's highly pluralistic officer corps remains both apolitical and professional, and New Delhi can draw upon superior fiscal and material resources.

A Tragic Victory

Though vaguely conceived, the idea of Pakistan did tie together the three major Muslim communities of British India: those of East Bengal, Punjab, and the United Provinces. The Pakistan movement was not strong in the Northwest Frontier Province or Sindh, or in India's south. For seven years, from the passage of the Lahore Resolution demanding a separate Pakistan in 1940 to independence in 1947, the differences between these groups were contained by Jinnah's leadership. He negotiated both with the British and with the Indian nationalists, winning enough victories at the polls to make the claim for Pakistan credible.[36]

Jinnah was fortunate in that the other two players in the drama were, at their core, liberal. The Raj was a far cry from the brutal French regime in Algeria, the Dutch in Indonesia, or the Portuguese in Africa. The Indian National Congress, too, was a liberal organization—like the Muslim League, it was led by a lawyer, and its firebrands were marginalized. While the League's fight for Pakistan has been mythologized as a titanic battle against two implacable foes, the Raj and the Congress, it was in fact not much of a struggle. This has contributed a great deal to Pakistan's later inclination toward constitutional structures and the rule of law—even when it has been unable to sustain them.

As the economist-scholar Shahid Javed Burki notes, "The new state was meant to achieve different things for different people: emancipation from the Hindu landlords of the peasantry of Bengal and Assam; the creation of new economic and political opportunities for the frustrated urban Muslim classes of Delhi, Bombay, and the United and Central provinces; and the establishment of an Islamic state" for the religiously minded in Sindh, Punjab, and the Northwest Frontier Province.[37] Pakistan as an idea was successful enough to command support from many, but not all, of India's Muslims; as a blueprint for a state it was to founder on the rocks of these different interests.

Ironically, a decision by the Indian National Congress helped turn the idea of Pakistan—a longshot or a negotiating tactic, at best—into reality. Whereas the Congress had supported Britain in World War I, in 1942 its members, led by Gandhi, decided to launch the "Quit India" movement and sat out the war in prison, demanding a promise of independence in exchange for their support. Some prominent members even sympathized with the Axis powers. As a result, the British relied on the Muslim League to help them recruit soldiers to the Indian army—Punjabi Muslims were the single largest recruitment class in the army—and gather Indian Muslims to its own cause.

The Congress's nonparticipation in the war made the British wary. Those in military and strategic circles in particular had to look after postwar British imperial interests and vastly distrusted Gandhi and the Congress Party. Though India was no longer the jewel in the imperial crown, Britain still had colonies to India's east and precious oil reserves to its west. There was also some concern that India, led by the "leftist" Nehru, might fall under Soviet influence.

The idea of Pakistan as an independent, pro-Western state remaining under Western (that is, British) tutelage was thus quite attractive. For many British strategists, the most secure foothold would be in an independent Pakistan, with its loyal army and Western-leaning Muslim League leadership.[38] Whereas Pakistanis tend to emphasize the injustices and discrimination that made separation necessary, Indian historians tend to regard Pakistan as partly the product of this British imperial strategy, not the result of a legitimate demand. The historical record is complex and rich enough to support both interpretations, and as with so many other events that conceptually divide the two states, debate continues to surround the partition of British India.

The Idea of Pakistan

When two cultures collide, does one flee from the other, accommodate it, ignore it, absorb it, yield to it, or try to destroy it?[39] Most Muslim rulers on the subcontinent eventually *accommodated* their Hindu subjects, but the coming of the British opened up the question once again, particularly for Muslims. Since Hindus took to British education more readily than Muslims, many Muslim elites felt overwhelmed by a devastating coalition of British power and renascent Hinduism, which had been energized by the tools of learning and power acquired from the British. Not only had the Hindus transformed themselves but their numbers were so great that Muslims could not even hope to maintain normal relations with them, which could only be realized if Muslims had equal status or access to skills, positions, and assets that would protect their special position in India. Perhaps, there was also some fear of Hindu revenge for crimes chronicled by Alberuni and others.

Though Iqbal may have considered Pakistan part of a larger Islamic rebirth, the spirit behind it also resembled the nation-state movement of the nineteenth century, as reflected in Zionism or the Armenian national movement. More recent comparisons would include the Chechnyan, Bosnian, and Palestinian movements, which also seek homelands for oppressed minorities, and which have been strongly supported by Pakistanis. The Indian National Congress, which made the comparison with Israel, noted that both Zionism and the Pakistan movement identified their members by religion and professed tolerance for religious minorities within the borders of the new state. Where they differ is that Israel opens its doors to all coreligionists while Pakistan restricts entry of Muslims from India and even Bangladesh. Even Jinnah did not foresee Pakistan as a homeland for *all* of India's Muslims.[40]

By making religion the basis for a separate nation-state, argued Pakistani nationalists, the new Muslim homeland would also be a progressive state because Islam, unlike Hinduism, is a modern religion with a proud position in history as the faith that brought to perfection the religions of the modern, advanced, scientific West, Judaism and Christianity. Islam is part of this tradition, whereas Hinduism belongs to another world, that of the complete nonbeliever. In the extreme view, Hindus lack even the revelations of the other "people of the book"; their accomplishments were historically interesting but are not to be regarded as modern or progressive.

This distinction between the world of Islam (in Arabic, world of submission or peace) and the remainder of mankind is central to Islamic political thought. As discussed in subsequent chapters, Pakistani ideologues believe that the acceptance of Islam and proper guidance enable man to create a society of peace and justice on this earth. By contrast, they contend, Hindus believe that Islam offers no hope of perfection, for the world is in an era of decay and destruction—*Kaliyug*. In this scheme of things, individual redemption through death and rebirth is a difficult and slow process. Hindus profess no real faith, only a cynical opportunism and a crude and misguided devotion to a thousand gods. As some Muslims argued at the time of separation, if they could not rule over Hindus, then they had to be shielded from Hindu influence, not by becoming a separate but equal society, but a separate and superior one.

For the more ardent supporters of Pakistan, the structure of the Hindu caste system was further empirical evidence of the incompatibility between Islam and Indian culture and of the need for a separate state. Like many non-Hindus, they associated caste with *varna*, Hinduism's theoretical four-fold social hierarchy. At the same time, some Pakistanis prided themselves on Rajput or other high-caste origins, although a great number were converts to Islam from lower Hindu castes. Thus they harbored a special resentment toward "Hindu Brahmin" dominance and arrogance flowing from being at the top of the system. Equally important in elite Pakistani circles was the view that regional discord stems from the "Hindu mind," which is often characterized as scheming and devious, and compelled to expand.[41]

Another distinctive component of faith that shapes the view Pakistanis have of their own country, its claims on Kashmir, and its relations with India is *Izzat,* meaning pride and honor. Islam calls on individuals to live honorable lives in accordance with their religious and moral principles. The Pakistan movement and subsequent relations with India (and other powers, especially the United States) suggest that Pakistan's honor, and therefore the honor of its citizens, is at stake in such issues as Kashmir, India's dominance, and Pakistan's autonomy.[42] Any prospective normalization of India-Pakistan relations and Kashmir affairs must address this factor, just as it must reckon with India's national identity.

Thus the idea of Pakistan rests on the elite Indian Muslim sense of being culturally and historically distinct. This view descends in part from the original Muslim invaders of the subcontinent, and in part from the willingness of some to abandon corrupt Hinduism for a peaceful and just Islam.

Although Islam is an egalitarian religion, the leadership of the Pakistan movement had difficulty accepting the democratic norm of one man, one vote. Jinnah and others tirelessly argued that without some restraint on majority power, Muslims would always be outvoted. Once the British left, who would check the majority Hindu community? Jinnah strongly opposed independence if it meant representative government based on numbers: "three to one," three Hindus for every Indian Muslim. Who, he asked, would interpret and enforce the terms of the transfer of power from Britain to India? "We come back to the same answer: the Hindu majority would do it, and will it be with the help of the British bayonet or Mr. Gandhi's 'Ahimsa' [strategy of nonviolence]? Can we trust them any more?"[43] Unyieldingly, Jinnah's answer was no, no, and again no. Sarcastically, he threw back Gandhi's claim that the two men were brothers, that Hindus, Muslims, Parsis, Harijans are all alike: "The only difference is this, that brother Gandhi has three votes and I have only one vote."[44]

As far as Jinnah was concerned, "a thousand years of close contact, nationalities which are as divergent today as ever cannot at any time be expected to transform themselves into one nation merely by means of subjecting them to a democratic constitution." And, Jinnah added, Muslims were not even minorities as the term is "commonly known and understood," since they were a majority in four of eleven British Indian provinces.

Majoritarian democracy had no attractions for a minority divided by language and sect, and with many coreligionists in the Congress Party itself. This fundamental structural objection to democratic politics explains why many Pakistanis of an older generation have strong reservations about democracy and democratic politics as an end in itself. Democracy threatened the minority Muslim community, forcing it to establish its own political order, Pakistan. But proponents of the idea of Pakistan had not looked too closely at the contradiction between the educated, Westernized leadership of the Pakistan movement (many of whom claimed descent from the original Muslim invaders) and the much larger numbers of the poor and the converted. Pakistan's leadership eventually split on the question of democracy—guided, basic, and otherwise—when the poorer (but more populous) half of Pakistan claimed its right to rule the whole state.

Glorious Past, Glorious Future?

The Pakistani movement bequeathed to the state of Pakistan a number of identities. First, Pakistan was clearly "Indian," in that the strongest supporters of the idea of Pakistan identified themselves as culturally Indian, although in opposition to Hindu Indians. This Indian dimension of Pakistan's identity has been systematically overlooked by contemporary Pakistani politicians and scholars. Even Pakistan's Buddhist heritage is ignored, even though a good number in both East and West Pakistan converted to Buddhism, and present-day Pakistan has many impressive Buddhist pilgrimage sites.

Second, the idea of Pakistan implied that Pakistan would be a modern extension of the great Islamic empires of South Asia, whose physical remnants still dominate the subcontinental landscape. From the Red Forts of Delhi and Agra to the Taj Mahal and the spectacular ruins of Golconda in southern India, there was compelling evidence of recent Islamic greatness. Many prominent Indian Muslim families traced their lineage back to particular invasions of the subcontinent, or to a distinguished ancestor's conversion from Hinduism to Islam.

Third, Pakistan was also a legatee of British India, sharing in the 200-year-old tradition of the Raj. This itself was a complex identity, as British India had incorporated Turkish, Persian, and Hindu practices into its own structure.

Fourth, because of its cultural links with Central Asia, strategists such as Jinnah viewed Pakistan as a boundary land between the teeming masses of India and the vastness of Central Asia. Such a Pakistan, with its strong military tradition, was to serve as the guardian of South Asia. In subsequent years Pakistani strategists and their American and British counterparts came to see Pakistan as a balance to both the Soviet Union and the pro-Soviet government of India (eventually, China came to hold the same view).

Fifth, since Pakistan was also to be part of the Islamic world, it would share in one way or another the *ummah*'s destiny. As a result, it had a special interest in the persecution of Muslim minorities in the rest of the world. Pakistan was, in brief, blessed with many assets, several great traditions, and a number of potential identities. It was Jinnah who wove these attributes together, arguing that without a separate Muslim homeland, South Asia would be mired in conflict and vulnerable to outside pressure. For him, the past pointed to the future. Pakistan would be a democratic, liberal, and just state. It would live peaceably with its minority Hindu population, and relations with India would be normal, possibly encompassing regional cooperation. How was this vision realized during the subsequent fifty-plus years of Pakistan the state?

CHAPTER TWO

THE STATE
OF PAKISTAN

The British plan to partition the Indian subcontinent into two dominions—India and Pakistan—was announced on June 3, 1947, and accelerated the time frame for independence by six or more months, with the date for transfer of power set for August 15. Few believed that a clean, uncomplicated break was possible in that shortened period. They were correct; of all the schemes that had been discussed over the years, the plan to create a single Muslim state with two wings, separated by 1,000 miles of Indian territory, was perhaps the most problematic to implement and certainly unprecedented. This kind of geography required perfect Indian cooperation to make the idea work, but many Indian leaders were all too eager to ensure that the new state of Pakistan would have a short life. The Indian leadership differed sharply on the entire question of partition: Gandhi opposed it, but Nehru and other Indian leaders such as Sardar Patel accepted it for fear the British might decide to give the hundreds of princely states the option of independence, which would certainly have weakened the coherence of their new Indian state. Moreover, they expected Pakistan to fail.

The State of Pakistan: Assets and Liabilities

In the event, Pakistan was the first state created after World War II, on August 14, 1947, and India's independence came one day later. Pakistan was immediately identified as a migrant state born amid massive bloodshed

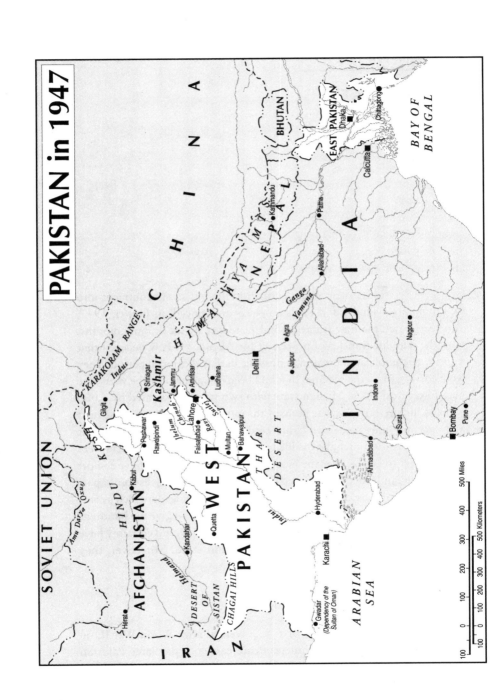

and carrying many liabilities. At the same time, it boasted a strong bureaucratic and legal tradition, an unthreatening military, a powerful uniting figure (Jinnah), and an important strategic position, among other assets.

The India Act of 1935 provided the legal framework for Pakistan until 1956, when the state passed its own constitution. The act had established parliamentary governments at the central and provincial levels and had divided power between them, also giving each the authority to collect taxes. In some areas—notably East Bengal, Punjab, Sindh, and the settled parts of the Northwest Frontier Province (NWFP)—the British had also established a comprehensive system of courts and local bureaucracies. Since much of the NWFP was the home of Pashtun tribes that had never been directly ruled by the British, however, it was allowed to keep a system of tribal governance, and the Pakistan government, like the British before it, sent political agents to deal with the population.[1]

The total strength of the pre-independence Indian civil service (ICS) had been no more than 1,400 individuals, and of these only about 80 came to Pakistan.[2] The service was renamed the civil service of Pakistan (CSP), and Pakistan recruited many former British officials to stay on in the civil services and police (7 of the top 27 senior civilian officials were still British in 1950). Most of the ICS officers who came to Pakistan were from northern India, or, in the case of East Pakistan, from the Bengal cadre of the ICS. While Pakistan remained short on manpower, those who did arrive were fully imbued with the British administrative tradition and within a few years replicated it, down to the tough recruitment standards and high-quality training academies.

Pakistan's strategic importance had been recognized by the British well before partition. With memories of the Indian National Congress's opposition to World War II still fresh and the likelihood that Pakistan would be cool toward Britain and its Western allies, the British thought it critical to maintain the remnants of their Far Eastern possessions. Americans, too, came to see the strategic value of West Pakistan's location—particularly as a possible bomber base on the Soviet Union's southern flank. This perception eventually led to close ties between the West and Pakistan's fledgling army, but for the first ten years the army was too small and too junior to play any role other than a military one; it did, however, become a conduit for Western influence.

Pakistan's aforementioned liabilities quickly made themselves felt. Not only did the government have to bridge two wings over a thousand miles of now-hostile Indian territory, but in large parts of the country it had little or no influence. Tribal leaders had the ultimate authority over who and what traversed their territory, and they managed tribal affairs by traditional laws through the tribal council, or *jirga*. This was especially the case in NWFP and large parts of Baluchistan and Sindh. These regions had either been lightly governed or not governed at all by the British and contained some of the most regressive princely states in the subcontinent. Fifty-seven years after independence, ordinary travel without government permission is discouraged in much of the NWFP and parts of Baluchistan, and in Sindh even government officials have to pay protection money to gangs.

Economically, Pakistan had no significant raw materials or exports other than jute (used for carpet backing and sacks). The jute industry, which had flourished during World War II, was soon challenged and then overtaken by other materials; in any case, there were few mills in the East Wing because the center of jute processing, Calcutta, had remained in India. To make matters worse, Bengal had just suffered a historic famine caused by British mismanagement of transportation and food supplies. Although Pakistan's breadbasket, the Punjab, was (and remains) very prosperous, until the 1960 Indus Waters Treaty it did not have a reliable flow of water for irrigation.

Jinnah of Pakistan

After August 1947, Jinnah of India became Jinnah of Pakistan, a man desperately trying to assemble a modern nation-state, a task that became monumental in the aftermath of partition. Jinnah's divisive rhetoric and acceptance of extralegal procedures suddenly gave way to a vision of a democratic Pakistan that would be tolerant of religious minorities, socially progressive, and constitutionally modern in the Western sense. Jinnah died appalled by the hatred and bloodshed generated by partition, desperately concerned about the difficulties that Pakistan would face in establishing a modern state.[3]

While he left no document outlining his plans for the new state, Jinnah had given several important addresses that constitute benchmarks in the history of both the state and the idea of Pakistan. The most remarkable aspect of these later speeches was their secular character.

Box 2-1. *Secularism*

In Pakistani parlance, Jinnah is not called a "secular" leader, although his personal habits were quite secular and he did advocate the practical separation of religion and personal life, even as he worked toward the creation of an "Islamic" Pakistan. Subsequently, the term "mainstream" has been used to describe Jinnah's mixture of Islam and secularism; the term "liberal" is often used pejoratively by self-proclaimed Islamists, as is "secular," both carrying the implication of not being fully committed to the idea of an Islamic state.

For a man who had emphasized the differences between Muslims and Hindus right up to independence, Jinnah pointedly urged the new Pakistanis—Hindu, Sikh, and Christian, as well as Muslim, to forget the past and work together "in a spirit that every one of you, no matter to what community he belongs, no matter what relations he had with you in the past, no matter what is his colour, caste or creed, is first, second, and last a citizen of this State with equal rights, privileges and obligations, there will be no end to the progress you will make."[4] (At this time Pakistan had a small Christian and Parsi minority, no more than 5 percent of the total. Less than a million Hindus stayed behind in West Pakistan, but East Pakistan's population was approximately 20 percent Hindu.) Whether Sunni, Shi'ia, Bengalis, Tamils, Pathans, Punjabis, or Hindus of any caste—not to mention Christians or Parsis—all residents of the new state were Pakistanis, Jinnah proclaimed, and he urged cooperation. Pointedly, he told the assembly that if India had been imbued with this spirit, it would have been independent years earlier. Without this sense of tolerance, he implied, the new state would be in danger.

Despite their import, Jinnah's fine words had little impact: they were delivered just as a historically unprecedented 6 million to 8 million refugees poured into Pakistan.[5] Jinnah had sought out and welcomed trained Indian Muslims but had not reckoned on a mass migration of the dispossessed, the fearful, and the deprived, many of whom fled to Pakistan not out of idealism but out of terror. A few speeches could not erase four decades of emphasis on the *differences* between Hindus and Muslims, and the threat to Muslims from the larger community. As Shahid Burki questioned, "How could Muslims cease to be Muslims and Hindus cease to be Hindus in the political sense when the religions to which they belonged were, in Jinnah's passionately held belief, so utterly different from one another? Was Jinnah giving up the two-nation theory, the ideological foundation of the state of Pakistan?"[6] The fact is, he was a pragmatic leader trained in the British constitutional framework, scornful of the religious leaders who had opposed the idea of Pakistan—and who in turn castigated him for being irreligious.

Jinnah's mission was to establish internal cohesion. On the surface, at least, he showed no concern about India-Pakistan relations, and he evidently had no Kashmir policy. He foresaw cooperation, despite the personal strains between him and the Congress leadership and the rivalry between the Muslim League and the Congress:

> The Dominion of Pakistan and the Dominion of India should co-ordinate for the purpose of playing their part in international affairs and the developments that may take place, and also it is of vital importance to Pakistan and India, as independent sovereign States, to collaborate in a friendly way jointly to defend their frontiers both on land and sea against any aggression. But this depends entirely on whether Pakistan and India can resolve their own differences and grave domestic issues in the first instance. In other words, if we can put our house in order internally, then we may be able to play a very great part externally in all international affairs.[7]

Jinnah's secular vision of Pakistan was embedded in the state's British-derived constitution. Though watered down over the years, the constitution has been carefully tended by a series of inventive legal minds, beginning with Jinnah himself, a lawyer by profession. They have maintained the façade of constitutionalism during each military takeover and the more repressive civilian governments. A key figure in providing such continuity was Syed Sharifuddin Pirzada, a Bombay lawyer who became Jinnah's personal assistant and legal adviser to every Pakistani military government since. Of the constitutional changes, the blasphemy laws and the laws declaring the Ahmediyyas to be non-Muslims are stains on the Jinnah-of-Pakistan model: they have been used to systematically persecute and punish Pakistanis who do not conform to a narrow, Sunni-dominated vision of Islam.[8]

Elements of Jinnah's latter-day secular outlook are also evident in Pakistan's courts, newspapers, and universities, despite decades of institutional decay. The large and influential nongovernmental organization (NGO) community also hearkens back to Jinnah's earliest dream of a society with a commitment to positive social change, although it also indicates that the Pakistani state failed to meet the basic needs of its citizens in the fields of health, education, civil liberties, and social equality—all areas emphasized by Jinnah in his final speeches.

Would Jinnah recognize the Pakistan of today? Perhaps, but just barely. Several of the religious parties that opposed him in 1947 now govern in two provinces, while Pakistan is governed by a politically powerful army, not by the mainstream parties of persuasion similar to his own; Jinnah would certainly see army rule and the disproportionate influence of the Islamists as an aberration, and he would undoubtedly be distressed about Pakistan's distorted economy and the loss of more than half of Pakistan after a civil war and Indian intervention. Perhaps most troubling, according to one perceptive student of Pakistani politics, would have been the way in which his image and his reputation were appropriated by those attempting to create a state at variance with his hopes and expectations; after all, Jinnah's "was a middle of the road approach which viewed Islam as a civilization and culture, a social order, and a source of law, rather than a set of punitive, regulative, and extractive codes."[9]

Out of India

Partition and the horrific violence that accompanied it had important consequences for both the idea and the state of Pakistan.[10] First came a mass migration that changed the power balance in what was to become West Pakistan. Support for the Muslim League and a separate Muslim state had been strongest in North India, where Muslims had been in a minority. However, Pakistan was established on the periphery of the subcontinent, where Muslims were in a majority but support for Pakistan was weak.[11] The upshot was that the strongest supporters of Pakistan migrated in huge numbers to the new state (significant among the minorities were the Mohajirs, Urdu-speakers from North and Central India, who flooded into the West Wing). These individuals were more educated, urbanized, professionally qualified, and experienced in the ways of the British Indian bureaucracy than the local population; the incoming trading communities possessed significant capital as well. The refugees thus gained control of the government, bureaucracy, and business in the West Wing, while the traditional Punjabi and Pathan leadership—the descendants of the Unionists who had controlled the politics of pre-independence Punjab—were frozen out. Also taking shape was the "triad" consisting of the army, the bureaucracy, and the feudal landlords that came to dominate the politics and social life of the Indus basin, and that today "continues to exercise inordinate influence over public and economic affairs."[12]

Second, partition confirmed many Pakistanis' worst fears about India, especially among migrants, who by 1951 constituted approximately 10 percent of all Pakistanis.[13] Though the Congress and Muslim League had struggled against each other in the courts and the legislatures of British India, they were both fundamentally oriented toward constitutionalism and unprepared for the violence unleashed by partition. Minorities were attacked on both sides of the newly drawn international border, and ethnic cleansing was commonplace. Memories of these events remain vivid from generation to generation, especially among the deeply affected populations of parts of northern India and the major cities of what was then the West Wing of Pakistan and is now the state of Pakistan.

Many refugees nurtured, as their descendants still do, a deep hatred against "Hindu India" or "artificial Pakistan."[14] From the perspective of the new Pakistani elite, the ensuing violence simply proved how right they had been to seek a separate country. Although they saw their struggle in historical and practical terms, not as a theological quest, and people differed over what it meant to be a Pakistani, the new state was the promised land and was rooted in an idea validated by the state's very existence. Subsequent wars were further evidence of the justness of their cause, representing further Indian attempts to strangle the state of Pakistan and renew Hindu oppression of Muslims. By 1965 and 1971 the vision of Pakistan as a homeland had long been supplanted by that of Pakistan as a fortress— an armed redoubt guarded by the Pakistan army, safe from predatory India. Nothing illustrated this more pointedly than the Kashmir conflict, which was both a cause and a consequence of India-Pakistan hostility.

Third, partition made evident how necessary the state's institutions were to protecting the basic interests of citizens of the new state. The Muslim League was ineffective in providing relief and rehabilitation aid to the West Wing. The task of protecting and caring for the émigrés hence fell to Pakistani bureaucrats and young army officers. They performed their impossible task with valor, and the experience propelled them to the new state's center stage.

The army further demonstrated its importance in October 1948, with the eruption of the first India-Pakistan war in Kashmir. The senior commanding officers were still British, thus limiting the scope of operations, but the army acquitted itself well and quickly assumed its place as one of Pakistan's central institutions. Although their former British commanders believed the officers who had come to the Pakistan army were not as well qualified on average as those of the new Indian army, the force did well enough, and subsequent retelling of the drama did much to burnish its reputation.

Partition had a fourth consequence that underscored the theme of betrayal in relations between the two new states, which carried back to when both the Muslim League and the Congress had struggled for independence while competing against each other. Pakistanis considered India's failure to adhere to the terms of partition as the supreme betrayal. India had not only defaulted on the division of assets, but it had also connived with the British to manipulate the international boundary between the two states and persuaded some of the rulers of the princely states to accede to India rather than Pakistan. Further, India had unfairly moved its forces to the princely state of Jammu and Kashmir (see the next section).

Ironically, though Gandhi and Jinnah had been rivals, it was Gandhi who undertook a fast unto death (begun on January 13, 1948) to protest India's retention of Pakistan's assets and Hindu and Sikh attacks on Muslims in India. Indeed, the Hindu extremist who assassinated Gandhi thought he was too pro-Pakistani. Such events demonstrate the tight linkage between separatism, terrorism, and foreign policy throughout South Asia.

Betrayal is a pronounced leitmotiv of Pakistani explanations for the state's problems perhaps because it runs through early Muslim history wherever experiments at statehood have failed. Like many other Arab and Islamic populations, Pakistanis have found it difficult to establish or retain a modern state. As Akbar S. Ahmed notes, Muslims feel that the West, having a hand in this outcome, has stripped them of dignity and honor, but they confusingly equate the restoration of honor with violence.[15]

Box 2-2. *Left Behind*

The creation of Pakistan made organized politics by India's large Muslim minority difficult. For decades they found a home in the Congress Party—then a Brahmin-led party that had great strength among both Muslims and the Scheduled Castes. Whenever a crisis with Pakistan has occurred, or whenever Kashmir flares up, all eyes have turned to India's Muslim population for their reaction. In some instances, such as cheering for visiting Pakistani cricket teams, it has been defiant, and intended to irritate Hindu nationalists; but when India normalized relations with Israel, few if any Muslim voices arose in protest. The loyalty of Indian Muslims is openly questioned by Hindu nationalists, including elements of the Bharatiya Janata Party, who also consider the Aligarh Muslim University (the intellectual base for the Pakistan movement) suspect. This has led to a fresh spurt of migration by educated Indian Muslims, not to Pakistan but to the West and to the Middle East. However, Indian Muslims have found a place in a few sectors, notably entertainment and films; some have ventured into politics, and India's wealthiest person, the software entrepreneur Aziz Premji, is Muslim. Furthermore, three Indian presidents have been Muslims, and the community is well represented in the diplomatic services, although its contribution to the army is small.

The fifth consequence of partition stemmed from the uneven migration of Indian Muslims to Pakistan and the large numbers left behind (see box 2-2). While some Pakistanis consider their state incomplete because it does not encompass all of the Muslims of South Asia, the fact is that India's remaining Muslims now constitute the world's largest minority population and may actually outnumber the Muslims in Pakistan. For a state whose creation was justified as necessary for the continued survival of South Asian Muslims, the presence of these Muslims on the other side of the border is inconvenient.

Sixth, partition transformed the economies of the regions that became Pakistan.[16] As mentioned earlier, at the outset Pakistan did not have a significant industrial and business sector. Furthermore, only 1 percent of its national income was generated in industries that used power and employed at least twenty workers. With the exception of the great trading communities in Western India, the Muslims in undivided India had played no part in industry and the capital sector. Whereas Hindu and Parsi businesses had collaborated with British industry and trade to take advantage of the new economic opportunities, the traditional business communities were the early competitors of the East India Company and thus subjected to biased trading practices.

Most significant was the absence of Muslims in banking, partly because Islam prohibited usury, but also because capitalism had not yet evolved in its communities. Though India's Muslim businesses used credit instruments extensively, there was no interest-bearing mass system channeling small savings into large investments. This incapacity to pool small savings to make large industrial investments has continued to haunt Pakistan: the country's savings rate has been significantly less than that of comparable economies in Asia.

Furthermore, the overwhelming majority of businesses in the regions of the subcontinent that became Pakistan had been owned by non-Muslims, most of whom had fled to India.[17] In West Pakistan as a whole, 80 percent of industrial firms had been owned by non-Muslims. In Karachi, the first city of Pakistan, 80 percent of the landed property and the overwhelming proportion of the foreign trade had been controlled by non-Muslims. In Lahore alone, 167 of 215 Indian-owned factories had belonged to non-Muslims. In East Pakistan, a Hindu trading caste, the Marwaris, had controlled almost all trade and industry—though the Hindu exodus from East Pakistan was not as dramatic or complete as from the West Wing. By way of example, Karachi's population of 600,000 in 1947 was equally divided between Muslims and Hindus, but by 1951 only 4,400 Hindus remained in a population then in excess of 1 million.

The exodus of Hindu merchants and business families living in what would become Pakistan was matched by a heavy migration of Muslim business families leaving India out of fear for their lives and property. The Indian state of Gujarat experienced the largest outflow, but Bombay and Calcutta also saw important families depart.

Gujarat, for example, had been home to the Muslim Habib family, which had been prominent in the finance and gold trading community in undivided India. Jinnah himself belonged to a similar community. The family's Habib Bank, founded in 1941, was the first to be owned by Muslims in the subcontinent. Mohammed Ali Habib, the head of the House of Habib and owner of the bank, reportedly presented Jinnah with a blank check to finance the new state until India delivered its share of financial resources, and Jinnah wrote in the figure of Rs 80 million.[18]

Other families that supported the Muslim League included the Ispahanis and Adamjees of Calcutta.[19] The Adamjees had set up a successful Indian-owned jute mill in an industry dominated by the British and decided to migrate because partition was going to separate their mills from the jute-producing lands of East Bengal. While they established new mills in East Pakistan, the family itself migrated to West Pakistan.

Another old Calcutta Muslim family that moved to Pakistan was the Saigols. Unlike the Adamjees and the Habibs, the Saigols were from Punjab, where they dominated the leather-tanning business, a trade avoided by Hindus because of the ritual pollution associated with handling animal hides. From leather the Saigols had expanded into the rubber industry and set up one of the first Indian-owned rubber factories. Following partition, the Saigols moved to Lahore in West Punjab to build the country's second textile mill, and Rafique Saigol, the son of patriarch Amin Saigol, became a cabinet minister. One Saigol brother remained in India to manage family businesses there, but the Indian government expropriated them as enemy property during the 1965 war.

Most émigré business families belonging to the traditional trading communities of Gujarat resettled in Karachi, turning the sleepy port city into the business capital of the country and eventually a huge metropolis. They quickly filled the gap left by Hindu traders. A smaller number of Punjabi-owned businesses resettled in the Lahore-Lyallpur (now Faisalabad) belt, making the first major investments in industry.

The contribution of these families should not be underestimated. Both the Bengalis in East Pakistan and the Urdu-speaking Mohajirs (together with the Punjabi working class and the Islamists) in West Pakistan protested the concentration of wealth in their hands, but it was the entrepreneurial skill and capital of these business communities that enabled Pakistan to develop the rudiments of an industrial sector after partition.

Though Pakistan did not inherit an industrial base, the areas that became Pakistan in 1947 produced large agricultural surpluses. The irrigation canal system built by the British in the Indus River basin had turned the arid plains of northwest India into fields of cotton, wheat, and rice, and many of the lands had been settled by retired officers and other ranks of the British Indian army. This created an enormous agricultural surplus in the region. The biggest cash crop in the area was cotton—a crop that Pakistan depends on to this day. The cotton fed the textile mills of Ahmedabad and Bombay. East Pakistan had a largely jute-and-rice economy similarly tied to Calcutta's jute mills and accounted for the bulk of the world's jute production.

Once the dust of partition settled, however, these earlier economic linkages were severed. The two countries could not agree on an exchange rate mechanism, effectively making it difficult to maintain integrated agricultural-business operations across the border, and both the cotton and jute industries came unstuck. West Pakistan could not process the cotton it produced, and East Pakistan could not process its jute.

The Pakistani economy may have had its prospects, but these structural problems stood in the way, as soon became evident. Pakistan suffered more than India; with the exception of Calcutta, which lost most of its hinterland and went into steep decline as a commercial and manufacturing center, India adapted reasonably well to the bifurcation of what once had been a vast, integrated economy.

The Kashmir Curse

All of the early arguments in favor of Pakistan and the experience of partition found their ultimate expression in the dispute over Kashmir, a Muslim-majority state ruled by a Hindu maharaja. After partition, the ruler was faced with an invasion of tribal warriors sent from the NWFP. He invited the Indian army to repel the invaders—but India first demanded his accession, which he provided. Thus Kashmir became the only Muslim-majority state in India.

Pakistani attitudes hardened when India reversed its pledge to the United Nations to allow a plebiscite in which Kashmiris could choose between India and Pakistan.[20] India had already sent forces in because it said tribal invaders had been dispatched from Pakistan's NWFP. Pakistanis acknowledge the move, but argue that it was done without Jinnah's knowledge, and that in any case India had also demonstrated its bad intentions by invading Junagadh, a princely state that had acceded to Pakistan, and by its reluctance to give Pakistan a fair share of assets from British India.

For first-generation Pakistanis, Kashmir was not a territorial or strategic concern—although it later became both as Kashmir came to symbolize the idea of Pakistan as a homeland for South Asian Muslims. India's reluctance to permit Kashmiri self-determination seemed to demonstrate both the correctness and justice of the two-nation theory, and to demonstrate the continued antagonism toward all of Pakistan and the cruelty toward its own Muslim citizens.

For many Pakistanis, but especially that first generation, Kashmir's captivity conjured up vivid images of oppression. Seven years before he became prime minister, the charismatic and demagogic politician Zulfiqar Ali Bhutto called Kashmir the "handsome head of the body of Pakistan" held by India "against all norms of morality" because it wanted to keep a Muslim majority area out of Pakistan, thus negating the two-nation theory.[21] Cruder and more virulent descriptions of Kashmir are also common, often supported by state propaganda organs.

This rhetoric resonated among Pakistanis who suffered during partition. It resonates even today. The staunchest advocates of the *idea* of Pakistan (in contrast to those who take a more relaxed view as *citizens* of Pakistan) feel that their identity is wrapped up in the fate of Kashmir, a region that reflects their own personal and political histories. For some, Kashmir is also the key to unraveling India. If India gave up Kashmir, then Indian Muslims would also come to Pakistan—or would at least achieve a separate status within a restructured Indian confederation. Whereas Indians regard the creation of Bangladesh as the death-knell of the two-nation theory, many Pakistanis now believe that the existence of two Islamic states in South Asia is compatible with the original Pakistan movement—a few hardliners even look forward to the day India might be broken up, adding to the list of independent South Asian Muslim states. In effect, they have come to agree with Choudhary Rahmat Ali's vision of many Muslim states in South Asia—Pakistan being joined by Bangladesh (he called it Bangistan), a new Kashmir, and perhaps an "Osmanistan" (the former princely state of Hyderabad, now incorporated in India's Andhra Pradesh), and others.

Interestingly, some of the most intense supporters of Kashmiri liberation are those who suffered under various military regimes or at the hands of Zulfiqar Ali Bhutto. Kashmir's liberation is a cause that justifies their uprooting and suffering; their anger at martial law during the Zia regime could be channeled into support for Kashmir. They see a link between their own private agony, India's policies on Kashmir, and the neutral or unhelpful policies of such countries as the United States. Because America failed to even acknowledge the brutal suppression of Kashmiri rights, it has, by extension, treated lightly the suffering of non-Kashmiris who supported the Pakistan movement. A good example of this reasoning is provided by Z. A. Suleri, a close associate of Jinnah and an active Muslim Leaguer.[22] For Suleri and his generation, the key issues were justice and truth, not strategy and security: "When the Quaid was asked about the economic viability of Pakistan he said: 'we will worry about that when the time comes.' We will worry about the impact of a free Kashmir when the time comes; you know, Kashmiris were never known as people who would fight, but look at them now!"[23]

To be sure, much of this vocal support is bravado, especially when coming from civilians. The army leadership would not risk the future of Pakistan over Kashmir, and until the 1989 Kashmir uprising, few thought that Kashmir's status would ever change (there is also a degree of cultural disdain, especially by Punjabis, for the nonmartial Kashmiris). Army officers speak of aid to the Kashmiri liberation movement but basically see it as a guerrilla struggle, which must therefore be waged by the Kashmiris, not outsiders. This has not prevented Pakistan from supporting Kashmiri militants and facilitating the movement into Kashmir (and India) of Punjabis and others who would like to join the fight against India, but the motive is as much to bleed India as to hope that Kashmir can be wrested from India.

For years, this seemed to be a no-lose position. If Kashmiris failed to achieve their freedom, then it was because they were insufficiently motivated, despite their just grievances against Indian perfidy. If Kashmiris *are* successful, then this can only be to Pakistan's advantage—it would validate the two-nation theory. There has thus been no serious civilian thinking about the actual strategic consequences of an independent Kashmir— how it would affect Pakistan's relations with Central Asia, Russia, Afghanistan, China, and India, and possibly other potential new states carved out of India or Pakistan, or how it would affect separatist demands from Sindhis or Baluch.

Pakistan has had a military strategy for Kashmir but not a political one, except to try to embarrass India in international forums. It has tried to wrest Kashmir away from India by force several times, and more recently it has used proxy war and militants to force India to come to the negotiating table. These policies have not worked, and Pakistanis have yet to examine carefully the kind of compromise settlement on Kashmir that they would be willing to accept.

Over the years, Kashmir has become part of the Pakistani identity—at least, of those Pakistanis who focus on strategic and security issues, notably the army—and it raises deep passions and emotions, especially among the large Kashmiri population in important Pakistani cities. The obsession with Kashmir for over fifty years can be said to have seriously damaged Pakistan's prospects as a state, but it is a cost that several generations of Pakistani leaders have been willing to pay, and the same can be said of their Indian counterparts.

The Struggle to Build a State

Pakistan was unstable from the outset. Jinnah's vision of a liberal Pakistan lacked roots, perhaps because he came to it so late, and was but one of the competing ideas put forth—especially by the Islamists and the state's various ethnolinguistic groups. (Ironically, this state created on the basis of religious fraternity chose Urdu as the national language, which was not the mother tongue of any Pakistani living in the provinces that became Pakistan, but of the Mohajirs who came from northern India.)

After independence no consensus emerged on the idea of Pakistan until one was imposed by the military, and even it proved elusive. Having failed to establish enduring and credible political institutions, Pakistan continued to face instability. Actually, a number of factors were to blame:

—The fledgling state suffered an immediate leadership crisis: Jinnah died on September 11, 1948, and his chief lieutenant, Liaquat Ali Khan, was assassinated on October 16, 1951.

—The Muslim League soon fractured: its leaders, newly arrived from India, lacked a political base in the provinces that became West Pakistan.

—In West Pakistan, the newly arrived Mohajirs favored a more or less secular state, laissez-faire economy, and liberal politics. By contrast, Muslim Leaguers from the NWFP, Punjab, Baluchistan, and Sindh tended to favor Islamization, a state-managed economy, and a go-slow policy toward land reform.

—In East Pakistan, 1,000 miles away, the Bengali wing of the Muslim League lost its influence in the party and national politics when ousted by a loose assemblage of opposition groups in provincial elections in 1954.

—There were deep differences between the populations of the East and West Wings: the former was almost entirely Bengali, while the latter was divided among several linguistic groups, with almost half being Punjabi.

—East Pakistanis (mainly Bengalis) were an overall majority and believed in the logic of majority rule, which put the less populous West at risk of permanent subordination to its Bengali fraction, which was poorer and in some quarters culturally denigrated.

Although it may not have lived up to its founders' expectations, Pakistan did move ahead economically, in stride with the much larger India, and established its own international identity. Three factors contributed to these successes.

First, Pakistanis had an intense underdog desire to disprove Indian predictions that their state would fail. The Indian National Congress had accepted partition grudgingly, expecting a fairly immediate collapse. By merely staying afloat, Pakistanis felt they were defying India. This psychology is evident even today in the third post-independence generation, particularly in cricket and sports rivalries and in public declarations of Pakistani nuclear prowess, which is why it was so difficult for the government to move against the hero of Pakistan's nuclear program, A. Q. Khan, when it was revealed in 2004 that he had been selling (as well as buying) nuclear secrets around the world.

Second, several policy issues it faced had the effect of strengthening the state and reinforcing the idea behind it. One of these was Kashmir. Of greater interest to West Pakistanis than those in the East Wing, Kashmir seemed to confirm the core rationale for Pakistan—that Muslims could not live peacefully or safely in a Hindu-dominated India. Further, their dependency on India, the upper riparian, united both East and West Pakistanis.[24]

Finally, Pakistan received significant outside economic and diplomatic support because it had early on decided to join two Western-sponsored military alliances, the Central Treaty Organization (CENTO) and the Southeast Asian Treaty Organization (SEATO). From 1954 to 1965 Pakistan was allowed to purchase weapons and received a mixture of military assistance in the form of grants and aid (weapons sold at concessional rates, or with reduced interest). This enabled it to build a modern army and a very efficient air force whose quality was enhanced by cooperative arrangements with several Gulf states. After Pakistan joined these Western-sponsored military pacts, however, the Indian attitude, never generous, hardened.

The Disinterest in Democracy

The difficulty of reconciling the idea of Pakistan with the requirements of a new democratic state was most evident in the failure to establish a functioning constitution or hold regular and consequential elections, both requirements for democracy. Although the idea of Pakistan included a nominally democratic Pakistan and there was agreement on the term, pressure began building to abridge or abort democracy. Most of the key power players in Pakistan respected democracy and wished Pakistan to be democratic, but they were not willing to make it so. These included the army, which admired democracy in the abstract but found it troubling in practice; civilian bureaucrats, who tended to equate democracy with civilian governments in which they played a major role; and the left, which advocated democracy in theory but also had authoritarian inclinations.

In fact, many groups in Pakistan lacked even a nominal commitment to democratic forms, let alone substance. The large landowners and rural elites, the so-called feudals of Pakistan, were dismissive of democracy, and many favored an undivided India—some had property on both sides of the international border and many had family and kin ties all over India. They rushed to join the Muslim League when it became apparent that the new state would come into being, but that was more to preserve their influence than out of ideological fervor.[25] As for the Islamic groups, most opposed this Western-imposed institution, and many were also not interested in Pakistan per se. They were conservative and generally apolitical, and for the most part not yet violent. That change would come twenty years later.

Pakistan's international supporters were ambivalent about democracy too. The American agenda was clear: a pro-Western Pakistan, a stable Pakistan, a prosperous Pakistan, and a democratic Pakistan were all desirable, but in that order. When democracy threatened to remove a leadership that was less than pro-American, the U.S. Embassy conveyed this priority to Pakistanis and for decades got a hearing—over the years the embassy, and most ambassadors, have been major participants in the Pakistani political process, even when they did not seek such influence.

The Objectives Resolution

Pakistan's constitutional history had begun before it was a state.[26] A Constituent Assembly met on August 11, four days before Pakistan came into being, and served as the federal parliament of Pakistan while it framed the new constitution. Jinnah was elected the first president of the assembly and became Pakistan's governor-general (the title for head of state that replaced the position of viceroy), snubbing Britain's Lord Mountbatten, who had wanted to be governor-general of both new countries.

The assembly took nine years to formulate a new constitution, but in 1949 it did try to define the idea of Pakistan in the Objectives Resolution, which is still in effect. As one analyst notes, "The Objectives Resolution was always there as the centre-piece to serve either as the preamble of a new Constitution or as a constitutional *Grundnorm,* and in 1985 it was incorporated as an operative part of the constitution."[27] The resolution defines both the state and the idea of Pakistan. The new country was to be a federal, democratic, and Islamic entity, but there was no mention whatsoever of a secular Muslim life, a secularized Islam, or even the term "secular."

In this constitutionally uncertain environment, Pakistan did not take long to move in an authoritarian direction. Rather than seek a fresh mandate from the people of Pakistan, the early governments hung on to power until displaced by the governor-general. Many Pakistanis, especially in the West Wing, felt comfortable with this arrangement for it was modeled on the Raj, which had been a benevolent and usually benign authoritarian system.

A Withered Judiciary

While the goals set forth in the Objectives Resolution and other statements of high principle had broad appeal, they offered little guidance on what to do when they conflicted, as they often do. Hence Pakistan's judiciary is regularly asked to rule on whether a coup, a parliamentary act, or an Islamic law is encompassed by the resolution. Pakistan has acquired a rich but convoluted judicial history, and its courts have become increasingly sensitive to political (and physical) pressures to bend their rulings in favor of the military or civilian government in power.[28]

Judicial power began to erode in 1955 when the then governor-general, civil servant Ghulam Mohammad, dissolved the Constituent Assembly and dismissed the government of Muhammad Ali Bogra. The courts then declared: "That which otherwise is not lawful, necessity makes lawful." This became known as "the doctrine of necessity," and subsequent courts have retroactively cited it to justify coups against civilian governments by generals Ayub, Yahya, Zia, and Musharraf. The Pakistani courts have thus sustained the "myth of constitutionalism" by pretending that military coups were legally and constitutionally justified.[29] They were activist judges in the sense that they exercised judicial review of government policies, but only to ratify coercive acts. One explanation for their actions may be that many of Pakistan's judges were Mohajirs and had a stronger ideological commitment to the new state than to constitutionalism. Nevertheless, their early pliability made it easier for subsequent civilian governments to break the law, and subsequent military governments to launch coups—all in the name of the doctrine of necessity.

At the same time, many have opposed the manipulation of the judicial system. Pakistan's various bar associations, especially those in Lahore, have been consistently critical of constitutional interference by the executive branch, the higher courts, and the military.[30]

Attempts at Building a Constitution

In its fifty-seven years, Pakistan has had three constitutions, those of 1956, 1962, and 1973. The 1956 constitution replaced the governor-general with a president, but with power in the hands of a prime minister elected by a national parliament. It preserved most of the British Indian constitutional structure and declared Pakistan to be an Islamic Republic. Other than that, there were no significant "Islamic" steps introduced, to the disappointment of the Islamic parties. The constitution of 1962 created a stronger presidency and an elaborate system of local government, presumably one that was party-free. The third constitution, that of 1973, reintroduced a prime ministerial system. All of these constitutions were amended significantly from time to time, most notably in 1985. Then, as Zia's martial law was being lifted, the powers of the president were increased in comparison with those of the prime minister, who could henceforth be removed by the president, and the provincial chief ministers by the governors. Prime ministerial authority was revived in 1997 by Nawaz Sharif, only to be once again subordinated to that of the president in 2002 by General Musharraf through an extraconstitutional Legal Framework Order (LFO). In early 2004, as a result of a year's negotiations, much of the LFO was incorporated into the constitution by a majority vote of Pakistan's electoral college (consisting of members of the national and provincial assemblies). At the same time, Musharraf promised to give up his army office at the end of the year, to seek election as president some time in 2007, and to retain the right to dismiss the prime minister after referral to the Pakistan Supreme Court.

As for elections, there was no shortage of these, although few were truly free. Pakistan did not hold its first national election until 1970, with subsequent ones in 1977, 1985, 1988, 1990, 1993, 1997, and 2002. The most calamitous of these was the first, which was also the freest (1970). It was followed by a civil war, Indian military intervention, and the breakup of Pakistan. Subsequent national elections were held under close military gaze.

To sum up Pakistan's democratic record, in its entire history it has had no successive elected governments—each such body was deposed by the military or dismissed by presidential fiat—and only Zulfiqar Ali Bhutto completed a term in office in 1977. Four presidents were themselves forced to resign by the army (Ayub Khan, Yahya Khan, Ghulam Ishaq Khan, and Rafiq Tarar), while a fifth, Farooq Leghari, was pushed out by Prime Minister Nawaz Sharif in 1998. Neither Pakistan's constitutional arrangement nor its political parties have attained a central place in the emerging Pakistani state-nation. Instead, the experienced bureaucracy and the young but ambitious army have perpetuated the notion that the politicians have let Pakistan down at moments when it faced its greatest threats from India.

Ayub and the End of Parliamentary Democracy

According to the American scholar Allen McGrath, October 28, 1954, marks the destruction of Pakistan's democracy, although democratic norms and practices had been deeply eroded from independence day onward. It was on this date that Governor-General Ghulam Mohammad ordered the police to bar the members of the Constituent Assembly from meeting in Karachi, where they were going to vote on the draft constitution approved at the assembly's previous session.[31]

As McGrath notes, Pakistan had no shortage of talented politicians then, and they did not lack political and parliamentary experience. However, they were disunited on the question of a constitution—the assembly's Bengali members, coming from the one region of Pakistan that had the most experience with parliamentary government, were especially at odds over the need for a new constitution. Some joined with the West Pakistanis to argue that Pakistan was not ready for "real" democracy and could only function as a tutored state, really an extension of the Raj. Unsure of their own political base, they were unwilling to give democracy a chance, and thus began Pakistan's long experiment with autocracy and oligarchy, with democratic tendencies bursting through from time to time.

In the view of many Pakistani liberals and constitutional scholars such as McGrath, the Pakistani elite, plus its foreign (largely American and European) supporters, effectively whitewashed Pakistan's failure to achieve constitutional normalcy largely on the grounds that a state under external pressure and still in internal disarray had no choice but to compromise on such niceties as a constitution.[32] Muhammad's decision was legitimized a year later by the Federal Court, thus leaving Pakistan in constitutional limbo: it was governed neither by the 1935 Government of India Act, nor by a new constitution. Pakistan stumbled forward under a weak parliamentary government until that was terminated in 1958 by General Ayub Khan.

Ayub's Coup

On October 7, 1958, in the face of continuing domestic disorder and political disarray, Pakistan's president, Major General Iskander Mirza, declared martial law and dismissed the central and provincial governments. Political parties were abolished and Ayub Khan was appointed supreme commander of the armed forces and chief martial law administrator. Mirza issued a statement noting that corruption, the unseemly struggle for power by the politicians, food crises, and the exploitation of Pakistan's masses had compelled his action. Mirza was himself soon bundled onto a waiting aircraft and flown to comfortable exile in London.

Thus began Pakistan's long experiment with military rule, broken only by spells of highly personalistic, sometimes autocratic, civilian governments, all of which were carefully watched—and eventually deposed—by the army. Military rule was bitterly opposed by a few Pakistani politicians, but most found a role in the new system or dropped out of politics.[33] Pakistan's army, at first assisted by the civilian bureaucracy and a group of experienced political elites, assumed the role of benevolent babysitter, watching over Pakistani politics and society. Later it was to assume the dominant role in "correcting" Pakistan, emulating the benevolent, all-encompassing role of *maa-baap* (mother-father, the colloquial name for the British Raj). Like the Raj, it justified its rule in strategic and moral terms. Under Ayub, grave matters of state security were taken out of the hands of the always untrustworthy political class—Pakistan was to undergo a transition from a homeland for Indian Muslims to a *fortress*, where its citizens could live more or less "Islamic" lives secure from the predatory India. Forty years later, this is still the dominant theme of Pakistan's politics.

From the 1960s, there was a growing linkage between the army and the ideology of the state. By the end of Ayub's rule, the security of Pakistan was seen as being in the capable hands of the military; the military itself became more and more closely identified with the two provinces that produced most of its officers and nearly all of its jawans, the NWFP and Punjab. Punjab was also Pakistan's breadbasket and the country's wealthiest province. This connection between the state, the army, and the province of Punjab was to have devastating consequences.

As for Pakistan's Islamic side, Ayub and his colleagues had no serious interest in Islamic doctrine or theory, even as practicing or orthodox Muslims. Their task, they thought, was to identify Pakistan's geostrategic threats and to formulate a strategy that would ensure Pakistani security. Islam was incidental to Pakistan, in the sense that it was the state that was challenged, and the state was the protector of Islam within its borders. If there was a role for Islam, it was to assist in the mobilization of the state apparatus, particularly the armed forces.

The image of Pakistan as a fortress had distinct features. First, the threat to Pakistan was now from a real state, India. This threat was situated in a global, strategic context. Delhi was portrayed as an ally of

Moscow. Thus if outside powers would not support Pakistan because of the justness of its cause, at least they would come to Islamabad's rescue out of strategic necessity.

Second, the Pakistani armed forces had the best understanding of the requirements of national defense and security. They were the dedicated, professional guardians of the fortress. Civilian politicians who interfered with the smooth operations of the armed forces, especially the army, might as well have opened the fortress gates to the barbarian invader.

Finally, regional peace was possible, but only if a military balance was achieved between India and Pakistan. If Delhi refused to recognize Pakistan's legitimate existence and denied the validity of the two-nation theory, it would meet a reality check administered by a well-armed Pakistan. The Indians were bullies, and bullies recognize superior power. The prime duty of Pakistanis was to keep the fortress intact, safe from external and internal enemies.

After he became president, Ayub took the lead in articulating this new vision of Pakistan. He would often begin with a framework that recalled Alberuni's catalogue of Hindu-Muslim differences:

> It was Brahmin chauvinism and arrogance that had forced us to seek a homeland of our own where we could order our life according to our own thinking and faith. They wanted us to remain as serfs, which was precisely the condition in which the Muslim minority in India lived today. There was the fundamental opposition between the ideologies of India and Pakistan. The whole Indian society was based on class distinction in which even the shadow of a low-caste man was enough to pollute a member of the high caste.[34]

Ayub explained that because of their hatred for Muslims, Indian leaders wanted to browbeat Pakistan into subservience.[35] This meant that Pakistan had to build a "deterrent force with adequate offensive and defensive power; enough, at least, to neutralize the Indian army. India can concentrate her forces against us without warning. We must, therefore, have a standing army ready to take the field at a moment's notice."[36] Under the influence of Zulfiqar Ali Bhutto, Ayub adopted a strategy of moving toward better relations with two of Pakistan's three giant neighbors (the Soviet Union and China). In the Pakistani view, China was no threat to India, and Ayub later also came to believe that Pakistan's membership in the U.S.-sponsored SEATO had been unwise.

Ayub further believed that East Pakistan, being surrounded on three sides by India, was practically indefensible. His dismissal of the defense of East Pakistan became a major Bengali grievance after the 1965 war with India. If Pakistani generals thought that East Pakistan could be sacrificed to India to save West Pakistan, why should Bengalis stay in the Pakistani federation? It was a question ultimately answered by the creation of Bangladesh.

From "Joint Defense" to War

One of Ayub's most important steps was to again offer India a "joint-defense" arrangement. This idea had a long history, going back to Jinnah's assumption that the two dominions would cooperate on security matters and the suggestion of several politicians that once outstanding disputes between India and Pakistan had been resolved, a joint defense arrangement would release money for development. Ayub raised the idea in 1959: "In case of external aggression both India and Pakistan should come together to defend the subcontinent."[37]

By this time Delhi was alarmed by its border dispute with China, and Ayub and his advisers felt the Indians might be more amenable to working on Kashmir, the canal waters dispute, and other issues. "Once these were resolved, the armies of the two countries could disengage and move to their respective vulnerable frontiers. This would give us the substance of joint defense; that is, freedom from fear of each other and freedom to protect our respective frontiers."[38] Ayub's proposal of joint defense would today be called a confidence-building measure. His intent had not been an alliance, but a large-scale troop withdrawal from the borders, including the disputed cease-fire line in Kashmir. This, in turn, would enable India to better meet the threat from China, while Pakistan could deal with its difficulties along the Durand Line, the long border with Afghanistan.

But, as Ayub correctly records, the Indians were suspicious of his motives. They envisaged a repeat of the 1947–48 infiltration of raiders into Kashmir, supported by regular Pakistan army troops. The Indians rejected the proposal, seemingly also misinterpreting it to mean a formal military pact. In turn, Nehru offered a "no war" agreement between India and Pakistan—which was rejected by Pakistan.

Ayub had exactly predicted the future, but so had the Indians. When the India-China war broke out in 1962, India delayed pulling its forces away from the border and cease-fire line with Pakistan until the United States and Great Britain offered assurances that Pakistan would not take advantage of the situation. (This led to a new American-British effort to address the Kashmir problem, an effort that collapsed by 1964.) New Delhi's apprehensions also seem to be justified: in 1965 Ayub was persuaded to support a rerun of the 1948 infiltration of raiders, in the 1980s Pakistan sponsored terrorists in Indian Punjab, and in the 1990s it supported them in Kashmir. Whether Pakistan would have taken this course had India responded seriously to Ayub's initiatives is an important but speculative question, for which there is no known answer.

Domestic Reforms

Shortly before Ayub Khan was forced from power, Samuel P. Huntington, an American academic subsequently well known for his popularization of the idea of the "clash of civilizations," declared that "more than any other political leader in a modernizing country after World War II, Ayub came close to filling the role of a Solon or Lycurgus, or 'Great Legislator' on the Platonic or Rousseauean model."[39]

It is easy to see why Huntington was impressed with Ayub. The Ayub years were a break from the chaos and disorder that preceded his coup, but they also represented a departure from the idealism of the Pakistan movement. With military precision, Ayub and his army colleagues set about creating a Pakistan that was both intellectually coherent and administratively effective in a way that served as a model for others and also received much praise. Ayub's pattern was copied by two of his three military successors—Zia ul-Haq and Pervez Musharraf—both of whom came to power in a coup and then sought to bring about a political, cultural, and social revolution.

Domestically, Ayub set about transforming a coup d'état into a revolution. In the words of one close observer, "The broad appeal in the revolutionary idea went very much further than answering to legal necessities. The notion was, in itself, stimulating, evocative, and altogether congenial. It signified a clear break with a past of which no one felt unduly proud; a past all too definitely associated with political gerrymandering, purposeless intrigue, corruption, internal unrest, incompetence, and loss of face abroad."[40] The army set about disinfecting Pakistan, and the army public relations apparatus played down the coup aspect of Ayub's takeover, emphasizing its revolutionary and popular dimension. Ayub promised that what would emerge would be a "sound, solid, and strong nation." He also gave an unequivocal pledge that he would restore power to the people of Pakistan via a new political system that would provide suitable checks and balances on political parties and politicians.

With support from America and Britain, Ayub accelerated the rehabilitation of refugees from East Punjab and revived interest in agriculture. Considerable American technical assistance made it possible to establish agricultural universities and extension services in both wings. Ayub also moved the capital from Karachi (seen by the army as a symbol of corruption and venality), building a new city in Islamabad, not far from his own home village.

Pakistan became a widely admired case study of nation-building directed by the army. Scrapping the 1956 constitution, Ayub eventually assumed the presidency, and his own constitution, promulgated in 1962, paid only lip service to the Islamic dimensions of Pakistan while trying to stabilize the country's geographical and linguistic diversity, addressing its uneven economic development, and retaining firm control at the center. This 1962 constitution created a presidency indirectly elected by 80,000 union councilors (Ayub also created his own "tame" political party, the Conference Muslim League, to provide a façade of democratization). Though much derided in India, it was an attempt to balance the popular desire for democracy with the seeming requirements of order and development.

Ayub had to create a new system because the existing order had no place for the army, especially the officer corps. Like the Raj, Pakistan was now governed by a civil-military coalition at the center, the difference being that in British India the civilians dominated the relationship whereas in Pakistan it was the generals, assisted by the bureaucracy, that did so. The politicians were expected to assume a modest stance, one appropriate to their record of failed governance and incessant speechifying.

Economic Gains

Ayub was a strong believer in free enterprise. Where legislative majorities had been unable to revive the economy, Ayub's military government instituted an export-promotion strategy that led to the strongest growth in the history of the Pakistan economy. Pakistan's exports during these years surpassed those of Thailand, Malaysia, and Singapore *combined*. Countries such as South Korea and Malaysia saw Pakistan as a model for export-led growth strategies. Today they are regarded as models for Pakistan. Pakistan was also the darling of the developmental world in the 1950s and 1960s, and massive American, European, and Japanese aid and investment flowed in, along with substantial military grants and sales from Washington.

The Pakistan economy had received an initial boost from the Korean War and the huge demand for cotton and jute. Between 1947 and 1954, West Pakistan's textile production capacity increased from less than 0.2 million spindles to 1.3 million. East Pakistan went from 0 tons to 55,000 tons of jute production during the same time.[41] Between 1949 and 1954, industrial output grew 34 percent a year in West Pakistan and 21 percent in the eastern wing (after the war, from 1955 to 1959, this slowed down to 12.4 percent a year in the west and 10 percent in the east). By 1959 the value of industrial output had risen from 1 percent to 6 percent of gross domestic product (GDP).[42]

Ayub's economic policy allowed the military to forge an alliance with the business community. His purpose in doing so was to reduce the power of the political classes, both popular politicians and the feudal landowners. Ayub's regime established the Pakistan Industrial Development Corporation (PIDC), which would finance the industrial growth of the 1960s. Between 1962 and 1969, the PIDC financed twenty-five large industrial projects in the private sector.[43] The PIDC was also used by the regime to discriminate against those who did not support military rule. Further, the government supported the formation of business associations in order to direct their growth and to maintain their political reliability. Other policy initiatives expanded Pakistani industry by allowing new businessmen to set up factories and mills, resulting in the entry of a new class of entrepreneurs that included Punjabi merchants, the feudal aristocracy, retired civil servants, and military officers.[44]

There was a downside to these economic policies. Ayub's government was highly business-friendly, with the result that wealth was concentrated in the hands of a few families: in a now famous speech in Karachi in 1968, the chief economist of the Pakistan Planning Commission and one of the country's foremost economists, Mahbub ul-Haq, said that 66 percent of the country's economy, 70 percent of insurance, and 80 percent of banking assets were controlled by twenty families. Haq later expanded the figure to twenty-two, and the number became a symbol of Pakistan's grave economic inequalities.[45]

The émigré business families who owned capital and dominated the economy captured the benefits of the growth. Real wages, for example, declined for the growing urban working class even as the economy continued to expand rapidly. Also troubling, the industrial licensing system was used to reward regime supporters and punish opponents. Ayub's policies were particularly negative for East Pakistan, where 53 percent of the population lived. The industrial licensing policy clearly favored West Pakistani businessmen over local entrepreneurs. The eastern wing received less than half the share of the country's resources.

The rapid economic growth under Ayub was responsible for the regional imbalance between the eastern and western wings of the country, which in turn contributed to the breakup of 1971. Ayub's policies also fomented economic populism in West Pakistan. Riding its tide, the next prime minister, Zulfiqar Ali Bhutto, nationalized big and small industries, persecuted the business community, and shattered the investment climate in Pakistan.

An Ideology for Pakistan

Pakistan's leaders never made a serious attempt to introduce Islamic principles of governance as they could not agree on *which* Islam would be widely acceptable. There were also sharp divisions between the highly Westernized few who ran the country and the remaining disparate population. Hence Pakistan evolved an ethos and a ruling elite that narrowed the range of debate over the nature of the idea of Pakistan, glorifying elements of the state, especially the army, and buttressing a political order that had little relevance to Islam, democracy, or any other system.

All nation-states indulge themselves as they develop an idealized history, passing it on to successive generations through the school curriculum and official media.[46] It was during the Ayub years that Pakistan began the process of official myth-creation in earnest. A large central bureaucracy was created to manufacture an ideology for Pakistan, one that glorified the army as the state's key institution.

As the British scholar Ian Talbot notes, the ideology of a monolithic Muslim community was erected to counter the "other" of Indian nationalism and "provincialism" within Pakistan.[47] The state controlled textbooks and electronic media, ran several newspapers, and had a coercive influence over the privately owned press. Even when the latter was not subjected to formal censorship, threats were made to withdraw official advertisements, an important revenue stream for most print media (in recent years the threats have escalated to beatings and physical intimidation of reporters and owners). K. K. Aziz, a leading Pakistani historian, has remarked on the government's xenophobic tendencies and glorification of the armed forces, especially the army.[48] Today, many young Pakistanis do not have access to an objective history of their own country.

The Pakistani state was deployed in the service of the two-nation theory, but the process of social indoctrination did not penetrate very far because of the weak school system and Pakistan's considerable ethnic and linguistic diversity. Nevertheless, ideological propagation grew over the years, the process reaching a peak under Zia when virtually everything was censored, even books that were favorably regarded by Zia himself.[49] A whole discipline, "Pakistan Studies," was established in the Ministry of Education and became the vehicle for the promulgation of an often-distorted vision of Pakistan, its origin, and other states, especially India.

Although the Pakistan government was thus able to launch mass campaigns to shape "public opinion," one regime after another found itself at the mercy of years of autoindoctrination. That is why Pakistan's government is often unable to move: in short, its own "public opinion," cultivated over the years, poses an impediment to fresh policy departures.[50]

Pakistan's Ruling Elite

Aristotle divided forms of government into three basic categories: the rule of one (monarchy), the few (aristocracy), and the many. Each form has a corrupt twin: tyranny, oligarchy, and mobocracy, and in each case the abuse of power could damage the interests of the polity.[51]

Of all of Ayub's achievements, the most enduring was not a particular policy, official state apparatus, or even an idea of Pakistan and its history, but an informal political system that tied together the senior ranks of the military, the civil service, key members of the judiciary, and other elites.

Subsequently dubbed the "Establishment," it resembles a classic oligarchy, and its roots lie deep in the psychology of the British Raj and the social structure of Pakistan's West Wing.[52] Huntington's praise of Ayub as a "Solon" was misjudged: instead of providing a legal framework that would regulate Pakistan, he established an oligarchy. Ironically, Ayub was himself removed by the military members of the oligarchy *cum* Establishment when he later faltered.

Writing in 1996, a contemporary chronicler of the Establishment, Syed Mushahid Hussain, pegged it at about 500 people, a small culturally and socially intertwined elite. Ayub's Establishment may have been smaller still, but it included those East Bengalis who were thought to be trustworthy. Other members of the Establishment included members of the business community; journalists, editors, and media experts; and a few academics and members of think tanks (most of which were and are government supported). At times, some foreign ambassadors with particularly close ties to the leadership were de facto members of the Establishment.[53] Military officers and civilian bureaucrats above a certain level were potential members of the Establishment but were not taken into confidence or fully trusted until they had proved themselves "loyal" to core principles; the Establishment has always been wary of mavericks, and few high-ranking Pakistani officials, civil or military, have publicly broken with the group consensus.

As Hussain notes, the informality of the Establishment ensures that occupying a particular post does not confer membership. This is not only because of the personalistic nature of Pakistan's politics, but because membership depends on adherence to a broad set of values and norms, including a particular understanding of the idea of Pakistan. Hence individuals who share these values and norms but who do not hold any official position—such as the legendary soldier-diplomat-spokesman Lieutenant General Sahabzada Yaqub Khan—may be part of the Establishment, while those who hold official positions but who might wander from these norms in some significant way or who cannot be fully trusted are not part of the inner circle or may drift in and out. Another long-time member of the Establishment, Syed Sharifuddin Pirzada, is now a senior cabinet member without portfolio. Pirzada was a young Bombay lawyer who came to serve as Jinnah's personal secretary. Over the decades almost every Pakistani government, certainly all the military ones, brought Pirzada into the inner circle: he gave legal advice to Ayub, Yahya, Zia, and Musharraf and provided the legal justification for all of the coups. Still active in 2003, he accompanied President Musharraf on an important visit to Washington.[54] Most recently, Tariq Aziz, a former schoolmate of Musharraf and an official in Pakistan's Income Tax service, has joined Musharraf as a core member of the Establishment. He has no special achievement in his professional record, but he is highly valued for his political astuteness and his advice on managing domestic politics.

The Establishment also has an important subset composed of Islamic nationalists that sometimes finds itself at odds with the core members. "Islamic Nationalism," which describes the politics of an increasing number of Establishment members, is rooted not in a desire to transform Pakistan into a state under Islamic law, the *Shariah,* but in a worldview that stems from nationalist and foreign policy motives. These are, above all, anti-Indian in character but also include a deep distrust of the United States and hatred of Israel. The Pakistani figures who currently epitomize Islamic nationalism include the former army chief, General Aslam Beg, and A. Q. Khan, one of the key figures in the covert nuclear program— and subsequently a national hero. Often personally secular, the Islamic nationalist worldview is shaped by the notion of grievance, not by the principles of Islam, although the policies of this group are justified as being supportive of the Muslim *ummah,* or community.

These positions bring them very close to the underpinnings of al Qaeda, another movement rooted in anger and a desire to punish the corrupt and powerful, be they Muslim leaders (of Saudi Arabia) or their American patrons. Islamic nationalists take literally the idea of cooperation among Muslim countries, pride in the idea of Pakistan being the world's most powerful and influential Muslim state, and considerable pleasure in being able to trick Pakistan's enemies, especially the United States and India. This group has steered Pakistan down some dangerous paths, notably its attempt to expand Pakistani influence in Central Asia, General Beg's "strategic defiance" of the United States, and A. Q. Khan's covert sale of nuclear technology to other countries.

The "operational code" of Pakistan's Establishment has changed somewhat over the years. Since its elements are examined in subsequent chapters, suffice it to say here that in Ayub's years it included the following precepts:

—India was the chief threat to Pakistan, and the armed forces were central to the defense of the state. Therefore the armed forces deserved a priority position in determining domestic political issues and in the allocation of state resources.

—Pakistan's security problem was first and foremost a military one: India had to be deterred from attacking Pakistan, and Pakistan itself had to be able to pressure India to force it to behave properly. Strategically, the defense of Pakistan lay in the west and Punjab was Pakistan's heartland.

—Military alliances were necessary because Pakistan could not afford to match Indian size on its own. "Borrowed" power was not something to be ashamed of; on the contrary, it was vital to the survival of the state and capabilities of the armed forces.

—Kashmir was an important issue even if the Pakistani masses did not think so. It was not only a strategically important territory, it was proof positive of Indian malevolence. Pursuing the cause of the Kashmiris, with the ultimate goal of incorporating them into Pakistan, would fulfill the original vision of Pakistan as a homeland for oppressed Indian Muslims. While the Establishment was sometimes divided as to how to deal with Kashmir, these were tactical not strategic differences.

—Other moderate Islamic states, notably Turkey and Iran, both of which were also secular, centralized, and Western-oriented, were Pakistan's natural allies and role models.

—Domestically, the armed forces were the model for the rest of Pakistan. The army was seen as selfless, disciplined, obedient, and competent. Denigration of the army was not allowed.

—Deep or rapid social reform, while theoretically necessary, was too risky for a state that was already unstable and pressed from the outside by dangerous enemies. The Establishment accepted Pakistan's low levels of literacy and the absence of serious social and land reform.

—The economy was problematic: Pakistan had great assets, but also a high defense burden, and the East Wing was very poor. One solution was the solicitation of massive military and economic aid—economic growth would march hand in hand with large amounts of foreign aid. This aid originally came from the West, especially the United States, but by the 1960s Japan was a significant donor and investor, and China emerged as Pakistan's chief arms supplier after 1970.

—Democracy was theoretically desirable, but the Pakistani people were "excitable" (President Zia's term), and the standards of education and public discourse had to be raised before the masses could be allowed to freely express their opinion in the ballot box or the press. Popular passions had to be channeled where they might not interfere with the efficient operation of the state. These restrictions applied both to "leftists" and extreme Islamists.

—The state's tight control over the media and academia ensured that the Pakistani masses were exposed to a correct history and that news was presented in such a way as to strengthen, not weaken, their faith in the idea of Pakistan and the legitimacy of the Pakistani state. Dissent and disagreement were suppressed or hidden from foreign observers.[55]

—Radical or violent Islamic groups were regarded with disdain by the Ayub generation, but Yahya Khan employed them in East Pakistan, thus beginning a pattern of tolerating them if they could be used as instruments of state policy, as demonstrated by Zulfiqar Ali Bhutto, Zia, both democratic governments during the 1990s, and Musharraf.

—The leftist vision of Pakistan was incompatible with that of the Establishment, and Pakistan's Western allies had to be shown that Pakistan was free from revolutionary impulses. The left was systematically suppressed and the Communist Party of Pakistan was banned. Ironically, oppression of the left continued after China became Pakistan's leading ally.

—The Establishment made gestures toward Islam but never took seriously the idea of imposing a standard Islam upon Pakistan or altering Pakistan's relatively secular and tolerant public culture (see chapter 5). The army was even less tolerant of Islamists than the civilians.

—By merely surviving, Pakistan could demonstrate that the Indian opposition to both the idea of Pakistan and the new state of Pakistan was misguided. Sooner or later the Indians would reconcile themselves to the facts and deal honestly and fairly with Pakistan.

As already mentioned, the Establishment's view of Pakistan borrowed heavily from the ideology of the British Raj, a paternalistic government that meant well and shared power only when required to do so. Like the British, the Pakistan Establishment did well by doing good, although the level of corruption in Pakistan far exceeded that of the Raj's latter years. The Raj had ultimately been accountable to London, and its soldiers were (after 1918) firmly under civilian control, whereas Pakistan's Establishment has had little check on its authority. Foreign governments do have leverage if they are providing arms aid and economic assistance, but Pakistan has tried to diversify its outside supporters to ensure that no single donor can compel it to move in any particular direction.

Thus the Ayub period saw the transformation of Pakistan from an ideologically defined but ethnically circumscribed state to one whose major purpose was to provide a shield against a threatening India. The continued hostility with India plus the benefits of belonging to two military alliances ensured the rise of a liberal praetorian state, a "basic" democracy that could hold its own alongside other hyphenated democracies. However, the system failed because good intentions and shrewd manipulation by a benevolent oligarchy were unable to prevent politics from again taking command or social aspirations from expressing themselves on the street.

The 1965 War and the Second Partition

Ayub might have occupied the presidency for many years more, but he fell seriously ill, his reputation was clouded by family-related scandals, politicians escalated their demands for a return to parliamentary democracy, and he made a serious strategic error in going to war against India in 1965. In this Ayub had been egged on by his activist foreign minister, the young Zulfiqar Ali Bhutto, who was ambitious, ruthless, and a charter member of the Establishment. The war's objective had been to put pressure on India to negotiate on Kashmir, and the Kashmiris themselves were expected to rise up en masse. Instead, India escalated the conflict across the international border, the Kashmiris did not stir, and a stalemate ensued. None of Pakistan's Western allies came to its rescue, and Pakistan's newest ally, China, only made sympathetic noises.

The 1965 war was devastating for Pakistani unity because it revealed to the East Wing that Pakistan was a Punjab-centric state whose army defined both the idea of Pakistan and the security parameters of the state of Pakistan in a manner that was incompatible with Bengali interests. When Ayub stated that the defense of Pakistan lay in the West, he effectively wrote off East Pakistan. Further, the army's overwhelming Punjabi-Pathan officer corps had never accepted the idea that Bengalis were militarily equal to them in terms of their "martial" qualities, so by assuming that half of Pakistan's citizens were militarily inferior, they also implied over half the country comprised lesser Pakistanis. In short, in the dominant West Wing the "idea" of Pakistan pertained to a martial people defending its Punjabi stronghold. Bengal and Bengalis only figured as an investment opportunity or source of foreign exchange.

Not surprisingly, the Bengali political leadership responded sharply to what they perceived as slights by the army-dominated West. Led by Sheikh Mujibur Rahman, the Awami League put forth a six-point agenda demanding a return to democracy, greater attention to East Pakistan's defense, a redistribution of assets, and in effect, the freedom to conduct relations with other countries as it saw fit. This was almost a return to one of the earlier partition schemes—which envisioned two loosely affiliated Pakistans that would be allies and friends, but virtually independent.[56]

The system created by Ayub was not flexible or representative enough to accommodate these pressures, and no other system was acceptable—neither a looser federation that would allow the East Wing to remain within the state, nor a move to mass democratic politics, nor a system of majority rule at the center. The first was blocked by the army, which saw it as a first step to the destruction of Pakistan. Mass democratic politics were opposed by many elites, fearful of socialism and Islam. And the notion of a Bengali majority was anathema both to the Punjabi-Pathan–dominated army and to the most prominent West Pakistani politician, Bhutto, who wanted the prime ministerial position for himself.

Ayub's successor was his army chief, Yahya Khan, a sincere but politically inept general. He had to address the demands of the East Wing while simultaneously trying to contain the charismatic Bhutto. The latter had turned against Ayub and emerged as the most popular politician in West Pakistan. However, Yahya lacked the necessary political skills; he was facing two strong politicians, Bhutto and Mujib; and the military-dominated Establishment itself could only think of force when dealing with a political problem. The three men share the responsibility for creating the conditions that led to open rebellion in the East Wing, Indian military intervention, and the formation of the separate state of Bangladesh.

Separation might have been averted by a more accommodating policy, but by 1970 the generals had decided that a whiff of gunpowder would overawe the meek Bengalis. The army treated the Bengal movement as a counterinsurgency exercise, not a political puzzle to be painstakingly and patiently solved. Furthermore, by treating the Bengali autonomist movement as an Indian creation, Pakistan's civil-military oligarchy lost the opportunity to hold its country together. Islamabad was right to be suspicious of India, but long before civil war broke out, the Bengali population had been thoroughly alienated.

The Aftermath

The impact of defeat in the 1971 war and the second partition on the Pakistani elite should not be understated.[57] Pakistan lost 54 percent of its population, and the army, the core of the Establishment, had been humiliated, with more than 90,000 officers and men taken prisoner. Pakistan's friends, including America, had done nothing to help it, and the widespread international support for India had been especially galling since most Pakistani strategists believed that from the beginning New Delhi was behind the East Pakistan separatist movement. However, the most important consequence of the loss of the East Wing may have been the way it affected Pakistan's identity as a state. Overall, three consequences were of major negative proportions.

First, the political balance shifted within Pakistan, leaving Punjab the overwhelmingly dominant province (see chapter 6). From 1972 onward, the most populous province in Pakistan was also its economically strongest and the major contributor of manpower to the politically important army. As reflected in the army's own teachings and doctrine, Pakistan became equated with Punjab.

Second, the loss of East Pakistan dramatically narrowed Pakistan's cultural and social diversity, to its ultimate disadvantage. Bengalis had been an important element in Pakistani cultural life and had added much to the old Pakistan. They were especially important in parliamentary debate, where they were among the "most bold, outspoken and non-conformist" elements.[58] While many West Pakistanis believed that shedding the garrulous Bengalis would make Pakistan a more homogeneous and stronger state, this turned out to be a serious error. One of Pakistan's early qualities was its cultural diversity, which had strengthened the country, not weakened it.

Third, the balance of power subtly shifted away from secular, "mainstream" forces toward the Islamists. The Islam of East Pakistan was on

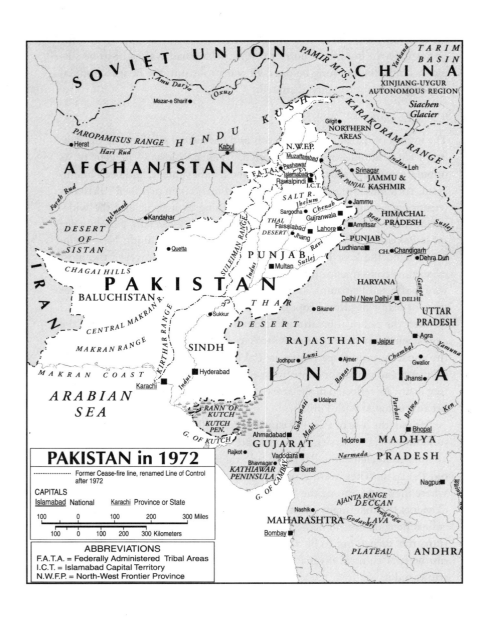

SOVIET UNION

Amu Darya
(Oxus)

Mazar-e Sharif ●

PAMIR MTS.

TARIM BASIN

CHINA

XINJIANG-UYGUR
AUTONOMOUS REGION

Yarkand

KUSH

Siachen Glacier

KARAKORAM RANGE

Indus

PAROPAMISUS RANGE HINDU

● Herat

Hari Rud

Kabul

AFGHANISTAN

Gilgit ●
NORTHERN
AREAS

N.W.F.P.

Muzaffarabad ●

F.A.T.A.

Peshawar ●
Islamabad ●
Rawalpindi ■
I.C.T.

● Srinagar

● Leh

PIR PANJAL

JAMMU &
KASHMIR

Forah Rud

Helmand

● Kandahar

SALT R.

Jhelum

● Jammu

Sargodha ■

Chenab

Beas

HIMACHAL
PRADESH

Sutlej

DESERT
OF
SISTAN

● Quetta

SULEIMAN RANGE

THAL
DESERT

Faisalabad ●
Jhang

Gujranwala ■
■ Amritsar

Lahore ■

PUNJAB

CHAGAI HILLS

PAKISTAN

PUNJAB

Indus

Ludhiana ■

Ravi

■ Multan *Sutlej*

CH. ● Chandigarh
● Dehra Dun

IRAN

BALUCHISTAN

MAKRAN R.

CENTRAL MAKRAN

MAKRAN RANGE

KIRTHAR RANGE

THAR

● Sukkur

DESERT

SINDH

Indus

HARYANA

Delhi / New Delhi ■ ■ DELHI

● Bikaner

Ganges

UTTAR
PRADESH

RAJASTHAN ■ Jaipur

■ Agra

Yamuna

Luni
Jodhpur ●

● Ajmer

Chambal

Gwalior ●

MAKRAN COAST

● Hyderabad

Karachi ●

Indus

INDIA

Jhansi ●

ARABIAN
SEA

*RANN OF
KUTCH*

KUTCH
PEN.

Banas

● Udaipur

Sabarmati

Parbati

Betwa

Ken

G. OF KUTCH

Ahmadabad ■

Mahi

■ Bhopal

Indore ■

MADHYA

Rajkot ●

GUJARAT

Vadodara ■

Narmada

PRADESH

PAKISTAN in 1972

·············· Former Cease-fire line, renamed Line of Control
after 1972

CAPITALS
Islamabad National   Karachi Province or State

| 100 | 0 | 100 | 200 | 300 Miles |

| 100 | 0 | 100 | 200 | 300 Kilometers |

ABBREVIATIONS
F.A.T.A. = Federally Administered Tribal Areas
I.C.T. = Islamabad Capital Territory
N.W.F.P. = North-West Frontier Province

Bhavnagar ●
*KATHIAWAR
PENINSULA*

■ Surat

G. OF CAMBAY

Nashik ●

AJANTA RANGE
DECCAN

MAHARASHTRA *Godavari*

Bombay ●

Nagpur ■

Wainganga

Penganga

LAVA

PLATEAU

ANDHRA

balance far more moderate than that of the Northwest Frontier Province or Baluchistan. The breakup of the country merely empowered the most regressive and conservative Islamists in the West.

East Pakistan's separation was seldom discussed in Pakistan after 1972, but on the thirtieth anniversary of the event, President Musharraf made a trip to the national memorial to the Bangladesh freedom fighters on the outskirts of Dhaka. Just before he arrived, the leaders of fifty-one Pakistani civil rights organizations issued a public apology to Bangladesh for the events of 1971, and in the visitors' book Musharraf wrote that Pakistanis "share the pain" of those events with Bangladeshis.[59] Going farther than any previous Pakistani leader, he repeated his words at a formal banquet, describing Pakistanis and Bangladeshis as a "family" with a common religious and cultural heritage.[60] The two countries then agreed to additional contacts. The Musharraf visit, and his near-apology, involved as much strategy as heart-felt reconciliation. Musharraf's bold advances toward Bangladesh were no doubt motivated mainly by the two states' shared concern about India.

For the army and its civilian supporters, the major lesson of 1971 was that Pakistan had the moral right, if not the obligation, to pay India back in kind. Obsessed with India's role in dividing the country, Pakistan's leadership showed little concern with the social and cultural losses its people had suffered, let alone an interest in strengthening cultural and political diversity in the new Pakistan. In the early 1980s, ten years after the East Pakistan debacle, Islamabad was finally able to achieve a measure of revenge by providing covert support for, first, the Khalistani (Sikh) separatist movement, and beginning in 1989, for militant Kashmiri separatists.

Zulfiqar Ali Bhutto: The Innovator

The loss of East Pakistan created widespread ferment and drove people to ask hitherto taboo questions: Was Pakistan going to survive? Had the dream of Pakistan proven illusory? Would there be another "Bangladesh" in the future? How could Pakistan protect itself against the newly victorious India? Zulfiqar Ali Bhutto had answers to all of these questions.

Bhutto had been a wunderkind, educated partly in the United States and attracted to leftist causes. A striking speaker, he had established the

Pakistan People's Party (PPP) in December 1967. Bhutto's appeal transcended provincial boundaries, and although a Sindhi, he was popular in Punjab as well. Bhutto finally came to power after Pakistan's surrender to India. He enjoyed more freedom than any other civilian leader before or since and set about implementing his own version of the idea and the state of Pakistan.

A new constitution passed in 1973 gave Bhutto, as the new prime minister, complete executive power and made the president a figurehead. Bhutto also wished to reduce the army's power, but fearful of a coup, he moved slowly. First, he ensured that pliable generals were in command of key army positions and then began laying the foundations of an alternative military force, the Federal Security Force, which would distance the army from internal security. He also initiated a nuclear weapons project to undercut the army's claim to being the ultimate defender of Pakistan. In addition, Bhutto appointed a War Inquiry Commission to look into the 1971 defeat. Its report, submitted in 1974 but never officially released, was eventually made public in 2002.[61]

The commission, headed by the chief justice of Pakistan at the time, Hamoodur Rahman, concluded that widespread atrocities, the abuse of power by Pakistani generals, and a complete failure of civilian and martial law leadership were responsible for the loss of East Pakistan. It recommended trials for senior generals implicated in the coup that removed Ayub and in the conduct of the war in East Pakistan. The report dwells on a range of sins, suggesting "Measures for Moral Reform in the Armed Forces" to address "lust for wine and women, and greed for lands and houses" by senior army officers. These included a ban on alcohol in the messes, moral instruction in officer training schools (setting the stage for Zia's Islamization of the officer corps), and a declaration of assets by all officers, including those acquired in the name of relatives.

Bhutto had commissioned the report in part to disgrace the army, but in the end he decided to avoid humiliating it; subsequent army leaders did not want to embarrass their former colleagues and commanders either, and of course every civilian government in Pakistan was afraid that releasing the Hamoodur Rahman report, or discussing it publicly, would only anger the army. The report was not officially released in Pakistan, and there was no public debate over the causes of the loss of East Pakistan. Belatedly, a few desultory histories of the East Pakistan war appeared, but most of these took the form of recrimination among and between the generals formerly in command in Dhaka.

Bhutto also challenged the army's concept of Pakistan as a fortress or redoubt for the Pakistani people. First as a young cabinet minister, then in opposition to the military government, and finally as prime minister, Bhutto forged a new identity for Pakistan. He sought a changed regional environment, a changed relationship with the United States, and a new identity that supplanted, but did not replace, the concept of Pakistan as a homeland or a secure fortress.

Bhutto did not disagree with the army's basic assessment of the threats to Pakistan. He saw that they came from India, either alone or in alliance with outsiders. America was thought to be indifferent, and perhaps hostile to Pakistan. Bhutto's solution to Pakistan's security dilemma was a masterful geopolitical innovation: an alliance with China. He broke with Ayub on this issue but eventually had his way when he became president (and then prime minister), negotiating military and nuclear agreements with Beijing that may have included assistance to Pakistan's nuclear weapons program. (To pay for this, Bhutto turned to Libya, then shopping for a shortcut to nuclear weapons, and dressed up the entire operation in language that referred to an "Islamic Bomb.")[62]

Bhutto also sought to dilute Pakistan's military dependence on the United States and the army's linkages to the Americans. He advanced a version of nonalignment for Pakistan, and to India's discomfiture later joined the Non-Aligned Movement, officially declaring Pakistan a nonaligned state. He later coined the term "bilateralism" to describe his foreign policy: it was nonalignment without subordination to the self-proclaimed leaders (that is, India), whose pretensions in these directions were ridiculed by Bhutto. Importantly, bilateralism did not exclude special ties with the Islamic world.[63]

As for the Establishment, Bhutto knew where to strike as he had worked within it for a decade. Bhutto eliminated the civil service of Pakistan, replacing it with a District Management Group, weakening the 200-year-old civil service tradition. He cynically merged the two ideologies that were anathema to the Establishment, socialism and Islam, proclaiming a vision of Pakistan as an Islamic *and* socialist state. Bhutto was an effective populist, and his slogan, "Roti, Kapra, Makan" (bread, clothes, shelter), set the tone for at least the early part of his six years in office. His populism echoed that of India's leader, Indira Gandhi, and of others in the nonaligned world, such as Egypt's Gamal Abdel Nasser, Indonesia's Soekarno, and Ghana's Kwame Nkrumah.

Nuclear Weapons and Pakistan's Identity

One of Bhutto's more fateful decisions was to initiate a nuclear weapons program. This eventually shaped Pakistani self-image and identity in unexpected and corrupting ways. Bhutto saw the program as a way of dealing with two problems: matching Indian military power and providing an alternative to the armed forces. By building the bomb, Pakistan would reduce the army's role and could face India on an equal footing. The program was eventually seized by the army, which also saw nuclear weapons as a way of providing top cover for probes against India.

The weapons program, which probably produced a deployable nuclear device by early 1990 and since then has produced fifteen to twenty bombs, had several important consequences. For one thing, it led the army to think of ways in which it could actively put pressure on India by interfering in Indian politics, and this generated support for the Sikh separatist movement in the 1980s, and then the Kashmiri separatists after 1989, by which time a nuclear weapon was near completion. For another, both civilian and military officials placed the nuclear program at the center of public propaganda, and a personality cult grew up around A. Q. Khan after his role was revealed in 1992. A university was named after him (he had already lent his name to his own laboratory), and fiberglass models of the 1998 test site, lit up by floodlights, decorate the outskirts of several Pakistani towns. The belief grew, especially after 1990, that the nuclear program proved the greatness of Pakistan's science and technology, and that Pakistan had assumed its rightful place as the most advanced Muslim country. The bomb confirmed the sought-for image of Pakistan as combining Islam and technology, never mind that most of the technology was either stolen from a European nuclear facility or provided by China.

The nuclear program thus warped judgments about Pakistan's real strengths and weaknesses. The truth was that Pakistan's bomb program was a triumph of espionage and assistance from a friendly power, not the product of a technologically advanced state. For purposes of deterrence and war fighting the difference is unimportant, but in the context of Pakistan's deeper security, political, and social problems, the bomb made it possible to perpetuate the delusion that this was a technologically advanced country. Strategically, it enabled Pakistan to put off the day of reckoning with India, by providing the appearance of equality between the two states.

The bomb was thought of as a magic bullet that could resolve any problem. It even united Pakistanis politically as a symbol of defiance of both India and the West—if Pakistan could stand up to both forces and prevail, there was no limit to what the country could do. Even the Pakistani left, which was antinuclear in principle, appreciated the way in which their country resisted the bullying Americans. In contrast, other new nuclear states such as China, Israel, and India did not allow the bomb to change their basic strategies or to warp their domestic politics.

Bhutto's Economic Experiments

The pro-business policies of the Ayub government created a working-class movement that contested the concentration of wealth in Pakistan. Rapid economic growth had not improved the living conditions of a population that was fast urbanizing, laying the foundations of shantytowns around Karachi, Lahore, and other cities. Moreover, the urbanizing working class comprised primarily Punjabis and some Urdu-speaking Mohajirs. Sindhis felt left out, especially from the Karachi boom inside their own state. After serving as the backbone of the new government, even the Mohajirs felt denied the breakthrough opportunities for their new generation.

Tapping the building anger and reflecting global trends, all the opposition parties participating in the 1970 general elections promised extensive nationalization of key industries such as insurance and banking. Even so, Bhutto was only able to consolidate power after the ruling alliance of military, bureaucracy, business, and feudals had been discredited by Pakistan's defeat in the 1971 war.

Bhutto began his onslaught on the concentration of wealth by personally attacking Mahbub ul-Haq's "twenty-two families." He seized the passports of the family members and even arrested some of the more politically active ones. Among his first acts as prime minister was to pass the Economic Reform Order, taking over thirty-two firms with a net worth of PRs 1.4 billion, the first act of mass nationalization of industry in Pakistan. A series of orders and ordinances that followed progressively brought more sectors of the economy under direct government control. New antimonopoly measures ended up creating new public sector monopolies in the cement, fertilizer, oil refining, engineering, and chemical industries. By 1974 the Pakistan government was believed to control 60 percent of the country's financial and nonfinancial assets, with direct authority over critical sectors such as banking, insurance, and heavy industry.[64] The government also instituted price controls to prevent hoarding and profiteering in essential commodities. The import of finished goods was stopped, though import duties were lowered to encourage domestic manufacturing and assembly of consumer products. The new economic program also removed export subsidies and fiscal incentives for large industry.[65]

Bhutto's nationalization program, along with his actions to diminish the power and influence of the military, was designed to permanently alter political power within the country. His radical agenda ignored the practical realities of economic and political life. For example, one Karachi industrialist whose business had been nationalized, found a way of stripping his company of its assets before the state took it over: "I owned the business in Pakistan that made [an important industrial product]. Before they took over our plants, I went to the ten best people in the organization, and set each of them up in business, stripping my company of its most important machine tools and people. The Pakistan government got a shell, and they have never been able to make a profit."[66] In the case of "Abbaji," Nawaz Sharif's father, the family moved to the Middle East to start anew. Sharif never forgave Bhutto and the PPP, and the family took out its revenge on Bhutto's daughter, Benazir, when she became prime minister.

Initially, Bhutto received widespread public support for his economic agenda, even from the small business community, especially the local, nonémigré traders who had been excluded from economic power for the first twenty years. But as nationalization progressed, Bhutto lost this support when he nationalized cotton-ginning, rice, and flour mills. Once the support of this class dwindled, the business community coalesced in opposition.

Bhutto also passed up an opportunity to move Pakistan into a promising new area of agricultural development. Several foreign governments and the Ford Foundation proposed helping Pakistan become an important source of high-value foodstuffs for the European and Middle Eastern market. One foundation official said he had tried to persuade Bhutto to turn the Indus Valley into a "machine" that would earn Pakistan huge amounts of foreign exchange. Frustrated by a lack of cooperation and interest, the foundation eventually pulled out of Pakistan.[67]

Guided by doctrine, not experience, Bhutto and his economic advisers had turned away from market economics. In response to Bhutto's policies, economic growth dropped to 4 percent after topping 6 percent under Ayub, driving out foreign investment and Pakistani capital alike. New investments all but dried up, and many émigré business families fled overseas, taking as much of their capital as they could. Some families deindustrialized, returning to trading, which required low capital outlays. While the impact of nationalization and slow growth were bad, worse was the business community's disillusionment with the idea of Pakistan. Having voted with their feet during partition and having used the opportunities presented by a new country, the businessmen felt betrayed. The combined effect of the 1971 war and Bhutto's nationalization certainly ended the domination of the top twenty-two families. It would be years before big business would trust the government enough once again to make new investments. Even today the PPP's official website shows a party stuck in the past, serving as an electronic reminder of Bhutto's dysfunctional economic policies.[68]

Bhutto's tenure as prime minister also revealed the inability of Pakistani businesses to influence government policy. Only after the nationalization of medium and small industrial units did the shopkeepers and small businessmen join big business to oppose the government's economic policies. The local political influence of these smaller businesses brought people out in the streets on behalf of the Pakistan National Alliance (PNA), the anti-Bhutto coalition. Politically, Bhutto fell back on the feudal landlords for support, but it was too late for him.

The six Bhutto years were traumatic. The economy, still recovering from the loss of Bangladesh, suffered further damage. This was masked by a rise in overseas remittances, especially from the Gulf, which merely made Pakistan increasingly dependent on a few Gulf states that took in large numbers of Pakistani workers.

The Zia Decade

Bhutto was arrested by the army on July 5, 1977. General Zia ul-Haq, the army chief, had been prodded into action by his restive corps commanders. They distrusted Bhutto's demagogic political style, resented his attempt to bypass the army, and were concerned about the chaos that had engulfed the government following opposition-led protests against Bhutto. To their surprise, Zia quietly established his own authority, leading the country in a new direction. Islam was at the center of his vision of a rejuvenated nation, the army at the center of his vision of a rejuvenated Pakistani state. Most of his fellow coup-makers were unaware of Zia's own agenda for Pakistan's future because he himself only came to it gradually.

Zia was the first Pakistani leader to take Islam seriously. He believed that Pakistan should be guided by Islamic principles and that Islam (or any other religion, if it was deeply held) made a man a better citizen or professional. Zia respected the secular professional but was convinced that a deeply religious scientist or soldier (of any faith) would be a better technician or fighter. While restoring the army's central role in Pakistan, he broke new ground as he tried to foster Islamic ideology in Pakistan, going so far as to declare that the "preservation of that Ideology [Pakistan ideology] and the Islamic character of the country was . . . as important as the security of the country's geographical boundaries."[69] As one analyst notes, Jinnah was reinterpreted as an Islamist, not a secular politician, and the *Ulema* (religious leaders) marginal in the struggle for the creation of Pakistan were "elevated to a vanguard role."[70] Jinnah's call for a state of all faiths and religions was erased from accounts of his life during the Zia years, and an attempt was made to show that Jinnah favored an Islamic state with rigorous Islamic codes and laws.[71] There were limits to what the basically secular army would accept, however, and Zia knew better than to impose a formalized Islam on his colleagues. He did improve the quality of the unit *Maulvis* (Muslim chaplains) in the military, and there was some evidence that more devout officers were being favored in matters of promotion.

Zia's closest and most trusted advisers were former generals, men who had taught him and whom he respected. He also relied on Establishment civilians who had advised Ayub and Yahya in the past. Lawyers, such as

A. K. Brohi, and the inevitable S. S. Pirzada, were brought in to rationalize Zia's martial law and his subsequent unilateral changes to the Pakistani constitution. Zia suppressed the political parties, stopped mass rallies, and tried to depoliticize politics. To balance the still-strong PPP, he entered into a temporary alliance with some of the Islamic parties, notably the Jama'at-i-Islami, only to dump them when the job was done. The result was a narrow political elite that drew heavily from the ranks of retired officers, shorn of idealism, suspicious of democracy, and convinced that it was the "savior" generation, rescuing Pakistan from grave domestic and foreign threats. Among other ironies, the army disbanded the paramilitary force that Bhutto had created and took control over the nuclear weapons program that Bhutto thought would some day balance the army's power.

Zia's economic policies also produced a new business class, and during his regime Punjab became increasingly dominant in Pakistan's politics, business, and social life. The Chinioti business houses, rooted in Jhang District in South Punjab, moved up in the ranks of the top twenty families.[72]

Culture Wars

Undoubtedly, Zia's most lasting impact on Pakistan was cultural and social. He pursued policies that seemed consistent but were contradictory. He was "pro-American" in that he reached a strategic understanding with Washington and worked closely with it in prosecuting the war against the Soviet Union in Afghanistan. Yet he was ruthless in dealing with the very social class in Pakistan that was most Americanized, instead patronizing the Islamists and obscurantists. The cultural divide in Pakistan deepened, a divide that runs north-south through the country, transcending provinces, and is most evident in the more cosmopolitan cities of Lahore, Karachi, and Faisalabad. This Pakistan includes a few discos, world-class restaurants, instances of fine modern architecture, television dramas that have conquered Indian audiences with their professionalism and seriousness, and colleges and universities that were strongly influenced by British models. The one artifact that Islamists and modernists, the urban rich and rural poor alike, share across this cultural divide is a love affair with cricket.

Despite their modernism, Westernized Pakistanis grew angrier with the United States during the Zia years, as U.S.-Pakistan relations took on the pathologies of a dependency relationship, marked by feigned interest on the American side and anger mixed with longing for the "good old days" on the Pakistani side. Elite Pakistanis felt a sense of abandonment—because American support was shaped by strategic considerations. Hence it bolstered successive military regimes, whether led by a Zia, Ayub, Yahya, or later a Musharraf. While the United States no longer praised the virtues of military rule (as it had during the Ayub years), its attempts to support civilian authority and power were hidden, at best.

Today, this feeling of abandonment grows even stronger among Pakistan's Westernized urban elite, for it now feels threatened from within as well as from without. The internal threat—from a spreading and virulent Islamization—is doubly hurtful because of American support for Zia and the mujahiddin in the anti-communist Afghan jihad. As pointed out by Iqbal's son, Javed Iqbal, a retired justice of Pakistan's Supreme Court, the preponderant majority of Pakistani Muslims are moderate by temperament, subscribe to Jinnah's liberal view of Islam, and believe in cultural pluralism, yet are being "held hostage" by the extremist minority that emerged with the American-supported Zia's encouragement.[73] This view is widely shared today by a younger generation of Westernized Pakistanis, notably women, who were a prime target of Zia's Islamization campaign. In Lahore, professional women recount stories told by their parents of the liberal city of the 1950s and 1960s. By contrast, in today's Lahore there are no-go areas for single women, dress codes are compulsory, assault and harassment are on the rise, and secular pleasures, ranging from blue jeans to alcohol, are indulged in only behind closed doors.[74]

Ten Years of Democracy

When civilian government did return to Pakistan after Zia's death in a still-unexplained plane crash, it was called democracy but was really one struggling regime followed by another, with the army again looking over the shoulders of its leaders, in this case Benazir Bhutto and Nawaz Sharif, the two most important civilian politicians of the "decade of democracy." There were elections in 1988, 1990, 1993, 1997, and 2002, but the actual turnout in each succeeding election declined from 50 percent in 1988 to a government-declared 35 percent (but probably closer to 26 percent) in 1997, and 25–30 percent in 2002.[75] Reflecting the elite nature of Pakistan's politics, turnout has generally been low—except when there have been provincial grievances, or during the Bhutto years. Many elections have been rigged—often with the connivance of Pakistan's ineffective Election Commission.[76]

By the 1990s the idea of Pakistan no longer included genuine democracy. Most Pakistanis would have settled for the appearance of democracy with a modicum of good government—they got neither. Both Benazir Bhutto and Nawaz Sharif were mainstream (that is, more or less secular) leaders. Neither challenged the consensus that had grown up around the idea of Pakistan as a Muslim or Islamic state, but neither made this the core of his or her policies. They were content with occasional gestures in the direction of Islamic unity, and both toed the line on Kashmir. Both understood that the army had placed certain limits on change when it came to relations with India, and both gave the army a free hand in the nuclear and missile programs. For ten years, the elected democratic governments of Pakistan accommodated and fronted for the army while gingerly attempting to expand their own authority and power. In the end neither leader built a political coalition strong enough to contain the army—such a coalition would have had to demonstrate competence in dealing with some of Pakistan's most pressing problems, especially the economy. It would also have had to include a wide spectrum of political forces and receive support from critical foreign powers, especially the United States.

Foreign Policy and Pakistan

During the Zia years and the subsequent decade of democracy, Pakistan's relations with other countries became an important factor in its own internal politics. Although America lost interest in Pakistan after 1989, the country's strategic significance did not diminish. Meanwhile China saw Pakistan as an important point of access to the Islamic world and a balancer of India. Pakistan preserved its already close ties with Saudi Arabia and China but also expanded them to North Korea (a source of military technology). Further, led by a few army strategists and their civilian counterparts, Pakistanis came to hold a strategic vision of themselves as the core of a new West Asian order. A key element of this vision was an active policy in Afghanistan and Central Asia, and Pakistani strategists spoke openly of inheriting the Raj's civilizing burden in Central Asia. This "forward policy" was also a part of Pakistan's long-standing attempt to match Indian power by acquiring "strategic depth." In addition, after 1990 Islamabad built and deployed a small nuclear force, whose purpose was to provide both status and a strategic umbrella beneath which low-level conflict could be fomented.

By the mid-1990s Pakistanis could boast a degree of independence and influence that more than made up for the sanctions and criticisms leveled against it by Washington. The strategic elite described Pakistan as a minipower on the march, in view of its nuclear weapons potential, democratic government, and ability to combine Western technology and organizational skills with an advanced form of Islam. Thus extending Pakistan's influence over Afghanistan and Central Asia was both a strategic imperative and a "civilizing" mission. Pakistan's Afghan adventure was attractive to one of Pakistan's key friends, Saudi Arabia. But Pakistani hawks could also argue that the strategy of pressuring India was working, while Pakistani liberals could say the country still had civilian governments, even if none of them functioned completely normally. The economy was stagnant, but remittances from the large overseas Pakistani diaspora masked structural problems. Social and political unrest was evident, as was the rise of Islamic extremism, but again this could be explained away as part of the cost of having an open, democratic system.

System Collapse

Things quickly went bad, and by 1999 many of the contradictions in Pakistan's political, economic, and social structure became painfully evident. The government's enthusiastic support for the Afghan Taliban and for Islamic militants in Indian-administered Kashmir eventually backfired when the Taliban wound up supporting al Qaeda. The Kargil war led to a civil-military crisis and the return of the army to overt political power. Pakistan's nuclear program alienated the United States, and its support for Islamic radicalism in Afghanistan (and at home) worried both America and Islamabad's most important friend, China, both of which began to court Pakistan's major strategic rival, India.

Pakistan also acquired an unhealthy reputation as a center for terrorism and violence. Its level of domestic violence places it among the small, negative elite of states regarded as "extremely risky" by the insurance industry. The group includes Saudi Arabia, Ethiopia, Zaire, Nepal, and

Colombia.[77] Foreign terrorists combined with Pakistan's home-grown sectarian terrorists to target foreign journalists, Christians, minority Muslim sects, and others (for a discussion of the sectarian terrorists, see chapter 5). In the words of the Human Rights Commission of Pakistan (HRCP), the country has seen "the unleashing of unprecedented violence within the country by terrorists," as dozens of Westerners and Pakistani Christians have been killed by militants' bullets.[78] The goriest of these episodes was the videotaped beheading of the American journalist Daniel Pearl, which shocked even those accustomed to political violence. Pearl's murder signaled to the world that Pakistan had become a more dangerous place than ever before.[79]

These events made the headlines, but Pakistan's day-to-day human rights record, chronicled in the HRCP reports and website, shows no improvement either. A great number of sufferers were women, often the target of "honor killings," and in several notorious cases villagers and peasants were attacked by the authorities while engaged in peaceful protest or were forcefully removed from their homes in the thousands and without alternative housing to make way for road construction projects such as the Lyari Expressway in Karachi. Perhaps the most brazen case of human rights violations was the kidnapping of an HRCP member from Hyderabad, along with a Hindu member, by "unknown" security agencies.[80] Recent HRCP reports document many more cases of violations of basic human rights, all the more egregious since the military-dominated government has not been seriously challenged.

American and other human rights reports parallel those of the HRCP. While the U.S. government has often reiterated its hopes that Pakistan will remain a moderate Islamic state, country reports issued by the Department of State are startling. Examining Pakistan in great detail, the report for 2003 observes that its human rights record remains poor, and despite improvements in some areas, "serious problems remained."[81]

Corruption, always present, became a major domestic and political issue in the mid-1990s, when Transparency International (TI) began to rank Pakistan near or at the top of its index of corruption.[82] The rankings initially came out during Benazir Bhutto's administration, which she angrily defended as "the most honest administration in Pakistan's history."[83] Recent TI reports show considerable progress since the appointment of a new economic team in 1999.

Official corruption was particularly widespread in Pakistan's Water and Power Development Authority (WAPDA), which controlled much of Pakistan's irrigation and power infrastructure. A retired chairman asserted in 2003 that line losses in Karachi were as high as 60 percent before the army took over WAPDA's management in 1999 (at Nawaz Sharif's request).[84]

By 1999 the inevitable comparison with India reinforced the judgment that the state of Pakistan was in deep trouble. India was advancing economically, it had a wide range of developed political and administrative institutions, and its leadership was capable of dramatic foreign policy innovations—including a series of nuclear tests in 1998 and the possibility of a new strategic relationship with Washington. Pakistan's economy, on the other hand, was flat or worse, its core institutions were in shambles, and its provocative limited war with India had led to American mediation and a condemnation of Islamabad. If anything, Pakistan was a case study of negatives: the state was seemingly incapable of establishing a normal political system; it was supporting the radical Islamic Taliban; it had mounted its own Islamist operations into India; and while its economic and political systems were deteriorating, religious and ethnic-based violence was dramatically rising.

9/11 and Pakistan

On the eve of September 11, 2001, Pakistan looked like a state that had lost its way, with a stagnant economy, a military government, international pariah status, and political and social institutions in disarray. Pakistanis debated vigorously such problems as corruption, bad governance, poor education, weak political parties, domestic disorder, and a malformed economy. They also discussed (in a press that was only partly censored by the military regime) the nation's ills: a dangerous flirtation with Islamic extremists, no consensus on the very purpose or identity of Pakistan, and a continuing and ruinous obsession with India and Kashmir. Mounting despair about the future was visible among the large number of educated Pakistanis leaving the country and those already abroad who had no plans to return.[85]

The events of September 11 affected Pakistan more than any other Muslim state except Afghanistan, yet prompted little domestic change apart from an incipient debate over the basic themes and policies that constituted Pakistan's identity. The Establishment-dominated system proved flexible enough to adapt to the new circumstances. Pakistan agreed to abandon the Taliban, provide extensive military and intelligence support to the United States, and allow its territory to be used by American forces fighting in Afghanistan—all major concessions. Islamabad once again became the capital of a "frontline" state, and its few five-star hotels filled up with the international press corps. Reporters from many countries told the world what informed Pakistanis already knew: this was a country rapidly slipping into extremism and violence, a scourge to all of its neighbors, and a potential threat to friends and allies such as the United States and China.

In 2001 the logic of the U.S.-Pakistan alliance dictated changes in Pakistan's domestic politics. If the new alliance was to be directed against terrorism, then Pakistan's relations with the groups of concern to Washington had to change, which included supporters within Pakistan itself. Even more striking was the pressure put on Pakistan to reduce its support for terrorist groups operating in Indian-administered Kashmir, though they had not usually targeted Americans. Because of its new relationship with India, the United States pressed Pakistan to end its support for cross-border terrorists moving across the Line of Control into Kashmir. This, along with some intense but secret India-Pakistan negotiations, led to the dramatic summit meeting between Indian and Pakistani leaders in January 2004 during the South Asian Association for Regional Cooperation (SAARC) meeting in Islamabad. After the May 2004 national election in India, the two countries resumed talks on nuclear issues and Kashmir.

American pressure on Pakistan worked for two reasons. First, Musharraf had already banned a number of extremist Islamic groups, in August 2001, although the order was enforced half-heartedly at best. When the United States and other countries insisted that Pakistan end its flirtation with terrorist groups, the military leadership had less difficulty acting: Pakistan absolutely needed international economic support to remain viable, and the West was clearly prepared to "crash" Pakistan's economy if the government did not cooperate. Second, Musharraf knew that if he did not accede to American demands, Washington had alternatives in South Asia. The new U.S.-India tie, forged by the Clinton administration and extended by George W. Bush, gave America unprecedented leverage over Pakistan. Musharraf promised to stop cross-border terrorism but reserved the right to morally and politically support the Kashmiri brethren, whose blood, he declared, ran through the veins of the Pakistani people.

These new policies were explained to the world and to the Pakistani people in a dramatic speech (delivered in Urdu) over Pakistan television on January 12, 2002.[86] In it, Musharraf bluntly set forth the goal of turning Pakistan into a moderate Muslim state—the word "secular" is still contentious. There was to be no internal extremism and no safe haven for terrorists operating across Pakistan's borders. A joke making the rounds in Pakistan after the speech was that if the pious, Islamic Zia *died* in 1988 he was finally *buried* on January 12.

However, the euphoria of Pakistani liberals and others who greeted Musharraf as a latter-day Ataturk (a comparison that he has himself offered) soon faded. There was a bizarre referendum on whether Musharraf should continue as president (he won, with 98 percent support, but very little turnout). This was followed by a manipulated election in which both major centrist political parties were denied seats in some provinces and the National Assembly. Pakistan was stuck between democracy and a military autocracy yet again, seemingly unable to move out of a zone of frustration and failure, despite Musharraf's claim that a new era had dawned. Pakistanis were weary of such claims, and Musharraf has governed without serious opposition. Some of his innovations (discussed at length in chapter 4) seem to have produced much movement but little fundamental change.

Fifty-Seven Years of Pakistan

If Jinnah had been less persistent, the Indian National Congress more accommodating, or the British more responsible in fulfilling their final imperial obligation, Pakistan would not have come into existence in the form it did. The state born on August 14, 1947, had deep structural problems: it was divided between east and west, its economy was torn by partition, and its major political movement, the Muslim League, had shallow roots in what became Pakistan. Further, Jinnah died early, and powerful groups, especially in the West Wing, propounded an alternative Islamic vision for the state. Finally, with the Indians openly hostile to the new state, the seemingly best way to offset Indian power was to turn to outsiders and to the army, thus elevating its influence and prestige.

Pakistan's social-economic order, old and new, has been dominated by a "triad" composed of the army, the bureaucracy, and the feudal landlords. Today this triad is known as the Establishment, although the key role in this amorphous, unofficial, but powerful body has shifted away from the bureaucrats toward the military.

Both the idea and the state of Pakistan are evolving in unexpected directions, forcing its leaders to explore new political and ideological territory. For a number of reasons, the original idea did not stick, although the perennial conflict with India certainly reinforced the notion of Pakistan as a necessary and safe haven for the Indian Muslim "nation" and as an Islamic state. One factor was that many Indian Muslims chose to remain in India, in some cases for lack of means. The comparable number of Muslims residing in India and in present-day Pakistan is a reminder that the original idea of Pakistan was ignored by as many as those who followed it. Despite the ghastly state-tolerated slaughter of almost 2,000 Muslims in India's Gujarat, most Muslims there live in relative security within the still-secular Indian political framework, and several have achieved positions of great importance. While Pakistani ideologues deride India's democracy as a sham, its performance has, despite some lapses, been better than Pakistan's in terms of protecting individual liberties, education, and economic prosperity.

Equally important, Pakistan has never come to closure on the Islamic dimension of its identity. The Objectives Resolution froze thinking on the idea of an Islamic state. The question has divided rather than united Pakistanis: there are fundamental sectarian differences and disagreement over the degree to which Islamic law should become the law of the state. The only area of agreement is negative—in that unorthodox sects, such as the Ahmediyyas, are not considered Muslims.

The loss of East Pakistan was another traumatic blow to the idea of Pakistan, as over half of all Pakistanis rejected it. Only now, thirty years after the event, are Pakistanis beginning to understand the idea's shortcomings, especially in the eyes of the disaffected, and applying the lessons to still-dissatisfied groups.

As for the *state* of Pakistan, it has faced a bewildering array of challenges. Like Russia, Turkey, and Germany, the state has suffered military defeat, both rising and falling as a major military power. However, Pakistan also resembles nineteenth-century Poland, the Austro-Hungarian Empire, and contemporary Yugoslavia—states that have been partitioned out of existence, lost a major war, or slipped into internecine warfare and destruction—the one obvious difference being that Pakistan still retains a major military capability, including a nuclear arsenal.

Pakistan also resembles some of the contemporary Central Asian republics or members of the former East European Soviet bloc now undergoing political and social "de-development." Like the Soviet system, Pakistan's martial law regimes provided a measure of order and stability (and in the case of Ayub's rule, rapid economic and educational advancement). Though subsequent regimes had some democratic intervals, they grew feebler and feebler, unable to prevent the vivisection of the country.

At the same time, Pakistan built a stable informal political structure in the Establishment. Originally a civil-military coalition, it eventually became military-dominated. The army's idea of Pakistan is once again being imposed on the rest of the nation, through economic, foreign, and security policies. As noted in chapter 3, the army boasts of being the best-qualified institution to run Pakistan, even though four major spells of military rule provide evidence to the contrary.

On the economic front, Pakistan's performance after 1972 was dismal, despite the expected upswing following the loss of the very poor East Pakistan and despite the approach tried—whether Bhutto's demagogic socialism, Zia's military rule, or ten years of chaotic democracy. The Musharraf years focused on fiscal reform, not growth, and it is yet to be seen whether Pakistan has passed the point at which real economic growth is possible.

As for Pakistan's trajectory in the area of civil liberties and political freedom, only rough measures are available, and these show no strong trend one way or another.[87] Freedom House's index of "free," "partly free," and "not free" countries over a thirty-year period shows Pakistan with twenty-one years as "partly free" and nine as "not-free," which makes it comparable to Indonesia by this measure.[88] It lags far behind India, which was "free" for eight of the thirty years and "partly free" for twenty, and even behind Bangladesh.[89] Taking a different methodological approach, Freedom House also ranked thirty countries that were at the "crossroads" in determining their political future. Alongside these states,

Pakistan consistently ranked very near the bottom on civil liberties, the rule of law, accountability, and anticorruption and transparency.[90]

These ratings match up with personal observation, although Pakistanis might argue that while their political and civil rights are curtailed, the population does not suffer from the extreme economic deprivation found in many other states, notably India. Even here, however, recent studies indicate that the health of Pakistanis has badly deteriorated in the last few years, and the relative prosperity of Pakistan, taken for granted when compared with India, may be a thing of the past.[91]

Pakistan's press, too, has been on a roller-coaster ride for fifty-seven years. Over the past twenty years press freedom has moved from nonexistent to quite impressive, and Pakistan now has one of the most lively and interesting presses in the non-Western world—all the more remarkable given its low literacy rates. Three major groups—Dawn, Jang, and Nawa-i-Waqt—dominate the media, each publishing in Urdu and English. Some of the new television and radio channels attempt to move beyond government propaganda and probe more deeply, but licenses for these are carefully regulated by the government.[92] There are several other English language newspapers, notably the very liberal and provocative *Daily Times* and its sister weekly, *Friday Times*. Along with the monthlies *Herald* and *Newsline*, these provide some of the most serious analytical reporting found in Pakistan, or all of Asia for that matter.

There remain, however, subtle and not-so-subtle threats to the press, and on occasion arrests, beatings, and mild torture, administered by both military and civilian governments (in some cases, noted journalists have alternatively been arrested and then elected to public office).[93] Pakistani academics and journalists lament that in their country freedom of expression is stronger than freedom after expression.

On the external front, Pakistan continues to be the only South Asian state to openly challenge India's hegemony. However, its once innovative approach to foreign policy is now a thing of the past, its freedom to maneuver narrower. It overreached by supporting the Taliban and attempting to extend its influence into Central Asia. At one time, it enjoyed the support of a wide range of allies—Britain, America, China, Saudi Arabia, and other Arab states—but its engagement with terrorist organizations troubles even its supporters, who wonder whether Pakistan is part of the problem as well as the solution.

Despite its obvious failings, what has not happened in Pakistan is also important. Pakistan's armed forces have remained disciplined and united, and so far there have been no mass-based religious movements, although in some regions ethnic politics is linked to Islamic political parties. Pakistan's future is not fixed, and in some respects it has fewer options than it did thirty or fifty years ago. As the next five chapters explain, a great deal will depend on Pakistan's major institutions, parties, and social forces, beginning with the army.

CHAPTER THREE

THE ARMY'S
PAKISTAN

For the foreseeable future, the army's vision of itself, its
domestic role, and Pakistan's strategic environment will be the most
important factors shaping Pakistan's identity.[1] While the growing Islamic
consciousness, ethnic and subnational rivalries, and maldeveloped political system are all important, time and time again the army's way has been
Pakistan's way. Pakistan is likely to remain a state in the possession of a
uniformed bureaucracy even when civilian governments are perched on
the seat of power. Regardless of what may be *desirable,* the army will continue to set the limits on what is *possible* in Pakistan.

This chapter explores the role of the Pakistan army and the core beliefs
of the officer corps. It first offers a glimpse at past, present, and future generations of Pakistani officers and then turns to their core strategic vision
for Pakistan, the prospect for their "Islamization," and their relationship
with the politicians.

Generations

Every year, throughout Pakistan, there is a search for approximately 320
young men between the ages of seventeen and twenty-two. The ones chosen succeed where almost 15,000 fail: they are to be cadets in the Pakistan
Military Academy (PMA) at Kakul. The selection process has several
stages: an initial interview and written test narrows the field to about
7,000 hopefuls; a medical examination, a review by the Services Selection

Board, and an intensive three-day examination and interview procedure then yield the successful candidates.

Of the 350 who entered the Pakistan Military Academy in 1979, approximately 275 graduated. Those who have not retired are among the army's 900 brigadiers and full colonels. Of these about 70 will go on to become major generals in the fighting branches (about 20 major-generals are in the technical arms), and no more than 20 of these will receive a third star—assuming the rank of lieutenant general and becoming one of Pakistan's nine corps commanders or senior staff members.[2] If President Musharraf retains his position as chief of the army staff until 2005, then his replacement could come from this group.

In terms of their ethnic and linguistic background, the 1979 cadre was about 70 percent Punjabi; the Northwest Frontier contributed 14 percent, Sindh 9 percent, Baluchistan 3 percent, and Azad Kashmir 1.3 percent. A small percentage of them were "Muhajirs," whose parents or grandparents had migrated from India and were, like General Musharraf, Urdu speakers. The percentages have not changed significantly over the years, although there have been slight increases from poorer provinces and districts. The heavy representation of Punjabis reflects the sheer size of that province, its military traditions, and its higher educational standards.

Armies are total institutions that mold the beliefs of their members for life. Thus the views and policies of most officers who have gone through "the system"—and in Pakistan the PMA is the only entry point into the system—are highly predictable. The collective views and assumptions of a particular generation of officers are formed by the curriculum of the PMA, the Staff College at Quetta, and (for the brigadiers) the National Defence College in Islamabad. These institutions provide a lens through which the officer views politics, strategic issues, neighbors, and even Pakistan's future. The social and class background of these officers, their ethnic origins, and ideological predilections are also important in shaping their worldview, as is their allegiance to the corporate identity and interests of the army itself.

Significant events also influence the outlook of an officer corps, especially its younger members. The 1947 partition and the defeat by India in 1971 influenced two different generations of officers in Pakistan. The "lessons" of these events were passed along to new officers in the army's schools, clubs, and officers' messes. The present crop of brigadiers had their own formative experiences. Some were involved in the embarrassing Kargil miniwar; all were caught up in the ten-month mobilization in response to the Indian buildup in 2001–02, and a few served on detachment to special service forces or with the Inter-Services Intelligence Directorate (ISI), working with irregular forces in Afghanistan and Kashmir. All were firsthand witnesses to ten years of wobbly democracy from 1989 to 1999, and almost to a man they were relieved when the army ousted Prime Minister Nawaz Sharif in a coup on October 12, 1999. (For a discussion of ISI and other Pakistani intelligence services, see box 3-1.)

The promotion system ensures continuity in the social and ideological makeup of the army. Promotion beyond the rank of major is by merit; the system is supposed to winnow out the unfit and advance only the best officers, but the process does give personal, family, or other connections a chance to play their role, especially at the higher ranks. As in most bureaucracies, senior officers tend to select and promote younger officers who are like themselves. This not only ensures that the changing biography of the Pakistan army officer corps can be traced over successive generations, it also displays remarkable continuity.

The British Generation

Three distinct groups of officers received their initial professional training in the British Indian army and had served in combat by the time of partition. They constitute the long-departed British generation. Some had entered the army in peacetime and received their training at Sandhurst (in the United Kingdom) or (after 1932) the Indian Military Academy (IMA), at Dehra Dun. Ayub Khan belonged to the former group, and his friend and successor as commander in chief of the Pakistan army, Mohammed Musa, to the latter. It is often assumed that the Sandhurst-trained officers were superior soldiers; however, there is substantial evidence to indicate that the IMA officers were better qualified and more professional in their outlook.[3]

All prewar officers and wartime-entry officers have long since retired, although a few members of this generation, such as Lieutenant General Yaqub Khan, have stayed on as influential advisers, key members of the Establishment. This generation of officers left an important legacy: they were responsible for founding and commanding the major training and educational facilities of the new Pakistan army, and for shaping the army itself.

Box 3-1. *Intelligence and Police Agencies*

Pakistan has two civilian intelligence agencies and two military intelligence services. The civilian Intelligence Bureau (IB) is responsible for national police affairs and counterintelligence; along with the police's Special Branch, it reports to the interior minister and prime minister. Overshadowing them, in part because the post of IB director is now filled by an army general, are the army's Directorate of Intelligence, responsible for military intelligence, broadly defined, and the increasingly influential ISI. Army intelligence now has a Corps of Intelligence, reflecting the tendency toward specialization and professionalization found in armies around the world. The ISI's head is a lieutenant general appointed by the army chief, but he reports to the prime minister (when there was no prime minister, the ISI director reported to General Musharraf in his capacity as chief executive). About 80 percent of ISI is drawn from Pakistan's three military services, and there is a small cadre of civilians; most of ISI's officers are on deputation from the army. The ISI only emerged as an important agency during the Soviet occupation of Afghanistan, and has remained a powerful political force ever since. It is not clear whether the rotation of officers from the army through the ISI tempers the ISI with more professional and military tendencies of the officer corps, or whether the ISI's mentality—typical of an intelligence service—has come to dominate the officer corps itself.

The ISI is responsible for foreign intelligence, which means, in practical terms, a dominant focus on India, but with some attention to Afghanistan, Iran, and other regional states. The year 1971 was a turning point in the history of the organization, with a considerable expansion of its activities. Because the Bengali IB officers could not be trusted in East Pakistan, the ISI was called upon and eventually recruited Islamist groups, including students, for counterinsurgency operations. Afterward Zulfiqar Ali Bhutto substantially increased the ISI's budget—he used it in Afghanistan and to spy on domestic opponents. During the Afghan insurgency, the ISI grew enormously, with funding coming directly from both Saudi Arabia and the United States, and its resources, influence, and foreign contacts expanded exponentially; it also expanded its authority to include domestic matters, and it now actively tries to manipulate the political parties, extremist groups, and the Islamists.

Although World War II exerted a major influence on Muslim officers who were to form the Pakistan army's core, the events immediately after the war had an even greater effect. In the aftermath of the decision to create Pakistan, many Muslim officers had to choose between Pakistan and

India.[4] For the group of able Muslim officers whose homes were in India (the Muhajirs), joining the Pakistan army meant moving their families, leaving ancestral homes and properties, and starting over in a new country as well as a new army. Why did they leave, and how did this decision affect their professional and political attitudes—and, in turn, succeeding generations of Pakistan army officers?

A central, recurrent motive for choosing Pakistan was a sense of injustice and fear in regard to the Hindu majority. Even though religion was rarely discussed in the British Indian army messes and Hindu and Muslim officers got along well, remaining friends for years, the vast majority of Muslim officers came to the conclusion that they could lead a better life in an Islamic state. The experience of partition—the killing, the bloodletting, the random cruelty exceeded only by the organized variety—confirmed their worst suspicions.

These mostly secular officers had commanded Hindu troops of all castes and regions as well as Sikhs and Muslims (there were no all-Muslim regiments). However, partition taught them that no one could be trusted when communal passions raged, even their former Hindu and Sikh colleagues. The reluctance of India to deliver Pakistan's allotted share of military stores, India's occupation of Kashmir, and its forceful absorption of the princely state of Hyderabad and the Portuguese colonies, and many other examples of Indian duplicity—real or imagined—became part of the Pakistan army's legacy. For Pakistani officers of all generations, this axiomatic distrust of India is as certain as is the existence of Pakistan. A common view, held by many Pakistani officers through the years, and taught at the Staff College, was that had Indian Hindus treated the Muslims fairly to begin with, there would have been no need for a Pakistani state.

The Pakistan army retained the basic structure of the old Indian army, and most of the new Pakistani officers continued to see their British predecessors as professional role models. Because there were no qualified Muslim officers, initially the position of commanders in chief and many other senior positions were filled by British officers who stayed on; this was especially the case in key training institutions. One of these, the Staff College (at Quetta), was intact, but a military academy had to be constructed, and Pakistan sought and received extensive assistance from several foreign countries, notably the United States, in creating a basic infrastructure.

Because Jinnah cared little for military matters—he told the first commander in chief of the Pakistan army, Sir Douglas Gracey, to run things together with Liaquat Ali Khan—and because the first two chiefs were British, the possibility of turning the Pakistan army into an "Islamic" army was never seriously considered. However, some young Pakistani officers admired the "liberation army" model of Subhas Chandra Bose's Indian National Army (INA) and early on there was an aborted coup, the Rawalpindi Conspiracy of 1951, influenced by revolutionary ideas.[5] At this stage, few had any interest in applying Islamic theories or doctrine to army organization or strategy, and the British (and then American) advisers serving with the army frowned upon both a politically radical or ideologically motivated army.[6]

The American Generation

After Pakistan joined the Baghdad Pact (later CENTO) in 1955 and developed close ties with Iran, Turkey, and the United States, a new generation of officers emerged. Three things set the "American generation" apart from its predecessors and successors.

First, its members were fully exposed to the American military. Many of them received training in America or from Americans, whereas their predecessors had received most of their professional training from the British in India and Pakistan; subsequent generations of Pakistanis (with a few important exceptions) were entirely trained in Pakistan.[7] The American connection led to a complete revision of the army's structure, the addition of an American-equipped armored division, four infantry divisions, one armored brigade group, and support elements for two corps.

Along with American equipment and training came American military doctrine and approaches to problem solving. While the infantry remained unchanged, armor, artillery, and other technical services and branches (especially the air force) were strongly influenced by American practices. In artillery alone, more than 200 Pakistani officers attended American schools between 1955 and 1958, and there was an important American contribution in the form of periodic visits by American nuclear experts to the Staff College in Quetta. As the official history of the college notes, a 1957 visit by an American nuclear-warfare team "proved most useful and resulted in modification and revision of the old syllabus" to bring it into line with the "fresh data" given by the team.[8] Present-day Pakistani nuclear planning and doctrine is descended directly from this early exposure to Western nuclear strategizing; it very much resembles American thinking of the mid-1950s with its acceptance of first-use and the tactical use of nuclear weapons against onrushing conventional forces.[9]

Another important contribution was American philosophy. After long emphasizing caution and the conservation of men and material, Pakistanis were exposed to mechanization, the lavish use of ammunition, and an informal personal style. To be "modern" was to emulate the Americans in their breezy, casual, but apparently effective ways. It took the Vietnam war to demonstrate that the American approach might not always work; this lesson, plus the virtual end of the U.S.-Pakistan military relationship by the early 1970s, led to a renewed search for a particularly Pakistani strategic and organizational style.

Second, officers of the post-independence generation had no adult experience with India and did not know many of their Indian army counterparts—except when they met abroad at foreign training institutions or worked together in UN peacekeeping operations. As a group, they acquired an exaggerated view of the weakness of both India and the Indian military. For this generation the 1965 war was a shock, and some came to believe that a conspiracy in Pakistan was responsible for the failure to achieve a clear-cut military victory. Needless to say, the events of 1971 were utterly devastating and intensified the habit of conspiratorial thinking.

Third, officers of the American generation had an exaggerated estimate of their own and Pakistan's martial qualities, with some believing that one Pakistani soldier equaled ten or more Indians. This seriously distorted the army's professionalism. The "martial races" myth, developed by the British in the nineteenth century, grew out of European theories that jumbled racial, climatic, cultural, and religious notions. The British used the idea of a militarily superior "race" to keep Indians out of the officer corps and to avoid recruiting from many Indian castes and regions said to be nonmartial and hence unacceptable for recruitment.[10] Pakistan adopted it as a way of demonstrating to foreign supporters and to Pakistanis themselves that a small amount of assistance to Pakistan could offset the Indian behemoth. If one Pakistani equaled ten or twenty Hindu Indian soldiers, then Pakistan could overcome the disadvantages of its apparent size and resources, and, if necessary, the Pakistan army could challenge India.[11]

Elevating the "martial races" theory to the level of an absolute truth had domestic implications for Pakistani politics and contributed to the neglect of other aspects of security, including technological innovation and interservice cooperation. The army's intoxication with its own mythology, excessive confidence in its strategic attractiveness to outside powers, and lack of interest in technology contributed to the country's permanent strategic inferiority, making it increasingly dependent upon other states even as these grew more unreliable.

A powerful Motivation Program amplified the army's illusions to a wider audience, transforming normal public relations into indoctrination.[12] This apparatus targeted the Pakistani population, India, and the outside world—particularly the United States—but it also influenced the military's judgment of its own competence and raised civilian expectations to absurd heights. When the military did falter (in 1965), the public relations (PR) programs were intensified, but when the army was broken (in 1971), the PR system collapsed, only to be revived in modified form under Bhutto. It is still in existence, and recently General Musharraf's former interservices public relations (ISPR) director, Major General Rashid Qureshi, spoke with greater authority than any civilian on a wide range of political, economic, and strategic issues—indeed, greater than any other ISPR predecessor.

The American contact also led Pakistan down new strategic byways. Influenced by the United States, Pakistan undertook a detailed study of guerrilla warfare and people's war. The American objective was primarily to *suppress* such a war, but Pakistanis studied it in terms of *launching* a people's war against India, or developing a people's army as a second line of defense.

A special forces unit was established in 1959 with American assistance, and the professional military journals explored the concept of low-intensity conflict in considerable detail. Studies were made of Algeria, Yugoslavia, North Vietnam, and particularly China; several of them concluded that guerrilla warfare was a "strategic weapon," a "slow but sure and relatively inexpensive" strategy that was "fast overshadowing regular warfare."[13] Maoist military doctrine was particularly attractive to many Pakistani officers because of Pakistan's close connection to China and that doctrine's apparent relevance to Kashmir. The prerequisites for people's war seemed to exist: a worthy cause; difficult terrain; a determined, warlike people (the Pakistanis); a sympathetic local population (the Kashmiris); the availability of weapons and equipment; and "a high degree of leadership and discipline to prevent (the guerrillas) from degenerating into banditry."[14]

Some of these tactics and strategies were employed in 1947–48 and 1965, although without much impact. Their first significant implementation was in East Pakistan, when civil war broke out in 1970–71.[15] There, irregular forces were raised among non-Bengalis and some Bengalis who were pro-Pakistan (primarily militant religious groups). The result of their brutal tactics was the further alienation of Bengalis and international notoriety. Pakistani veterans of that conflict point out, however, that they were subject to acts of extreme cruelty, including the torture and execution of prisoners by Bengali guerrilla forces.

Pakistan's next attempt at what has acquired the euphemistic name "special operations" was the massive 1980–89 U.S.-Pakistan effort to dislodge Kabul's communist regime and force the departure of Soviet forces—or at least to make them pay a high price for occupying Afghanistan. This was very successful in purely military terms and emboldened the Pakistan army. Its officers were deeply involved in supporting the Afghan mujahiddin, providing them with logistics and training, and serving as the prime conduit for American, Chinese, and other weapons. In 1984 there was a small operation, eventually terminated, that provided support for Sikh separatists in India. In 1989, however, after a major rebellion in the Indian-administered parts of Kashmir, the Pakistani strategy of support for a people's war—Indians call it simple terrorism—had a major impact.

America's on-again, off-again relations with Pakistan and its periodic flirtation with the hated India had a deep impact on this generation of Pakistani officers. They had no doubt about their enemies but were less certain about their friends. As realists, they were aware of the difficulties of alliance with the Americans; on a private level, however, many retained affection for the country that was so intimately involved with their professional and personal development. Pakistani officers even today replay for Americans what is taught in the military schools: that there had been a historical "friendship" between the United States and Pakistan, and it was the Americans who had abandoned Islamabad. They dismiss as "compulsions of state" Pakistan's deceptive behavior regarding its own nuclear program, recent revelations about the nuclear and missile links to North Korea, and Pakistan's support for Afghanistan's Taliban. Had the United States not abandoned Pakistan, they argue, such activities would not have been necessary. Increasingly, Pakistan's problems are blamed on conspirators: the devious Indians, the liberals and Zionists of American politics, or their own politicians. As discussed at length next, there is a touch of paranoia in the army's assessment of its relations with the outside world, although it cannot be denied that this is a paranoid state with real and powerful enemies.

The Pakistani Generation, 1972–82

The outstanding characteristic of those who joined the Pakistan army in the post-Bangladesh years was that they were the most purely "Pakistani" of all. They were more representative of the wider society in class origin, had less exposure to American professional influence, and believed the United States had let Pakistan down. They joined the army when its reputation and prestige had plummeted, and their professional careers and world outlook were shaped by the 1971 debacle.

The experience of 1965 had not been subjected to critical analysis, and this lapse may have contributed to the disaster of 1971, as did the army's involvement in politics. After 1971 the authority of senior officers was no longer accepted without question, being openly challenged on several dramatic occasions.[16] The 1965–71 period came to be known as the "sawdust years," during which military honor and professionalism slipped away from the Pakistan army. The myth of the army's invincibility was shaken in 1965 and shattered in 1971, and its corollary, the corrupt ineptitude of the Indian army, was no longer taken for granted.

When Zulfiqar Ali Bhutto became prime minister, he systematically pointed out the failings of the senior military leadership, ridiculing those responsible. His goal was to create in Pakistan a kind of professional but docile army like India's by reducing the power and prestige of the army without reducing its fighting capabilities.[17] Bhutto also emulated the Indians when he tried to build up a paramilitary force—the Federal Security Force—that would stand between the army and the police but also serve as a foil to the military if necessary. His secret nuclear program was also intended to balance the power of the army by giving Pakistan a new way of offsetting India's military superiority, and the bomb program was run by civilians until Bhutto was overthrown in 1977.

Bhutto's reforms were welcomed. The Pakistan army knew that professionalism had slipped under Ayub and deteriorated under Yahya. One officer who focused on reprofessionalization was General Mohammed Zia ul-Haq, whose tenure as chief of the army staff brought the military back to power, but also saw reforms at all levels. Zia began a program of sending combat officers to universities in Pakistan for postgraduate higher education in such nonmilitary subjects as history, psychology, and political science, as well as strategic studies. A number of officers went to foreign civilian institutions for training, often on an ad hoc basis, and at the new National Defence College (NDC), Pakistani officers have close contact with a number of foreign officers, most from the Middle East and Islamic world.[18] The NDC still runs two courses: one is purely military, dealing with higher military strategy; the other, lasting for ten months, is designed to educate Pakistani civilian bureaucrats and officials and has a mixed civilian and military student body.

While the education provided to officers is generally comparable to that of many western military schools (the Staff College is reportedly computerized and paperless), its presentation of India remains defective. Indian strategic objectives are said to be fixed, rooted in communal attitudes and illusions of great-power status. The syllabus is often factually inaccurate, and instructors do not encourage debate or discussion on the subject. The analysis drives home one important point: Indian intentions are subject to rapid change; hence the Pakistani military planner must focus only on the already substantial (and growing) Indian capability and not on the fluid nature of Indian intentions. Pakistan does have a real security problem in relation to India, but the Staff College and the National Defence College offer their students a stereotyped, reductionist theory of Indian motives and strategy.[19]

Zia's long tenure as chief of the army staff and president inevitably shaped the officer corps. Some argued that a Zia generation became embedded in the army, and that it was socially more conservative, more "Islamic" in its orientation, and not too concerned about the army's role in politics. Furthermore, inasmuch as this generation's chief foreign policy experience was the 1971 humiliation, it was seen as vengeful as well.

In India it is widely and incorrectly believed that from about this date onward, all cadets at the Pakistan Military Academy were required to take an oath swearing revenge against India for the loss of East Pakistan.

There is no strong evidence that Zia's tenure created a distinct group in the army. However, his influence was important in three respects: his emphasis on Islam, his stress on irregular war or low-intensity conflict, and his acceleration of the nuclear program, which permanently altered South Asia's strategic landscape.

Zia's emphasis on Islam, in an already conservative society, encouraged Islamic zealotry in the army. Several senior officers of the post-Zia era blame him for damaging Pakistan, and some close to President Musharraf insist that they do not want to repeat the Zia experiment. They do not question his personal sincerity, but they do point out that Zia opened the door to intolerant bigots and fanatics; during his spell as army commander a number of subordinates suddenly "got religion." A harmful legacy of the Zia years was the attempted coup in September 1995, led by Major General Zahir ul Islam Abbasi, who spoke publicly about the need to "Islamize" both Pakistan and its army. He wrote in the Staff College's professional journal of the importance of "Islamization" and resisting the domination of an aggressive, sinister India and other foreign, anti-Muslim states.[20]

Abbasi's actions prompted a much closer watch on "bearded" officers, and those suspected of religious zealotry were weeded out by being put in posts with little prospect of promotion to higher command.[21] Even before that, Asif Nawaz Janjua, who had been army chief from August 1991 to January 1993, had slowly pushed back politicized Islam in the army and reasserted the tradition of making Islam a component of professionalism, not a separate and equal criterion for making policies and judging officers. This, however, may merely have driven the more committed and shrewder Islamicists underground. As Hasan-Askari Rizvi notes, Pakistan's middle and junior level officers were the product of an era when "public display of Islamic orthodoxy and conservatism was an asset" and even a method of career enhancement.[22]

Zia's second major contribution was the revival and legitimization of irregular or covert warfare, launched on two fronts: the major covert war in Afghanistan, blessed by a wide range of states, including America, China, and many Islamic countries; and the limited support provided to

Sikh separatists after 1984. The latter program diminished as the Indians reestablished control over the state of Punjab but the army later revived support for Indian dissidents in the late 1980s when India lost control over large parts of Kashmir.

In addition, Zia pushed Pakistan's nuclear program ahead, bringing it under army direction. This was to give Islamabad the ultimate deterrent against Indian conventional and nuclear threats and also allowed Pakistan to engage in more intensive low-level warfare against India; it also led the army to develop new nuclear and low-intensity warfare doctrines.

The Next Generation

The officers who will occupy top staff and command positions over the next several years have a different orientation toward society. Many come from the middle class and joined the army simply to improve their standard of living. Comparisons are not easy, but socially they resemble their Indian army counterparts. Neither army attracts many individuals from families of high social status, but both are seen as a vehicle for social mobility; in Pakistan's case, the army is also seen as a path to social and political power, as it claims to be the country's ultimate savior—a role that no Indian army officer would dare contemplate. Some of these officers tasted power during the Zia years; others have managed a variety of civilian institutions—from airports to Pakistan's power supply. They consider themselves to be less well off, but no less deserving than their generational predecessors, and they appear to be as professionally competent.

This generation entered the army in the 1970s, during a period of great agitation in the universities and schools of Pakistan, and like the broader society they did not share the idealism of the first generation of officers. The army is now considered just another profession, and the ablest members of the Pakistani elite, including graduates of the best public and private colleges, head elsewhere, especially for opportunities that lead to an education or a career overseas. Nevertheless, a core of fine officers remains.

The opportunities open to this generation of officers are not as plentiful as they would have been twenty years ago. Few Gulf armies need them for training missions, UN peacekeeping assignments are rare prizes (many other countries, including Bangladesh, actively compete for these tasks), and in Hasan-Askari Rizvi's judgment, the military will have to maintain a strong reward and benefit system "to keep them quiet."[23] Rizvi, a close observer of the army, notes that the distinction between the public and private domains is fast disappearing, as senior officers misuse official transport, manpower, and regimental resources and facilities. For junior officers, there is greater latitude to do the same, and the incidents of disregard for civilian laws are increasing.

This Zia and post-Zia generation stands on the brink of political and strategic influence. As with previous generations, those who will get to the top will be promoted on the basis of merit, but also by the informal and subtle criteria established by senior officers who tend to favor younger candidates just like themselves. For the most part, extremists, including those who are blatant in their Islamist professions, are not moved up, nor do officers have the opportunity to acquire demagogic skills.

However, interactions between the army and civilians have greatly expanded in two areas: in the management of various civilian institutions, and in the always-present but increasingly blatant behind-the-scenes manipulation of politicians, as discussed in the next section. The difficult question is whether the next generation of officers has imbibed the notion of the army as a corporate entity. If the sense of corporateness should weaken, it will be easier for civilians to divide the army along ideological, class, or personal lines. It will also increase the risk of an ideological split within the officer corps.

Islam and the Army

Several widely held images, almost verging on stereotypes, muddy an outsider's understanding of the relationship between Islam and the Pakistan army. One is that the Pakistani soldier goes into battle dreaming of death and heaven or that he pursues an "Islamic" strategy in conjunction with Muslim brethren in other states. Neither statement is wholly true, although the army has on occasion issued the cry of Islam and has tried to coordinate policies with other Islamic states. The army does employ "Islamic" slogans ("Fighting in the name of Allah . . . is the supreme sort of worship, and anybody who does service in the armed forces with the intention of doing this job in worship, his life is a worship"). The army has also used Islam as a motivating force. During the fight for East Pakistan, for example, the local commander, Lieutenant General Tikka Khan, quoted freely from Islamic texts in his talks to the beleaguered West

Pakistan garrison, reminding his forces of the great battles against infidels as "proof of what the Muslims could do." At the same moment, Yahya Khan, then commander in chief and president of Pakistan, urged his soldiers on with the message that the Mukti Bahini (the Bangladesh guerrilla movement) was a *Kaffir* (nonbeliever) army, and that they (the Pakistanis) were upholding the highest traditions of *mujahiddin*—soldiers of Islam. As one senior officer recalled, "expressions like the 'ideology of Pakistan' and the 'glory of Islam,' normally outside a professional fighter's lexicon, were becoming stock phrases. . . .. The Service Chiefs sounded more like high priests than soldiers."[24] More recently, a number of senior officers have been outspoken in their "Islamic" interpretations of Pakistani security and openly critical of the United States, Israel, and, of course, India— arguing that these three states form a kind of cabal that threatens "Islamic" Pakistan.[25]

Historically, the Pakistan army has used Islam in the service of a professional goal, but Islam, or Islamic models of strategy, military organization, or even personal behavior have not displaced the essentially professional orientation of the army. However, because of Pakistan's ideological origins, some have always argued that an Islamic state needs an Islamic army.

Islamic Roots

How Islamic should the army of an Islamic state be? Before partition, the only important Muslim leader to speak of an Islamic army was Sir Mohammed Iqbal. In his important address to the All India Muslim League in 1930, he dealt at length with Pakistan's Islamic identity and its strategic prospects. "In Islam," Iqbal told his audience, "God and the universe, spirit and matter, Church and State, are organic to each other."[26] The problem with the West was that it had lost touch with its spiritual Christian moorings; in a future Muslim state in South Asia, this could not be allowed to occur.[27]

Jinnah's approach was very different. After independence his primary concern, and that of the fledgling Pakistani military leadership, was to establish a rudimentary capability, not to promulgate an ideology. The Quaid stressed the necessity for obedience to established authority and dealt in generalities: the military were to be the guardians of the new state and were to protect its Islamic democracy and Islamic social justice.[28]

Other than gradually replacing British-inspired symbols and slogans with Islamic ones, and introducing a stock history of the Pakistan movement, Jinnah called for little change. It was enough that the army served an Islamic state; after all, even he had encouraged the *non*-Muslim officers and men in the Pakistan military to "serve the ideal of Pakistan"; if Christians and Hindus could be good Pakistanis, then there was no need to press the question.[29]

This laissez-faire attitude suited most officers of the British generation and many who came to professional maturity during the American years. Slowly, however, things began to change. Several political and military failures, coupled with officer recruitment from increasingly conservative sectors of Pakistani society, led to an extended inquiry into the linkage between the army and the state in a predominately Muslim and self-professed Islamic country. Officers began to ask what international models might be more appropriate than the secular British or American patterns. Because it still resembled the Indian army in many ways, there had to be a sharp differentiation between the two. How could Pakistani soldiers come to view their state correctly in an Islamic way, and how could the military reflect or contribute to that Islamic character? It took many years for this transition to occur, but the surprising contours of an "Islamic Pakistan army" are now clear.

The Zia Years

It was Zia who oversaw the transition from a largely secular army with an occasional nod in the direction of Islam to a still-secular army that paid more attention to Islam, but whose major innovation was the use of Islam as a strategic asset at home and abroad. Pakistan is not a laboratory for the application of Islamic theory, but the officer corps is clearly more "Islamic" than it was thirty or forty years ago, and more openly supportive of Islamic forces and groups. Nineteen retired generals attended the 1991 convention of the Jama'at-i-Islami in Islamabad, and there are strong links between the army and various Islamist groups, especially among retired ISI officers who have joined their former "clients."

If the Pakistan movement was a struggle to turn Indian Muslims into Pakistanis, Zia's question was: "How can Pakistanis be turned into good Muslims?" As he grappled with this problem, he took Israel as one of his models. Publicly critical of Israel, Zia argued privately that it was a good example of the power of faith to enhance professional competence as well as solidify a nation's identity. He firmly believed that one could be a secular scientist, soldier, or scholar, but that a man who was truly religious would be a better professional.[30] During his years in power Zia extended and reinforced the Islamization of Pakistan out of the belief that a more devout country would be a better country. Extending the Islamic "reforms" introduced by Zulfiqar Ali Bhutto, Zia allowed the Tablighi Jama'at (an Islamic missionary society) to operate freely within the army and was the first politician, not just the first army chief, to appear before the Tablighi's annual convention at Raiwind. He also developed a tactical alliance with the Jama'at-i-Islami to balance the more secular and liberal parties, especially Bhutto's Pakistan People's Party, which was the strongest opponent of his regime.

Many officers only tentatively supported these policies. Privately, some of Zia's junior colleagues wondered whether Islamization was seriously being pursued or whether it was being used to pacify religious extremists. Yet some around Zia took Islamization seriously. Zia and his closest military advisers believed they were being progressive and enlightened when they argued that harsh Islamic laws (condoning practices such as public whipping and chopping off hands) were necessary because Pakistan was not a fully developed or modern society. Their mission, as it had been for the British, was to civilize the Pakistani people, to raise them to their own educated and sophisticated level.

As mentioned earlier, the aborted "Islamic" coup of Major General Abbasi led to a concerted attempt to reduce the overtly Islamic nature of the officer corps. The 1999 coup that placed General Musharraf in power was not justified in "Islamic" terms. Indeed, President Musharraf is perhaps one of the most secular officers in the army, and even his more devout colleagues, such as Lieutenant General Mohammed Aziz Khan, are professional in their orientation, so there is no interest in Islamizing the Pakistan army itself. Of the thirty or so generals and lieutenant generals in the Pakistan army, Aziz is the only one identified as "fundamentalist."[31] However, the army continues the practice, begun by Yahya and perfected by Zia, of using Islamic political parties and radical Islamic groups as pawns in domestic and international politics.

Islam and Military Organization

What of the officers of the Pakistan army? Is their recruitment, training, and behavior regulated in some special way by Islam? There is no short answer to this question.

The typical Pakistani officer is highly Westernized in appearance and values, yet he rejects much of what reflects the degradation of the West. However, Islam does not provide a complete model to these highly informed and cosmopolitan individuals. Zia's approach was to draw upon his own professional experience: if good government works within the military, via adherence to regulations, law, and tradition, then the broader society should be amenable to the same kind of orthosocial control. By the end of Zia's life, he and others around him knew that they had not persuaded many Western-educated Pakistanis of their view, but for some, this only confirmed the degree of un-Islamic rot in Pakistan and the need to persevere.

The officer corps as a whole cannot be characterized as "orthodox" or literalist in their view of the Quran, but individual officers can; others (probably the great majority) are devout Muslims and would, on a pragmatic basis, like to adapt their professional lives to Islam, and they do so when it is professionally convenient. Meanwhile, they live as reasonably orthodox Muslims within the military. Of a dozen officers sitting in the officers' mess in the late afternoon with a guest, one or two may excuse themselves or just slip away for prayer. There is no compulsory praying in the military (except for one unit prayer each Friday, a practice that dates back to the British). This might be just as well, for a certain percentage of officers are quite irreligious in the sense that they used to drink alcohol freely in the messes and in their homes before Bhutto imposed prohibition in 1977. A number still do drink, although the habit has ended the career of more than one promising officer.

A recurrent theme in the military literature is that the officer should be careful about his religion; it is one way he may preserve his honor. The distinguished retired general Attiqur Rahman argued this view in his comprehensive critique of Pakistan's military and security policy. Although he had very little to say about Islam otherwise, he did assert:

> As a beginning [to framing a code of honor for the military] what better source have we at hand than our Holy Book? It should not be

difficult to codify certain aspects of military honor from these sacred pages. Those verses that pertain to the duties of man to man—the treatment of prisoners—telling the truth regardless of consequences; uprightness; the treatment of women . . . [o]nce these are known by all cadets passing out of their parent institutions—and if those who disregard them are punished severely—then some idea of honor will find its place in the armed forces.[32]

Islamic teachings were introduced in the PMA, but only to complement regular professional and academic subjects. With Zia's encouragement, they became part of the curriculum at the Staff College. Of the themes that found their way into various courses at Quetta, particularly notable were those lectured on by Colonel Abdul Qayyum (ultimately printed in book form with a foreword by Zia), which provided the intellectual basis for training changes.[33] According to Qayyum, those educated in a Western tradition are in an especially difficult position in Pakistan—they are caught between being Muslim and being non-Muslim. This basic dichotomy is one from which they must push forward or retreat because there can be no split between life and faith, career and religion. In words echoed by Zia and others, Qayyum wrote that the gift of Western education should not be considered an end in itself and that the Pakistani must not be merely "a professional soldier, engineer, or doctor" but must use this to become "Muslim soldiers, Muslim engineers, Muslim doctors, Muslim officers and Muslim men."[34]

An Islamic Army?

The PMA looks today very much the way it did thirty years ago, except for some newly constructed buildings and a much-improved library, the result of the expansion of the army under Zia. In 2001 the directing staff (DS) was virtually identical in outlook and demeanor to its predecessors. These young officers serve as the role models and instructors for the future generations of the army and are an impressive group. In a recent year, only one DS member wore a beard; his colleagues jokingly referred to him as "our bearded one." He did not shave, he said, in order to save two or three minutes each day ("These add up, you know") and because his wife liked the look.[35]

As a group, the DS, like their charges, differ widely in their adherence to Islam. Some are devout, others less so, and one suspects that a few have a taste for alcohol. But all are expected to meet a fairly tough professional standard, and to communicate that standard to the cadets. The result is a professionally competent army, especially when it comes to basic infantry and low levels of technology, and one that is still largely secular. The passions of the young officers are political and cultural, not ideological. Recruits are taught the standard version of Pakistan's history and know no other. For them India is a "Hindu" threat, abetted by the Christian and Zionist powers of the world, while Pakistan and its few true allies (including the most un-Islamic China) stand as lonely defenders of a high ideal.

The Islamic missionary society, the Tablighi Jama'at, has grown in influence in the officer corps, just as it has expanded its activities in Pakistan and wherever there is a large Muslim population, including India (see chapter 5). Historically, it was viewed not as a radical Islamist venture, but as a pious, loosely organized proselytizing group, analogous to Mormon missionaries, and opposed to the doctrinaire Wahabis of Saudi Arabia. There is no evidence that the Islamist political party, the Jama'at-i-Islami, has infiltrated the army, but there are reports of Islamist groups targeting the army and the armed forces, as well as the police and Pakistan's burgeoning paramilitary organizations. Zia tried to ensure that the Jama'at and other Islamist groups were kept out of the army. He may have thought that religiosity was desirable, but he never formally introduced Islamic criteria for promotion or recruitment; this did happen briefly under his successor, Aslam Beg, although this policy was reversed by *his* successor, Asif Nawaz Janjua.

As Rizvi notes, several developments did accelerate the Islamization of the officer corps. The Islamic revolution in Iran (1979) had a profound impact on civilians and soldiers alike, and the Afghan experience "reinforced Islamic conservatism among Army personnel. A good number of them worked in collaboration with Islamic parties and Afghan resistance groups, and the ISI was responsible for arming the resistance and offering strategic advice." [36]

The officers who came into the army in the Zia years now hold the rank of major or colonel and are undoubtedly more conservative in their outlook than their predecessors. A few were recently discovered in

Afghanistan supporting Taliban fighters, in direct contradiction of official Pakistani policy.[37]

Although no systematic survey is possible, contacts with a number of officers and conversations with retired officers and close observers of the army paint a picture of a rather simplistic approach to questions of Islam and military professionalism. Drawn increasingly from rural Pakistan or from smaller towns and cities, such officers often begin with a distorted image of the West, reflecting the deepening anti-West sentiment prevalent in the country. Pakistani officers have come to believe that the West has targeted the Islamic world and Pakistan in particular. Like many Islamists, they think that Muslims are subjected to discrimination and military oppression throughout the world—in Palestine, Bosnia, the Philippines, Iraq, and Chechnya—simply because they are Muslims. The more simplistic ones assume a "Zionist"-American alliance, and despite their favorable view of the United States as a land of opportunity, many believe that Washington favors Hindu India and thus is no longer an ally, but a strategic threat to Pakistan.

These beliefs are deeply entrenched in the officer corps, and changing them will require extended contacts with the West and a more liberal social and educational environment. If the Pakistan army does move further down the road of Islamic parochialism, one reason will be that it was cut off from those Western contacts that had been a liberalizing force for its first thirty years. In a sentence, younger officers reflect the larger society, and to this extent they are becoming more "Islamic" and anti-West.

Islamist trends could be important in the future if they were linked to one of Pakistan's Islamist parties, and if social disorder were to accelerate. However, the central army-society issue in Pakistan is not, for the moment, Islam, but whether the army should redefine and restructure itself in such a way as to reduce itself in size, maintain its professionalism, and make the army attractive to smart, ambitious Pakistanis. Here, the army is responding to the same social, economic, and technical challenges facing other armies created on a prenuclear, low-technology, infantry-intensive model. Educated Pakistani youth need to see the army as leading to a useful career later in life, not just as a means of developing martial skills that cannot be marketed in later years. However, should domestic disorder and violence continue to grow, then these skills will have a use among the sectarian and ideologically driven gangs and jehadist guerrilla groups emerging in several parts of the country.

Islam and Strategy

The Pakistan army has also explored its Islamic heritage in search of strategic guidance. More intense than in comparable armies, notably India's, is the strong linkage between honor, revenge, and force. The Code of Honor inculcated in the Military Academy and through regimental legends has been adjusted to emphasize the "Islamic" dimension of strategy and the importance of fighting for the honor and memory of previous generations, as well as the larger Muslim community.[38] Part of the army's legacy is the idea that any insult or slight must be avenged, not only to punish the aggression of an enemy but to honor the sacrifices of earlier generations.

Although Zia encouraged attempts to synthesize Islamic and Western theories of warfare and some writing along these lines appeared in earlier years, the bulk of the army remained unconvinced. Twenty years later, the army has retreated from any effort to develop an "Islamic" approach to strategy and military doctrine. Indeed, even much of the writing inspired by Zia merely used Islamic terminology to justify military doctrines and strategies already in place. For example, Pakistani strategists writing as Islamists were careful to point out that Islam was a more humane and balanced religion when it came to the question of fighting a war.[39] A comprehensive study of war and Islam came to the same conclusion. Its most interesting argument pertains to the link between terror and the Islamic conduct of modern war:

> Terror struck into the hearts of the enemies is not only a means, it is the end in itself. Once a condition of terror into the opponent's heart is obtained, hardly anything is left to be achieved. It is the point where the means and the end meet and merge. Terror is not a means of imposing decision upon the enemy; it is the decision we wish to impose upon him.[40]

This conclusion is derived from a reading of a number of Quranic passages citing the word "terror." For example, Anfal (Sura 12), is read as "Remember, the Lord inspired the angels (with the message), 'I am with you: give firmness to the Believers: I will instill terror into the hearts of the

Unbelievers.'"[41] This is not dissimilar to J. Dawood's translation: "Allah revealed His will to the angels, saying: 'I shall be with you. Give courage to the believers. I shall cast terror into the hearts of the infidels.'" Yet in a comprehensive edition of the Holy Quran, praised by Zia himself, the word "terror" is often replaced by "awe," or in the example of Anfal, 12, "fright," which gives the passage a different emphasis: "Remember how thy Lord (appeared to) urge the angels: 'I am with you—hold ye fast the Faithful; anon, I shall instill the hearts of infidels with fright!'"[42]

This exploration of terror as a means of warfare helped justify covert Pakistani support for militant groups operating in Indian-administered Kashmir, and perhaps India itself. If terror was sanctioned by the Quran, then it was a legitimate instrument of state power. This position may not be publicly flaunted, but it is widely held in the army. Many officers draw a connection between the concept of terror and Pakistani strategy. In their view, a strategy that fails to strike terror into the heart of the enemy will suffer from "inherent drawbacks and weaknesses; and should be reviewed and modified." Furthermore, this standard must be applied to "nuclear as well as conventional wars," thus making terror an adjunct to Pakistan's nuclear strategy. Pakistan has an elaborate strategic framework for the use of nuclear weapons. Pakistani officers have written of escalation ladders, limited nuclear war, and first strikes against an onrushing Indian armored invasion, but they also note the importance of deterrence, and the threat to retaliate by striking Indian cities. So, indeed, has every other nuclear weapons power, the difference being that in Pakistan a deterrence strategy that includes the destruction of large populations is also justified in Islamic terms as a suitable way of employing "terror" in warfare.

The strategy of nuclear deterrence, "in fashion today," cannot work unless it is capable of striking "terror into the hearts of the enemy."[43] To do this, his faith must be weakened, whereas the Muslim soldier must adhere even more firmly to his own religion. Neither nuclear nor conventional weapons are to be used on a random, haphazard basis, but they must support and strengthen this central objective of Islamic war. Terror will weaken the enemy's faith in himself, and that in turn will lead to his destruction. War is a matter of will and faith, and even instruments of mass destruction have a clear-cut and (in one sense) limited pinpoint role in war.

Pakistan army officers therefore strongly object to their nuclear program being called "crazy" or irresponsible. They see their weapons in terms of military strategy, not theology, although few (especially civilians) would hesitate to describe these weapons in apocalyptic terms. Officers in the nuclear weapons program insist that there will be a rigorous chain of command, with irresponsible people kept away from the nuclear trigger. Islam, they argue, provides moral guidance, a set of principles for going to war. However, no Pakistani strategist has yet gone as far as some Iranian officials who state that nuclear weapons and other weapons of mass destruction are un-Islamic.[44]

Pakistan shares the dilemma that all other nuclear powers face. By their very nature, nuclear weapons have the potential for mass destruction, which enhances their value as "terror" weapons—ideal city-busters. By any moral standard, however, the use of such weapons is problematic. Neither Western deterrence theory nor Islamic doctrine offers clear guidance for the resolution of this moral and strategic dilemma.

Pakistani military strategists have also explored the idea of jihad. While it has always been used at the rhetorical level as a way of motivating Pakistani troops, there are quite different views on the relevance of jihad to contemporary Pakistani strategy.

One of Zia's closest advisers, the lawyer A. K. Brohi, wrote extensively on jihad, attempting to link it to just war theory. For some Islamist writers, jihad is a "religious duty inculcated in the Quran on the followers of Mohammed to wage war upon those who do not adopt the doctrines of Islam."[45] Brohi, however, offered the liberal Islamic interpretation: the Quran commands man to struggle against the forces of evil and to defend the interests of believers by jihad, "a word which is untranslatable in English but, broadly speaking, means, 'striving,' 'struggling,' 'trying to advance the Divine causes or purposes.'"[46] There are many aspects of jihad, and force is only the most extreme and intense form; in fact, while urging jihad, the Islamic tradition also proclaims that "the ink of the scholar is more holy than the blood of the martyr."[47]

The Strategy to Defend Pakistan

By the mid-1950s the increasingly powerful army and its civilian allies had settled on a strategy that remains at the core of Pakistan's foreign and military policies. If India was its most serious threat, and Kashmir both a symbol of enduring Indian hostility and a moral and strategic objective, a variety of policies suggested themselves. With decisionmaking under army domination, Pakistan has pursued all of them with varying degrees of success.

The core assumption behind Pakistani strategy is that the Indian threat was existential in every sense of the word. India was not only a much larger country and a military challenge, but it denied the very idea of Pakistan—that India's Muslims formed a separate nation—and would see to the destruction of Pakistan if it could. The 1971 war confirmed the worst fears of Pakistani strategists, civilian as well as military. The army could see Pakistan becoming another Poland, partitioned out of existence, or a West Bangladesh pliantly joining a South Asian security regime dominated by hegemonic India.

Pakistan faced an ideological threat as well. Though Kashmir is a constant refrain in Pakistani strategic writing and Pakistanis argue that it is the only serious dispute that prevents normalization between the two states, this argument is disingenuous to the degree that Kashmir is also a very important component of the Pakistani identity. The military, especially the army, also offers geostrategic reasons for Kashmir's importance, although in the final analysis these could be dealt with if the two states ever wanted to reach an agreement.[48]

Since Pakistan could not compete militarily with India, as B. R. Ambedkar pointed out in the 1940s, it had to "borrow" power from other sources. This meant a close relationship with Britain, then an extended alliance with the United States, and subsequently a remarkable military tie with China. The latter was especially important because China, unlike the British and the Americans, was also interested in balancing Indian power.

The American contact brought in new, more aggressive thinking about strategy, including the idea that a proactive, even preemptive strategy was appropriate when facing a large, implacable, but slow-moving and inept enemy. A minority of Pakistani officers went further, arguing that since India was unviable, Pakistan only needed to give it a push and this artificial "Hindu" state would implode.

The United States ceased being Pakistan's most important foreign ally after the 1971 debacle. From that point on, Pakistan began to entertain nonalignment and flirt with China and a number of other states. The first and second Afghan wars again brought America and Pakistan together, but the army's core assumption—shared by many in the Pakistan

Establishment—is that America is a fickle and naive state, that it does not understand India, and that it cannot focus on an important country or region for more than a short period of time. Thus the American tie is important and must be cultivated, but Pakistan cannot ever allow itself to be dependent upon Washington.

Pakistan also sought out second-tier powers. Military relations were established with Turkey, Iran, and Iraq via the Baghdad Pact (later CENTO), and then with North Korea. These links were as "pragmatic" as those with the Americans and Chinese. The Iran-Turkey relationship was ostensibly an alliance of moderate anti-communist states, but Pakistan also entered into a close military relationship with totalitarian North Korea.

At the same time, Pakistan also pursued close relations with important Gulf states, especially Saudi Arabia. They were part of British India's sphere of influence and had many social and economic ties with Pakistan. Moreover, they were part of the "Islamic world," so Pakistani strategists expected them to be supportive. The Saudi tie endured because the two states each offered something important to the other. The Saudis bankrolled Pakistani military programs and provided grants for oil purchases, while Pakistan trained Saudi forces and cooperated on intelligence matters. The two countries worked closely together in Afghanistan during the war to expel the Soviets, and then to support the Taliban. The tie appealed strongly to all sectors of the Pakistan armed forces, including the army, bringing material gain and close relations with the guardian of two of Islam's most important holy places.

Strategic Innovations

After the mid-1980s, Pakistan began to innovate at the highest and lowest levels of force. At the high end was the nuclear program, with a weapon that could not be used but had to be built and deployed; at the low end was "low-intensity conflict," guerrilla warfare, and support for dissident ethnic and tribal groups in neighboring states and Kashmir—a war that could be fought but required organizational innovation.

Many officers in the Pakistan army, including Pervez Musharraf, acquired considerable expertise in this kind of warfare, and it expanded the kind of training and changed the career patterns for many of them. Originally an artillery officer, Musharraf shifted to special forces while a colonel. Although the army remained largely conventional—relying on tanks, guns, and infantry—the cutting edge was in special forces. This required a new kind of officer, one with good language skills, initiative, and political judgment. The task of special forces is the proxy application of force at low and precisely calculated levels, the objective being to achieve some political effect, not a battlefield victory.

The army also turned to nuclear weapons as a way of overcoming its strategic inferiority and to match India's conventional dominance. From an early stage, it thought such weapons could provide an "umbrella" under which Pakistan could pressure India at lower levels of conflict.[49] The army is now grappling with the implications of being a nuclear weapons state. As the Kargil miniwar demonstrates, being a nuclear power does not bring political and strategic wisdom. Pakistan mounted a serious provocation, but the threat of escalation to nuclear war did not prevent India from responding by conventional means, and the blame for the conflict fell squarely on Pakistan. Being a nuclear power, the army is discovering, may ensure that India will not dare threaten Pakistan's existence, but it is the kind of power that is hard to translate into political advantage. Kargil may have been tactically innovative—it caught the Indians by surprise—but it was a strategic catastrophe in that it brought the United States into the conflict on India's side.

The Kargil war also emphasized other weaknesses of the Pakistan army, notably its lack of interest in joint service operations and its weak technological base. The army is not only the dominant political power in Pakistan, it does not share this power with the other services, treating them strategically like a junior partner. The multiplier effect of combined air-ground operations or the importance of sea power are not well understood, or at least are not reflected in military budgets and planning. While Pakistan has had a joint staff system for more than twenty years, it is army headquarters that makes all important decisions. As for the army's weaknesses in technology, this reflects the poor scientific and technical capabilities of Pakistan itself, the low-technology capabilities of its major military supplier (China), the tight budget, and the reluctance of the United States and the European Community to become major military suppliers to Pakistan.

Pakistan also has a home front, which is not surprising in a country largely governed by the military and in a perpetual cold (and sometimes hot) war with two of its neighbors. The army demands a united front at home on security issues, especially Kashmir and, until recently, Afghanistan. The army thus supported restraints—self-imposed and official—on the press, political parties, and even academia.

Thus the army sees Pakistan as a threatened, peace-loving, and status quo power pursuing a defensive strategy heavily dependent upon the support of friends and allies of uncertain reliability. It does not accept the de facto partition of Kashmir and seeks to break India's hold on the state. Kashmir is not considered an international issue as much as an extension of domestic politics and the remnants of a flawed partition.

The Army and Politics

One military intervention in fifty years could be seen as an incident and two as an aberration, but four spells of military rule indicate deeper systemic problems. The army's relationship with the political process can be characterized as a five-step dance. First, the army warns what it regards as incompetent or foolish civilians. Second, a crisis leads to army intervention, which is followed by the third step: attempts to "straighten out" Pakistan, often by introducing major constitutional changes. Fourth, the army, faced with growing civilian discontent, "allows" civilians back into office, and fifth, the army reasserts itself behind a façade of civilian government, and the cycle repeats itself. A number of retired army officers and scholars, notably Hasan-Askari Rizvi, have carefully documented the process. Ayub's autobiography, published while he was still in office, sets forth his own views on the army's role in politics.[50]

The interventions have had different objectives. Ayub Khan's was the first and turned out to be the model for the 1999 coup. Ayub seized power on October 27, 1958, and governed through a lightly applied martial law regime for four years. Ayub dominated Pakistani politics until March 1969, when ill and out of favor he handed over power to General Yahya Khan.

Ayub's 1962 constitution foresaw a disengagement of the military from politics and a transition to civilian rule by a "careful tailoring" of Pakistan's political institutions and processes, and a co-option of a section of the political elite.[51] The new political and constitutional arrangements reflected the army's organizational ethos of hierarchy, order, and discipline and attempted to regulate political activity. The Establishment was in place and the continuity of key personnel and policies from military rule evident. Ayub's system rested upon a patron-client relationship, not a partnership, with major institutions and political (and economic) forces drawing their power from proximity to the chief. The president was to be elected indirectly by an electoral college, and the cabinet was unaccountable to the federal parliament. Ayub was also commander in chief, with the power to declare war or make peace without consulting the National Assembly.

The most atypical military intervention was that of Yahya Khan, who displaced Ayub and declared a new martial law on March 25, 1969. Yahya's coup was exceptional in that he had no plans to reform or straighten out Pakistan's political order. Pakistan's third coup, led by Zia ul-Haq, again opened the door to political experimentation. Zia declared martial law, ruled with a firm hand, and tinkered with the 1973 constitution. He and his colleagues wanted to set Pakistan "straight," or, as Zia used to say, correct the politicians' *qibla,* or direction of prayer. Zia's Islamic, conservative orientation broke with that of his predecessors. It was partly out of conviction but also used to obtain the support of the Islamic parties, especially the Jama'at-i-Islami.

Like Ayub, General Musharraf sought to impress upon Pakistan a political framework derived from an army model. Spurred on by the belief that the army is Pakistan's leading institution (an assertion that may be true only because other institutions have badly decayed), Musharraf has introduced educational qualifications for officeholders and nonpartisan local elections. In addition, Musharraf created a constitutional role for the army via the new National Security Council. The council, which first met in June 2004, will have only four military members, but their presence will be decisive since "national security" can be defined to include the economy, foreign policy, and domestic matters as well as hardcore security issues.

What separates Musharraf's military rule from Zia's, in the army's view, is that it was more liberal and humane, not driven by a narrow ideological perspective. The real model for Musharraf and his colleagues is Ayub's tutelary regime. They are eager to make social and political changes that will be good in their own right but will make it less likely that the armed forces will intervene in the future.

The army-politician relationship (explored further in chapter 4) is one consequence of the most recent army interventions. Initially welcomed by many Pakistanis as a relief from corrupt politicians, the armed forces, especially the army, are now being seen in a different light. Criticism of the military per se, once rare, has become widespread and well informed. During Zia's martial law regime, he was widely despised, but the army was held in high esteem; after four years of Musharraf, his position is criticized within the army, and his former popularity was diminished even before the several attempts to assassinate him after 2002.

Why Intervention?

Four important arguments are still used to justify the army's intervention. They revolve around professionalism, patriotism, power, and honesty.

First, the army's sheer professional competence compared with the incompetence and corrupt nature of the civilian sector is reason enough to justify periodic military interventions, says the officer corps, especially in a state with many problems. As a major general responsible for one of Pakistan's key military training institutions put it, "We are recruited and promoted on the basis of merit, we go to many schools such as this one, we have to pass a series of tough tests, and only the best of us reach higher rank."[52] Civilians, he added, needed no formal education to attain public office—it was not surprising that one of Musharraf's reforms was to insist that all candidates for provincial and national legislatures have a minimal education. Officers also serve as instructors in the various schools and academies; at one point in their career they may manage a civilian organization, or help run an armaments factory or defense production facility. An officer acquires skills in logistics, planning, leadership, and a wide variety of other topics via practical experience and the various schools of higher education, and a few have earned advanced academic degrees. Despite the army's insistence that it has better managerial skills than civilians, this view has not been carefully studied. Some would argue that the military is no better at running Pakistan's economy than civilians.[53]

Second, officers stake a special claim to power because of their undeniable patriotism and their commitment to the people of Pakistan. As young officers, they are taught that their profession is managing and applying force, and that this may one day entail their own deaths. The cantonments are thick with reminders of past battles and fallen comrades, and every year the units muster for regimental and unit memorial ceremonies, each officer being reminded that he may yet have to make the ultimate sacrifice if called upon. Most officers have relatives, friends, or comrades who were captured, injured, or killed in the line of duty. All of this strengthens the moral position of the officer in comparison with his civilian counterparts.

This position is further enhanced by the officer's close relationship with Pakistan's "sons of the soil," the peasantry. In most branches, officers work closely with ordinary soldiers in their cantonments and on maneuvers. This, they claim, makes the officer more sensitive to the abuses of Pakistan's politicians, corrupt civilian bureaucrats, and feudal aristocracy. In many cases there is a class basis for the army's sense of noblesse oblige; unlike many politicians, who have a wealthy urban or feudal aristocratic background, a large number of officers are not that far removed from the upper peasantry since many of them are from families of modest background. They were socially elevated by joining the army, and the single most common background is that they were the sons of junior commissioned officers who became officers. As they progress up the military ladder, their social status also advances, but many believe that they understand the "people" better than the politicians, the urban professionals, or the landed aristocracy.

Third, the typical officer also claims that he understands the "national interest" better than civilians. Having studied history and strategy in the service schools and written papers on the subject, most officers believe they are well grounded in the military arts—important for a state under siege—and have a good understanding of contemporary world strategic problems. What civilians have routinely gone through this experience? Very few. Further, many officers serve abroad or with foreign armies, where they have developed contacts important to Pakistan's future. In some Pakistani embassies and high commissions, the defense attaché may be more important than the ambassador if he has a better professional understanding of military-related issues and closer contacts with weapons suppliers and his host military counterparts. More than most states, Pakistan has sent former officers abroad to serve as ambassadors and provided them with many opportunities for postservice employment, especially in the state's own corporations and institutions.

The army's fourth reason for claiming the role of political watchdog is that politicians are seen in a negative light. By contrast, the army was for many years free of charges of corruption and often described by foreigners and Pakistanis alike as the only organization that functions at an acceptable level of competence. Many recent military interventions, overt and behind the scenes, were justified on the grounds that corrupt politicians were ruining Pakistan. Both Benazir Bhutto and Nawaz Sharif are now effectively banned from direct participation in politics because of alleged corruption.

The armed forces do not believe that ruling Pakistan is good *for the army*. Rather, as Musharraf argues (and Ayub before him), the army is the only institution that can fix Pakistan's political problems while defending its borders. However, the military's claim to efficiency and honesty is more apparent than real. The armed services are shielded from public scrutiny, and only recently has the weapons acquisition process been subjected to informed criticism. In 2002 one retired navy admiral was found guilty of massive corruption but given a light punishment. Other arms purchases have been criticized, as has the vast and unaccountable system of military farms, factories, and foundations. Many of these have routinely broken the law, and few have been brought to justice. The army's reputation for honesty is coming under criticism, and the media, especially the English press, are no longer wary of looking too closely at "sensitive" subjects.

The Army and Pakistan's Future

Despite the army's considerable accomplishments over the past fifty-four years, Pakistan is a state hopping on one strong leg. That leg, the army, retains its élan and professionalism, but this does not always translate into political and strategic success. Its educational system produces officers who are unwilling or unable to challenge long-held strategic and political beliefs. This may create stability, but many of these views relate to an earlier era and not contemporary realities. The better officers are impressive by any standard, but many are afflicted with strategic tunnel vision.

Still, through its political preponderance, the army remains the single most important political force in Pakistan, and civilians of all stripes have to face an army-defined reality. Because it believes it is Pakistan's guardian, and because it has the means to enforce this belief, the army will remain the most important institution in Pakistan for many years. Previous military regimes thought they could return to the barracks after a spell of military rule, but Musharraf has demanded, and obtained, a formal role for the armed forces in all day-to-day decisions that affect a vaguely defined "national interest."[54] Since the army thinks it has the only true professional ability to handle national security or the national interest, Pakistan is likely to be in for a long spell of direct and indirect military rule. Therefore the beliefs of the officer corps will shape both Pakistan's domestic and foreign policies.

Looking to Pakistan's near-term future, it is easier to say what the army will *not* do than what it *will* do:

—The Pakistan army is unlikely to become "Islamic," but Islam will continue to play a role in its approach to domestic politics and foreign policy. Even the secular Musharraf found common cause with the Islamist parties. Like Zia, he uses them to balance and pressure more liberal or centrist forces.

—The army is unlikely to split apart and a civil war is unlikely. The corporate identity of the army remains very strong, and there are few factions or divisions in it, certainly none based upon ethnic, religious, or sectarian differences.

—Officers of Musharraf's generation show no sign of changing Pakistan's overall orientation. Recent events—the ten years of wobbly democracy and India's unyielding policies—confirm their belief in the centrality of the army in domestic and foreign affairs.

—As for the chief enemy, India, Pakistani officers no longer boast that one Muslim is worth five or ten Hindus. However, the dominant view is that Pakistan can continue to harass "soft" India. With nuclear weapons, missiles, and a tough army, Islamabad can withstand considerable Indian pressure and will usually find powerful international supporters to back it up.

—The army's image of itself, its role in Pakistan, and Pakistan's place in the world—especially the threat to the state from India and the potential threat from the United States—is unlikely to change soon. The army has a strategic and political role legitimized by religion and geopolitics. From the army's perspective, Pakistan needs a safe environment, so some risk-taking is acceptable abroad if it makes Pakistan more secure and stable at home.

Turning from the unlikely to the possible, the following would seem to be in store for the army:

—Because the present attempts at restructuring Pakistan's domestic political and economic order are likely to be disappointing at best, further experiments are likely. As I discuss in chapter 8, it is conceivable that Musharraf (or more likely, a successor) will attempt to change the pattern, perhaps declaring a new martial law, or adopting a demagogic political style, or even, like Zia, flirting with Islamic ideology. None of these are likely to be any more successful than the present arrangement.

—The army may one day become a route to political power, but its preoccupation with purely military problems—especially the conflict with India—will ensure that its professional orientation will dominate. However, the perquisites of power, already an important side attraction to officers, can only increase with an expanded military role in setting domestic agendas.

In summary, to reverse Pakistan's decline, Pakistan's military leaders must come to a better understanding of the new international environment and a more objective assessment of India, as well as Pakistan's own deep structural and social problems. Pakistan is a case in which an excellent army depends upon a failing economy, a divided society, and unreliable politicians. The army lacks the capability to fix Pakistan's problems, but it is unwilling to give other state institutions and the political system the opportunity to learn and grow; its tolerance for the mistakes of others is very low, yet its own performance, when in power, has usually dug the hole deeper.

CHAPTER FOUR

POLITICAL
PAKISTAN

Pakistan's politicians confront three problems as they attempt to shape the future of their state. The first is simple: how do they come to power and hold on to it given the army's historic role as ruler or power broker? Two prime ministers—Zulfiqar Ali Bhutto and Benazir Bhutto—came to office after events that temporarily reduced the army's role; they were the most prominent politicians at those moments and had wide popular support. Two (Sharif and Benazir in her second term) came to office through normal democratic elections, but at least two (Mohammed Khan Junejo and Mir Zafarullah Khan Jamali) were the product of elections shaped by the intelligence services.

The Pakistan army practices a policy of divide and rule when it comes to dealing with the political parties. The army shifts its support among and between the "mainstream" and religious parties, and between the national parties and those whose power base is confined to one province. Thus even when it believes it has the army's support, a party in power is insecure since this support can be withdrawn at a moment's notice.

Given the army's deep distrust of the politicians, the latter have pursued several survival strategies. They have attempted to accommodate the army, to divide it, and to supplant it. These dynamics of the civil-military relationship remain central to Pakistan's future.

The second problem facing Pakistan's politicians is how to practice their craft in the face of resistance, and even hostility, from Pakistan's myriad ethnic and linguistic groups, religious factions, business and labor, and of course the army. Here, politicians have pursued different strategies. Some have attempted to build a cadre-based party, others tried and failed to build coalitions, and many indulged in coercion and threats against political opponents and the press. All were eventually removed because they were unable to govern effectively, appeared to be incompetent or corrupt, were seen to be threatening widely held values, or had challenged the army itself. This record, no better in the last decade than the previous four, raises the question of whether *any* path will lead to a stable and effective political order.

Of equal concern, Pakistan's politicians must address the many real problems facing their country. How can economic growth be stimulated? How can the federal balance be maintained so that dissident provinces or subprovincial groups feel more comfortable within Pakistan than outside it? How do they address Pakistan's "identity" issue, balancing competing visions of Pakistan as an Islamic state and Pakistan as a modern state? How do they approach the third rail of Pakistani politics, foreign policy, in such a way that the army feels that vital national security interests are safeguarded? Here again, a variety of strategies have been attempted, ranging from an embrace of Islam and socialism (both, in Bhutto's case) to free market economics, détente with India, hostility toward India, and maintaining a close relationship with Washington—or distancing Pakistan from it. On the question of federalism, the tendency, after the East Pakistan–Bangladesh debacle, has been to come down hard on provincial separatist movements, notably in Baluchistan and Sindh.[1] The question remains—can Pakistan's politicians address these long-term questions if obsessed with the short-term ones of countering the army's influence and staying in power?

This chapter surveys the politicians' approach to these three tasks—balancing the army's power, building political support, and addressing critical long-term problems. The emphasis here is on the major centrist parties and politicians—reserving for subsequent chapters the avowedly religious parties and separatist movements—and on the stratagems employed by Pakistan's latest general-politician, Pervez Musharraf. The prospects for a stable civil-military relationship are also assessed.

Pakistan's Evanescent Parties

Some political parties are vehicles for a powerful personality, special interest, or region of a country; others are ideological in their orientation.

Then there are *aggregative* parties that attempt to unite a diverse range of class, economic, ideological, and geographic interests for the purpose of attaining political power. Pakistan has seen the rise (and often the fall) of each kind of party, but it has produced only one enduring aggregative political party, the Pakistan People's Party (PPP). The only other major mainstream party, the Pakistan Muslim League (PML), is notable more for its tendency to split and fragment.[2]

The Pakistan Muslim League

Today's PML is a different organization than the Muslim League that was founded in 1906 as the All India Muslim League and evolved into a nationalist movement. The original Muslim League never had deep roots in the provinces that eventually made up Pakistan; it was an elite party with an undemocratic structure. When Mohammed Ali Jinnah died and his chief lieutenant Liaquat Ali Khan was assassinated, the party was deprived of experienced leaders who might have managed the transition from political movement to political party.

Ayub Khan's system of "basic democracies" circumscribed party growth and banned thousands of politicians. Three years later political parties were allowed to function again, but the ban on thousands of select politicians was extended (thirty years later Pervez Musharraf did much the same thing when he exiled several leading politicians and imposed educational qualifications for elected office, thus excluding others). Ayub revived the Muslim League party name and became its president on December 24, 1962, with Zulfiqar Ali Bhutto, then one of his trusted ministers, as the party's secretary general.

Shortly thereafter, the League re-formed into two separate factions, one headed by Ayub. This faction faded when he resigned as president in 1969. The other faction disappeared after Pakistan's first free national election in 1970, when Bhutto's PPP swept the polls in the West Wing.

Zia's martial law regime nurtured a new political party with an old name, the Pakistan Muslim League, and used it to balance the PPP and regional parties, some of which were openly secessionist. The army also fostered the growth of splinter parties, pitting former allies against each other.[3]

Mohammed Khan Junejo was the reborn PML's leader. After his death in March 1993, Mian Nawaz Sharif, a protégé of Zia, took over the party and it became the Pakistan Muslim League-Nawaz (PML-N). Junejo had represented powerful landed and feudal interests, while Nawaz Sharif was an exemplar of the new business and industrial classes favored by Zia that had grown up in Pakistan, especially in urban Punjab.

Seven years of leadership by Nawaz Sharif and his extended family saw few changes in the party itself. It remained a party of the elite, a combination of large landowners (the "feudals"), the urban business community, former bureaucrats, and office-seekers, all glued together by the prospect of sharing the rewards of office. This came to an abrupt end in October 2000 when the military forced Nawaz and his family, including his brother Shahbaz (referred to by some as the "smarter Sharif") and their father Abbaji, to withdraw from politics and to move to Saudi Arabia.

Meanwhile, the party split once more, now with a pro-military branch, the Pakistan Muslim League-Quaid-i-Azam (PML-Q), and an "opposition" branch, the PML-N, under whose banner Nawaz's remaining supporters contested the 2002 election. The PML-N did poorly at the polls. It had little time to prepare for the election; many of its leaders were lured away to the PML-Q; and of course, Nawaz and Shahbaz Sharif were not allowed back into Pakistan to campaign for office—Shahbaz being unceremoniously expelled from Pakistan when he flew to Lahore in May 2004. In an attempt to further marginalize Nawaz and his supporters, those elements of the PML that backed the Musharraf government were united amid much fanfare and praise from the president himself. The "unified" PML is being encouraged to celebrate 100 years of party history in 2006—even though the present PML has no organic or historical relationship to the original Muslim League.[4]

The prognosis for the PML-N remains more of the same. It lacks an ideological core, a cadre, or roots in the Pakistani middle class, let alone the urban masses. It is badly splintered—several of its factions joined the Musharraf-led government after 2001—and it has no mass political base outside the Punjab. It was, and remains, an important vehicle for members of Pakistan's aspiring industrial and business community, but little else.

Pakistan People's Party

The PPP is characterized by ideological, regional, and class consistency and a degree of all-Pakistan influence unmatched by any other party. It was born out of the disillusionment following the 1965 war, which had been portrayed as a great military victory by Ayub's government but which only pulverized and polarized Pakistan. Zulfiqar Ali Bhutto had been Ayub's foreign minister (and had contributed to the calamitous misjudgment that led to the war) but resigned his office on June 16, 1966, launching a sustained critique of Ayub and his policies.[5] Around the same time a group of Pakistani intellectuals and liberals drafted "A Declaration of the Unity of the People," a statement of the major steps needed to improve Pakistan's political, economic, and social condition, which had deteriorated significantly. Bhutto joined forces with this Lahore group, and after a year in the political wilderness, they founded the PPP in Lahore on December 1, 1967, electing Bhutto as chairman.[6]

"Zulfi" was a compelling personality. He was also a slogan-meister, and he and his liberal-left supporters quickly adopted four basic PPP principles: "Islam is our Faith, Democracy is our Politics, Socialism is our Economy, All Power to the People." The PPP also promised "the elimination of feudalism in accordance with the established principles of socialism to protect and advance the interests of peasantry," lofty goals reflecting the leadership's core liberal-left beliefs.[7]

After Ayub resigned in March 1969, an interim military government took over and announced elections for October 1970 (postponed two months because of a cyclone). Borrowing heavily from the populist rhetoric of Indira Gandhi and others, Bhutto and his supporters contested the election with a new slogan, *Roti, Kapra, aur Makan*: bread, clothes, and shelter.

The PPP won 81 of the 138 seats allocated to West Pakistan in the National Assembly (a total of 300 seats were contested in both wings of the country), coming in second to the East Pakistan–based Awami League of Mujibur Rahman. At the provincial level, it won a majority of seats in the Sindh and Punjab assemblies.

After the 1971 war, the PPP found itself to be the dominant political force in a shrunken Pakistan. However, Bhutto's personality and his politics, including his early reliance upon left ideologues, soon managed to unite other forces, including the army, against him. From the perspective of his liberal supporters:

The ruling Establishment and the elite of Pakistan, of which we did not form a part, had an attitude of hostility and contempt for the new government. Our political noses could smell the hostility in the air. The treasury was empty. Indian forces were within our borders. We had few international allies. Landlords and industrialists, religious and ethnic groups, national and international press, leaders of labour unions and leftists parties, were all stoutly against us. We believed that the most formidable of our ill-wishers were to be found in the senior ranks of the civil and military bureaucracies.[8]

The PPP was in power from December 20, 1971, to July 5, 1977; it promulgated a new constitution and initiated a number of long-overdue social and political reforms. Nevertheless, these steps, and Bhutto's personality, galvanized a nine-party Pakistan National Alliance (PNA) opposition, which included several important centrist parties as its members, as well as the religious parties, notably the powerful cadre-based Jama'at-i-Islami. Over time, Bhutto slowly lost the support of his left and liberal constituents, too.

In March 1977 the PPP then stole an election it had won, returning 155 PPP candidates to the 200-strong National Assembly (the PNA won only 36 seats). Election fraud was widely suspected, and the PNA, taking to the streets, called for military intervention. The army obliged, and General Zia ul-Haq's coup of July 5, 1977, removed both Bhutto and the PPP from power, despite an agreement that had been reached between Bhutto and the PNA for fresh elections.

Driven underground and persecuted by the martial law regime, the PPP went into angry opposition to the Zia regime. Members were intimidated, assaulted, and arrested by the government, often with the support of the Jama'at-i-Islami and other Islamist groups. While the party had lost many key and influential supporters, especially on the left, it remained Pakistan's only credible political organization through these years. The PPP was the dominant member of the Movement for the Restoration of Democracy (MRD), formed in 1981. Then Zulfiqar's daughter, Benazir, returned to Pakistan to assume the leadership of the PPP in 1986, and two years later Zia's death in August 1988 transformed the landscape.

The PPP did well in the election of November 1988, emerging as the single largest party in the National Assembly having won 92 of the 207 contested seats. The party secured a majority in Sindh, and with the support of the leading Mohajir Party, the Muttahida Quami Movement (MQM), Benazir Bhutto formed a government at the center. Her government was never given a chance. It was regarded by the Pakistan Establishment,

Table 4-1. *Seats Won in National and Provincial Elections, 2002*
Number of seats unless otherwise indicated

Party	National Assembly[a]	Punjab	Sindh	NWFP	Balu-chistan
Pakistan Muslim League (Q)	77 (25.7)	130	10	6	10
Pakistan People's Party Parliamentarians	63 (25.8)	63	50	8	1
MMA (six-party Islamic Alliance)	44 (11.3)	8	9	48	14
Pakistan Muslim League (Nawaz)	14 (9.4)	33	0	4	0
MQM	13 (3.1)	0	32	0	0
National Alliance	12 (4.6)	12	11	0	3
Nonpartisan/independent	28 (14.1)	33	3	15	6

Source: BBC and Pakistan Electoral Commission. Small parties have been omitted.
a. Numbers in parentheses are percent of total National Assembly votes.

notably the army, as too soft on India and too close to the Americans. Benazir was dismissed by President Ghulam Ishaq Khan on August 6, 1990. In the next election, held on October 24, 1990, the PPP lost to Nawaz's Islami Jamhuri Ittihad (IJI) coalition, but Benazir came to power again on October 19, 1993, only to be forced out again, this time by her own hand-picked president, Farooq Leghari, on November 5, 1996, in large part because her government was ineffective and suspected of corruption.

In 2002, despite being constrained by the government, the enforced exile of Benazir, and splits engineered by the military regime, the party was still the largest single vote-getter. Today, despite continuing disillusionment with it and with Benazir, the PPP remains the only all-Pakistani political force of any consequence, and hence a prime target of the military. Even though it was the largest vote-getter, it received fewer seats in the National Assembly than the PML-Q, while the army-favored alliance of Islamic parties, the Muttahida Majlis-e-Amal (MMA, United Action Forum) did much better in the assembly than its percentage of votes. Table 4-1 summarizes the results of Pakistan's most recent national election.

Asserting Political Authority: Five Strategies

Since 1972 five people have served as prime minister of Pakistan: Zulfiqar Ali Bhutto, Mohammed Khan Junejo, Benazir Bhutto, Nawaz Sharif, and

Zafarullah Khan Jamali. With the exception of Zulfiqar Bhutto, none completed a full term: one (Jamali) resigned at the suggestion of the army, two (Zulfiqar Bhutto and Nawaz) were removed by military takeover, one (Zulfiqar Bhutto) was hanged while in his second term, two (Benazir and Nawaz) left Pakistan under threat of prosecution, and three (Benazir twice, Nawaz once, and Junejo) were dismissed by the president (with army encouragement). Each pursued different strategies toward the army and other political rivals, and somewhat different economic and foreign policies. How did they fare, and what lessons for the future can be extracted from this record?

Zulfiqar Ali Bhutto and the Failure of Left Charisma

Bhutto tried almost every imaginable strategy to stay in power over six and a half years. He had come to power by virtue of the fact that he was the only Pakistani politician of stature remaining after the country was divided in 1971, even though he was partly responsible for creating that division.[9]

After the war with India, the disgraced army turned to Bhutto out of desperation, making him interim president and chief martial law administrator. With a powerful intellect and many international contacts, Bhutto was seen as the only man who could rescue the much-reduced Pakistan and prevent further disintegration, while fending off the Indians. Seven years later, the army removed him from power and later hanged him.

Bhutto was born into Pakistan's Establishment and knew it better than any of his successors. The son of a prominent Sindhi landowner, he was for many years Ayub Khan's favorite, eventually serving as his foreign minister. Bhutto had remarkable personal qualities: he was intelligent, a fine speaker, and politically shrewd and charismatic. He could be manipulative too, and while he praised democracy and criticized the army government he served for many years, he was himself highly autocratic. Though not a Punjabi, he built a political organization that was strong in southern Punjab—thus he had a powerful base in two provinces, Sindh and Punjab.

One foreign diplomat who knew Bhutto well and admired his talents, characterized him as a flawed angel, a Lucifer, with a ruthlessness and capacity for ill-doing that "went far beyond what is natural." Bhutto's life was tragic in the classic Greek sense of the word; his very talents and abilities made him intolerant and scornful of lesser individuals, and lacking humility "he came to believe himself infallible, even when yawning gaps in his own experience . . . laid him—as over the 1965 war—wide open to disastrous error."[10]

Having come to power, Bhutto pursued domestic and foreign policies that he was convinced could transform what remained of Pakistan. Most were also designed to strengthen his status and power while weakening that of the Establishment and the army. While some of his policies alienated many of his more scrupulous supporters, the party was strong enough to survive his death, and remains, barely, the largest party in Pakistan today.

Bhutto may have failed, but he left a greater imprint on Pakistan than any other civilian, including postindependence Jinnah. He pursued six broad strategies, many of which were picked up by his successors.

OUTFLANKING THE ARMY. Bhutto was from Sindh, a region that produced few soldiers or officers, and his military credentials were nonexistent. The army regarded him as a useful stone to hurl against the Indians in the United Nations and other fora but did not take him seriously. Aware that he was not the army's favorite but merely their last resort, Bhutto moved quickly to forestall a coup against him. He first tried to promote pliable officers to key positions. The 1976 appointment of Zia ul-Haq was thought to be especially clever, as Zia had earlier shown himself willing to enforce Bhutto's policies; but even Zia was to eventually turn against him.[11] Bhutto also altered the military's higher command structure, reducing the status of the army chief, elevating that of the other two services, and creating a new "joint chiefs" structure that would serve as an additional layer of authority between the prime minister and the head of the army.[12] Other important innovations included the formation of an alternative paramilitary called the Federal Security Force (FSF), the nuclear weapons program, and a push toward weapons autarky.

The FSF was to insulate the army from popular discontent and prevent situations in which the army would be called upon to put down public protests, especially in the Punjab. Controlled by the Interior Ministry, the FSF, instead of the army, was also available for more "political" tasks, and on several occasions its excesses raised alarm.[13] Bhutto expected the FSF to decrease his dependence upon the army in suppressing internal dissent.

The covert nuclear program also partly stemmed from domestic political calculations. Bhutto had earlier called for an "Islamic Bomb" and had broken with Ayub on the issue.[14] The latter had opposed nuclear weapons on the grounds that they would alienate Pakistan's major ally, the United States, but Bhutto saw a bomb as a device to erode the army's central military role and increase Pakistan's international freedom of movement. The army had no technical capability to produce a nuclear weapon, so the program would have to be run by civilians. Bhutto negotiated military and nuclear agreements with Beijing, turned to Libya for financial support (the Libyan leadership was then shopping for a shortcut to nuclear weapons), and approved A. Q. Khan's scheme to steal the plans for an enrichment facility and build a uranium device. None of this was widely known until several years after Bhutto's death, and it was one of the many ironies of his life that the program, originally designed to undercut the central role of the army, came under its control.

Bhutto also pursued a policy of strengthening the defense sector. He had admired India's policy of seeking autarky in weapons production.[15] Although he recognized the difficulty of rapidly achieving self-reliance, he went ahead with a major program of defense production with assistance from China and France. Like the FSF and the bomb, this expanded defense production infrastructure was also designed to cut off the army's ties to foreign military suppliers, especially the United States. It also created a large bureaucratic-industrial force with huge possibilities for patronage that would have come under Bhutto's control had he lived.

Bhutto thus sought to divide, balance, and supplant the Pakistan army. His goal was to bring it under his own control and to whittle away its claim to be the sole defender of Pakistan. While Bhutto regarded India as Pakistan's major military threat, there was no doubt about his views on the threat to *his* rule, and to civilian authority, in Pakistan itself.

REDUCING AMERICAN INFLUENCE. Bhutto's view of Washington and its role in the subcontinent was summarized in one of the chapter titles of *The Myth of Independence*: "American Policy to Bring Pakistan under Indian Hegemony."[16] For Bhutto, America's decision to stop arms sales and aid to both India and Pakistan after 1965 was proof that it tilted toward the larger India; Pakistan's security could only be maintained in South Asia by a military balance between the two states. The Americans failed to apply the lesson of their own détente with the Soviet Union, a détente that grew out of such a balance. Bhutto also rejected the idea that Pakistan and India were under a heavy defense burden: the imperatives of national security came first, and Washington's pretense that it was trying to ease the military burden on both sides by its arms cutoff merely masked a pro-India tilt.

Bhutto's anti-Americanism was not personal, but a matter of strategic and political calculation. By shrinking what he saw as a grossly inflated American role in Pakistan, Bhutto also struck at one important America-Pakistan tie. Eventually, the policy spread to the army, once the bastion of pro-American feelings.

ASSERTING FOREIGN POLICY LEADERSHIP. Complementing his other policies, Bhutto sought to use his own expertise and wide international experience to further marginalize the army and its claim to be the ultimate protector of Pakistan (it was Bhutto who made a sensational, marathon defense of Pakistan before the United Nations Security Council during the war in East Pakistan, breaking down and crying, then walking out in feigned anger). Bhutto did not challenge the army's view that the chief threat to Pakistan came from India in collusion with the West. Once in power, he did try to persuade it that Ayub Khan had wrongly placated the West by aligning against China when India was the threat:[17]

The idea of becoming subservient to India is abhorrent and that of co-operation with India [referring to American suggestions], with the object of provoking tension with China, equally repugnant. . . . If India, notwithstanding her differences with China, is reluctant to become a party in a major conflict with China, it is all the more necessary for Pakistan to avoid a fatal conflict with a country that gave proof of its friendship by coming to our assistance when we faced aggression from India. It would be catastrophic for Pakistan to be dragged into such an alignment.[18]

After the 1971 war Bhutto negotiated directly with Indira Gandhi for the return of 90,000 Pakistani prisoners of war and reached a historic—but still contested—agreement with her at the Simla Summit in 1972. No other Pakistani civilian had the expertise and reputation to carry off such talks and retain some shred of dignity for Pakistan. Bhutto used these skills to impress upon the military that he was the indispensable man of the hour. As noted in the next section, his successors did not have this stature, and when one of them, Nawaz Sharif, attempted his own détente with India, he was bypassed and then removed by an army confident of its own power and its own judgment about what was best for Pakistan. As noted in chapter 2, Bhutto coined the term "bilateralism" to describe his foreign policy. Bilateralism included special ties with the Islamic world and selective alignments elsewhere.[19]

As for Pakistan's traditional Western allies, Bhutto divined in their policies a continuation of the old notorious divide and rule strategy. He argued that underdeveloped states could be divided into those that were pliable and those that were "nonpliable" to the West; particularly vulnerable were states such as Pakistan, whose leaders had joined alliances, thus making their countries susceptible to economic and military exploitation. Thus even "aligned" states were vulnerable.[20]

Bhutto's views on foreign policy became those of Pakistan. Zia ul-Haq and his successors all concurred in Bhutto's analysis of India as the threat, America as unreliable, and China as Pakistan's major strategic ally—with Zia extending this sentiment to the Saudis. Above all, Bhutto taught Pakistanis the importance of "flexibility," that is, of not taking any foreign commitment too seriously (except, perhaps, that of China), and being willing, when necessary, to deceive formal allies and putative friends about Pakistan's real intentions and capabilities. In doing this, Bhutto was merely applying to Pakistan's foreign policy some of the principles that had become endemic in domestic politics: trust no one, power alone counts, and principles can be compromised.

TRANSFORMING THE ECONOMY AND WEAKENING THE FEUDALS. With the loss of East Pakistan it appeared that a truncated Pakistan might be far more economically viable. There was hope in the international community and among Pakistan's own distinguished economists that the country could move ahead very quickly. In 1972 Bhutto, like Ayub before him, made gestures in the direction of land reform. These slashed the permissible individual holding to 150 acres of irrigated or 300 acres of unirrigated land. In 1977 the ceiling was further reduced to 100 acres of irrigated and 200 acres of unirrigated land. This alarmed Pakistan's "feudals," often hereditary landowners, who managed to circumvent the reforms in the

---

Box 4-1. *The Feudals Today*

As many journalists and scholars have noted, the "feudals" stay on in power, close to the Establishment. While their present natural party is the Pakistan Muslim League, they are to be found in the Pakistan People's Party as well. Now in their second and third post-independence generation, and often with degrees from American and British universities, many retain the mentality of their grandparents, which is to preserve their properties and lands by whatever means possible. As their forefathers were wary of the British and the introduction of representative government to the wilder provinces of British India, they are wary of the United States and schemes for "local self-government" promulgated by various NGOs.

The power and survival skills of this landed aristocracy are evident from one startling fact: despite many years of pressure from the International Monetary Fund or other international financial institutions and foreign aid donors, no Pakistani government has ever imposed an agricultural tax. The feudals have also successfully resisted attempts to introduce social change and reform, let alone education and economic development. Even many of the Western-educated generation are content to return to Pakistan to carry on the family tradition, deploying their Western education to acquire a privileged place in the Pakistan Establishment. They are opposed to the military, however, and often regard the *faujis* as coming from an inferior social strata. Bhutto could not remove them, nor could Ayub or any other general, and they seem likely to withstand any effort to build democracy "from below," as they have unmatched political resources based on their control of land and property.

---

time-honored practice of putting holdings in the name of distant relatives, servants, and friends. Bhutto thus managed to alienate a powerful political force without actually reaping the benefits of the reforms.

UNDERCUTTING THE CIVIL BUREAUCRACY. As Bhutto knew, the most enduring component of Pakistan's Establishment was the old-line civil service, which was a direct descendant of the Indian civil cervice. Bhutto eliminated the civil service of Pakistan, replacing it with a District Management Group. Then, as in subsequent attacks on the higher civil service, the bureaucrats struck back. Files did not move, decisions were not implemented, and the bureaucracy found a thousand ways to delay and deny Bhutto's wishes. The PPP could not replace the bureaucracy, nor could the army be brought in.

PLAYING AN ISLAMIC CARD. Finally, Bhutto ventured into troubled waters when he tried to present himself as a born-again Islamic reformer. Bhutto approached the Islamic world for aid, offering nuclear technology in exchange. This conversion was so transparently insincere that it fooled few people. His portrayal of his policies as Islamic as well as socialist made no impression on Pakistan's Islamist parties, further alienated his leftist supporters, and only set a precedent for successors: when in trouble turn to Islam. Bhutto was too clever by half, and gave political opportunism a bad name in Pakistan.

Bhutto's Legacy

First as a young cabinet minister, then in opposition to the military government, and finally as prime minister, Bhutto forged new policies and a new identity for Pakistan. Bhutto took on the Establishment by cynically merging the two ideologies that had been anathema to it, socialism and Islam, proclaiming a vision of Pakistan as an Islamic *and* socialist state. He sought a transformed regional environment, a changed relationship with the United States, and an identity for Pakistan that supplanted, but did not replace, the concept of Pakistan as a homeland or a secure fortress.

Bhutto's views were eventually absorbed by Pakistan's foreign service and army, once the most pro-American institutions in the country. Here are the roots of present-day anti-Americanism in Pakistan. Zia ul-Haq and his senior political and military advisers concurred in Bhutto's analysis of China as Pakistan's major strategic ally and shared his skepticism about American reliability. They, too, spoke the language of geopolitics, alliance, and strategy. Whatever the causes of Indian hostility, they could not be addressed from Islamabad—but Islamabad could acquire the military might to ensure that India would not again attempt to defeat and divide Pakistan.

These years also saw the army deployed against Baluch dissidents, the expansion of radical Islamic groups, an attempt to destabilize Afghanistan, and abusive treatment of domestic opponents. Despite the hope that Pakistan would do better once it had shed the poor East Wing,

Bhutto managed to generate mass opposition to his policies, damage the economy, and most dangerous of all, challenge the army's own self-image as Pakistan's ultimate defender. After Bhutto, every Pakistani politician had to contemplate the consequences of a too-ambitious program of reform and transformation. Bhutto's life was both ironic and tragic. All of his successors, even his daughter, were more modest in their ambitions and more cautious in their means.

Junejo and the Failure of Gradualism

Mohammed Khan Junejo—a respected but undistinguished large landowner from Sindh—became Zia's choice for prime minister in 1985, as Zia responded to international pressure to democratize his regime and held carefully controlled nonparty elections. Junejo assumed office on March 23, 1985, and Pakistan's state of emergency and martial law were lifted at the end of that year. Junejo's term in office was brief—he was dismissed by Zia on May 29, 1988, when Zia also dissolved the national and provincial assemblies and ordered new elections. But Junejo's term was long enough to highlight the limited tolerance of the military for politicians who sailed into controversial areas.

Not corrupt or incompetent, Junejo was a member of the Establishment, but he did question Zia's (and the army's) grand strategy. He wanted to exert his constitutional authority in the area of foreign policy, especially the negotiations aimed at removing Soviet forces from Afghanistan. Most Pakistanis were tired of the war. The country was overrun with guns, drugs, and Afghan refugees, and Junejo understood this popular anxiety. To the army, however, the war was sustainable, and Pakistanis would have to tolerate it for a while longer, given the larger strategic objectives at stake. These included the expansion of Pakistani influence into Central Asia. For Zia and the military, Junejo had exceeded his authority by venturing into foreign and security policy affairs—especially Afghanistan—and he was peremptorily dismissed. The Junejo case showed that even an unpopular army chief could defy public opinion and the wishes of a close ally (Washington was pressing for Pakistan's democratization) and fire a weak prime minister. This happened again in 2004, when a weak prime minister (Jamali) was pressured to resign by an increasingly unpopular army chief (Musharraf).

Benazir Bhutto and the Failure of Liberal Accommodation

Benazir first came to office on December 2, 1988, and was dismissed on August 6, 1990. Like her father, she came to power unexpectedly—as a direct result of Zia's death in an air crash on August 17, 1988. Also like her father, she had a political organization, the PPP, and a degree of popular appeal unmatched by any other politician. There was another precedent as well. Fatima Jinnah, Mohammed Ali Jinnah's sister, had also run for office (against Ayub) and generated massive popular support. But Benazir's fate was to be only marginally better than that of Fatima Jinnah. She was elected prime minister, but the army and Zia's successor as president, Ghulam Ishaq Khan (an Establishment pillar), ensured that she could not govern.

Benazir was extremely intelligent, had strong contacts abroad (especially in the United States), and was the PPP's undisputed leader. She also inherited two grudges—and grudges are as important in Pakistan as in any other state. One went back to 1972 when her father had nationalized the Ittefaq Foundry, the heart of the Sharif family's industrial empire. This set the Sharif family against her, and their distrust was shared by the entire Pakistani business community. The second grudge was that of the army. Its people doubted her professional competence, were intensely suspicious of her since she was not part of the Establishment, and feared that she might seek revenge for her father's death.

Benazir avoided a head-on clash with the army-centered Establishment under advice from friends. She adjusted her policies toward India, reversing her pro-dialogue position and adopting a demagogic policy on Kashmir, and gave her assent to a low-intensity proxy war against India.[21] She also professed support for the American tie, still unpopular among many of her leftist supporters, although she was not, in her second term in office, above deceiving her American interlocutors about Pakistan's support for the Taliban. She did anger the army, though, when she made some revealing statements about the nuclear program in Washington, a program she could not have stopped even if she had tried.

Benazir's second term in office lasted just over three years (October 19, 1993, to November 5, 1996) and ended in her dismissal, this time by the very man she had elected to the presidency, Farooq Leghari. By then, she had lost much support. Many of Pakistan's liberals were disappointed by her policy compromises, the right was suspicious about her willingness to forgive and forget her father's death, and everyone was astonished at the degree to which she gave a free hand to her husband, Asif Zardari, who was widely believed to be corrupt. Although psychological explanations might help explain her toleration of her husband's financial dealings, Benazir had lost many of her earlier supporters. She now lacked credibility, her policies were badly compromised, and Nawaz Sharif again seemed to be a reasonable alternative. Above all, she had not come to grips with the fundamental problem of reducing the power and influence of the military-bureaucratic complex, notably the much-expanded intelligence services. Benazir's qualities are discussed further in Chapter 8 in the context of the emergence of a new type of political leader in Pakistan.

THE LIBERAL CONUNDRUM. Benazir's fate illustrates the problematic situation of liberalism in Pakistan. Benazir, even more than her father, represented this perspective: progressive social and economic policies; accommodation with India; good relations with all of the major powers, including the United States (where she had many supporters); gender empowerment; and a commitment to parliamentary democracy and a free press. Her first act as prime minister was to end press censorship. By and large it remains uncensored, although her civilian successor, Nawaz Sharif, was not above roughing up a few English-language journalists, and the military regime that followed Nawaz kept a close eye on the politically more influential Urdu press. She also expanded the role of important non-governmental organizations, especially in the area of women's rights and education, and this remains widely accepted in Pakistan except among the conservative Islamist groups.

Despite an enduring impact in some areas, Benazir could never muster the political support to move forward on key parts of her agenda. This was partly a result of one of the most disturbing aspects of Pakistani liberalism—its steady decline. While Pakistan's Islamists have enthusiastically cultivated international ties and contributed much to Islamic thinking (including influencing Egypt's Muslim Brotherhood), Pakistan is an ideological ghetto, especially as far as its liberals are concerned. They are cut off from their natural allies in India, and many are bitterly anti-American because of Washington's support for one military regime after another. The liberals' natural support—and the core support base of the PPP—is in Pakistan's trade unions, the universities, educational and professional communities, the Westernized English-language press, and the NGO community. Except for the latter two, all are in retreat as the state has starved education of resources, the unions decayed along with Pakistani industry, and many professionals migrated abroad. Pakistan's minorities (made up of Parsis, a small Christian population, some Hindus and Sikhs, as well as minority Islamic sects) also contributed much to Pakistani liberalism, but they, too, have lost influence over the past ten years as sectarianism and regional and ethnic loyalties assume greater importance.[22]

Ironically, Pakistan's numerous and highly competent liberal NGOs have been used by the Musharraf government to further fragment Pakistani politics, establish central control, and weaken the political parties.[23] The NGOs have a special, not a general constituency, and unlike political parties, they rarely aggregate diverse interests. They receive governmental support and encouragement and in exchange inadvertently undercut the ability of political parties to develop ties to a broad range of social forces. Further, the foreign connections of many NGOs (many are funded by expatriate Pakistanis, the United Nations, and private foundations) prohibit them from acquiring political legitimacy within Pakistan, further depoliticizing Pakistani politics. They can be easily attacked as being foreign-influenced, and thus subversive toward Pakistani and Islamic values.[24]

One key tenet of traditional Pakistani liberalism, the normalization of relations with India, became a nonissue after the 1998 tests—tensions between India and Pakistan made such a position look weak and unpatriotic. Few now publicly oppose the Pakistani nuclear program, and Pakistan's security managers, who built a national security state based on opposition to India, continue to benefit from the sixteen years of India-Pakistan crisis that began in 1987.

As for relations with the United States, where many of Pakistan's liberal community have professional and personal ties, they are fast diminishing. Events after September 11 turned Pakistani liberals against the United States for several reasons: they believed America was strengthening Pakistan's military regime, using brutal force in Afghanistan, and, most hurtful, discriminating against Pakistanis per se. U.S. immigration and visa authorities have singled out countless Pakistani professionals and journalists, generating a fresh wave of anti-Americanism among the educated. The best publicized case involved the arrest and maltreatment of Ejaz Haider, a respected journalist and at the time a resident visiting scholar at the Brookings Institution.[25]

Nawaz Sharif and the Failure of Manipulation

Whereas Benazir was handicapped by being from outside Pakistan's Establishment, Mian Nawaz Sharif was a product of that Establishment and knew how to "work" it. Nevertheless, he failed as miserably as his predecessors to build his own power base and reduce the army's.

Nawaz was brought into politics by Zia ul-Haq, serving as the Punjab province's finance minister from 1982 to 1985, and then (with some brief interruptions) as chief minister from 1985 to 1990. Nawaz assumed control of the Pakistan Muslim League after Junejo's removal from politics and thus had a nominal party base, especially in his home province of Punjab. More important were his family connections. He was the son of one of Pakistan's most successful businessmen, Mian Mohammed Sharif, who remained a force behind Nawaz for the latter's entire career. His brother, Shahbaz, perhaps more capable and certainly more articulate, became chief minister of Punjab when Nawaz went to Islamabad for the second time.

Nawaz's first term as prime minister was a product of the manipulated election of 1990; it ran from November 6, 1990, to July 18, 1993, at which point he was dismissed by Ghulam Ishaq Khan. It was a conformist and accommodating prime ministership, although Nawaz did attempt to woo some elements of the army by various inducements.

Nawaz's second and more remarkable tenure began on February 17, 1997, and ended on October 12, 1999. This time he was swept into office by a huge majority—nearly 50 percent of the vote and 66 percent of the seats in Pakistan's lower house. Nawaz pursued pro-business policies, built a number of freeways and toll roads, and initiated a popular but fiscally ruinous own-your-own-taxicab scheme. As much as these schemes added to Pakistan's debt, it was his other policies that proved to be his undoing.

First, Nawaz set out to systematically eliminate or weaken his political opponents. He looked into charges of corruption against Benazir and her husband, creating a national *Ehtesab* (reform) commission for the purpose. This commission laid the groundwork for subsequent charges against Nawaz and his family by the military-appointed National

Accountability Bureau. Nawaz also purged the PML of rivals, and he crudely pressured the press, arresting and beating several noted English-language journalists who had been critical of his government.

More worrisome were his attempts to bring the government under his total control. In his second term, bolstered by a large majority, he stripped the president of the constitutional power to dismiss the parliament and thus by default remove the prime minister, appointing a political cipher, Rafiq Tarar, as president. He further purged the bureaucracy, freely transferred judges, and manipulated local elections, but certainly the most blatant assault on the rule of law took place on November 28, 1997. On that date Nawaz's supporters undertook a physical attack on the Supreme Court of Pakistan in Islamabad. They invaded the court's premises and intimidated the judges with security cameras recording the entire event.

Nawaz Sharif's most provocative step was an attempt to reduce the army's influence. Sharif told one Pakistani colleague in the PML that the plan was "to induct 50,000 soldiers into WAPDA and the Railways each, and the next year to bring them into other areas, and at the same time make peace with India, thus reducing the effective size of the army and its main mission."[26] If this was a plan, it was ineptly implemented.

His next step in regard to the army was to remove the amiable and professional army chief, Jehangir Karamat, because Karamat had proposed a National Security Council that would include representatives from the services, the bureaucracy, and the cabinet to deal with a wide range of issues. Karamat had been concerned about Pakistan's economic problems, its domestic sectarian violence, and the growth of corruption, arguing that the armed forces needed to have a voice in policies affecting these matters as well as "high" national security concerns such as Pakistan's nuclear and foreign policies.

Nawaz, concerned with civilian supremacy, calculated correctly that Karamat would go quietly. Karamat had not intervened in the matter of the Supreme Court, and Nawaz judged him to be weak. Karamat did resign. He was criticized within the army for not standing up to Nawaz, but he defended his resignation as the "right" thing to do since he had lost the confidence of a constitutionally elected prime minister.

Nawaz's next move against the army stemmed from important policy differences that put him in opposition to Karamat's successor. Nawaz saw India quite differently from the army's more hard-line elements. Believing that every country, bureaucracy, or individual had a price, he thought he could do business with India and met with Indian prime minister Atal Behari Vajpayee in Lahore in February 1999. The army, then commanded by General Pervez Musharraf, was upset with the Lahore summit, especially because the original communiqué made no mention of Kashmir. A reference to Kashmir was inserted at the army's insistence, but even then the service chiefs declined to accord full honors to the Indian prime minister, failing to turn up to greet him at the border crossing where he entered Pakistan.

That spring, when the Pakistan army crossed the Line of Control in the Kargil region of Kashmir, precipitating a determined Indian response, Nawaz flew off to China and Washington seeking a way out of the crisis. He met with Bill Clinton on July 4 and on the president's advice asked his generals to retreat from Kargil. The army was infuriated at what they regarded as a betrayal by an uninformed civilian, especially since they claimed that Nawaz had been briefed fully on the operation. He had, but probably did not fully understand the implications of what he was being told by the generals.

Sure that a coup was coming, Nawaz tried to preempt it by removing Musharraf while the latter was away on a visit to Sri Lanka, ordering that Musharraf's Pakistan International Airlines flight land outside Pakistan. Simultaneously, he appointed a successor (the then director of the ISI) as army chief. Musharraf's replacement came from the engineering branch of the army, an unlikely source for a service dominated by infantry, armor, and artillery. The preemptive move failed. Instead, Musharraf's subordinates moved against Nawaz, arresting and charging him with attempted murder and corruption. In the end, after a trial and a year in jail under a sentence of death, Nawaz was exiled to Saudi Arabia, pledging that he would not reenter politics.[27]

Though the charge against him was subsequently dropped, after the coup the army made much of Nawaz's attempt to "murder" General Musharraf and others on the diverted aircraft, and the corruption of his government. By then, however, Nawaz Sharif's attempts to gather all power in his hands had already alienated many Pakistanis. He had done much to damage Pakistan's feeble democratic institutions, and his departure was greeted with wary relief by many. Still, he might have stayed on had he not attempted to interfere in army matters and in foreign and security policy. In the eyes of the army, he compounded his sins by bringing a foreign power, the United States, into Pakistani politics. Of the many ironies of Nawaz's downfall, this was the most poignant: in the past it was the military that had powerful foreign ties, in this case it was the civilian government, but these were not enough to protect him from a coup and may have emboldened Nawaz to go too far.

The entire experience was disillusioning to informed and knowledgeable Pakistanis. If Nawaz Sharif was the best their political system could produce, and if he failed, was there hope for Pakistan? General Musharraf brought the military back to power, and there was initial relief that he had done so, but as he stayed on in power, the best defense that his supporters could muster was that all other alternatives were worse, including the alternative of a civilian government unconstrained by the army.

Mir Zafarullah Khan Jamali and the Politics of Survival

Nawaz's fall, after eleven tumultuous years of democracy, left Pakistan's political community in disarray. Nawaz and Benazir had been exiled, no left movement of any consequence had emerged, the few major regional parties (in Sindh, NWFP, and Baluchistan) showed little capacity to work together, and none had a counterpart in the dominant Punjab. Thus when the Supreme Court ordered General Musharraf to hold elections in October 2002, it took over a month to form a government, and the new prime minister, Zafarullah Khan Jamali, did not take office until November 23, 2002.

Jamali appeared to be another early Junejo—a politically inconsequential and highly deferential Baluch politician from a landed aristocratic family. In his first months in office, Jamali was even more cautious than Junejo, in part because he was dependent upon the army's manipulation of the coalition-building process.[28] As a condition of coming to office, Jamali was required to accept Musharraf's choice of interior, finance, and education ministers. His foreign minister, Mian Khurshid Mahmood Kasuri, a genial Punjabi politician, dared not challenge the army's foreign policy even if he wanted to—he was not even invited to accompany Musharraf on the latter's swing through Western capitals, and neither Jamali nor he were invited to attend the Camp David Summit in mid-2003. There were reports of divergence on Kashmir policy between the army and Kasuri's ministry, but Jamali and his ministers knew that they could not roam far from orthodoxy.

Like lawyers for the defense who do not not look too closely at the guilt or innocence of the client, the Jamali government did not look too closely at the policies it had to implement, suppressing possible doubts on the grounds that the client deserves the best possible defense. Perhaps even more cautiously than Junejo, it followed a strategy of wait and hope, fending off the Islamic parties, the PPP, and regional parties and content at being the buffer between the army and the country. Aware that the army's domestic intelligence agencies could instantly stir up an "agitation" that could bring down his government, Jamali carried on, presenting the best face possible on a difficult case. He did not inquire too closely about whether the ultimate power in Pakistan, the army, was guilty or innocent of such deeds as support for terrorism, spreading nuclear technology to other states, and rising sectarian violence. As solid members of Pakistan's Establishment, Jamali and his ministers were individually agreeable but collectively ineffective and constrained by the strong-willed dominant partner, the army, represented by the increasingly vocal Musharraf.

In the end, this low-profile strategy was not enough, and Jamali was encouraged to resign the prime ministership on June 26, 2004, after nineteen months in office. His interim replacement, Chaudhry Shujaat Hussain, the president of the PML-Q, served only long enough for Musharraf's favorite, Finance Minister Shaukat Aziz, to run for election, become a member of the National Assembly, and then be named prime minister. Aziz's appointment could have come much earlier, and may have been precipitated because Jamali (a Baluch) had doubts about the ongoing anti-terrorist military operations in the NWFP and Baluchistan; it certainly represents a further weakening of even the facade of democracy and a move in the direction of technocratic government.

Musharraf's New Order: The General as a Politician

Shortly after the 1999 coup, then "Chief Executive" General Pervez Musharraf was advised to turn power over to civilians as quickly as possible. His response was a firm "no," on the grounds that the system had to be cleansed, once and for all, and thoroughly reorganized to ensure that the military-civilian balance was maintained and that civilians would never again lead Pakistan into disaster.

Musharraf had a few ideas as to how this might be done, beginning with a commitment to the appearance of democracy, as long as checks and balances prevented a dominant political force from emerging. Other useful measures would be to discipline the politicians, give the military a permanent and constitutional role, rely upon technocrats, and build a new system of government that would effectively link Islamabad to "the people" of Pakistan.

Musharraf already had one instrument at hand. Prime Minister Nawaz Sharif had established a process of Ehtesab, or reform, with a commission that was empowered to investigate political and economic irregularities. In practice, this turned into an instrument to coerce political rivals. One of Musharraf's first steps was to convert the commission into the National Accountability Bureau (NAB), which used the Ehtesab Commission's files as the basis for going after corrupt officials and politicians. Over a four-year period NAB claims to have uncovered Rs 90 billion in fraud and prosecuted 164 politicians, 294 bureaucrats, 56 businessmen, and 8 members of the armed forces.[29] Its most famous case was the plea-bargain of a former Pakistan navy chief, resulting in the return of $7.5 million.[30] The NAB, international human rights groups complain, bypasses the regular judicial process, has its own closed courts, and is clearly used as a political tool by the government. For example, elected district Nazims (local officials) and appointed officials fear a NAB prosecution if they are politically uncooperative, since almost all Pakistani officials have been compromised at one time or another, and NAB's prosecutions can range back to the year 1985.

To acquire a degree of legitimacy, Musharraf organized a national referendum on the military takeover in June 2002, winning 98 percent of the votes in a sham election widely derided by Pakistani and foreign observers alike. Five months later he went ahead with national and provincial elections. These were organized under the close supervision of the military and intelligence services, and without the presence of the PPP's and PML's most important leaders, Benazir Bhutto and Nawaz Sharif.

The elections were manipulated at many levels. The PML was encouraged to break into several factions, including one openly favored by the military (the PML-Q faction). Nominations of pliable politicians were supported, and there was interference by the security forces and the bureaucracy on polling day. The elections, as planned, produced no clearly dominant party at the center or in Pakistan's four provinces, the only surprise being the greater-than-expected votes for the Islamist parties, which had ridden a wave of anti-Americanism, especially in the NWFP, and were encouraged to form an electoral alliance.

Not only did the new military regime discipline the politicians and declare an attack on corruption, it launched a transformation of Pakistan's governmental structure and its law and order mechanism, ensuring that the military would have a seat in any future government. Musharraf came to power intent on bringing about a fundamental change in Pakistan's political order, but with no clear idea about what had to be done. As in other areas, he commissioned a retired official, in this case Lieutenant General (ret.) S. Tanwir Naqvi, to head a new National Reconstruction Bureau (NRB) and come up with a scheme that would rebalance Pakistan's politics. There were no specific guidelines, except that Musharraf placed great emphasis on "checks and balances" and the need to moderate the excesses of the politicians. A scheme was put together by a team of experts and consultants, which included the U.S.-trained Daniyal Aziz, who succeeded Naqvi as head of the NRB.[31]

When it was created by the military government, the NRB was described as a think tank, but it acquired a momentum of its own and conceived the new district government (Nazim) system, which remains its major achievement. The Nazim scheme was never widely discussed, nor did the parties provide any input. Nazims were to operate in a political vacuum, excluding national and provincial legislators and Pakistan's own services from local government. Not surprisingly, politicians and bureaucrats opposed the system. The Nazims and the elected assemblies, on the other hand, were promised autonomy and were content with an arrangement that delivers money directly to them, bypassing the bureaucracy and the provincial legislators.

On one level, with its discussion of transparency, openness, accountability, devolution, responsibility, and public accessibility, the new system is a mélange of contemporary theories of public administration. On another level, it very closely resembles the earlier "basic democracies" scheme of Ayub Khan. On a third level, and the one that counts, it does several things.

First, the Nazim system further weakens the power of the bureaucracy, much distrusted by the army and given only an ancillary role in the new system. It is hard to tell whether this was the purpose of the reforms, or whether, in the words of one senior civil servant, the bureaucracy was merely "road kill"—an incidental casualty. Second, by providing block grants at the local level it weakens the provincial governments, which have little or no fiscal control over what happens in the districts.[32] Perhaps the real purpose of the exercise is to curry political favor by creating a class of local notables who owe their position to Army Headquarters, and who are unconstrained in how they spend the funds allocated to their district, as long as things square with the interests and concerns of the local military commander. As one Nazim commented, "There is no check on us, the government funds are our own funds; we are not audited; if we do anything that the government might not like, we can be reported to NAB." "For us," he remarked, "this kind of chance comes only once. The district Nazims are becoming multimillionaires."[33]

NRB's involvement in these issues was, and remains, a constitutional aberration as both local governance and policing are provincial functions. After uniform laws were crafted for all the provinces, the NRB conceded that the provinces could amend these in accordance with their peculiar situations. It would have been constitutionally correct to allow the provinces to iron out the rough edges in the new structures. This would also have given them a hitherto lacking sense of ownership, which, rather than enforcement from Islamabad, would ultimately determine the success or failure of the new systems.

When Pervez Musharraf came to power, he stated often that one of his major goals was to end the sectarian violence that plagued Pakistan. As a Mohajir from Karachi, he was well aware of the corrosive impact of such fury. His army colleagues knew from their own experience in "aid to the civil operations" that Pakistan's law and order situation had reached a state of crisis. By the 1990s Pakistan also had a critical small arms problem, reflected in the growth of private police forces, some of them armed militias, with at least 200 security services commercially operating in the country.[34]

Pakistan's crime data are notoriously unreliable, but this speaks to the larger problem of policing in Pakistan.[35] Over the years, Pakistan's police forces have been significantly weakened, with encroachments by both the military and local politicians. The police are also constrained by a lack of resources, and crime-reporting activity is among the first functions thought of as dispensable.

Following Musharraf's takeover, Pakistan's police force was targeted for reform. Pakistan's police are poorly paid, poorly trained, and widely feared and distrusted by ordinary Pakistanis. The NRB was asked to formulate a new police system to address the crime problem. The Japanese Public Safety Commission was proposed as a model for the federal, provincial, and local police. However, the Japanese police are politically neutral, whereas the Pakistan police have long been an instrument of political harassment, electoral manipulation, and graft during military *and* civilian regimes. Furthermore, under the new dispensation the police were to be responsible to the district Nazims, who in turn were elected in accordance with the police's own instructions and guidance from provincial and national officials.

Few expected this scheme to work.[36] Inevitably, the touted "reforms" were deferred or put on hold under the Musharraf government, and any likely successor will continue to treat the police as an important instrument of control. Indeed, the last thing that any Pakistan government wants is police accountability, except in the occasional case that gets international attention or when a member of the elite is inadvertently arrested, beaten, or kidnaped without explanation.

Yet another Musharraf idea was that the role of the armed forces in government had to be constitutionally regulated—they had to be brought into the system to prevent them from having to take it over again. Under the new order put into effect in 2004, the military acquired a formal constitutional role through membership in the National Security Council, and Musharraf will continue on for one year as both army chief and president, after which he will yield his army position and remain president until 2007.[37] The arrangement was negotiated between Musharraf and his Establishment supporters, on the one hand, and the six-party Islamist alliance on the other; most of the mainstream parties boycotted the talks. In the end they are also likely to accept the arrangement.

Musharraf's supporters—and they are numerous—argue that this arrangement will once and for all regulate Pakistan's civil-military dilemma—keeping the military out by bringing it in; nothing less than this will end the military's "random interference" in civil affairs. This open, overt role is necessary, they insist, because the army's role as a "silent partner" in governance did not guarantee that it would stay out of politics, owing to the politicians' venality and incompetence.[38] People close to Musharraf claim that he *learns*; he eventually figures out that policies adapted on impulse and without careful analysis are not enough. The hope of such supporters is that Musharraf's combination of political naiveté, secularism, and realism will get Pakistan through the next few years.

An "Armored Democracy"

While the role of the armed forces is settled in most former colonial states, political-military tensions remain at the core of Pakistani politics.[39] In the final analysis, Pakistan's politicians must pass a competency test administered and graded by Pakistan's army, not its voters. The more ideological and ambitious generals would raise the bar very high, but even the most moderate and professional of them believe that the politicians must be held to a minimal standard.

The only Pakistan army chief ever to voluntarily resign from his position, Jehangir Karamat, acknowledges that the army has been assertive and "interventionist" but attributes this tendency to historical circumstances. Defending his service, he has argued that the army has a better understanding of its role than do civilians: "Since 1988 . . . every army chief has tried to make the system work and to somehow keep democracy afloat and to encourage the governments to complete their tenures." With the exception of Benazir, Karamat attests, all recent politicians failed to "work" the institutional system effectively because they lacked expertise and self-confidence and had a "fear of being dominated by the military."[40]

Other generals are not so kind to the politicians. They roundly condemn them as incorrigibly corrupt, venal, and incompetent and eagerly compare the army's own high standards of integrity with the politicians' abysmal record. Karamat spoke for the vast majority of his fellow officers when he lamented that the politicians have let the army down. Furthermore, in Pakistan the military assumes that it must veto any civilian decision that affects "national security," a concept defined so broadly by President Musharraf as to be meaningless. Even Karamat noted that the notion of "national security" has greatly expanded from a purely military idea, now including economic policy, budgets, and domestic issues. Karamat himself had proposed a National Security Council that would institutionalize the military's de facto voice in such issues. Clearly, Pakistan's centrist, mainstream political parties cannot hope to come to real power, and govern effectively, unless several indicators point in the same direction at the same time.

First, the army's historic dominance of Pakistan and its central role in the Pakistan Establishment must be severely weakened before any politician can hope to come to real power on his or her own; alternatively, the army must have enough confidence in a civilian leader, or party, to allow them to come to power. The former condition occurred only in Zulfiqar Ali Bhutto's case, and to some extent Benazir's first term.

Then, once in power, a civilian government must demonstrate its competence to the military and meet criteria drawn up by the army. When Karamat attempted to formalize this relationship, Nawaz panicked, fired Karamat, and created deep distrust between him and the army. Pakistan thus has a real chicken-egg problem when it comes to civil-military relations. Under present circumstances, it is impossible for politicians to master the arts and science of democratic politics, to grow and mature in their profession. Once in office, it is equally difficult for them to govern without fear of the army's encroachment or a blatant army takeover.

In short, any civilian government that consistently takes bold steps in a new direction, especially foreign policy, must have army consent. Such issues as Kashmir and India are especially sensitive, and a government that fails to work out a strategy in concert with the armed forces will run enormous risks. Politicians must learn the limits of their own freedom but then must attempt to expand these limits. The army, on the other hand, will have to understand the limits of its own capacity to govern.

Seeds of Change?

The fact that Pakistan has four times followed a cycle of military intervention, military government, military misrule, a return to civilian government, civilian floundering, and renewed intervention, does not mean that the future must look like the past. With each new cycle, fewer and fewer parties are willing to play the role of "King's party" and be manipulated by the armed forces. Thirty-nine years ago, in 1965, all of the political parties supported Ayub's provocative policies toward India; in 1971 all of the West Pakistan political parties supported the army in the east. In 2002, however, Pakistan's parties have shown a degree of independence from the army and the Establishment, and a number of them have linked support for Pakistan's strategic policies with changes in the army's domestic political role.

As chapter 5 indicates, the Islamic parties disagree strongly with Musharraf's alignment with the United States, especially his professed support of the war against terrorism and his reversal of Pakistan's Afghanistan policy. They also insisted (successfully) that he give up either his civilian or his military positions. Benazir's PPP goes along with the army's new strategy in Afghanistan but also insists that the military leave politics; finally, while the PML-Q supports the army without qualification, the other remnant of the PML, the PML-N, is critical of its continuation in power.

The differences among the parties also manifested themselves in the reaction to the army's changes to the Pakistan constitution, embodied in a Legal Framework Order (LFO), with most of them united in opposition to the LFO, but the PML-Q still supportive. Thus even while there is growing discontent with the army's direction of Pakistani foreign policy, and some criticism of its changes to the constitution, there are no issues on which all the parties are aligned on the same side. This, coupled with their rivalry and the army's greater capacity to manipulate elections and electoral coalitions, seems to ensure that Pakistan's parties are further from power now than they have been for many years.

The only civil-military strategy that will work in Pakistan, short of a revolution, military defeat, or ideological transformation, is one in which a *staged* transfer of power and authority takes place over a period of years, spanning the tenures of more than one prime minister, and more than one army chief. Unless that happens, Pakistan's democracy will always be qualified or limited. In this case "staged" is meant both in the sense of a timed schedule and a theatrical event: at each stage both the symbolic and substantive accoutrements of power have to gradually shift from the armed forces to the political parties. As explained in chapter 8, it is questionable that the conditions for such a shift will soon arise.

Islamic
Pakistan

Until 1947 no other state with a predominately Muslim or Islamic population had been founded as a homeland for coreligionists. Most such states had an earlier cultural or civilizational identity *before* they became Muslim: this was notably true of those with Arab and Persian populations. Pakistan was the product of a classic nationalist movement with a geopolitical vision that sought a protected area where Muslims could live unthreatened lives. As for Pakistan's identity, the (personally) secular Jinnah and the Muslim League wanted Pakistan to be a state for Muslims, rather than an Islamic state. Being lawyers brought up in the British tradition, many Muslim League members had practical and political, not theological, concerns and thus were more inclined toward electoral politics and the rule of law.

For the most part, those who fought for Pakistan assumed that Islam would bind together the citizens of the new state regardless of their geographic origins. Pakistanis were to have more in common with each other as Muslims than they did with Hindus, Sikhs, Christians, or Bengali Hindus (who spoke the same language). The Pakistan movement highlighted the idea of the Muslim as victim, subjected to discrimination by a Hindu majority. While the Muslim League did promise a state that would be guided by Islam, this was couched in vague and general terms with no specific blueprint for the future. It was enough to break away from the Hindus.

Box 5-1. *Muslim, Islamist, Secular*

As used here, a "Muslim state" refers to a state whose citizens are entirely or predominately Muslim; "Islamic," refers to the belief that a Muslim state can be made to follow Islamic guidelines, however defined. "Islamist" refers to the groups that advocate an Islamic state, and "Islamism" is an Islamic-flavored version of totalitarianism, seeking to impose a sustained program of various Islamic practices on a society. "Secular" is used to describe the belief that Muslim states can borrow from other cultures and societies, especially the West, and reduce Islam to the private sphere.*

  *Some of these are modified from Daniel Pipes's categorization, "Distinguishing between Islam and Islamism," Center for Strategic and International Studies (www.danielpipes.org/article/954 [June 30, 1998]).

Many who came late to the idea of Pakistan, however, were skeptical of the League's secular vision. They rejected the idea of Pakistan as a nationalist movement, and—when they finally came to support Pakistan—envisioned it as an Islamic state. Before independence, their goal was to change the way Muslims lived—to make them more Islamic, to see their lives regulated by the *Shariat*. After independence, they moved to a larger canvas—Pakistan itself, their mission being to liberate India's remaining Muslims from Hindu dominance.

In several respects—ethnic and cultural pluralism, not to mention religion's role in both the state and citizenship—Pakistan resembles Israel.[1] Like Israel, Pakistan had an assimilation problem, in the form of a million migrants from India. It also had to choose among interpretations of the dominant religion, determine which interpretation should receive state support, and accommodate minority religions and secular coreligionists. In both countries, relations between secular and orthodox have been strained, with the former fearing encroachment by the well-organized orthodox, and the latter resenting what they regard as cultural and social slurs by a secular (in Pakistan, "mainstream") majority. The states differ in that many of Pakistan's founding fathers considered it a model for coreligionists elsewhere, the first modern Muslim state, a beacon of enlightenment for other Muslims.

Pakistan's multiple identities can be categorized on the basis of religion and state. One category takes in the nation's several million non-Muslims (mostly Christians, Parsis, Hindus, and, according to Pakistani law, the Ahmediyya sect). Another encompasses Muslims with secular leanings, most of whom have roots in the territorial state of Pakistan. Yet another consists of Muslims with a close affinity to other South Asian traditions— Hindu, Sikh, Indian Muslim, and Afghan. A fourth category is composed of Muslims who want to turn Pakistan into an Islamic state, and a fifth, of Muslims who would like to bring the message of Islam to other states, by force or by peaceful means.

These are not hard and fast distinctions, and there is much interplay between and among the "cultural," "homeland," "Islamic state," and "Islamic vanguard" identities. This complexity ensures that Pakistan's politics will always carry an extra burden. Its leaders must not only govern effectively and develop a satisfactory relationship with the dominant army, they must solve the ideological puzzle: reconciling the different permutations of state and religion in a country with widespread ethnic and linguistic conflict and a dysfunctional oligarchic political order. How Pakistanis cope with the competing demands of ideology, power, and statecraft will in part determine the future of their state. This chapter focuses on these tensions and the solutions advanced by its increasingly important Islamic parties and movements.

The Islamists and Pakistan

India's Muslim communities were well organized long before 1947, and they were also quite varied. Their members ranged from sophisticated and highly cultured remnants of a number of major Muslim states (and several active ones, notably Hyderabad) to highly Westernized Muslim intellectuals and professionals, to peasants and farmers with their own version of folk Islam. North-south and east-west differences were also evident. The one-quarter of India that was Muslim supported a wide range of associations built around mosques, *madaris* (religious schools often attached to an important mosque), pilgrimage sites, and individual teachers, scholars, and other religious figures, as well as a rich and varied cultural life.

After the 1920s, in response to Hindu attempts to reconvert Muslims to Hinduism (the Shuddhi movement) and the activities of Christian missionaries, Muslims formed several missionary groups of their own. One of them, the Tablighi Jama'at (TJ), has endured and prospered, and it functions throughout South Asia, the Muslim world, and in Great Britain and other Western states.[2] The TJ is usually regarded as apolitical. Other Muslim groups supported a united India, notably the Jama'at-i Ulama-i-Hind.

Maulana Kalam Azad (1888–1958) was the first to tie the fortunes of the Muslim community of India to an organizational solution, and he supported the Hizbul'llah (Party of God), which was charged with the revival of Muslim religious consciousness while protecting Muslim political interests. The organization never amounted to much, and Azad eventually joined Congress, but the idea of an organization that was both a moral beacon and an effective political force appealed to many Muslims, including Maulana Mawdudi.[3]

Mawdudi and the Jama'at

Maulana Mawdudi (1903–79) was the most influential of Pakistan's Islamists. In his view, Pakistan was not just to be a Muslim homeland but had to be perfected along Islamic lines. A scholar and educator, influenced by the Deobandis in northern India, Mawdudi's popularity never approached Jinnah's, yet today his writings are widely propagated and the organization he founded is still strong. His writings also influenced Egypt's Muslim Brotherhood, which in turn has produced pan-Islamic doctrines of revolution and change and indirectly influenced the present day al Qaeda.

Mawdudi came of age just after the failure of the Khilafat movement (which sought to restore the Islamic Caliphate in Turkey), at a time when accommodationist strategies seemed to have reached their limits and Hindu nationalists were active in North India. Mawdudi was an early supporter of the TJ. He then grew critical of its unwillingness to move beyond opposing reconversion and take a more active stance against the British, the Hindus, and the secular but Hindu-dominated Congress Party. A train ride with a leading Hindu politician in 1935 reportedly convinced Mawdudi that Hindus and Muslims could not live together.[4] He was, in his biographer Vali Nasr's words, a "Muslim communalist" at heart.[5]

Mawdudi remained intellectually active but politically disengaged for fifteen years. He was motivated by a distrust—if not hatred—of Hindu politicians and society. Indeed, Mawdudi was not so much pro-Pakistan as anti-Hindu, and during the years before partition he proposed two schemes as alternatives to the creation of Pakistan. One was the bifurcation of India into Hindu and Muslim majority provinces within the framework of a single India; the other envisioned one large Hindu province and thirteen smaller Muslim ones, again within a larger Indian context. It was not until the Muslim League promulgated the Pakistan Resolution at Lahore in 1940, raising the prospect of a separate state, that he organized what went on to become South Asia's most important Islamist organization, the Jama'at-i-Islami (JI), on August 26, 1941.

Unlike Jinnah, whom he scorned, Mawdudi set forth a doctrine that addressed the question of how Muslims could live as a minority and eventually shape the state in which they were the majority. Mawdudi's vehicle, the JI, was to be a tightly knit organization. It was structured along the lines of what a Leninist would call "democratic centralism," with strong leaders (*amirs*) at each level, active member participation, and obedience to the organization's decisions.

The Jama'at was to be more than a party; it was, in Nasr's phrase, the "vanguard" of the Islamic revolution in Pakistan. Each of the seventy-five original members stood up and followed Mawdudi's lead in professing the Muslim testament of faith (*shahadah*), thereby reaffirming their Muslimness and forming a new holy community.[6] The JI cadres were required to be good Muslims, shunning corruption and engaging in charitable and public services, and the JI spread quickly throughout India, partly because of the social services it offered to members and nonmembers. In this way it resembles the militant Hindu organization, the Rashtriya Swayam Sevak Sangh, which also helped dislocated refugees and sought to inspire others by its members' discipline and exemplary behavior. The JI cadres were expected to be more disciplined and effective than the state, and it was Mawdudi's expectation that the JI would win both the minds and the souls of Indian Muslims, eventually supplanting the Muslim League.

Mawdudi's expectations were unrealistic. Jinnah was a world-renowned figure, supported by many wealthy Muslims and traditional leaders, and he had the ear of the British. The Jama'at did not even contest local elections in 1945, and at the time of partition, Mawdudi found himself on the wrong side of the new border. He had to be escorted by Pakistan army troops to Lahore from the JI's headquarters in Pathankot.

The Jama'at then split into separate Indian and Pakistani national organizations.[7] Today, it stands apart as an Islamist party, following no particular Islamic sect, disciplined, and intellectually attractive, especially to Pakistan's middle classes.

The Islamists and the State of Pakistan

The Islamist groups played an important role in helping Pakistan recover from the devastation of partition, and this gave them additional organizational skills and helped them establish a link to many new Pakistanis—especially the migrants from India. The pattern was to be repeated forty years later when many Islamist groups worked with millions of Afghan refugees who poured into Pakistan from 1980 onward.

Immediately after independence, a wide spectrum of groups began to press the Muslim League government to turn Pakistan into an Islamic state. Mawdudi developed the argument that the Muslim League had wrought a state ruled by Muslims—a Muslim state—whereas an Islamic state conducts its affairs in accordance with the revealed guidance of Islam and accepts the sovereignty of Allah and the supremacy of Allah's laws. The Islamists were not content with an ingathering of Indian Muslims; they wanted to eliminate vestiges of the British-derived civil and criminal laws and create a state based upon *Shariat*. Most liberal Pakistanis continue to reject the imposition of *Shariat* law, but the demand is pressed incessantly by all Islamist parties.

Although not enthusiastic about Pakistan's creation, the Islamists were also the first to demand that Islamic, and sometimes highly sectarian, provisions be included in the yet-to-be-adopted constitution. Rigid and conservative, they hampered efforts to reach a constitutional consensus. Mawdudi led this campaign, arguing that his party alone possessed the understanding and commitment needed to accomplish this cherished goal. The JI also led the battle to ban "foreign" or alien cultural influence—especially from India.[8]

The Establishment's Islam

The Establishment's views of how to organize a society were greatly affected by the interplay between traditional Islamic forms of charity, education, and law, on the one hand, and practices inherited from a "colonial" past, on the other. [9] That is to say, Pakistan's institutions were the result of adapting to a British-dominated environment, while simultaneously supporting and exploiting traditional allegiances and structures. This had been particularly evident in the army, where traditional modes of valor and loyalty had been harnessed to a British strategic cause, and in the process traditional forms were refined, standardized, and given some degree of influence.

The battlegrounds for these competing conceptions of how to order the state range from vital structural issues, such as Pakistan's legal codes and the degree to which *Shariat* is adapted, to questions of attire (were Lady Diana's knees too visible, for example, when she visited Lahore's largest mosque?).[10] The Pakistan government also created a number of new identities and organizations for its own purposes—mostly to counter regional nationalist movements and the left. This of course required the creation of counterforces, in an endless attempt to balance forces set in motion by the state, but energized by traditional values and organizations.

In response to Islamist forces, but also because of its own commitment to an Islamic Republic, the Muslim League and its leaders slowly moved to "Islamize" the state. While largely secular or "mainstream" in outlook, they viewed Islam as an acceptable (if untried) vehicle for nation-building. During the struggle for Pakistan, Jinnah and other leaders had assured Muslims that the constitution of Pakistan would be based upon the Quran.[11] Strategically, there was also a desire to draw a sharp distinction between India and Pakistan. Islamic Pakistan, as soon portrayed by Jinnah and other leaders, was a trustworthy link to the Islamic world and the Middle East. Pakistan's Islamic identity was thus a useful way of distinguishing the new state from the larger and more famous India.

Between them, the army, the Muslim League, regional and ethnic parties, the intelligence services, and Pakistan's scholars forged an Establishment view of the link between the state and Islam. Its core concept was that a wall should separate the individual and civil society, on the one hand, and many Islamic practices (especially a codified *Shariat*-based law), on the other. This view is in gradual but steady retreat, and Pakistan has become increasingly Islamic. That is, many Western social practices have been altered or abandoned in the name of religion, notably the public consumption of alcohol, gambling, and coeducational classrooms, except in some of Pakistan's most Westernized cities, such as Islamabad, Lahore, and Karachi.

Although the Establishment has not reached a consensus on how far and how fast Islamic principles can be introduced, there is general agreement on two points. The first is that abandoning Western-derived practices for unproven Islamic ones is a risky business. Can an Islamic banking system or educational system produce the wealth or the kind of people able to function in the modern world? The second major objection is simply, "Which Islam?" Many interpretations of the *Shariat* exist, as evidenced by the often bitter disputes among Pakistan's Islamic parties and theologians.

All of these issues arose early in Pakistan's history. The first major compromise between the Islamizers and the mainstream secularists was the Constitutional Assembly's Objectives Resolution of 1949. Its Preamble read: "Sovereignty over the entire universe belongs to God Almighty alone, and the authority which He has delegated to the State of Pakistan through its people for being exercised within the limits prescribed by Him is a sacred trust." However, this left some questions unanswered. Was the *Shariat* to be introduced? How were Pakistan's minorities to be treated? Which sect of Islam would provide guidance? As soon as Liaquat Ali Khan, reflecting the views of the overwhelming number of Pakistanis, insisted that Pakistan would not become a theocracy, the debate with the Islamists was joined. In another concession, the government assigned different rights of citizenship to Muslims and non-Muslims (the latter could not become prime minister or president). Subsequent Pakistan governments, including those of Ayub, Yahya, and Bhutto, continued to seek compromise with the Islamists. They indulged in the rhetoric of Islam, but none were serious about implementing an Islamic blueprint, even if one could be defined to everyone's satisfaction.

Ayub Khan regarded the Islamist parties, especially the well-organized Jama'at, as a dangerous nuisance. The Jama'at was banned, and Mawdudi was imprisoned, a move that only enhanced his personal status. Seen to be suffering for their religious beliefs, Islamist leaders portrayed themselves as heroes and martyrs, invoking the memory of the great martyrdoms of early Islam. The government responded by pitting the conservative ulema against the Jama'at and its political allies, playing to the issue of their support of Jinnah's sister, Fatima Jinnah, in the 1965 presidential election.[12]

The rough treatment gave some of the Islamist parties, notably the Jama'at, a new respect for constitutionalism and civil liberties, and generated among them an animosity toward the whisky-drinking army.

Ayub viewed Islam as an adjunct to Pakistan's security policy. For Ayub, "man as an animal is moved by basic instincts for preservation of life" but longs for an ideology that can command his allegiance—for which "he should be able to lay down his life."[13] He saw Islam as such an ideology and felt that Pakistan had become vulnerable internally and externally because its citizens had drifted away from the cause that had united them in the first place. For Ayub, the problem was simple: reformulate Islam so that Pakistanis could understand it. He did this in a private note on April 12, 1959, with a nine-point outline of "the ideology of Islam." Bypassing the ulema, he opted for a bureaucratic approach to the problem of reconciling the laws of the state to the Quran and the *Sunnah*.[14] Under Ayub's sponsorship, a panoply of captive research and teaching institutions was established, all state-sponsored and directed, none of which achieved popular support, let alone support among Pakistan's Islamist parties. Preoccupied with strategy and reshaping Pakistan's domestic political order, his government said little afterward about Islamizing Pakistan.

With the failure of Ayub and his successor, General Yahya Khan, who lost half of Pakistan in 1971, the army's pragmatic approach to Islamic issues also fell into disgrace. It is often noted that the loss of East Pakistan changed Pakistan's ethnic and political balance, but it also changed the ideological balance. What shocked many West Pakistanis was not the behavior of the Indians or even the Americans, but the betrayal of Pakistan by East Pakistanis themselves. In trying to explain this, many concluded that the Bengalis were not "truly" Pakistanis. That is, they were not truly Islamic or Muslims—theirs was a moral and religious failure, not a political one. Compounding this feeling of betrayal was the fact that even the Islamic world had not intervened to prevent the vivisection of an Islamic brother.

The idea of an Islamic Pakistan was seized upon by Zulfiqar Ali Bhutto. Aware of a growing Islamist movement, which had gathered steam by opposing both Ayub and the blatantly irreligious Yahya Khan, Bhutto advanced the idea of "Islamic socialism."[15] He was transparently insincere about the Islamic component of this ideology, but it was politically expedient, given the resurgence of Islam as a political issue. Bhutto put the state at the service of Islam, introducing a ban on alcohol and gambling and making Friday a nonwork day (a decision reversed years later by Nawaz Sharif). His 1973 constitution made further concessions to Islam: in 1974 he supported a move to declare the Ahmediyya sect non-Muslim, and he instructed the army chief, Zia ul-Haq, to Islamize the Pakistan army. Bhutto was later to admit that promoting and encouraging the pious Zia was the biggest mistake of his life.

Bhutto also applied Islamic rhetoric to Pakistan's foreign and strategic policy, hosting a major Organization of the Islamic Conference meeting in Lahore in 1974 and approaching "Islamic" states such as Qadhafi's Libya for support for Pakistan's nuclear program, described by Bhutto as an "Islamic bomb." He also supported several extremist groups in opposition to the Afghan government. These later played a major role in the war against the Soviet Union and were eventually displaced by the Taliban.

Most striking, though, was that Bhutto began turning Pakistan's back on South Asia, looking to the Middle East for aid, ideology, and strategic cooperation. After 1972 the Indian presence—in the form of business, trade, and culture—diminished, and India was regarded as a state that could teach Pakistan nothing, except revenge. Under Bhutto's admittedly insincere Islamization, Pakistan's non-Indian identity was emphasized. This may have been important in forming a separate Pakistani identity, but it also meant that Pakistan ceased to learn from the one state that it most resembled. When, twenty-five years later, India began to reform critical sectors of its economy, Pakistan could not follow suit.

Zia and Islamism

It was under Zia's effort to launch Pakistan's moral rearmament that Islamization acquired legitimacy and the backing of the state. Zia combined religious zeal and a shrewd political mind. With a more attractive personality he might have been more popular among Pakistan's urban middle classes, but his ten years as president suggest a template that might yet be applied by some future leader.

As discussed in chapter 3, under Zia, Islamization went beyond the ban on alcohol introduced by his predecessor, General Tikka Khan: more officers grew beards, and a number of hortatory signboards quoting the Quran and the Prophet were placed around the cantonments. Of greater importance, evaluation forms included a box for comments on an officer's religious sincerity. For Zia, a more truly Islamic Pakistan would have the moral qualities necessary to stand up to India, since its scientists, generals, and politicians would be strengthened, not weakened, by their faith. Zia also cynically used Islamic groups internally against leftist opponents, especially the PPP, though he was not above betraying them when he felt the alliance had outlived its usefulness.

Zia left an enduring mark on Pakistan's civilian schools and institutions. He introduced a core curriculum inculcating a particular interpretation of Pakistan, South Asia, and the world. Bhutto had begun the process of wrecking Pakistan's colleges and universities by nationalizing private schools; Zia continued the process by encouraging them to become seminaries.

The worldview that they were instructed to teach was very close to that of Zia's new ally, the Jama'at-i-Islami. A new field, "Pakistan Studies," was made compulsory for all degree students, including those at engineering and medical colleges. In 1981 the University Grants Commission (UGC) issued a directive to prospective textbook authors, "to demonstrate that the basis of Pakistan is not to be founded in racial, linguistic, or geographical factors, but, rather, in the shared experience of a common religion. To get students to know and appreciate the Ideology of Pakistan, and to popularize it with slogans. To guide students towards the ultimate goal of Pakistan—the creation of a completely Islamicized State."[16]

One analysis of Pakistani textbooks notes that three Islamic-related events were discussed in detail: the Objectives Resolution, the presentation to the government of a program of Islamization by thirty-one ulema in 1951 (it became the manifesto of the Jama'at), and the implementation of Islamic principles by General Zia.[17]

However, even this was not enough for some of the Islamizers, including a few in the military. One brigadier called for a revival of "the spirit of Jihad," including compulsory military training for all Pakistani men and women, and a thorough transformation of Pakistan itself.[18] Even under Zia this was a fringe position, but such writing showed how the trauma of 1971 had created fertile ground for the idea that the *new* Pakistan, shorn of its poorer and partly Hindu East Wing, could be guided by the mission of perfecting Islam itself in Pakistan. Pakistan was not a mere refuge, it was to be an Islamic outpost with a long-term historic mission that transcended South Asia.

An Islamic Foreign Policy

The more Islamist members of the Establishment could take solace in a special strategic and foreign policy derived from the fact that Pakistan is an Islamic state. "Pakistan is an ideological miracle and not a geographical landmark"; therefore its strategic doctrine is primarily ideological and only secondarily geopolitical. Pakistan was created as an Islamic state by a people whose political interests were not confined to the India-Pakistan subcontinent but extended to the entire Muslim world. Thus Pakistan should not be an introverted state confined to South Asia, but an "outward looking extroverted Islamic State which was to be the harbinger of the independence of the Muslim States of Asia and Africa."[19]

These views, which paralleled those of the Jama'at, were encouraged by Zia's successor as army chief, General Aslam Beg. For Beg and the more Islamist members of the Establishment, such as Beg's Inter-Service Intelligence Directorate (ISI) head, Lieutenant General Hamid Gul, Islam was the ideology, and Jihad was its instrument. Gul (a Jama'at member) and Beg, reflecting widely held views on the Islamist side of the political spectrum, believed that Pakistan needed to rapidly industrialize in order to oppose the superpowers and to create a balance with India. Pakistan also needed to push forward in Afghanistan by promoting a fundamentalist regime, and to liberate Muslim areas under non-Muslim domination (such as Eritrea, Arakan [Burma], South Philippines, the Muslim republics of the Soviet Union, Sinkiang in China) and Muslim areas under Hindu domination (such as Jammu and Kashmir). Some of the strategic Islamists argued that they had to organize an international Jihad brigade to take the offensive against both India and the Soviet Union by using as an available asset the Muslim populations in those countries—a way that would also "absolve [the] Pakistan government of all responsibilities."[20] Pakistan also had to develop the latest military technology (a euphemism for nuclear weapons and missiles, then being secretly developed) and, where possible, share this technology with less-developed (but often oil-rich) Islamic states. The army Islamists also wanted to convert the Pakistan army from its British-based structure "to an Islamic army," modeled along the lines of the soldiers of Islam from the time of the Prophet to the Caliphate.

For most of the army, the latter suggestion went too far, as did the call for a dedicated corps of jihadis. After Beg's retirement, the army sharply limited the influence of overtly "Islamic" officers. Beg was the last army chief to see Pakistan's regional security in Islamic terms; all of his successors, while no less religious than he, saw the dangers of eroding traditional professional standards, even though they enthusiastically used Islamist groups as strategic instruments of power.

The Democratic Interregnum

During the ten years of shaky democracy that followed Zia's death, the Pakistan Establishment treated the Islamic question with great caution. On one level, it offered enthusiastic public support for "Islamic" causes, especially the rebellion in Kashmir and the activities of the Taliban. The latter assistance was undertaken by Benazir Bhutto, who was vulnerable to Islamist attacks because many Islamists did not believe that women were fit to govern. Nawaz Sharif was more forthcoming on the domestic front, and in 1999 he tried to make *Shariat* part of Pakistan's constitution. The bill passed the lower house, where the Muslim League had a commanding majority, and he was expected to complete the process when the Muslim League gained control over the Senate in 2000. Why did Sharif pursue this domestic Islamist agenda when he already had a commanding majority in parliament? Some speculated that he was responding to the wishes of his Islamist father, but he was probably more interested in outflanking the parties on his ideological right. Playing the Islamic card would have enabled him to determine what was "Islamic," thus complementing his already formidable executive powers with the sanction of religion. The army stayed aloof on the matter and remained neutral as long as *Shariat* was not imposed on them.

The greatest assistance Benazir and Nawaz offered the Islamists lay in what they did *not* do: they made no attempt to rebuild Pakistan's school system, allowing it to deteriorate further after Zia's twelve years of neglect. Unable to send their children to Pakistan's disappearing public schools, many families, especially the poor, took advantage of the madaris, many of which offered free room and board as well as an Islamic education. Toward the end of the decade of democracy, Shahbaz Sharif, the Punjab chief minister and Nawaz's younger brother, commissioned a study of the madaris, but by then the Islamists had struck deep roots.

More recently, many members of Pakistan's Establishment have reverted to an earlier theme that Pakistanis are discriminated against because they are Muslims. Whether ostensibly this is a result of Islamabad's nuclear program or the Western reaction to September 11, it is felt that the West (in collusion with India) is unfairly attacking Pakistan for its fresh adherence to Islam and Islamic principles. According to the biographer of A. Q. Khan, the "father" of Pakistan's Islamic bomb, "propaganda" against Pakistan "is a lot stronger than the one carried out against Hitler during World War II," and the West still demonstrates a crusader mentality in dealing with the Islamic world.[21] Even before 9/11, the more Islamist elements of the Pakistan Establishment held that the rest of the world, especially Christians, Jews, and Hindus, feared Islam's progressive, reformist qualities and were intent upon keeping Islamic countries backward. Thus Pakistan's material and military backwardness is easily explained: it is due to Pakistan's religious and social greatness, and to a worldwide conspiracy to prevent it from acquiring modern technology and weapons. Thus the threat to Pakistan increases as it becomes purer, more Islamic; Islamic *superiority* explains Muslim *inferiority*.

That is why Pakistan's Establishment was ambivalent about greater Islamization of the state. Zia was an enthusiast, and he and Aslam Beg linked Pakistan's security and foreign policy to various domestic and foreign radical Islamists. Both Bhuttos, personally very secular, cynically used Islamic causes for short-term political gain. All Pakistani governments from Zulfiqar Ali Bhutto onward neglected public education, indirectly strengthening the Islamist counterculture.

Resurgent Islam

Reflecting Islam's heavy emphasis on volunteerism and community responsibility for the less fortunate, many Islamic groups and parties support apolitical charitable organizations, notably hospitals, medical clinics, and feeding centers, as well as disaster relief and other programs. In Pakistan the most important and visible charities have been those of the Aga Khan Foundation. It runs an important hospital and medical school in Karachi and is engaged in development work in some of Pakistan's isolated mountainous regions—where many members of the Ismaili sect live. On a smaller scale, but still widely respected and highly effective, are the activities of the Edhi Foundation, run from Karachi by the saintly Abdus Sattar Edhi.[22] It is important to distinguish between these and apolitical missionary activities, on the one hand, and those of the politically oriented Islamists and Islamic radicals, on the other. The former are noncontroversial, although at times charities have been used by militants to fund their activities, and some militant organizations have charitable branches.

As for the missionaries, the Tablighi Jama'at remains important in Pakistan (and in many other countries).[23] Theoretically, the society could serve as a recruitment base for more radical groups or could spin off a more militant faction operating under the cover of the widely respected Tablighi, or it could become more militant itself. So far there is no evidence of any of this happening.[24]

The Islamist parties and movements that do have a political or revolutionary agenda are very diverse. Most are Sunni groups, but some are Shi'ia, and a few, such as the Jama'at, are nonsectarian (in some cases the Sunni-Shi'ia classes are directly linked to ethnolinguistic differences, not theological ones, as discussed in chapter 6). They range from the center-right groups dominated by the Jama'at to a few radical groups seeking to bring about a global Islamic revolution.[25] Most of the Islamist political and revolutionary groups are anti-American, not only because of Washington's support of Israel, but because of its support for successive moderate Pakistani governments over the years, including those dominated by the army.

Some of the radical groups would readily wage a jihad in India to liberate its 150 million Muslims, and some have close ties to remnants of the Taliban and al Qaeda. Though small in numbers, some radical Islamic groups have employed deadly force within Pakistan against liberals, "secularists," Shi'as, and now Americans. While they represent a threat to public order and are capable of assassination and murder, they do not have broad political support. Their vision of Pakistan is so radical that they are held in contempt by the political and military branches of the Establishment.

The Jama'at and Centrist Islamism

In terms of organizational integrity and electoral and street power on a national level, the Jama'at remains Pakistan's most important Islamic group. Although the JI has not done well at the polls compared with Pakistan's two mainstream parties, the PPP and the PML, it has a wide following among Pakistan's urban middle classes—including the army, the bureaucracy, and professionals.

The Jama'at has had a long connection with the Pakistani military and intelligence, especially the more "Islamist" officers. Recently, a number of retired generals joined the JI, including two former ISI directors, Lieutenant General Hamid Gul and Lieutenant General Javed Nasir, as well as A. Q. Khan, a central figure in Pakistan's nuclear weapons program. It also has close ties to some Afghan militant Islamists who were influenced by Mawdudi's writings when they were students; the JI subsequently channeled military aid to them from the ISI; in turn, they trained young JI students as fighters in Afghanistan. The JI also has a hand in education, operating a national chain of schools and playing a large role in the Saudi-funded International Islamic University in Islamabad, which is co-joined with the spectacular Faisal Mosque in Islamabad.

One of the Jama'at's great strengths has been continuity in leadership—it has only had three amirs since 1941: Mian Tufail succeeded Mawdudi in 1972, and Qazi Hussein Ahmed replaced him in 1987. In addition, its reputation for being corruption-free, its internal democracy, and the discipline and dedication of its workers set the JI apart from other parties. Unlike sectarian groups, the Jama'at appeals to the intellect, and Mawdudi's writings are still widely read, and quoted by the party faithful. It has an especially strong student wing. In several discussions about politics, society, and Islam in a Jama'at-dominated Punjab University department, a group of young Jama'at students, including women, robotically repeated the party catechism on a wide range of social issues even as a group of students in another, more liberal department angrily protested the severe intolerance and harassment from Jama'at militants that they faced on campus. Subsequently, the Islamic faculty of the university proposed that English be removed as a compulsory subject from undergraduate arts and science programs, further isolating the beleaguered English department. As the Pakistani American scholar Mahnaz Ispahani notes, control of education and control over women are the sine qua non of the Islamization of Pakistan, and Pakistan's "current catacomb" of educational systems in English and Urdu, in madaris and public and private schools, "is producing a highly compartmentalized citizenry with few shared values or skills."[26]

The JI's core positions can be summarized in the following way:

—Islam will keep Pakistan united and turn it into a powerful, *modern* state that can more than hold its own with India. Paralleling Lenin, the JI envisions the marriage of Islam and electricity. Nuclear weapons, for example, are the ultimate expression of modernity, and Pakistan, as an advanced Muslim state, was right to acquire them.

—The Jama'at has reinterpreted Jinnah as an Islamist, claiming that his speech of August 11, 1947, has been read out of context by those who would make him a "secularist."

—Ethnic separatism is illegitimate and must be opposed by any means. The Jama'at was part of the army's strategy to clamp down on Bengali separatism in 1971, and it has fought separatism among Sindhis, Baluch, and Pashtuns. Its opposition to ethnic politics cost it support among some who drifted to the Muttahida Quami movement (MQM) in the 1990s.

—India remains Pakistan's chief enemy, but the Jama'at's opposition to India is nuanced, and like most Pakistanis, it believes that a major war would be ruinous. There are recent hints that the Jama'at might support a political dialogue with India over Kashmir; its position is very close to that of the government, which in late 2003 also moved in this direction.

—The JI recognizes America's dominant position but strongly disagrees with past American support for Pakistani military regimes, Israel, and India; while the Jama'at leadership maintains links to America, it has joined the chorus that accuses Washington of being hostile to Islam and Muslims.[27]

—The party is militant but strongly opposes military rule. Pervez Musharraf is especially scorned by the Jama'at leadership; after the 1999 coup, the Jama'at led the call for a restoration of civilian government, subsequently insisting that Musharraf resign one of his positions—either army chief or president.

—The Jama'at leadership has close ties to the military but would like to restructure Pakistan's armed forces, which it sees as one of the last vestiges of the colonial era.

—The Jama'at differs markedly from most of the other Islamist parties in that it strongly favors women's education, albeit strictly within "Islamic" guidelines. Many highly educated Pakistani women are JI members, and one of Qazi Hussein's daughters was elected to Pakistan's National Assembly in 2002.

—The Jama'at leadership craves acceptance in the international community and seeks to present a moderate face to the world. It has played host to many foreign officials, including several American ambassadors, and it operates a sophisticated public relations apparatus. Qazi Hussein has addressed a number of foreign research centers and think tanks, including the Brookings Institution, and he was the first leader of a religious party to address Pakistan's Ministry of Foreign Affairs.[28]

Two other qualities of the JI deserve special attention. One is its ability to work with other parties in an alliance; the other is its intermittent resort to violence.

The Jama'at has a long history of forging alliances with disparate parties, including potential rivals. During the Zia years, the Jama'at formed the Movement for Restoration of Democracy, and once Zia died and the PPP came to power, the JI joined another coalition, the Islami Jumhuri Ittihad (IJI, Islamic Democratic Alliance), sponsored by the intelligence services to keep the PPP government in check. The IJI consisted of conservative parties, notably the Pakistan Muslim League (PML), their common interest being hostility to the PPP and a desire to come to power. This ISI-brokered alliance worked, even though the PML had been a staunch supporter of the Zia regime. Recently, the JI became a critical member of the Muttahida Majlis-e-Amal (MMA), a six-party alliance, and its partners include five other Islamic parties. Their theological orientation is at variance with that of the Jama'at—most of them are highly sectarian, attached to one or another Islamic school.

The Jama'at has allied with more radical Islamist groups, and has its own violent history as well. The Jama'at's student wing, the Islami Jami'at Tulabah (Islamic Society of Students, IJT) was officially formed in February 1947 and is especially influential in Punjab University in Lahore. Many future Jama'at leaders, including the present amir, Qazi Hussein, were once IJT activists. Although one 1989 estimate placed the IJT's core membership at only 2,400, it had nearly a quarter million workers under looser discipline.[29] Originally conceived as a missionary movement for students, it came under the influence of the radical Muslim Brotherhood of Egypt and turned into an anti-Left student militia in the 1950s, moving from egg-tossing to violent street confrontations. The IJT was further radicalized between 1969 and 1971 when it became the "main force behind the Jama'at's national campaign against the People's Party in the west and the Awami League and Bengali secessionists in East Pakistan."[30] The IJT, with its Mohajir elements in the forefront, engaged in paramilitary operations in East Pakistan under the direction of the Pakistan army and its intelligence services. This completed the transformation of the IJT from a missionary and religious organization to a militant force.

The Jama'at also has links with one of the most important militant groups in Kashmir, the Hezbul Mujahideen.[31] In 2003 the Jama'at was also implicated in the operation of several safe houses for al Qaeda and Taliban leaders hiding out in Pakistan. Suspiciously, the government gave the JI a clean bill, and the ISI held an unusual press conference absolving the JI of any connection with captured al Qaeda operatives.[32] It is not known whether this represents a new flirtation with terrorism, whether the Jama'at was accommodating some of its alliance partners, or whether this was an aberration, with local JI cadres acting on their own.

The possible linkage of al Qaeda to the Jama'at raises many other questions. Is this a new development, or one of long standing? Are there sleeper cells of al Qaeda embedded in the JI membership, or did this connection—if it is significant—come about as a temporary consequence of the JI's new alliance with parties that had closer ties to the Taliban and al Qaeda?[33]

Equally problematic, for a party that professes constitutionalism and seeks to portray itself as the moderate face of Pakistan's Islamic movement, the JI has long been a close supporter of the notorious Gulbuddin Hekmatyar. When Hekmatyar was a student at Kabul University in the early 1970s, he was influenced by the ideas of Mawdudi, the JI founder, as was another hard-core Islamist, Burhanuddin Rabbani.[34] Hekmatyar worked closely with the JI during the Soviet occupation of Afghanistan, and under ISI sponsorship many JI cadres joined the mujahiddin, as many Afghans were trained by the JI in Pakistan.[35] Hekmatyar subsequently fought the Taliban, and for a while ISI was supporting both Hekmatyar and the Taliban, but he is now allied with the Taliban in opposition to the new Afghan regime of Hamid Karzai, just as the JI finds itself in alliance with the Taliban's main supporter, the Jamiat Ulema-e-Islam (JUI).

The JI cannot yet compete at the polls nationally, as it is a dominant presence in only a few parts of Pakistan—notably the urban areas, where it has elected a number of Nazims (local officials). In many ways, it resembles India's Hindu nationalist Bharatiya Janata Party of several years ago, before the latter's meteoric rise to power.

If the JI is to advance politically, it will have to tone down its religious-nationalist expressions and ally with regional and even mainstream political parties, not just other Islamist groups. This will be impossible if the JI leadership continues to insinuate that some Pakistanis, notably

Ahmediyyas, Parsis, Hindus, or those with foreign ties, are less than trust-worthy. Some of Qazi Hussein's statements, and those of the MMA alliance, have raised strong criticism about the Islamists' intolerance of non-Muslims and Islamic sects including such respected groups as the Ismaili Aga Khan Foundation.[36]

A much-debated question about radical or extremist groups is whether participation in a democratic political process can have a moderating effect on them. On one side of the aisle are those who think the cure for bad democracy is more democracy, on the other, all those who believe illiberal democracy is damaging to true democracy and produces corrupt and authoritarian regimes.[37] Developments in Pakistan shed little light on the issue. The Jama'at is poised to move in either direction. If it cannot come to power through peaceful means, might it revert to its street-fighting days? This remains a strong possibility if instability should again break out in the country, but this time it will also have to face the footsoldiers of the ulema parties. Several scenarios by which the Islamists, particularly the Jama'at, might come to power at the center are discussed in chapter 8.

The Ulema Parties

Each major Islamic movement in Pakistan gave rise to one or more political groups, sometimes referred to as the Ulema parties. These are usually linked to a particular theological school, and often to a specific chain of mosques and madaris.

Numerically, the moderate Barelvi school has the largest number of adherents, encompassing a large majority of rural Pakistanis.[38] The Barelvi movement, which controls about a quarter of Pakistan's madaris, was influenced by mystical Sufi and Indian-Pakistani folk traditions. The main Barelvi political organization is the Jamiat Ulema-e-Pakistan (JUP). However, some Barelvi groups, especially in Karachi (such as the Sunni Tehreek) are involved in sectarian violence against Deobandis, in a turf war over control over the city's mosques.[39]

The largest group of mosques and madaris belongs to the Deobandi sect of Islam (the name is derived from Deoband, the Indian town where the movement arose in the late nineteenth century). Deobandis control an estimated 65 percent of Pakistan's madaris. The main Deobandi-based party is the Jamiat Ulema-e-Islam-F (JUI-F), headed by Fazlur Rahman and a component of the MMA alliance.

In June 2003 Rahman made a highly publicized trip to India, to visit Deoband, and met with Indian prime minister Atal Behari Vajpayee, announcing that a solution to the Kashmir problem was possible and desirable. The JUI's political base is in the Northwest Frontier Province (NWFP), and it has never felt as strongly about Kashmir as developments in Afghanistan.[40] An alliance partner but bitter rival is the Jamiat Ulema-e-Islam-S (JUI-S), Samiul Haq's breakaway group.

The Deobandis are among the most militant of Pakistan's Islamic groups and demand that the Pakistan state become truly Islamic (as they would define Islam). They were also in the forefront of the movement to declare the Ahmediyyas to be non-Muslims and are behind much of the anti-Shi'ia sectarian violence that plagues Punjab and Karachi. Several Deobandi groups have been linked to sectarian violence, including off-shoots of the JUI, and one, the Harkat-ul-Mujahideen (HUM) was the first Pakistani organization to be put on the U.S. list of terrorist organizations.[41] Its chief ideologue was Maulana Masood Azhar, who, after his release from an Indian jail as part of a deal that freed hostages from a hijacked Indian airliner, briefly toured Pakistan to triumphal crowds until his intelligence handlers instructed him to go underground. Azhar then founded Jaish-e-Mohammad, which was subsequently banned by the government of Pakistan. Ahmed Omar Saeed Sheikh, a British national of Pakistani origin and an associate of Azhar, was linked to Daniel Pearl's murder and now faces a death sentence.[42] Despite his past activities, Azhar was not charged with any criminal activities (for that matter, he spent twelve years in India without being charged or tried for any crime).

Another movement dating back to the nineteenth century is the Ahle Hadith reform movement, which is closely linked to Saudi Arabia and is the "most orthodox and stringent school of interpretation and follows the lead of the Saudi Ulema."[43] The militant or "jihadi" wing of the Ahle Hadith produced the notorious Lashkar-e-Taiba (LeT), which has been implicated in a number of terrorist acts in India. LeT is banned by the government of Pakistan and is on the American list of terrorist organizations as well. The Ahle Hadith has had a stunning increase in membership since the 1980s, directly traceable to increased private Saudi support for their madaris.[44]

Pakistan's beleaguered Shi'ia (about 12 percent of the population) have also produced a number of militant organizations, almost all in response to the growth of militant Sunni groups in the 1980s.

As this narrative indicates, there has been a proliferation of sectarian and religious groups in Pakistan over the past fifteen years, many of whom were energized after Zia ul-Haq gave substance to Zulfiqar Ali Bhutto's promise to turn Pakistan into an Islamic state. As in the case of analogous left- and right-wing movements in the West, these radical groups are often closely linked to more "public" and moderate organizations, and some are splinter factions that leave their parent organization to strike off on their own.

Religious Education: A Vision of the Future?

In Pakistan these groups have a specific institutional base, the *madrassah*, or Islamic seminary (plural = *madaris*), and their growth and effectiveness is directly linked to the rise of these institutions. The madaris were the major source of religious and scientific learning and teaching in Islamic states, especially between the seventh and eleventh centuries. They were apolitical religious schools, with important centers in Baghdad and Damascus. In South Asia the madrassah tradition continued, restricted to the religious domain. These schools did produce some outstanding scholars and teachers but were also instrumental in chopping up Islamic thought along sectarian lines and in some cases narrowing, not broadening, the outlook of their graduates.

At the time of partition, there were only about 250 religious schools in Pakistan; by 1987 there may have been 3,000. Current estimates range from 10,000 to 45,000, of which some 10 to 15 percent preach a particularly virulent kind of hatred or provide military training.[45] The madaris range in size from a few students to several thousand. One of the largest, the Dur-ul-Uloom Haqqania in Baluchistan, has a student body of 1,500 boarding students and 1,000 day students, aged six and upward, and was the school that taught the Taliban leadership.[46] As a result of the state's official support (or exploitation) of traditional institutions, the number of scholars, Arabic teachers, students, and clerics far exceeds Pakistan's requirements. Moreover, they are ill-adapted to find a job in the modern world. This has created a class of religious lumpen proletariat, unemployable and practically uneducated young men who see religious education as a vehicle for social mobility, but who find traditional avenues clogged and modern ones blocked.[47]

Box 5-2. *Sects in Islam*

Like other major religions, Islam is amenable to a variety of interpreta-tions, and many of these have produced their own sects or movements. They sponsor educational institutions, mosques, charities, and political par-ties. Among Pakistani Sunnis, the most important sects are the Deobandis and the Barelvis. The puritanical Wahabis are also influential; though based in Saudi Arabia, they have funded many Islamic schools in Pakistan and elsewhere and are closely related to Deobandism ideologically. The Afghan Taliban were influenced by both sects and received their training in a Pak-istani Deoband madrassah. *Salafism* is not a sect per se but describes a sim-plified version of Islam, in which adherents follow a few commands and practices; it is also often associated with anti-West and anti-Jewish beliefs. Salafism, a creed founded in the late nineteenth century by Muslim reform-ers, states that Muslims should follow the rightly guided precedent of the Prophet and his companions; it is nearly identical to Saudi-originated Wahabism, except that Wahabism is far less tolerant of diversity. The founders of Salafism maintained that Muslims ought to return to the orig-inal textual sources of the Quran and the Sunnah, thus breaking away from slavish reiteration of earlier interpretations of Islam, a back-to-the-basics movement.*

*See Khaled Abou El Fadl, "The Orphans of Modernity and the Clash of Civili-sations," *Global Dialogue* 4 (Spring 2002): 1–16.

Violence against the state is recent, although the madaris had shown their mobilization potential during several demonstrations in the past, and they had been helpful in overthrowing Bhutto in 1977. Hundreds of Islamic students took up arms in Malakand in November 1994, and their support for the Taliban after the American attacks demonstrated the growing number of young men willing to go off to battle in the name of jihad. This is polarizing Pakistan, with the western (Jamal Malik calls it "colonial") sector of the Pakistani press portraying the "mullahs" as mil-itants, and in negative terms.[48]

The madaris expanded when Zia's government began to deduct *zakat* (an Islamic religious tithe) from bank accounts. The tax was used to fund local institutions deemed worthy by religious leaders, and this created an incentive to open new schools. At the same time, funding for the govern-ment's schools was cut. It was during this period that money from the Gulf states, especially Saudi Arabia, began to flow into the madaris, largely to schools that taught a mixture of Wahabism and Deobandism, a combustible mixture of conservative theologies.

The growth of these schools reflected a stagnant economy, a collapsed state school system, a desperate situation on the part of many parents, and the dead hand of tradition. This did not matter during Pakistan's first twenty years, when the number of madaris was very small, but their growth under Zia was detrimental to both the state and society. Even when not indoctrinated with religious extremism, madrassah students were deficient in subjects such as mathematics and science and were ignorant of basic events in human history.

One Pakistani study of the madaris concludes that militancy and intolerance do differ markedly within Pakistan's different types of schools.[49] When asked whether Pakistan should take Kashmir from India in an open war, 58 percent of the students taught in Urdu and 64 percent of those taught in English said no, but 59 percent of the madrassah students said yes. Questions about support of jehadi organizations and whether Pakistan should support cross-border infiltration into Kashmir elicited similar answers. Tolerance was measured by questions about members of the Ahmediyya sect; students in Urdu- and English-language schools agreed that they should be shown tolerance in the workplace (46 percent and 65 percent, respectively), but 82 percent of madrassah students said no. Similar replies were given to questions about providing equal rights to women: where English was the medium, students were the most liberal, followed closely by those taught in Urdu, with the madrassah students overwhelmingly conservative in their answers. As Rahman observed, the survey showed how polarized Pakistanis had become: "Perhaps what is most disturbing is that madrassa students should be so militant, so intolerant of minorities and from such poor families. . . . Are we about to witness the revolt of the dispossessed using the idea of religious superiority? Will this revolt turn Pakistan into an intolerant state on the warpath against everyone else? And if this happens, can Pakistan survive?"[50]

The madrassah problem was identified in Nawaz's second term by his brother, Shahbaz Sharif, then Punjab's chief minister. He developed a plan to rein the schools in. Because many madaris had developed local political ties, however, reforms were feeble, usually in the form of attempts to standardize the syllabus. This approach was also taken by General

Musharraf, but most close observers of the system feel that the madaris are so out of touch with the modern world that reform holds out no hope. They would support a combination of disbanding the more radical madaris, reforming others under state direction, and shrinking their over-all enrollment by massive investment in the subsidized public schools while encouraging the formation of small store-front schools that would offer parents an alternative nongovernmental system. With competition in the school marketplace, the role of the madaris would be reduced dra-matically, and they would be limited to providing a religious education for a small sector of Pakistan's population.

The rapid growth of madaris correlates with the decline in basic pub-lic education, the rise of sectarian violence, and massive funding from private and official Gulf sources. In the view of Islamists, a modern, sec-ular education is the enemy, to be countered by ideologically driven solu-tions to Pakistan's comprehensive economic and social problems. Only the middle- and upper-class Jama'at places a high premium on education, even for women. Essentially, the expansion of these seminaries and their upper-class counterparts, the English-language private schools, were in part a free-market response to the inability of the Pakistani state to address the issue of education. The madaris have assumed a lower profile since 9/11 and the war in Afghanistan, and some have abandoned their militant curriculum, but enrollment was on the rise by 2002, perhaps to take in the backlog of applicants that had built up.

The Pakistan government has declared that it has introduced a number of programs to address the more dangerous dimensions of the madaris. It has developed a standardized curriculum that includes modern subjects, claims to have restricted the entry of foreigners into the madaris, and has announced an expansion of public education. So far, the impact of these programs is very limited. When asked to register, only 1 percent of the madaris complied; the government still has no accurate count of the total number, let alone their influence over what is taught or who attends them. With a shortage of funds and strong resistance from the madaris, such reforms are token efforts. Under the completely new system of local self-government, the provincial authorities lack the capability to enforce them even if the funds were available. Problems also surround foreign aid pro-grams designed to provide a modern alternative to the more sectarian madaris because there is no effective system of monitoring where and how the funds are spent. Another obstacle in NWFP and Baluchistan is the government's lack of enthusiasm and poor security, which means foreign donors cannot verify that their funds are being spent appropriately. The best reform, in the view of one government official who has studied the issue, would be to eliminate them. The government's policy legitimizes madaris, but it cannot enforce the reform policy.

Ethos of the Radical Islamic Groups

Islamic militancy has several factors working to its advantage in Pakistan. A fundamental one is that the madaris are producing narrowly educated individuals who are incapable of thinking for themselves or operating in the modern world, but who form an increasingly large body of obedient footsoldiers. Another is that the elites educated along Western lines, though seemingly "modern" and capable of functioning in a modern and Western context, have narrow and unsophisticated political views lacking in originality; they, too, are soldiers. Most important is the militant doctrine perfected by Islamic ideologues, which has declared war on the West and its supporters in Pakistan, particularly the Establishment and the non-militants.

The big question is the degree to which the growing orthodox community serves as the recruiting ground for Islamic militancy. More and more militants are coming from there, even from the Tablighi, which has become increasingly political in its own right—in the 2002 elections it openly supported the MMA alliance.

As to the goals of the militants, some have modest Pakistan-related objectives, others are seized with sectarian hatred, and others are criminals posing as religious crusaders. The JUI's primary concern is the governance of Pakistan, with secondary emphasis on foreign policy and relations with the Islamic world, especially Afghanistan, Iran, and Saudi Arabia. Most of the Shi'ia groups are also engaged in sectarian violence against the Sunnis, notably the Sipah-e-Sahaba Pakistan (SSP), possibly an offshoot of the JUI whose members were used by the army to counter pro-democracy forces in the 1980s.

The theological origins of these groups inherently divide them. All have a tendency to splinter in ways reminiscent of religious or extreme right and left movements elsewhere. These groups also disagree in their diagnosis of Pakistan's political, economic, and social problems. In

NWFP and northern Baluchistan, they have become the vehicle for Pashtun fury, displacing the traditional Pashtun political parties. Most radical groups, including those assisted by Washington during the war against the Soviet forces, are unabashedly anti-American. They part company with the dominant Islamic party, the JI, which acknowledges that Pakistan has benefited from its American tie and must maintain some links to the world's sole superpower if the country is to emerge as a developed Islamic state.

A few groups are delusional and believe that terrorism can bring down the "American empire"; even more believe that selected acts of terror will demonstrate the artificiality of India as a state, that India's Muslims are seething with discontent and must be liberated through jihad. Others would direct their anger at the Pakistani state, arguing that it is still not truly "Islamic" and that the *Shariah* must be immediately imposed, with Pakistan returning to a purer form of Islam and purging itself of corrupt Western and Hindu cultural trappings. Generally, those who hold these views are Deobandis, while Shi'ia radicals are more defensive in nature, drawing their moral (and perhaps material) support from extremist elements in Iran. What, then, are the overall objectives of Pakistan's militant Islamists, where do they overlap, and where do they diverge?

The Parliamentary Strategy

Historically, Islamist parties have done badly at the polls. Until 2002 no avowedly Islamic political party captured more than 5 percent of the national vote, and together, they got about 9 percent. (In the 1970s the JUI participated in a nine-month coalition government in the NWFP.)

In the October 2002 election, the MMA alliance polled 11 percent of the vote, which yielded 62 seats, or 17 percent of the assembly's 342 seats. This gave the MMA considerable influence as a member of the opposition. At the provincial level, it did best in the Pashtun-dominated NWFP, where it won 47 percent of the seats and formed a government; in Baluchistan, the MMA is a member of a coalition government. A combination of ethnocultural factors, the U.S. invasion of Afghanistan, and the operation of American intelligence services within Pakistan, as well as the tacit support of the Pakistan government (and the difficulties that it placed in the way of the mainstream parties) led to this unexpected electoral victory.

The success of the MMA shows that mass discontent, good organization, the tacit support of the government, and the disarray of mainstream
parties can produce electoral results for the Islamists, at least in the thinly
populated provinces that have long been out of the Pakistani mainstream
(NWFP and Baluchistan). However, most Pakistani observers regard the
MMA six-party alliance as artificial, held together by anti-Americanism
and a desire for power—two points they can agree upon. The Jama'at
does not share much with its MMA allies beyond Islamist rhetoric and
will want to maintain a separate identity and organization apart from its
alliance partners. The constituents of the MMA resemble Leninists and
Trotskyites jockeying with Mensheviks, and sooner or later they attack
each other, or split (as two of the ulema parties, the Jamiat Ulema-e-Islam
and the Jamiat Ulema-e-Pakistan, have already done along personality
lines). It remains to be seen whether the desire for power will overcome
the natural tendencies to split and pursue individual objectives at the cost
of coalition coherence. So far, the MMA has displayed remarkable cohesion, and according to some close observers, even the ISI has been unable
to weaken the alliance.

An expert Pakistani judgment on the future of the Islamists, in the context of recent Islamist successes in Turkey, Pakistan, and Bahrain, was that
"their success d[id] not necessarily mean that dogmatic Islamic movements of Islamic-fundamentalist groups will take over the state, nor are
they likely to succeed in transforming these societies on dogmatic and
puritanical Islamic lines."[51] However, they have tried to move ahead with
some programs.

In 2002–03 the MMA government moved quickly to impose Islamic
practices in the Frontier through a Taliban-like agenda. They demanded
that provincial banks stop charging interest, that music be banned on
buses, and that a ministry be created for the promotion of virtue, all in the
name of introducing the *Shariat*.[52] In the process they managed to forfeit
several hundred million dollars in foreign aid, as some of their policies
affected women and women's programs sponsored by the World Bank.
However, they have been constrained from imposing their reforms, and
the leaders of the Islamist parties complain that the center holds them
back—this provides a good excuse for not carrying out what would
certainly be unpopular steps for many Pakistanis and would further alienate foreign donors and allies.

Perhaps the greatest weaknesses of the Islamists are their limited and distorted international contacts, their poor strategic understanding of how Pakistan is situated in the world, and their limited knowledge of modern science and economics. Many of Pakistan's Islamist parties and groups have extensive international ties, but these are almost always with other "Islamic" counterparts, and none of the parties, except the JI, has attempted to reach beyond the Islamic world for contacts and information. Even the JI has a limited range of such contacts and a very poor grasp of economic realities.[53] Like true believers elsewhere, they follow a set "line" on how to address problems such as economic stagnation, social violence, sectarianism, and even foreign policy. It is based on a very short list of prescriptive guidelines that have little substance. For example, the prescribed solution to Pakistan's economic problems is to apply the *Shariat* and strictly adhere to Islamic law, but leaders of the JI cannot point to any Muslim state that provides a model along these lines; in the case of foreign policy, such issues as the Palestine-Israel question are not subjected to serious analysis ("a solution will come when the Arab states are united and foreign powers leave, and the Jews can then live in peace"), and when asked which state might provide a model for Pakistan, they point to Japan, because it has been able to maintain a distinctive culture while modernizing and prospering.

The Islamists' superficial knowledge of the modern world is especially alarming in the area of science—this is surprising, since Islam had an early and vital relationship with the scientific temperament.[54] Its followers possess little understanding of the basic principles of science, such as the notion of testing and rejecting competing explanations and using rigorous criteria for the admission of evidence and data. This lack is evident in their approach to military strategy and nuclear weapons, which is akin to a kind of worship of Pakistan's nuclear program.

Islamists' Concept of Foreign Affairs

The Islamists' success in NWFP and Baluchistan has important strategic implications. If they should manage to stay together, and if they are successful in implementing components of *Shariat* without alienating the tribal and urban population of these provinces while maintaining law and order, they will be able to claim that their path works.

Pakistan's Islamists, including many with ties to the Establishment, make no distinction between "foreign" and "domestic" matters where Afghanistan and Kashmir are concerned. Like India, which has significant ethnic and linguistic overlap with all of its neighbors, Pakistan's Kashmiris, Pashtuns, and Baluch spill over into neighboring states or, in the case of Kashmir, a region still in dispute between India and Pakistan. There are also cross-border ties between Sindhis and Punjabis, but these are less weighed down with religious or Islamic passions (see chapter 6).

Pakistan's relations with Afghan-based radical Islamists are complex. At one level there was a strong ethnic affinity between the Afghan Pashtun tribes and their Pakistani counterparts, as well as a long history of Pakistani intelligence and party engagement with them. The JUI, the Jama'at, and other Islamist parties worked with Afghan counterparts, and the Taliban was born out of JUI-run madaris on the Afghan border. The JUI was instrumental in the Taliban's early successes as it has a strong Pashtun component. The ultraviolent Lashkar-e-Jhangvi based in the Punjab had ties to the Taliban and operated in Afghanistan and Indian-administered Kashmir.[55] The government of Pakistan used these Pakistani groups to train, fund, and in some cases assist the Afghan mujahiddin. The tie continued after the Pakistan government opted to support the Taliban. With the Taliban now officially off limits, the Pakistan government has renewed its ties to other Pashtun groups, which receive support from several of the Islamist parties, including the JI.

The Taliban grew out of a generation of leaders who had received their education in Pakistan's border madaris in NWFP and Baluchistan. It was a Pashtun movement that sought to gain power in Afghanistan and then purify it of contaminating elements. Their success was due in part to support from Pakistan intelligence, and from various Pakistan militant groups, especially the JUI. Perhaps guided by their radical Pakistani supporters, the Taliban saw Pakistan itself as a ripe target, and before Pakistan reversed its support for the Taliban, there was growing concern about Taliban influence in the Sindh, NWFP, Baluchistan, and Karachi.[56] Later when Afghanistan came under attack in 2002, thousands of Pakistanis were recruited to the cause, and hundreds may have perished in the subsequent fighting.

Whereas the agenda of Pakistan's Islamists is local and regional, this is not the case with al Qaeda, the Arab-dominated movement founded in

Afghanistan in 1989.[57] Al Qaeda is a jihadi-salafist movement, born out of the Afghan jihad that drove the Soviet forces out of Afghanistan.[58] The movement was beyond the control of any state, and its first doctrinal principle was to rationalize the existence and behavior of militants. Alienated by repeated military intervention, and repelled by the obvious corruption of the mainstream political parties, a few educated Pakistanis were attracted to jihadist-salafism, and al Qaeda.

They had anti-Americanism in common, as well as a distaste for corrupt pseudo-Islamic governments, be they in Saudi Arabia or Pakistan. Pakistan intelligence did work with al Qaeda, their common ally being the Taliban. Al Qaeda did not need Pakistani money or support, but it did develop a following in Pakistan among middle- and upper-class Pakistanis, including a number of physicians who volunteered their services in Afghanistan, and perhaps some army officers, who were implicated in al Qaeda–related activities in August 2003.

For his part, Osama Bin Laden was eager to win Pakistan's favor, since it was one of the Taliban's key supporters and a potential source of recruits for both the Taliban and al Qaeda. Osama therefore had a four-pronged strategy for Pakistan. He maintained close ties with the Pakistan army and intelligence, had equally close ties with the ulema and religious parties, established training camps in Afghanistan for Pakistani citizens who were fighting in both Afghanistan and Kashmir—as well as Islamic causes elsewhere—and cultivated the Pakistani press, and through it Pakistani public opinion. Osama was portrayed as an Islamic Robin Hood, a man of faith and action, and even Western-oriented Pakistani opinion was open to such an appeal. When American attacks on al Qaeda bases in 1998 killed a number of Pakistanis training in Afghanistan and in a few cases in Pakistani territory itself, many educated Pakistanis, as well as the Islamists, thought Osama was justified in defying an anti-Islamic America. Several prominent Pakistani intellectuals and professionals became pro-Taliban and pro–al Qaeda; in the words of one young woman, an employee of a major Western information service, "I don't care if the Mullahs make me wear the chador and keep me off the street, it would be worth it to rid ourselves of your [American/Western] control over us."

From al Qaeda's perspective, Pakistan was surpassed only by Afghanistan as an ally. Not only did it have the active and covert support of serving and retired intelligence officials, many of the latter openly supportive of both Taliban and al Qaeda, but the two civilian leaders who dominated Pakistani politics from 1988 to 1999 were willing to look the other way when it came to the Taliban, even after the Taliban entered into a symbiotic relationship with al Qaeda.[59]

Pakistan's Islamists also have limited but potentially important ties to a third set of overseas Muslims, those living in the advanced industrial states. Besides the large émigré community concentrated in the Gulf, Great Britain, and the United States, who return to Pakistan for personal or business reasons, a special subset of Westerners, often but not entirely of Pakistani extraction, feel an affinity with Pakistan. These are the individuals who seek a pure form of Islam and an opportunity to act upon deeply held, if sometimes confused, beliefs. Omar Saeed Sheikh's brief career as a radical Muslim is portentous.[60]

Sheikh was born into a prosperous British-Pakistani family in the United Kingdom and was educated at an elite Lahore college and the London School of Economics. He was drawn into radical Islamic causes along the way and went to South Asia, where he participated in the kidnapping of foreign tourists in India and probably the kidnapping and murder of Daniel Pearl in Pakistan. Sheikh seems to have been a Salafi, a follower of a simplified form of Islam, often attractive to new believers, with an answer to every question. Sheikh's understanding of Islam was superficial, but he was strongly motivated by a perception of injustice. Does his career as a radical Muslim represent a trend among nonresident Pakistanis? Britain, the United States, and other Western countries may not produce large numbers of radicals but they could yield a few dedicated cadres, and the hijackers of 9/11 seem to have been drawn from the same strata of angry, professional, and Westernized Muslims. They are all the more worrisome because of their ability to function in Western society, but so far they have had little systemic consequences for Pakistan.

Terrorism as a Strategy

Although they would reject the label, many of Pakistan's radical Islamists are deeply involved with terrorism. Because of the risk that a terrorist act might trigger a new war between India and Pakistan, it is important to examine how Pakistan's homegrown terrorists, as well as its "guest" militants, have made Indian-administered Kashmir their most important theater of operation. Conceptually, the terrorism literature has often compared terrorism to theater: the terrorists are playing to an audience. However, this audience is composed of three groups of people.

One is the enemy. For many terrorists, especially suicide-bombers who regard themselves to be on a holy mission, hurting the enemy is both a goal in itself and a means of forcing the enemy to change its policies (in the case of India in Kashmir), or even to leave Pakistan or change its religious beliefs (which is the purpose of sectarian violence within Pakistan). In Kashmir, some terrorist attacks are designed to provoke the Indian government into retaliatory measures that decrease its own legitimacy and make the terrorist or freedom fighter the defender of Kashmiris. In practice, this has degenerated into random terrorism, often against the Kashmiris themselves.

The second group, the "bystanders," constitutes the largest audience. The goal of the terrorist is to use an extreme act to change the way in which this group sees reality. Thus the terrorist is literally a bad actor, a bit player in a drama that seeks to change reality by a theatrical performance of increasingly unimaginable horror. As in the case of violence in literature and films, the level of horror has to increase over time to attract the attention of bystanders, who have their own mechanisms of coping with the awful. In Pakistan the most important bystanders include the army. It, however, must not be alienated by terrorist acts, but merely shown the moral and practical superiority of violence over parliamentary methods in achieving important and shared objectives.

The remainder of the audience consists of potential recruits to the cause. In this, suicide plays an important role: it helps to undo the moral damage caused by terrorism's obvious targeting of innocents. The death of many innocents who happen to be on the side of evil can thus be rebalanced by the death of a few martyrs who are on the side of good. The message of the terrorist is also that "small is beautiful," that a few dedicated cadres can take on and defeat the much larger enemy—thus the cause is not hopeless and is worth supporting, even at the expense of one's life.[61] In Pakistan the potential supporters include the large pool of unemployed graduates and college students; with a stagnating economy and an out-of-control population growth rate, their numbers are increasing.

The State and Radical Islam

Some state regimes may be threatened by radical Islamists, but in Pakistan the state, especially the army, almost always allowed them to function on a wider stage, equipping and training them, and providing overall political and strategic guidance. While the Pakistan government frequently commits itself to reining in radical groups, inevitably their "disbandment" or "banning" means a name change, or the temporary suspension of operations.[62] Such bans have been declared many times, but neither the membership nor the leadership of these groups is affected.[63]

Though many in Musharraf's generation of army officers oppose the army's Islamization, they use the radical Islamists as an instrument of policy. In this, they are just following the lead of their predecessors. Radical and violent Islamic groups were first exploited by the state in East Pakistan in 1970–71 when the Pakistan army drew upon Islamic militants, notably Jama'at cadres, to terrorize, torture, and murder Bengali intellectuals, politicians, and other supporters of the Bangladesh movement. Many of these militants were drawn from the "Bihari" (non-Bengali) community of East Pakistan. Thus began a long and sordid history of the Pakistani state and its intelligence services using Islamist radicals to terrorize regime opponents, ethnic separatists, the moderate politicians, and, where necessary, other radical Islamists.

The tie was made explicit after Zia ul-Haq became the first army chief to openly praise Islamic groups. He developed political ties with the JI and also provided massive arms and economic support for some of the most noxious and radical (but militarily effective) Afghan Islamic groups in the jihad against the Soviet forces.[64] Many of these had ties to counterparts in Pakistan and most were based in the Pakistani city of Peshawar, where ISI had assembled a seven-party alliance of mujahiddin.[65] There, and elsewhere in the NWFP, they developed ties to Arab and other Islamic volunteers in the jihad.

These ties deepened in the late 1980s when Pakistan's leading intelligence service, the ISI, began to train Kashmiri dissidents, many of whom had fled to Pakistan after the rigged Kashmir election of 1989. ISI also allowed various Pakistani-based Islamists to operate in Kashmir, and some of these groups found a role a few years later in their support of the

Taliban. Some were also active in sectarian disputes, and the army had to step in from time to time to limit their operations.

Radicals against the State

Within two years after Zia's death, civilian government returned to Pakistan, Soviet forces withdrew from Afghanistan, America imposed new sanctions on Islamabad, and a separatist uprising broke out in Indian Kashmir. In the army, a handful of zealots thought that Pakistan itself was ripe for an Islamic coup.[66] The Soviet withdrawal from Afghanistan and India's problems in Kashmir contributed to their euphoria. They believed they had support within the wider Pakistani society, and a few officers surmised that the Indians could be the second target of an Islamic jihad, now that the first (Soviet) one was out of the way. To carry out this agenda they had to take control of Pakistan. This led to a failed coup attempt in September 1995. The goal had been to establish a strict Islamic order in Pakistan and carry the jihad more vigorously to India and, via the Taliban, to Central Asia. (In this they shared some of the policy goals of the government, which from the late 1980s believed that an assertive, forward policy in Afghanistan and Kashmir could extend Pakistan's influence to Central Asia and weaken India's hold on Kashmir.)

As noted in chapter 3, there is no evidence that the army seethes with Islamic radicalism, that an Islamic cabal might seize power, or that the lower ranks of the officer corps are any more "Islamic" than would be expected in a society where Islamic sentiment has steadily grown over the past two decades. This does not put them above using the radical Islamists, since the Kashmir dispute, like Pakistan's relations with Afghanistan, is viewed as a domestic matter, vital to Pakistan's own society and security. This, however, raises the question of blowback, a subject that has generated considerable debate in Pakistan.

Blowback Pakistani Style

During the first Afghan war, the ISI's strategy was to support hard-line Islamic groups, and with American concurrence, the ISI characterized the war against the Soviet intruders as a religious struggle against atheistic communism. Again with American encouragement, young Muslims were recruited to the "cause" from the Arab and Islamic world, inadvertently creating a cohort that was to eventually form al Qaeda.

For Pakistanis, including some army officers, the negative consequences of the war in Afghanistan were palpable. An increase in domestic and sectarian violence, the appearance of a drug culture, increased availability of guns, and general social breakdown were attributed to the growth of violent Islamists in Afghanistan. All these had ties to counterpart groups in Pakistan, especially in the NWFP, Baluchistan, and Karachi.

The blowback effect of Pakistan's support for the mujahiddin, the Taliban, and now for Kashmiri separatists and terrorists (called freedom fighters by the Pakistan government) is self-evident. Pakistanis are sharply divided about the consequences of these struggles. On the one hand, Pakistan's liberals and many in the Establishment are deeply concerned about the rise in sectarian violence, guns, and disorder; on the other hand, radical Islamists praise these operations as true jihads and discount the costs to Pakistan itself. A new round of violence occurred after Islamabad turned against the Taliban in 2002, this time led by anti-Musharraf elements among the militants. Many of these banned groups continue to operate as before, often under a new name or in a new location.

Portents and Possibilities

Pakistan would seem to be a candidate for membership in the "axis of evil": it has terrorists, nuclear weapons, an increasingly influential group of radical Islamists, and a stagnant economy. With some Pakistanis already sympathetic to al Qaeda's ideology and others supporting the Taliban, it could become a new Iran, a center of Islamic revolutionary activity. This portrayal of Pakistan is widely held in India and, increasingly, America, but it is not accurate.

While most Pakistani Muslims are devout, they are not radical, and for much of its history, Pakistan's politics has been dominated by ethnic, linguistic, and economic issues, not religious ones. Further, Pakistan's ethnic, cultural, and regional boundaries do not match up with divisions among its Islamic sects. The power of religious parties derives more from their nuisance value and from state support. The dominant Islam practiced in Pakistan is strongly influenced by Sufism and thus far has not been amenable to radicalism. There are also competing visions of an Islamic state. Indeed, the most important conflict in Pakistan is not a civilizational clash between Muslims and non-Muslims but one between different concepts of Islam, especially about how the Pakistani state should implement its Islamic identity.

Until 2002 the religious parties did poorly at the polls, and there is reason to doubt that their street power will threaten any military regime or democratically elected government, or that they have the votes to win a free national election.[67] In other countries, successful Islamist parties and radical movements are often the sole outlet for angry and resentful ethnic or linguistic subgroups. In Pakistan, the centrist political parties, as feeble as they are, articulate a wide range of views and positions. However, this can change—the growth of religious extremism is inversely related to the capacity of the Pakistani state to meet its basic obligations. And the political parties have been failing spectacularly in their attempts to address the grievances of Pakistan's citizens; the army, with its monopoly of state power, has done no better. In part, the radical Islamists are products of a political vacuum. As Pakistani society becomes more and more turbulent, the recruiting base of its Islamist radicals is likely to expand.

Pakistan's Islamists have also benefited from events across Pakistan's western border. Many Pakistanis, especially the Pashtuns, were shocked at the rapid defeat of the Taliban by American and allied forces. The spectacle of ultramodern firepower defeating an Afghan army was awesome and unexpected. Also working in favor of Pakistan's Islamists is the growing suspicion of Pakistanis in the West. Upper-class educated Pakistanis, including nonresident Pakistanis, are now being subjected to more careful security regulations, bordering on harassment, and the feeling that Pakistanis are victims of discrimination, always present, is ballooning. If this process continues, it will only be a matter of time before more Pakistanis will come to share the Islamists' assumption of a civilizational war between Islam and an unholy Christian-Jewish-Hindu alliance. To the degree that the militants think the government of Pakistan is supporting the West, it is also at risk from terrorism.

The situation has developed into a vicious cycle. Each increase in religious extremism leads some talented Pakistanis to leave the country and deters many more from actively participating in politics; in turn, this emboldens the militants in their utopian vision of an Islamic revolution within Pakistan. Because the Islamists are especially strong in the NWFP and Baluchistan, their growth may also increase provincial separatism, and it will certainly further isolate Pakistan from the international community as foreigners increasingly see these provinces, and some urban areas, as "no go" zones.

The Army and Islamists

Ironically, the army is Pakistan's chief barrier against Islamic radicalism, even as it remains an obstacle to democratization. Under present circumstances, it is immune to the lure of an alliance with the more undisciplined, cruder Islamists. For their part, Pakistan's militant outfits regard the army as tainted by its British past, its contacts with foreign military organizations, and its un-Islamic structures and procedures. Their desire to purify Pakistan of foreign and "un-Islamic" practices is rejected by the security managers, as is the call to wage active war against India. The army wants to balance and counter India, but it does not want to provoke a war with Delhi or allow Islamist extremists to acquire significant power in Pakistan.

Assassinations of politicians or army brass would only confirm the army's institutional view that it remains Pakistan's last best hope, and that civilians—including radical Islamists—must not supplant the armed forces. Such activities will not keep the army and its intelligence services from manipulating militants for domestic and foreign policy purposes. This may not be an ideal way of running the state of Pakistan, but it is the army way. Although it ensures that Pakistan will not rapidly reform itself, it also ensures that Pakistan will not be radicalized soon. However, blocking secular and ethnic channels of expression—by a fresh ban on political activities—tends to open the door wider for radical Islamic groups who are capable of operating in informal channels, especially via their network of mosques and madaris.

The one scenario involving the army that would bring radical Islamic groups to a position of influence would be a decision by army leaders themselves to embrace militant Islam, as discussed in chapter 8. This appears unlikely to happen over the next few years, as the present generation of army leaders is openly critical of Zia's Islamic experiments; however, should the quasi-secular Musharraf be removed, and the state lose its capacity to govern, one future option might be a pseudo-coalition between some radical outfits and the military.

Islamist Strategies

Elsewhere Islamic movements were successful when they were able to catch the political system by surprise, translating general discontent into a mass movement.[68] This happened in Iran, but in Pakistan the political system has been accommodating enough to prevent surprises, and the Jama'at's long engagement in the political process has inoculated Pakistan from the comprehensive claims of Islamist groups, although the latter have won many concessions over the decades.

Will Pakistan's rapidly changing political and social order favor the center-right Jama'at-i-Islami, or will it enhance the power of the radicals, squeezing the JI between the secular parties on one side, and the militants on the other? A strategy open to the Jama'at, but practically no other Islamist group, would be to tone down some of its demands for the introduction of Islamic law and move toward the center to pick up support among Pakistanis who have hitherto backed the secularist PPP and PML. Party leaders must weigh this move against the possible loss of ardent workers, since it would require the party to turn away from Mawdudi's dictum that "the Jama'at-i-Islami is not only a political party, but also an ideological one." Such a shift would be difficult, but not impossible. Reaching out to the discontented but not ideologically driven middle classes of Pakistan, and developing a rhetoric and mass appeal that has been absent up to this point, is one route open to Pakistan's best-organized and most disciplined political party. Doing so would require the party to come to an understanding of the limits of utopian politics in a state that was only recently on the brink of collapse.

The Jama'at is capable of such a movement, but it fears being outflanked by the ulema parties, on one side, and absorbed into the Pakistan Establishment, on the other. The ulema parties have popular support in the NWFP, and the Jama'at needs an alliance with them to come to power; further, while the Jama'at's support is widespread, it lacks a powerful base in any one part of Pakistan, holding its own only in a few Punjab districts and parts of Karachi. In addition, the leadership fears becoming just another corrupt party, thus forgoing the considerable support that flows from its high moral reputation.

As for the sectarian Islamist parties, especially those involved in violence and steered by a compass set to an Islamic utopia, their most likely route to power is to wait until moderate forces have withered away. There is little prospect that radical Islamists will threaten present or future governments of Pakistan for many years. Their influence has largely been derived from government patronage, their attempts to infiltrate the Pakistan government have been feeble and easily countered, and they do not have street power outside of the NWFP. The army remains an insuperable obstacle to their coming to power and would reject any party that wanted to turn Pakistan into a comprehensively Islamic state. The prognosis is that such groups will continue to exert influence, constituting a fringe element in Pakistan's political system, but that institutional, economic, social, and political decay will have to accelerate if they are to emerge as an independent political force soon. Pakistan's extreme Islamists may be Bolsheviks, but Pakistan is not (yet) late Czarist Russia or the Shah's Iran.

While nothing can be ruled out in Pakistan's medium-term future, and the case of Iran shows that Muslim countries can undergo a real Islamic revolution, Pakistan is likely to follow another path. No single Pakistani Islamist leader has Khomeini's status, nor are Pakistan's Islamic parties faction-free—although they did demonstrate an unexpected capacity to suppress their differences and work toward a common goal, namely, to come to power. The open question is whether they will follow the example of religious movements and communist and leftist parties elsewhere and splinter along sectarian or personality lines. If, improbably, they avoid this fate, it may turn out that they could become Pakistan's second most important political force.

CHAPTER SIX

REGIONALISM
AND SEPARATISM

It is often forgotten that Pakistan is one of the world's most ethnically and linguistically complex states. Each of its provinces is associated with a single ethnolinguistic group: Punjab with Punjabis, Sindh with Sindhis, Baluchistan with Baluch, and the Northwest Frontier Province (NWFP) with Pashtuns. Some also have significant minority representation, and Pashtuns and Punjabis are found throughout the country (see table 6-1). Pakistan's tribal population is concentrated in the Federally Administered Tribal Area (FATA) and Azad Kashmir.

Ethnic and linguistic groups, identified by cultural markers, often claim they are a "people" or a "nation." Some seek independence and want to form an ethnically or linguistically homogeneous state; some seek greater autonomy within a state or province, and others move back and forth between these two goals or remain ambiguous.[1]

In December 1971 Pakistan became the first former colonial state to undergo a partition along ethnolinguistic lines when its East Wing became the new independent state of Bangladesh. Even after the loss of the East Wing, Pakistan had four major ethnic communities, several distinct linguistic groups, and a number of tribal and ethnic micro-peoples. Bengalis were not the only dissatisfied ethnolinguistic group: at various times active secessionist movements have sprouted in NWFP, Baluchistan, and Sindh. All these have links to neighboring states: NWFP to Afghanistan, Baluchistan to both Afghanistan and Iran, and Sindh to India. Another separatist group consists of Kashmiris seeking independence from both

Table 6-1. *Language Distribution in Pakistan's Main Districts*[a]

As a percent of total

District	Language (percent)	District	Language (percent)
Northwest Frontier Province		*Sindh*	
		Karachi	Pashto (8.7) Punjabi (13.6) Urdu (54.3)
Peshawar	Hindko (6.85) Pashto (87.54)		
Abbotabad	Hindko (92.32) Pashto (3.68)	Hyderabad	Sindhi (56.48) Urdu (28.10)
Swat	Kohistani (8.67) Pashto (90.28)	Larkana	Baluchi (6.98) Brahvi (5.92) Sindhi (78.43) Siraiki (5.04)
Mardan	Pashto (97.17)		
Punjab		Jacobabad	Baluchi (21.34) Sindhi (69.13)
Lahore	Punjabi (84.0) Urdu (13.4)	Sukkur	Punjabi (6.37) Sindhi (73.54) Urdu (12.66)
Rawalpindi	Punjabi (85.0) Urdu (7.5)		
Faisalabad	Punjabi (98.2)	*Baluchistan*	
Multan	Punjabi (43.8) Siraiki (44.7) Urdu (10.5)	Quetta	Brahvi (17.13) Pashto (36.47) Punjabi (18.85) Urdu (11.17)
Gujranwala	Punjabi (97.6)		
Jhelum	Punjabi (97.5)	Chagai	Baluchi (57.08) Brahvi (34.80)
Jhang	Punjabi (96.5)	Sibi	Baluchi (15.09) Pashto (49.77) Sindhi (20.12)
		Gwadar	Baluchi (98.25)

Source: Tariq Rahman, *Language and Politics in Pakistan* (Oxford University Press, 1996), appendix F, pp. 265–66.

a. National data are not available, but these are Pakistan's largest districts. Data based on the 1981 census reports on districts. Minor languages have been ignored.

India and Pakistan. In addition, two autonomist movements have been active in Punjab, Pakistan's largest province, and one of its most important ethnolinguistic minorities, the Urdu-speaking Mohajirs, have agitated for an autonomous Karachi. Table 6-2 provides available provincial data on each province.

This chapter provides a short survey of Pakistan's separatist and subnational movements, followed by a discussion of the ways in which the Pakistani state, especially the dominant army, dealt with them, and a preliminary estimate of their likely course over the next several years. Briefly, by themselves, Pakistan's separatist movements are unlikely to be able to repeat the Bangladesh example. However, they will pose a significant challenge to the state of Pakistan if they intersect with growing Islamist sentiments, the further decay of the Pakistani state apparatus, or enhanced ties to ethnolinguistic groups across Pakistan's borders.

Ethnonationalist Pakistan

Pakistan originally comprised five major ethnolinguistic groups, whose unity Liaquat Ali Khan signified with a clenched fist.[2] These were Bengalis (an absolute majority in the new state, although the poorest), Punjabis, Sindhis, Baluch, and Pashtuns. The predominately Urdu-speaking migrants from the United Provinces, the Mohajirs (named after the migrating companions of the Prophet Mohammed) constituted a sixth important group.[3] Along with East Punjabis (who also had to leave their homes and flee to Pakistan), the Mohajirs experienced the greatest hardships when the new state was created. They also included some of the best-educated and most pro-Pakistan of all Indian Muslims.

The leaders of the new state assumed that Jinnah's leadership and a common faith would override any differences between the major ethnolinguistic groups. This was a real concern, since support for the Pakistan movement was tepid among Sindhis, Pashtuns, and Baluch. North Indian Muslims had strongly supported the Pakistan movement, but it was mostly the leadership and the professional classes who had undertaken the harrowing migration after partition.

Like leaders in many other former colonial states, Pakistan's leaders developed an ethnolinguistic-nationalist narrative. It begins with a glorious

Table 6-2. *Provincial Population Data*[a]

Percent unless otherwise indicated

Feature	Pakistan	NWFP	FATA	Punjab	Sindh	Baluchistan	Islamabad
Area (km^2)	796,096	74,521	27,220	205,345	140,914	347,190	906
	(100)	(9.4)	(0.034)	(25.8)	(17.7)	(43.6)	(0.001)
Population (thousands)	132,352	17,744	3,176	73,621	30,440	6,566	805
	(100)	(13.4)	(0.02)	(57.7)	(23.0)	(0.05)	(0.006)
Male	52.03	51.22	52.01	51.74	52.88	53.4	53.93
Female	47.97	48.78	47.99	48.26	47.12	46.6	46.07
Male/female ratio	108.5	105	108.4	107.2	112.2	114.6	117
Under 15 years	43.4	41.3	25.9	42.5	42.76	46.67	37.9
15–64 years	53.09	53.9	24.3	53.5	54.47	50.81	59.4
65 years and older	3.5	4.8	1.8	4	2.77	2.52	2.7
Economically active	22.24	19.4	...	22.6	22.75	24.05	23
Unemployed	20.19	26.8	...	19.1	14.43	33.48	15.7
Urban	32.5	16.9	2.7	31.3	48.8	23.9	65.7
Density (person per km^2)	166.3	238.1	116.7	358.5	216	18.9	880.8
Average annual growth, 1981–98	2.69	2.82	2.19	2.64	2.8	2.47	5.19
Age-dependency ratio	88.34	85.6	114	86.9	83.58	96.79	68.4
Literacy ratio	43.92	35.4	17.4	46.6	45.3	24.83	72.4
Male	54.81	51.4	29.5	57.2	54.5	34.03	80.6
Female	32.02	18.8	3	35.1	34.78	14.09	62.4
School enrollment ratio	35.98	41	...	39.4	32.78	23.53	57.5
Male	41.19	5.2	...	43.8	37.35	29.49	57.7
Female	30.25	21.3	...	34.6	27.7	60.4	57.3

Source: Government of Pakistan, Statistics Division.

a. Figures in parentheses are percentages of the national total.

precolonial state-empire when the Muslims of South Asia were politically united and culturally, civilizationally, and strategically dominant. In that era, ethnolinguistic differences were subsumed under a common vision of an Islamic-inspired social and political order. However, the divisions among Muslims that did exist were exploited by the British, who practiced "divide-and-rule" politics, displacing the Mughals and circumscribing other Islamic rulers. Moreover, the Hindus were the allies of the British, who used them to strike a balance with the Muslims; many Hindus, a fundamentally insecure people, hated Muslims and would have oppressed them in a one-man, one-vote democratic India. The Pakistan freedom movement united these disparate pieces of the national puzzle, and Pakistan was the expression of the national will of India's liberated Muslims.

This narrative barely acknowledged Pakistan's separatist and autonomist movements. Statements by Pakistani leaders before and after 1970 show remarkable continuity. Each stressed the importance of a strong center and criticized the idea of greater provincial autonomy. Jinnah spoke of a Pakistan that was not Bengali, Baluch, Punjabi, Sindhi, or Pashtun, but a new nation, exhorting his listeners to remember the lessons of 1,300 years ago, when Islam came to India and unified it:[4] "You have carved out a territory, a vast territory. It is all yours: it does not belong to a Punjabi or a Sindhi or a Pathan or a Bengali. It is all yours. You have got your Central Government where several units are represented. Therefore, if you want to build yourself up into a nation, for God's sake give up this provincialism."[5] Ayub Khan was intolerant of regionalism, and as a military man saw the need for a strong center to hold the country together. This was also the case with Ayub's successor, General Yahya Khan, who managed to destroy Pakistan by refusing to contemplate greater provincial autonomy.

The loss of more than half of Pakistan's population in 1971 did not alert the leadership to the dangers of ignoring local "nationalist" sentiment.[6] After the loss of East Pakistan, Zulfiqar Ali Bhutto pursued a tough state-centric policy, moving forcefully against the Baluch and triggering a rebellion among a powerful linguistic group, the Mohajirs. Zia agreed: when asked in 1978 about the possibility of introducing a multinational Pakistan in which the Baluch, Pashtun, Sindhis, and Punjabis would be entitled to local self-rule, he expressed his dismay at "this type of thinking. We want to build a strong country, a unified country. Why should we talk in these small-minded terms? We should talk in terms of Pakistan, one united Pakistan."[7]

On paper, Pakistan has a tolerant view toward its ethnolinguistic groups. However, every Pakistani leader, whether from the Punjab or a less populous province, has vehemently opposed "nationalist" or ethnolinguistic sentiments, which they consider a threat to the state. For the leadership, an important challenge to Pakistan comes from ties between India or Afghanistan and disloyal Pakistani ethnolinguistic communities. The greatest danger to the state would be a coalition of such foreign and domestic enemies.

Pakistan's ethnic and linguistic minorities often cite the founding document of Pakistan, the Lahore Resolution, as legitimizing their claims to greater autonomy. Although the resolution does not include the word "federation," it does say that the independent state it called for should have "constituent units" that would be "autonomous and sovereign."

This poses the classic federal dilemma for Pakistan's Establishment. Are calls for national self-determination or autonomy by ethnolinguistic minorities really calls for separate statehood, and the breakup of Pakistan? Or are they part of a bargaining game, in which such groups profess such goals in order to satisfy their own maximalists but would really be willing to settle for greater autonomy or some special privileges? This is the same situation faced by India in Kashmir and Nagaland, where "separatists" privately suggest that their demands are set forth for purposes of bargaining with the central government.

Autonomism and Separatism Today

As noted in previous chapters, once the constitutional process was short-circuited, Pakistan became a highly centralized state. It became a more complex one as well. While the movement for Pakistan had been built upon a shared antagonism toward Hindus, Pakistanis today are not uniformly anti-Indian—for many, fear of India is offset by fear of domination by other Pakistanis.

In the 1960s the deepest fault line had an east-west orientation, as Bengalis came to regard the Punjab-Mohajir Establishment and the military as stifling. Since 1971 the fault lines have become more difuse, with the autonomist-separatist movements draw their energy from Baluch, Pashtun,

Table 6-3. *Ethnonationalist Movements: Patterns of Conflict* [a]

Group	Period	Location	Description
Bengali	1960s–70	East Pakistan	Language riots, 1952; dismissal of elected governments, regional disparities, army behavior, Indian intervention, 1971
Sindhi	1950s–90s	Rural Sindh	Opposition to Punjabi settlers, 1940s–50s; Son of the Soil movement against Mohajirs; demographic nationalism, suppression of Sindhi language, Indian patronage
Mohajir	1985–2003	Urban Sindh	Loss of preeminence in politics, bureaucracy, and industry; absence of presence in army; loss of identity after migration to Pakistan; abandonment of Biharis; punjabization of central government; declining role in army and civil service, Indian support.
Pashtun	1947–58 1973–77	NWFP	Reaction to dismissal/resignation of elected governments, 1947 and 1973; Afghan irredentist movement
Baluch	1947, 1958, 1963, 1973–77	Baluchistan	Antiannexation, 1974, and assertion of separate statehood; dismissal of elected governments, 1973, 1988; received Soviet and Afghan support

a. Adapted from Mohammed Waseem, "The Political Ethnicity and the State of Pakistan," paper presented to the International Conference on the "Nation-State" and Transnational Forces in South Asia, Kyoto, December 9–10, 2000; cited with permission of the author.

Mohajir, and Sindhi resentment of the dominant Punjab, sometimes in coalition with other ethnolinguistic minorities.

The creation of Bangladesh strengthened several existing separatist-autonomist groups. Table 6-3 offers a snapshot of the spread of ethnic separatism and nationalism. Outside of Punjab, there were movements for a Sindhudesh, an independent Baluchistan, a NWFP tied to Afghanistan, and even (for the Mohajirs) a Karachi that might become another Singapore.[8]

Although Pakistan's subnational and ethnolinguistic groups have some common features, they also differ in significant ways.

—All have different connections to the land; some have histories that can be traced back one or two millennia, and others, such as the Mohajirs, are newcomers to Pakistan. In several cases, notably Karachi, internal migration has changed ethnic and cultural balances, destabilizing local political and administrative patterns.

—Their narratives regarding their ties to the idea of Pakistan vary widely. The Mohajirs were in the forefront of the Pakistan movement; others were disinterested or marginal to it.

—All of these groups have a different relationship with the dominant Punjab. Some are fairly close, such as the Pashtuns; others, such as the Baluch, were alienated to the point of open warfare, with the Sindhis and Mohajirs having a mixed history.

—Some of these groups are entangled in mutual enmity, usually involving Punjabis as the third side of the triangle. Sindhis, like the Bengalis, resent the Mohajir-Punjabi nexus but are also pressed upon by the Baluch; the Baluch have been subjected to in-migration from Pashtuns; and the Mohajirs have come to regard Sindhis and Punjabis as threats to their identity and prosperity.

The Sindhis

Migration creates strange bedfellows. Karachi, once a cosmopolitan but Sindhi-dominated city is no longer a Sindhi city after decades of migration. Like other cities in Sindh, it has become a byword for rivalry, social dislocation, and revenge.[9] Ironically, Sindhis themselves are noted for their willingness to migrate in search of economic betterment.

The paramilitary Pakistan Rangers are on constant deployment in Karachi, even on the campuses of several universities. Even so, each year between 400 and 600 political murders occur. Of special concern are the murders of Shi'ia doctors and professionals, gunned down by sectarian Sunni hit squads, who want to cleanse Pakistan of its highly educated Shi'ia minority.[10] This has led to a mass migration of Shi'ia businessmen and professionals from Pakistan. Given that Karachi is Musharraf's own hometown, the lack of response to these killings is surprising; after the 2003 murder of a prominent Shi'ia doctor neither the government nor Musharraf said a word.

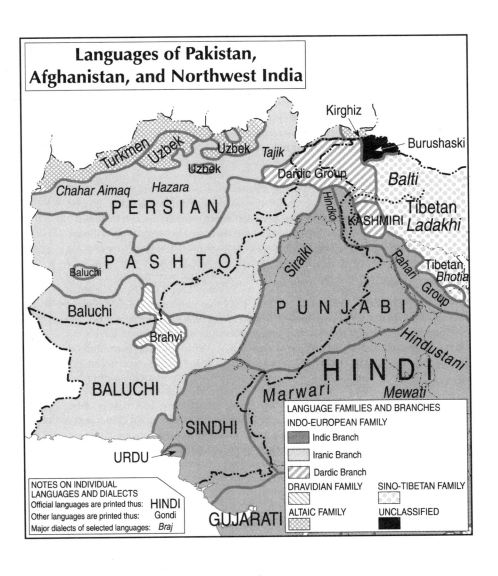

Languages of Pakistan, Afghanistan, and Northwest India

Kirghiz

Burushaski

Turkmen

Uzbek

Uzbek

Uzbek

Tajik

Dardic Group

Balti

Chahar Aimaq

Hazara

PERSIAN

Hindko

KASHMIRI

Tibetan
Ladakhi

PASHTO

Siraiki

Pahari
Group

Tibetan
Bhotia

Baluchi

PUNJABI

Baluchi

Hindustani

Brahvi

HINDI

BALUCHI

Marwari

Mewati

SINDHI

URDU

GUJARATI

LANGUAGE FAMILIES AND BRANCHES
INDO-EUROPEAN FAMILY

Indic Branch

Iranic Branch

Dardic Branch

DRAVIDIAN FAMILY

SINO-TIBETAN FAMILY

ALTAIC FAMILY

UNCLASSIFIED

NOTES ON INDIVIDUAL
LANGUAGES AND DIALECTS
Official languages are printed thus: HINDI
Other languages are printed thus: Gondi
Major dialects of selected languages: *Braj*

Box 6-1. *Karachi*

Karachi is Pakistan's most industrialized city, the commercial and financial capital, and hosts its two ports.* Its population of 12 million to 14 million will increase to 20 million by 2015. Half of all Karachites live in slums and temporary settlements. The city is sharply divided between its original residents, Sindhis and Baluch, the migrant Mohajir community, and Punjabis and Pashtuns, who came later. The Sindhi-Baluch and the Punjabi-Pashtun coalition are about 3 million each, the Mohajirs number about 5 million to 6 million, and there are 2 million illegals.

Sindhis and Baluch claim Karachi as their native city, but in the 1997 elections, they won just 1 of the 12 National Assembly seats from the city, and only 27 of the 110 Sindh Provincial Assembly seats from Karachi. Nawaz Sharif's gerrymandering, done with the collusion of Pakistan's ineffective Election Commission, gave preference to Mohajirs and Punjabis.

Pakistan's federal governments have alternated between using and fighting the Mohajir party, the MQM, to achieve greater control over the city. The MQM itself split into factions in the early 1990s, producing at least 1,000 casualties a year among the factions and the security forces, and the de facto division of the city. While the Pakistan People's Party government stabilized the situation in 1993, in 1995 four employees of an American multinational company were believed to have been killed by the MQM, and in subsequent years assassination attempts and bombings have been directed against American-owned hotels, a French technical team, and the U.S. consulate. Following the military coup in 1999, Musharraf accommodated the Mohajir leadership, allowing significant devolution of power, but violence in Karachi has worsened. Sectarian murders are common, as are bombings of Western (especially American) facilities, and in May, there was a concerted attempt to assassinate the Karachi corps commander. Meanwhile, protection, kidnapping, and extortion rackets are common, leading many Punjabi businessmen to move their industries to Central Punjab. The Citizen-Police Liaison Committee reported 219 major kidnappings (involving high-profile persons such as prominent businessmen and their families) in the city between 1990 and 1998.

*For sources, see Mehtab Ali Shah, "Criminalisation of Politics: Karachi, A Case Study," *Ethnic Studies Report* 19 (Winter 2001): 99–137; "Karachi Cops," *Herald* (Karachi), June 2003; Peter Gizewski and Thomas Homer-Dixon, *Environmental Scarcity and Violent Conflict: The Case of Pakistan* (Washington: American Association for the Advancement of Science, 1996). For an Indian analysis, see Wilson John, *Karachi: A Terror Capital in the Making* (New Delhi: Rupa/Observer Research Foundation, 2003).

Sindh was brought into the Raj in 1843 by General Charles Napier, who seized the province without authorization. Legend has it that he sent the message (in Latin) to Calcutta, *Peccavi* ("I have sinned").[11] Four years later Sindh was absorbed into the Bombay Presidency. The province was always on the periphery of empire, a distant part of the Mughal system and then for over a hundred years a British Indian backwater. While administratively part of Bombay, most of the Bombay Legislative Council legislation had not applied to Sindh, which had its own system of government and judiciary.[12] Its social structure and leadership were largely intact at independence, as was its feudal order, one of the subcontinent's most socially repressive.

By 1913 the Karachi business community, then overshadowed by Bombay, had begun calling for separation, which finally took place in 1936. Despite its Muslim-majority population, Sindh was not an ethnically pure region. Bordering the Arabian Sea, it had long been accustomed to traders, invaders, and migrants from nearby regions. There were large Punjabi and Baluch communities in Sindh, and the ruling family, the Talpur tribe, had Baluch origins, although its members and many other migrants had assimilated into Sindhi culture.

Like Punjab, Sindh produced a secular regional political party dominated by large landowners and feudal elites. As independence (and Pakistan) loomed, the Sindh elite had to choose between allying with the Congress or the Muslim League. The former posed a threat to the Sindhi feudals because of its liberal social policies and the potential for greater Hindu domination over the province's commercial and professional life. The Muslim League was somewhat more attractive: it was more elitist than the Congress, and in the early 1940s "Pakistan" did not imply a single separate state but could have meant that Muslim-majority provinces like Sindh might find a place within the larger India.

Several prominent Sindhis who had been opposed to the formation of Pakistan found their fears borne out after partition.[13] Seventy-three percent of the migrants to the new state of Pakistan in 1947 were Punjabis, and most of these settled in Pakistan's Punjab. The small number of Urdu speakers who migrated to Punjab had little difficulty settling there, mostly in dispersed groups; while they retain Urdu as a mother tongue, most are fluent in Punjabi. The problem for Sindh, which received only 20 percent of the Indian migrants, was different. The bulk of the migrants to Sindh were Urdu-speakers from Uttar Pradesh, Delhi, Hyderabad (Deccan), and Bihar, and they moved to Karachi, Hyderabad, and other cities where they made only a limited effort to assimilate. Their identity as Mohajirs was strengthened when Urdu was declared Pakistan's national language, and Karachi, which had been Sindh's largest and most affluent city, was stripped from the province to become Pakistan's capital on July 27, 1948. By 1951, the Sindhi-speaking population of the province had declined from a pre-partition level of 87 percent to about 67 percent.[14] Sindhis had also become a minority in Karachi, whereas 57 percent of its population was now Mohajir. Therefore, while partition had strengthened the ethnic homogeneity of Punjab and NWFP, it had created a new ethnic divide in Sindh and sown the seeds for fresh Sindhi grievances.

For the legendary G. M. Sayed, a politician who once supported the Pakistan movement, Pakistan and the two-nation theory became a trap for Sindhis—instead of liberating Sindh, it fell under Punjabi-Mohajir domination, and until his death in 1995 he called for a separate Sindhi "nation," implying a separate Sindhi country. Sayed had not been a Muslim nationalist, but a Sindhi one. In 1948 the fledgling Sindhi nationalist movement joined with Bengalis, Pashtuns, and Baluch to form the People's Organization. It was succeeded by the Pakistan Oppressed National Movement (PONAM), but both stopped short of openly calling for the dissolution of Pakistan.[15]

A second grievance was the imposition of the One-Unit scheme in 1955, which combined all of West Pakistan's provinces into a single political unit. Originally introduced to offset East Bengal's numerical majority, but rationalized in the name of administrative efficiency and as a way to counter "provincialism," the arrangement put Sindh at a disadvantage. Third, Sindhis were materially affected when Ayub allotted newly irrigated Sindhi land to retired military officers and bureaucrats. Over a million acres of this land went to non-Sindhis, and today as much as 40 percent of Sindh's prime agricultural land is held by non-Sindhis, mostly Punjabis and Mohajirs.[16] Fourth, Sindhis also claim that Punjab violated the pre-independence agreement between Punjab and Sindh for the distribution of waters when Punjab built new irrigation works without Sindh's consent. The water dispute between Sindh, the lower riparian, and Punjab remains a live issue and the subject of widespread Sindhi agitation.[17] Fifth, Sindhis were underrepresented in Pakistan's civil services and the military. As of the 1981 census, Sindhis were 11.7 percent of Pakistan's population, but their representation in the senior ranks of the civil service was a mere 3.6 percent in 1974, rising, after reforms in the quota system, to 6.8 percent in 1983.[18]

Government policies also drove a wedge between the Sindhis and the Urdu-speaking Mohajirs. A quota system favorable to the Mohajirs had been introduced in 1948 to redress regional inequities in public employment. With one of Pakistan's two official languages being made Urdu (the other was English), the Mohajir community had another special advantage, especially in civil service exams.

The Mohajirs were well represented in Pakistan's ruling national elite. By distributing selective rewards to their middle class, usually at the expense of the Sindhi middle class, the Mohajir leadership promulgated an extraterritorial nationalism, in which they were self-described as the real creators of Pakistan. They had been in the forefront of the movement for the new state, while Sindhis were at best half-hearted supporters. With Urdu as the new national language, and possessing considerable administrative and political skills, the Mohajirs came to regard themselves as a people apart in Sindh, and the integrative process ground to a halt. The 1970 election saw the rise of Mohajir identity defined in terms of the denigration of Sindhis, and Mohajirs turned to Islamists for political leadership, electing a conservative mullah from each of its National Assembly constituencies while the Sindhis were voting overwhelmingly for Bhutto's Pakistan People's Party (PPP).

In 1972 a movement began among the Sindhis that would make Sindhi the medium of instruction in schools; compel government employees to learn Sindhi; raise a Sindhi-speaking paramilitary force; return land taken from Sindhis in the resettlement program; regain provincial control over railways, the postal service, and electronic media; increase Sindh's share of the Indus waters; and declare Pakistan to be "four nations living in a confederation."[19]

While Bhutto was a national politician with strong support in the Punjab, Sindh was his core political base. He faced strong economic and administrative demands from these two states. The presence of a Sindhi prime minister and the termination of the One-Unit scheme emboldened Sindhi politicians and students, whose immediate target was the large (20 percent) Mohajir minority living in Sindh. This led to ten years of open rebellion in Sindh and a bitter dispute between two self-professed "nations" competing for the same geographical space.

However, the PPP, banned by Zia after the 1977 coup, was an all-Pakistani party, not a Sindhi party, and conflict between Sindhi and Mohajir deepened. A Sindhi nationalist movement evolved, taking the name of Sindhudesh (land of the Sindhis), and was promptly suppressed by the government of Pakistan.

By the mid-1970s the Sindhi ethnoseparatist movement was weakened. Sindhi was made an official provincial language, more university admission slots were reserved for Sindhis, and they were allocated a substantial number of the province's civil service positions. This came at the Mohajir's expense, but the most likely case of separatism in Pakistan after East Pakistan was defused.[20] Like Bengal, Sindh had a highly developed language and culture, it bordered the sea, and would have been economically viable. Yet because an independent Sindh would have blocked the access of the rest of Pakistan to the sea, separatist movements there were intolerable to the central government, and a mixture of inducement and punishment was applied to keep "nationalist" sentiments in check.

Sindhi separatist feelings still exist today, and political unrest runs deep. On top of old grievances, Sindhis bemoan a new development: the expansion into their province of radical Islamic movements, mostly from Punjab. Sindhi intellectuals and officials speak of a string of radical madaris established in Sindh, connecting the Punjab to Karachi. For many, this is just a contemporary manifestation of the old Punjab-Mohajir alliance, now backing the Islamists.

Sindhis are persuaded that Punjabis and Mohajirs are trying to further divide their state because they are the only real opposition to Punjabi domination of Pakistan. Thus, Punjabis have settled in Sindh, they have tried to implant Biharis (non-Bengali Pakistanis trapped in Bangladesh) in Sindh, and they have encouraged the migrant Mohajir population to attack Sindhis and Sindh culture in a strategy of divide and rule.[21] As a result, subnational politics, not regional or interstate politics, dominates their thoughts and their concerns. Even Sindhis (and Baluch) hold a special view on Kashmir: they see some justice in the Kashmir cause in relation to India and connect the dots between their own grievances and those of Kashmiris seeking independence; Pakistanis/Punjabis are as much the oppressors as the Indians/Hindus.

Would Sindh be a viable, independent state? It has a superb port, some natural resources, but it is a lower riparian to Punjab, and Sindhi independence could only come about with Punjabi acceptance.[22] Even an independent Sindh would have to accept a degree of subordination to India and might face a massive return of Hindu Sindhis.

The Mohajirs

Closely linked to Sindh's fate, the Mohajir movement is unique in two ways. First, it is not tied to a particular territory, although Mohajirs and Sindhis compete for power and position in Sindh; and unlike the Sindhis, Baluch, Pashtun, and Bengalis, the Mohajirs were part of Pakistan's elite until marginalized in the 1970s. During Pakistan's first twenty-five years they accounted for only 3 percent of the population but held 21 percent of government jobs and were prominent in the army (at least two army chiefs have been Mohajirs, including President Pervez Musharraf).[23] Seven of the twelve biggest business houses were controlled by Gujarati-speaking Mohajirs. As a blessed minority—they had made the trek from India—they operated at the national, not provincial level.

This changed markedly after Pakistan's first free election, held in 1970, which unleashed potent ethnolinguistic forces throughout the country. The Bengali separatist movement did not directly affect the Mohajir community in the west, but it was devastating for the non-Bengalis who lived in the east. The so-called Biharis were loyal to the west but trapped in the east and constitute one of the great tragedies of contemporary Pakistan. Following the loss of the East Wing the government of Pakistan refused to take most of them back, and those who did not flee or make it to Pakistan in the first few months after the war found themselves stateless and trapped in Bangladesh internment centers. Over a quarter million of them still live in Bangladesh, mostly in camps around Dhaka, yet Pakistan has only allowed a token number to repatriate to the country where they have no economic or social links.[24]

The Bihari calamity was closely observed by their West Pakistani counterparts, the Mohajirs. Many Indian Muslim families who had decided to migrate to the new state of Pakistan had faced a choice between going to the East or the West Wing, and some families found themselves in both wings. If a fiercely loyal segment of the population could be abandoned to their fate by the Pakistani state, could this ever happen to the Mohajirs? Already envied by many less well-off groups, they felt the full blast of the revival of ethnonationalist sentiments in Sindh, especially after Bhutto's PPP came to power in 1971. Mohajirs responded by an all-pervasive change in their own identity, which was first expressed through a Mohajir student organization in 1978 and then in a political party, the Muttahida Quami Movement (MQM, or United National Movement) in 1984.[25]

Although the Mohajirs were considered usurpers by the Sindhis, they themselves started feeling pressured when later migrants came to Hyderabad and Karachi. Karachi had 5.5 million Urdu- and Gujarati-speaking Mohajirs, 2 million Punjabis, 1.5 million Pashtuns, 2 million foreigners (including Iranians, Sri Lankans, Bangladeshis, Burmese, and others), and less than a million Sindhis and Baluch. It was this ethnic rivalry that provided the context of Mohajir political mobilization, exacerbated by the stagnant economy and tales of Biharis in Bangladesh concentration camps.

From the mid-1980s onward, the MQM, led by Altaf Hussain, developed a tightly organized political party structured along Leninist lines, complete with a hierarchy of commissars; it had a penchant for torture, kidnapping, and murder. The only political organization in Pakistan to have raised the issue of the stranded Biharis, the MQM focused on preserving a disproportionate number of places at universities and in the provincial and national civil services—especially important positions in the context of a stagnant economy. While very successful in local elections in urban Sindh and Karachi, where the educated and professional Mohajir community is concentrated, the movement was suppressed in the wake of massive urban violence, which finally drew the attention of the army in 1992. Altaf Hussain then fled to London where he lives in exile. The party is now on autopilot, run from London by Hussain, who has on several occasions said that the creation of Pakistan was a mistake. The end result is that MQM members can neither return to India nor find a place in Pakistan.

The community even now debates whether an earlier generation of North Indian Muslims was wise to support Pakistan. At the same time, stories of murder and persecution of Indian Muslims in Gujarat and other regions of India, plus the rise of militant Hinduism, seem to provide fresh justification for Pakistan. Because of their high educational levels and large network of contacts, many Mohajir families have undertaken a second migration to the Middle East, Europe, or the United States, where they are doubly unhappy, scorning both India and Pakistan.

The MQM remains strong for many reasons. For one thing, it represents the Mohajirs in interethnic rivalry. For another, Sindh province is unable to deliver basic civic amenities to the largely urban Mohajir community, and the community feels threatened both by new immigrants and the resurgent Sindhis. Note, too, that elite Mohajirs still hold important positions in Pakistan, but very much like Sri Lanka's Tamils, newer generations are anxious about the community's slow decline in influence and their own prospects in a struggling and increasingly violent Pakistan, especially when much of that violence is directed against them.

The Frontier

The separatist group that poses the largest threat to Pakistan today is perhaps the Pashtun nationalist movement. It was active well before Pakistan's creation, then faded for twenty years, and now is experiencing a resurgence. Like Kashmir, the pre-independence NWFP had a popular leader, Khan Abdul Ghaffar Khan, known as the "Frontier Gandhi" for his support of nonviolence and stewardship of a powerful organization, the Red Shirts. He and Kashmir's Sheikh Abdullah both favored provincial independence over accession to either India or Pakistan. Fearing that Muslims leaving India would come and dominate NWFP, Ghaffar Khan demanded and received a referendum that would determine his province's destiny, but the last British viceroy, Lord Mountbatten, refused to put the "third option" of independence on the ballot, and the Frontier Gandhi boycotted the vote. Although NWFP voted for Pakistan, Ghaffar Khan persisted in expressing views that Jinnah and the Pakistan leadership interpreted as separatist, whereupon they set a trend that "characterizes Pakistan politics to the present day . . . by imprisoning him."[26]

The Pashtun movement went into slow decline and was virtually nonexistent even before the Soviet Union invaded Afghanistan in late 1979. Ghaffar Khan's Red Shirts and its successor National Awami Party (NAP) led by his son, Wali Khan, were strong in just four of the six settled districts in NWFP—Peshawar, Kohat, Bannu, and Mardan—and had little reach among Pashtuns in the Federally Administered Tribal Areas or elsewhere.[27] The demand for Pakhtoonistan did not have significant middle- or lower middle-class support in urban areas. Lower middle-class Pashtuns in rural areas were tied to the Pakistani state through a long history of military service and an even higher percentage of soldiers than the Punjab. Also, a number of prominent officials, especially retired generals, were Pashtuns (Ayub Khan being the most prominent, although he was from a minor tribe). Furthermore, the NWFP economy was closely integrated with that of Punjab, and Karachi became a favorite destination for Pashtuns. Pashtuns came to dominate Pakistan's trucking industry, and they have found an important niche in Pakistan's legal and illegal economies.

The Soviet invasion put a nail in the coffin of Pashtun irredentism. Before the invasion, Hafizullah Amin, the leftist Afghan prime minister, held out the prospect of a greater Pakhtoonistan; after it, with Soviet occupiers in charge, Kabul backed away, adopting Moscow's view that Pakistan should not be dismembered. For the past twenty years, successive governments in Kabul have been too busy trying to stay in power to bother playing the Pakhtoonistan card with Pakistan.

From Islamabad's perspective, the Taliban provided the perfect instrument to end forever the idea of Pakhtoonistan. Trained in Pakistan's madaris, the Taliban was certainly Afghan and Pashtun, but it was also under the influence of Islamabad, both directly via Pakistani intelligence, and indirectly through the Islamist parties, notably the Jamiat Ulema-e-Islam, one of the Taliban's tutors. The destruction of the Taliban regime in Kabul by American forces in 2002 removed the first-ever Afghan government that Islamabad could regard as friendly.

During Pakistan's democratic decade—the 1990s—it had appeared that the relatively secular and national political parties had edged out irredentist and separatist movements, including the Islamists and the NAP. The election of 2002 reversed this trend, and the alliance of six Islamist parties, the Muttahida Majlis-e-Amal (MMA, United Action Forum), swept into power. They did so for three reasons. First, the more mainstream but conservative Muslim League, always the main rival of the Islamists, was both divided and prevented from organizing an effective campaign. There were also allegations that the ISI, or at least elements of the ISI sympathetic to the Islamists, initially put the MMA alliance together. Second, Pashtun sentiments were outraged by what they saw as a massacre of fellow Pashtuns by Americans with official Pakistani connivance—Islamabad had provided airfields and bases for American forces operating in Afghanistan and subsequently provided useful intelligence about the location of al Qaeda and Taliban leaders. The Islamist parties themselves put aside their quarrels and theological debates long enough to campaign on a common platform—one that was anti-American and pro-Taliban and Pashtun—and pooled their votes against mainstream parties that had a more benign view of the United States.

The emergence of an Islamist government in the NWFP (and as a coalition partner in Baluchistan) raises the possibility of a very different kind of separatist-nationalist movement in the NWFP, one based on religious symbols and alliances. It also raises anew the prospect of a clash with the new government of Afghanistan, which is openly wary of Islamists in the NWFP and Baluchistan. The Islamists protect and shield the Taliban, and any weakness in Afghanistan will be quickly exploited by the Pakistan-based Taliban and their newly powerful Islamist allies. Further, the government of Pakistan's pledge of support for the new Afghan government is highly questionable; if the opportunity arose to ensure that Afghanistan once again has a pro-Pakistan government, Islamabad would seize it.

This situation is not lost upon the Afghans. They have privately indicated that such a move could be met by a strategy of turning ethnonationalist sentiments against Pakistan, via support for Pakhtoonistan in the expectation that ethnic sentiments are more powerful than religious ones. Thus a Pakhtoonistan movement may yet emerge, but it is difficult to predict whether the sponsors will be Pakistani Pashtuns, in the guise of the MMA, or Afghanistan, seeking to counterbalance Islamabad by encouraging separatism in Pakistan itself.

Baluchistan

The Baluch tribes are settled on bleak lands that straddle Pakistan, Afghanistan, and Iran. One of their historic claims to fame is that their ancestors decimated the army of Alexander the Great as he tried to make his way back to Greece from India.

Baluch separatism was the brainchild of a few tribal chiefs (the sardars) and a student movement. The problem in Baluchistan was potentially serious in that it sought to generate separatist and nationalist sentiment within a culturally distinct ethnolinguistic group that had its own autonomous history and had not changed much under British rule.

Despite Baluchistan's distinct culture and tradition, not to mention its size (it constitutes 42 percent of Pakistan's landmass), the Baluch are weakly organized in modern terms. The province's vast spaces are home to only 5 percent of Pakistan's total population, and the educational level is very low: the best, and undoubtedly inflated, estimate puts literacy at barely 24 percent, with female literacy at an astonishingly low 5 percent. Further, Baluch is no longer the dominant ethnolinguistic group in large parts of the province now that northern Baluchistan's population is swollen with large numbers of Pashtun refugees from Afghanistan (many of the madaris that trained the Pashtun Taliban were located in Baluchistan). In addition, significant numbers of Baluch are assimilated in South Punjab and northern Sindh.

Since partition there have been four miniwars between the Baluch and Pakistani forces. The first two occurred in 1948 and 1958 and lasted a few months each, ending in a Baluch surrender, the imprisonment of the then Khan of Kalat for fifteen years, and the execution of other rebels.

Baluchistan's third civil war began in 1962 and ended in 1968 and was fought between Baluch tribals and Pakistani paramilitary forces. It ended with the Baluch taking huge losses in livestock through shelling and air attacks; this was merely a prelude to a far bloodier war at the peak of Baluchi separatism during the insurrection of 1973–75, sparked by Bhutto's dismissal of local administrators. After an alliance of an Islamist party (the JUI) and the NAP came to power in Baluchistan and the NWFP in 1972, two powerful and respected Baluch leaders, Mir Ghaus Bakhsh Bizenjo and Sardar Ataullah Khan Mengal, became governor and chief minister, respectively. This arrangement ended after ten months, when Bhutto dismissed the NAP-JUI governors, accusing the NAP leaders in Baluchistan of arming their followers, seeking the further breakup of Pakistan, and undermining the government effort to modernize the province through the construction of roads and schools and the maintenance of law and order. When the Baluchistan and NWFP governments resigned in protest, Bhutto ordered the Pakistan army to suppress the Baluch separatist movement and launched a full-scale military operation.[28] The army and paramilitary forces numbered about 80,000 troops, reinforced by helicopter gunships, armored vehicles, and mortars from Iran. This was the first occasion on which Pakistan's elite Special Security Group (SSG) commandos saw battle. On their part, the Baluch could only field some 1,000 guerrillas, armed with ancient rifles. Their forces suffered about 3,300 casualties, and some 7,000 families took refuge in Afghanistan.[29]

Bhutto was overthrown before the revolt could be crushed, and the army decided to withdraw its forces and reach an accommodation with the Baluch leadership. Zia released the NAP leaders from prison, and hostilities ceased. Mengal retreated to London, where he lives in exile as convenor of the Pakistan Oppressed Nations Movement.

Any possible future Baluch revolt was countered by a strategy of divide and rule, in which the sardars and other tribal leaders were played off against each other, or co-opted with contracts, grants, and the power to control the allocation of resources flowing from the center to their population. Zia's government also struck a bargain with the sardars to slow the pace of modernization, including education, since rapid social change undercut the traditional bases of tribal and clan authority.

In the Baluch case, like that of the FATA, the government is torn between intervening in the affairs of a tough tribal society that will resist outsiders with force and speeding up the process of modernization and development. A liberal but undemocratic central government is trying to modernize a very conservative tribal society, whose leaders are highly autocratic, but whose power rests upon the authority of tradition. The British were reluctant to interfere too much in Baluchistan and the NWFP tribal areas, but successive Pakistani governments cannot ignore the tribal areas. Islamabad fears cross-border support for separatists from India and Afghanistan, just as it once came from the Soviet Union and Afghanistan. The preponderant Pakistani view is one of a sense of noblesse oblige, a duty to bring the wild and untamed tribals into the "mainstream."

The Baluch and the tribal Pashtun, Pakistani officials contend, are easily led astray by fanatic tribal leaders who are uninformed about the modern world. In this picture the conservative Islamist parties have a role; they can appeal to the tribals on theological grounds and as part of a "modern" Pakistani political system can also serve as tutors to the tribals.

All in all, Baluchistan is an unlikely candidate for a successful separatist movement, even if there are grievances, real and imagined, against the Punjab-dominated state of Pakistan.[30] It lacks a middle class, a modern leadership, and the Baluch are a tiny fraction of Pakistan's population— and even in their own province are faced with a growing Pashtun population. Further, neither Iran nor Afghanistan shows any sign of encouraging Baluch separatism because such a movement might encompass their own Baluch population. However, there is little probability of this occurring; unlike the Kurds, divided between Turkey, Iraq, and Iran, the Baluch have few valuable resources in the areas they inhabit and are even less well organized than the Kurds. Only India might support a Baluch separatist movement, but absent a direct land link and considering the difficulty of controlling the Baluch, such an effort could only meet with tactical success—unless, as to be discussed in chapter 8, there was a general weakening of Pakistan's political order.

Pakistan's Micro-Nations

A cluster of ethnoreligious groups have also expressed some desire for greater autonomy and might under certain circumstances seek independence or create severe law and order problems for Islamabad. The best known of these is in the Siraiki-speaking region located in southwest Punjab and northern Sindh. Siraiki is a distinct language, spoken both by Punjabis and Sindhis, and its speakers claim to be a fifth of Pakistan's total population but are probably closer to 10 percent (there is also a rich Siraiki literature, including a translation of the Quran).[31] The Siraiki movement is largely cultural and social; it was once based in Bahawalpur, where it had received court patronage, but its center is now in Multan.[32] Although still in the stage of identity formation, its members voice economic grievances and some claim they would be better off if separated from Punjab.

Other potential separatist movements are to be found in Pakistan-administered Kashmir and the Northern Areas. Both regions exhibit a strong cultural identity and a sense of alienation from the Pakistan Establishment. "Azad" Kashmir, on the Pakistani side of the Line of Control, is culturally as close to Pakistan's Punjab as it is to Indian-administered Kashmir. Azad Kashmir is unlikely to opt to leave Pakistan, as is true of the Northern Areas such as Gilgit and Baltistan. Yet grievances do exist. The Northern Areas contain a high percentage of Shi'ia, some tribal in their ethnic origin and many Ismaili—the sect led by the Aga Khan and considered heretics by hard-line Islamists. The Pakistan government has routinely cracked down on "nationalist" groups in this region, targeting one called the Northern Areas Thinkers' Forum, which advocates the formation of two independent states in the northwest region of the subcontinent. The first would include the Pakistan- and Indian-administered parts of Kashmir, minus Ladakh; the second would include the Gilgit-Baltistan-Ladakh areas.[33] Another group seeks to create "Balawaristan," and wants statehood for Baltistan, Gilgit, and Dardistan. Claiming to be an "oppressed people" owing to sectarianism, intolerance, poverty, terrorist camps, and the theft of resources, the movement actually has a tiny population linked by their opposition to the alarming expansion of Sunni sectarianism into the region.[34]

Like similar movements elsewhere in Pakistan, and many more in neighboring India, these are constrained by the power of the central government. There might be circumstances under which they would achieve greater autonomy within Pakistan itself, but the next step—separate statehood—could only be achieved in the context of a major change in the region's strategic environment and Islamabad's loss of power.

Punjab and Its Army

Conversations with leading Sindhi and Baluch intellectuals and politicians quickly reveal their conviction that regional conflict is largely the fault of militaristic Punjabi leaders, who will not normalize relations with India because they want to maintain a large army. In the view of regional autonomists and separatists, the Punjab-dominated Establishment, in league with a few Mohajirs and the Pashtuns, use foreign and defense policy as a club to beat the lesser provinces, notably Sindh and Baluchistan.

A few years after submitting his report on the loss of East Pakistan, Chief Justice Rahman raised the issue of Punjabi dominance in Pakistan in a lead article in the army's professional journal. Justice Rahman reminded his readers that the main culprits in the corruption that led to the disintegration of the old Pakistan were invariably Punjabis, and that "this gave rise to a feeling of Punjabi domination which in its turn propelled into prominence regionalistic and parochial aspirations.[35] Nevertheless, most Sindhis and Baluch recognize that independence is not practical. With their feudal aristocracy, poor peasantry, and small middle class, these provinces lack the social and economic infrastructure for a successful nationalist, separatist movement; they particularly lack military skills, as is evident from the small number of Sindhis and Baluch in the army.

But what is the collective view of Punjab's elites about further major changes in Pakistan? On one hand, Punjab is clearly Pakistan's wealthiest and most populous province, with a commanding position in Pakistan's core political and military institutions. Punjab's centrality was enhanced by Pakistan's acceptance of military rule for half of the years since 1971. Indeed, the nation's army remains by and large a Punjabi army with regard to both the officer corps and other ranks.

Political style and culture merely reinforce a Punjab-centric system. Punjabis can best be described as a cross between Texans and New Yorkers. They exude a brashness and zest for life (reflected through their rich stock of "Punjabi" jokes) and also include some of Pakistan's best-educated and cultured elites, all of which can be irritating to non-Punjabis. For Punjabis, only the Pashtuns can compare in martial qualities and valor; attitudes toward Baluch are dismissive, and toward Sindhis, contemptuous.

The focal point of Punjabi domination was and remains the army.[36] Seventy-five percent of the army is drawn from three Punjab districts (Rawalpindi, Jhelum, and Campbellpur) and two adjacent districts in the NWFP (Kohat and Mardan). These districts contain only 9 percent of Pakistan's male population. The officer corps is drawn from a wider, more urban base but is still predominately Punjabi, often the sons of junior commissioned officers. Pakistan's air force and navy are drawn from a much wider base.

The composition of a state's security bureaucracies—the police and the army—is important for symbolic and practical reasons. The symbolism is obvious: a Pakistani who cannot share equally in the obligations and rewards associated with vital central institutions in a state that is dominated by the army and the security forces does not have full rights (or opportunities) as a citizen, whether the state is a democracy or a liberal autocracy. If ordinary citizens, farmers, and peasants from Sindh or Baluchistan do not make good soldiers—or if they are not interested in participating in the defense of the country—what does this imply about their loyalty to the state of Pakistan and about the loyalty and officer-like qualities of Baluch or Sindhis who join the officer corps? Although the process of "nation building" is not the same as the eradication of provincial and local loyalties (and in a state as diverse and complex as Pakistan, a federal system with multiple allegiances is inevitable), when one province is so much more powerful than the others, as is the Punjab, even a fair representation of its members in the armed forces may give the appearance of conspiracy.

The practical aspects of representativeness are no less important. With a stagnant economy and few opportunities for social advancement, access to the armed forces is a tremendous accomplishment for ordinary citizens. Once they have a relative in the military, especially the army, a certain aura surrounds the family or clan—other state institutions are likely to be more accommodating, be they the local police, civil servants, or petty officials. Retired officers, in particular, benefit enormously from the military association, through appointments to government posts, assistance in starting up new businesses (with government contracts), and assignments to the police and paramilitary forces. Hence Punjab has an enormous vested interest in keeping the army connection open, and this will not change until the Pakistani economy begins to expand rapidly, with new opportunities for retired jawans and officers.

Another reason offered for Punjab's dominance is its strategic value. The Staff College teaches that every country has a heart or core area, which in Pakistan's case is the Punjab, whereas the other three provinces constitute invasion routes. This logic is analogous to that of Ayub Khan's declaration that East Pakistan could be defended by maintaining strong forces in West Pakistan.

Might Punjab accept or initiate a major structural change in Pakistan's federal order? This is unlikely, although there have been proposals to create twenty-five or thirty smaller administrative areas in the interest of efficiency and building national loyalties—exactly the reasons advanced for the One-Unit scheme fifty years ago. Such a move would be bitterly resented by non-Punjabi ethnolinguistic groups, and even Punjabis would fear the breakup of their province, with the Siraiki region being the first to depart. As for administrative efficiency, Pakistan's problems in this area stem more from a demoralized civilian bureaucracy, a lack of funds, and a very high level of corruption.

All for One and One for All?

Barring a cataclysm in Pakistani politics or a war between India and Pakistan, there is unlikely to be a second Bangladesh or ethnolinguistic breakup. Nor is it likely, except under certain circumstances, that any single province will break away from Pakistan, or that a major reorganization of the state will take place to provide subnational groups with greater autonomy. The district-level Nazim experiment is likely to stagger on for several years, with a further breakdown in administration and law and order and hence a greater emphasis on central rather than provincial authority. The future growth (or diminution) of Pakistan's ethnolinguistic separatist and autonomist movements seems to hinge on four factors: the existence of a national identity that accommodates such movements, the extent of Pakistan's structural imbalance, the influence of international factors in Pakistan's domestic politics, and the mind-set of Pakistan's ruling Establishment.

Pakistan's historic identity as a homeland for oppressed Indian Muslims is, ironically, one factor that will continue to reinforce separatism. The notion of Pakistan as a homeland worked its way through the new state in a devastating fashion. If Muslims needed and deserved a separate space in which they could achieve personal and community fulfillment denied to them by Indian Hindus, what about those Pakistani Muslims who found themselves dominated politically, militarily, and culturally by other Pakistanis? When it became clear that equality was not possible between East and West Pakistan or between Punjabis and non-Punjabis, the concomitant idea that Pakistan itself might be composed of two, three, or even four nations spread first to East Bengal and then to Sindh, Baluchistan, the Northwest Frontier Province, and even the Punjab and Kashmir. It was accelerated by Pakistan's vehement support for the idea of national self-determination in the case of the Kashmiris.

What is special about Pakistan is the reluctance of its leadership to modify this narrative in the face of the reality of an ethnically unbalanced and very complex state. "Homelands" and "national self-determination" are powerful words, and dangerous ones when the state has generated enormous unrest among its own people. Pakistan needs a new organizing idea that will provide more space for subnationalism and an identity defined in terms other than fear.

Second, Pakistan remains structurally problematic. The old Pakistan broke up because political power was unbalanced, even though East and West Pakistan were approximately equal in numbers. The majority of Pakistani citizens lived in the East Wing (and voted as a block), but real political power lay in the hands of the overwhelmingly West Pakistan army. The leaders of West Pakistan, notably the army, believed that if they gave up power in an election, an East Pakistan–based majority would pursue policies detrimental to Pakistan's vital interests. There was enough consensus on this point in West Pakistan to form a common front against Sheikh Mujib and his Awami League, and to declare war on the East Wing rather than find a compromise. Further, no organization—not a single political party and certainly not the army—reflected the interests of East *and* West Pakistan.

The East Wing had been homogenous, united by territorial and ethno-linguistic interests, while the West Wing was far more diverse. The demise of the Muslim League and the army's unrepresentativeness made the situation structurally unstable, for East Pakistan did not have enough diversity to allow for cross-cutting allegiances and ties, whereas the West Wing did. Thus, while Punjab dominated West Pakistan, the issue of East versus West united the West. When East Pakistan was removed from the state, it not only let loose a fresh wave of ethnolinguistic demands, discussed earlier, but also created a new political geometry.

The present situation is structurally quite different, in that one province is clearly dominant and political power overlaps with economic and military power. Although this makes Pakistan extremely strong in terms of preventing separatism, it fosters resentment against the center among the less populous provinces and minorities such as the Mohajirs.

Pakistan's federal system works well when non-Punjabis are regularly inducted into the Establishment, through a form of ticket-balancing that ensures some senior posts will go to non-Punjabis. Baluch served as prime ministers under Zia and Musharraf, and Sindhis find a place in ministries and senior appointments. Although such appointments do not automatically confer power on a given province, they do help to co-opt regional elites. As already mentioned, the provincial assemblies have also been dramatically weakened by the new system of local government, which routes payments directly to the districts, bypassing the provincial governments.

Because many of the districts are not economically viable—especially the poorer rural ones—a better arrangement for genuine decentralization would be to break up the provinces into their constituent units, which is not the district but the division. A divided Punjab would not only provide more accessible and fiscally viable governance to individuals and groups at the district level but it would ease the concerns of other provinces. It would also go some way toward resolving some of the key disputes over issues such as the distribution of the waters of the Indus; right now, this pits the Sindh against Punjab in an uneven contest, but there are different water-related interests within the Punjab, and a new reordering along divisional lines would allow for trade-offs of different kinds of interests between roughly equal contestants.

Musharraf's goal is to weaken provincial power and further centralize politics. He is gambling that the increased direct control over the Nazims (via payments to the districts) will compensate for the decline in provincial responsibility. However, the experience of India and other complex society-states indicates that the gain may be illusory because of the difficulty of running a megastate from the center.

There is also an international dimension to separatism. From Islamabad's perspective, grounds for concern are ample because every Pakistani ethnolinguistic group has had cross-border ties. Other states, especially India, and potentially Afghanistan, may find it expedient to encourage autonomist and separatist movements. India and Pakistan treat ethnic separatist movements as instruments of foreign policy—in this region one's own national security and a rival state's domestic insecurity go hand in hand. The intelligence services of India and Pakistan are organized as much to meddle in their neighbor's affairs as to provide intelligence and information. Pakistan itself has supported Kashmiri separatists for years and housed terrorists on its soil. It also provided active support to Sikh separatists in the mid-1980s by way of a legitimate response to India's open support for Bengali separatists. Not surprisingly, Pakistani officials lament the vulnerability of their own ethnic minorities but calculate that the nation can withstand Indian (and perhaps Afghan) pressure indefinitely. That may be the case, but it is hard to determine where domestic resentment ends and foreign encouragement begins. This has made Islamabad ultra-suspicious of autonomist movements, and encourages the view that expressions of resentment are a false front for a "pro-India" group.

Pakistan's leaders do not seem to have fully grasped the point that in a multiethnic state, most politics is identity politics and closely linked to issues of pride, status, jobs, and social equality. They seem convinced that ethnolinguistic demands are an economic, not a political, problem, and if other means fail, a military problem. Almost all of Pakistan's ethnolinguistic revolts were triggered by the center's dismissal of a provincial government, notably in East Bengal and Sindh in the 1950s, Baluchistan in 1973 and 1988, and the NWFP in 1947 and 1973. Elections and representative government do confer legitimacy at the provincial level, and provinces tend to revolt whenever the central government is perceived to have violated those norms of constitutional behavior designed to constrain the powerful and protect the weak.[37] Instead, both sides tend to see Pakistan's ethnic politics as a zero-sum game. In the case of Sindh and the Mohajirs or the Baluch and Pashtuns, it involves intraethnic conflict, with the center sometimes egging on one side against the other.

Although its separatist or autonomist movements are unlikely to succeed, Pakistan will continue to be plagued by separatist-autonomist sentiments, and some political and structural scenarios are explored in chapter 8. A more pressing question for the center is how much economic and social trends will influence these sentiments over the next five to ten years.

CHAPTER SEVEN

DEMOGRAPHIC, EDUCATIONAL, AND ECONOMIC PROSPECTS

The previous four chapters offered both a history and an assessment of key Pakistani political and social forces, including the army, the political parties, regional elites, and the emerging Islamist movements. This chapter returns to the broader approach of chapters 1 and 2 to consider Pakistan's prospects in view of its alarming demographic and social indicators, the much-battered educational system, and uncertain economic circumstances. Factors of this nature are intertwined: when they are in a positive direction, they reinforce each other in a virtuous cycle; when they are negative, the cycle becomes vicious—and a state may spiral downward or stagnate. Where possible, comparisons are drawn with a select group of "peer" states—countries that have several important features in common with Pakistan and that face similar problems and opportunities.

Demographic Trends

Pakistan's demographic future is likely to shape its economy, social structure, and even its identity in powerful ways. The population of the area that is now Pakistan grew from an estimated 17 million in 1901 to 32 million at the time of partition, 34 million at the time of the first (1951) census, and about 140 million in recent years. Whereas Punjab is densely settled and the beneficiary of a major irrigation system, the other three provinces—Sindh, Baluchistan, and the Northwest Frontier Province (NWFP)—are sparsely populated and in places desert-like. For fifty years

231

Table 7-1. *Comparative Population and Growth*
Millions, except as indicated

Year	Pakistan	Bangladesh	India	Iran	Turkey	Indonesia
2000	141.3	137.4	1,008.9	70.3	66.7	212.1
2015	204.3	183.2	1,230.5	87.1	79.0	250.1
Rank in world	5	8	2	16	18	4
Total fertility rate[a]	Very high	Moderate	Moderate	High	Moderate	Moderate

Sources: UNESCAP, Human Development Report Data, www.unescap.org/theme/poptab03.htm.

a. Very high = total of more than 5.0 children per woman; high = 3.5–5.0; moderate = 2.1–3.5; low = < 2.1

Pakistan's population grew at a rate of almost 2.9 percent annually, a figure much greater than South Asia's average (1.9 percent) and one of the highest in the world. Its population is expected to reach 219 million by 2015 (making it the fifth largest country in the world, behind China, India, the United States, and Indonesia), 255 million by 2025, and 295 million by 2050, at which point it will surpass Indonesia (see table 7-1).

This demographic growth has been matched by massive urbanization in the past few decades. According to conservative estimates, Karachi, the largest city, had 9.9 million residents in 1998, or 7 percent of the country's total population. Today this figure may well stand above 14 million and is expected to reach 20 million or more in 2015.[1] Lahore, Punjab's capital and most important city, will also join the ranks of mega cities (those with a population of more than 10 million) by 2015. Karachi and Lahore are not even the fastest-growing cities, which are Punjab's Gujranwala and Faisalabad.[2] Overall, Pakistan has eight cities with a population of more than 1 million, and its urban population will surpass 103 million by 2015.[3] Its rate of urbanization between 2003 and 2004 has been higher than all but one of the peer group—Bangladesh.[4]

Pakistan's dramatic population increase has been propelled by high fertility rates.[5] The average Pakistani woman has only marginally fewer children than twenty years ago, the total fertility rate (the total number of children born per woman) having slipped only from about 6.4 in 1970 to 5.6 in 1998. Strong cultural and socioeconomic pressures in favor of male children have kept fertility rates high. It was only in 1992–93 that Pakistan's fertility rate started to decline, far later than was the case in India

Figure 7-1. *Annual Population Growth Rates, 2005–50*

Percent

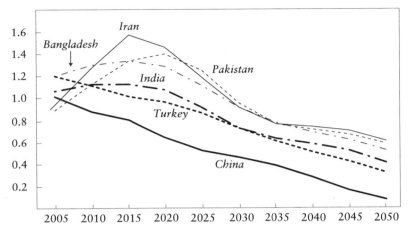

and Bangladesh. Yet without significant social investment in health care, education, and family planning, maximalist projections of Pakistan's population structure are likely to be realized. Figure 7-1 compares Pakistan's demographic future with some of its peers.

The demographic pressure on Pakistan is only likely to increase because of the youth bulge in age group 15–24 (figure 7-2). Although the number of young people on the whole is expected to decline in Pakistan and its peer countries, the current high rate of population growth will keep Pakistan in the midst of a youth bulge well into 2025. This could pose a serious problem since this situation, in combination with urbanization, lack of education, and high unemployment, is usually a recipe for social unrest. Further, none of these trends are manageable by ordinary means in the short to medium term.

Comparisons with a group of other Islamic countries shed light on Pakistan's demographic challenge. Pakistan is one of five Islamic countries with truly astounding population growth rates.[6] Such growth, Fuller suggests, makes it difficult to meet the demands of a younger population even in the long term. Initially, those demands create pressure on education and social management for public order and subsequently on employment,

Figure 7-2. *Median Age of Population, 2000–50*

Years

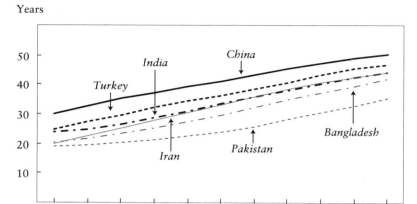

housing, and social services. Then the effects of the youth bulge pass through the generation with an echo effect in the following one. When the same group in the youth bulge begins to have children, the population growth will be high even if total fertility rates have dropped.

Speculatively, the causes of Pakistan's demographic plight can be explained in part by such economic and cultural factors as low levels of education, a lack of industrialization, a strong bias against family planning, and a strong patriarchal tradition. Clearly, Pakistan's political and social elite—the Establishment—have never paid much attention to the population problem. Their overriding concern is a perceived threat from a much larger and a faster-growing India. In their eyes, Pakistan is a *relatively* small state; to some degree the elite have never shaken off the minority complex that was embedded in the Pakistan movement. For some of the Islamists, a nation of Islamic warriors backed by an Islamic bomb represents an unstoppable force, which means a large population is a strategic asset.

A large population that cannot find opportunity within Pakistan but is unable to leave the country in sufficient numbers produces masses of young men (and a few young women) who are ripe for political exploitation. To some degree this can be balanced by an increase in the police and security forces, but there is just as likely to be a rise in political parties and leaders who recruit these young people to extremist political causes.

Optimistically, the Pakistani economist Shahid Javed Burki argues that although Pakistan does have the youngest population of the fifteen most populous countries, this demographic situation presents an extraordinary opportunity: if Pakistan could train and educate its young to fit the demographic gap that has opened up in the developed world (characterized by an aging population), its youth bulge could turn out to be a productive asset contributing to economic growth, more level economic distribution, and poverty alleviation. Pakistan, Burki writes, needs not only to increase literacy and education at the primary and secondary level, but also to train people to fit into key technical, service, and industrial sectors where the developed world is likely to experience gaps, especially in health services, education, and finance.[7]

It is true that an educated and mobile younger generation can lead a country in the direction of democratization and liberalization, and it might have the talent to take advantage of niche opportunities presented by the global marketplace. In the Middle Ages in Europe after the Black Death, the youth bulge in countries such as Spain and England found employment in overseas exploration. In Iran, a new, young generation, educated and aware of the world, presses the conservative regime for democratization and social change, and in India, the youth bulge is being channeled into burgeoning public and private institutions designed to place young Indians in a world market.

However, it is unclear whether Pakistan can replicate these achievements. The Middle East, traditionally a popular destination for job-seekers, is less likely to provide opportunities for Pakistanis with the skills to take advantage of them; Saudi Arabia, in particular, faces its own youth explosion and is systematically reducing the role of expatriates in the economy. If the Gulf and the Middle East can no longer welcome young Pakistanis, those who do not have the skills to compete in the West may join the flow into Kashmir and Afghanistan, where young, unemployed Pakistanis have joined the ranks of militants and paramilitary forces in substantial numbers; absent a genuine peace agreement in Kashmir and stability in Afghanistan, opportunities for employment as jihadis or ordinary mercenaries will continue to grow. About the only exportable human asset that Pakistan has in abundance is "boots on the ground." Its professional army could be used more extensively for peacekeeping operations in the Middle East or other strife-torn regions, but a significant expansion of this role for Pakistan would have to wait until the conflict with India is dampened.[8]

Education: The Future of the Future

A modern state that neglects education will have all the more difficulty adapting to changing circumstances, including new economic opportunities, changes in the physical environment, and new strategic alignments. This point is especially important to make when a country already has several strikes against it in the form of high levels of ethnolinguistic conflict and sectarian discord, as in the case of Pakistan. That is to say, its educational system must be of high enough caliber to help bridge the cultural and civilizational divides that already exist without producing new divisions, and in addition produce a trained cadre of future leaders able to navigate a nuclear-armed Pakistan through a rapidly changing global and regional environment.

Educational Traditions

Pakistan inherited a well-established primary and secondary educational system, especially in the urban centers and much of Punjab, although it had been predominately manned by Hindus, many of whom left for India after partition. The major educational assets Pakistan inherited were situated in Lahore, where a number of elite state and missionary schools had taught several generations of Hindus, Sikhs, and Muslims, producing many of India's and Pakistan's future leaders.

In 1947 Pakistan's First Educational Conference recommended universal primary education and an improvement in quality, but at the time the state's resources were concentrated on the industrial and economic infrastructure, including communications, railroads, water and power, and defense, with education and health receiving low priority.[9] For the next fifty years, the pattern remained much the same. Like India, Pakistan tended to emphasize higher education and showed little interest in spreading literacy and basic education, the difference being that India had many more centers of excellence of equal or better quality than those in Lahore and Karachi. Further, Indian states such as Kerala, Goa, Himachal

Pradesh, and Karnataka stressed primary education and technical training on their own, even as the Indian government poured resources into a number of elite institutions. For many years, India was justly criticized for its neglect of basic education, but its investment in higher education and English-medium schools paid off when India found itself well placed to take advantage of the information revolution. As a result, India has become a niche power in software: it is now the "back office" of the world and could become a major force in biotechnology.

Other peer states, notably Iran and Turkey, have done even better (table 7-2). Pakistan's one notable educational accomplishment, the increase in spending on pre-primary and primary education, from 36 to nearly 52 percent of total educational expenses, may be a statistical artifice: many of the schools established in the 1990s turned out to be "ghost" schools, without teachers, buildings, or students.[10] According to one Oxfam report, Pakistan, which once accounted for 27 percent of South Asian children out of school in 1995, will account for 40 percent in a few years.[11]

President Zia is often held responsible for the deterioration of Pakistan's educational system. It is true that he and his colleagues regarded the universities and colleges as hostile territory and had contempt for the "poets and professors" of Pakistan. However, the neglect continued during Benazir Bhutto and Nawaz Sharif's terms in office. In the decade of democracy, requirements for health, education, and other social services competed directly with the military's budget, so even well-meaning politicians who recognized that Pakistan was grossly underinvesting in human capital were reluctant to press the issue for fear of affronting the army. It was enough to have a school or even a technical institute in a constituency; beyond that there was little concern that the declining quality of education was weakening Pakistan's international competitiveness.

More recently, the Pakistan government did allocate considerably more money for education in 2002–03, increasing it by almost 80 percent to about Rs 3.1 billion. Nearly a third of this is to be spent on the Tawana Pakistan program, intended to improve female enrollment in schools and improve nutritional support. The project aims at providing about 0.5 million girls access to education in about 5,300 primary schools in poverty-ridden districts.[12] This touches only a tiny part of the problem, and it is yet to be seen whether the provincial and local governments have the administrative integrity to run even this small a program efficiently.

Table 7-2. Commitment to Education
Percent

Indicator	Year[a]	Pakistan	Bangladesh	Iran	Turkey	Indonesia	India	China
Comparative HDR ranking (out of 173)	2002	138	145	98	85	110	124	96
Public education expenditure								
Proportion of GNP	1985–87	3.1	1.4	3.7	1.2[b]	0.9[c,d]	3.2	2.3
	1995–97	2.7	2.2	4.0	2.2[e]	1.4[f]	3.2	2.3
Proportion of total government spending	1985–87	8.8	9.9	18.1	n.a.	4.3[c,d]	8.5	11.1
	1995–97	7.1	13.8	17.8	14.7[e,d]	7.9[f]	11.6	12.2[d]
Preprimary and primary, proportion of total expenses[h]	1985–86	36.0	46.1	42.0	45.9	n.a.	38.0	29.5[g]
	1995–97	51.8	44.8	29.0	43.3[i]	n.a.	39.5	37.4
Secondary, proportion of total expenses	1985–87	33.3	34.7	37.9	22.4	n.a.	25.3	33.2[g]
	1995–97	27.9	43.8	33.9	22.0[i]	73.5[c,i]	26.5	32.2
Tertiary, proportion of total expenses	1985–86	18.2	10.4	10.7	23.9	n.a.	15.3	21.8[g]
	1995–97	13.0	7.9	22.9	34.7[i]	24.4[c]	13.7	15.6

Source: United Nations Development Program, *Human Development Report 2002: Deepening Democracy in a Fragmented World* (Oxford University Press, 2002).

n.a. Not available.

a. Most recent year available during the period specified.
b. Excludes expenditure on tertiary education.
c. Ministry of Education only.
d. Year or period other than that specified.
e. Data may not be strictly comparable with those for earlier years as a result of methodological changes.
f. Central government only.
g. Excludes expenditure on midlevel specialized colleges and technical schools.
h. Current public expenditure on education. Expenditures by level may not sum to 100 because of rounding or the omission of the categories "other types" and "not distributed."
i. Expenditures previously classified as "other types" have been distributed across the different education levels. Includes capital expenditure.
j. Combined expenditures for preprimary, primary, and secondary levels.

Primary and Secondary Education: The New Wasteland

Pakistan has at least four types of primary and secondary educational institutions, and they produce very different kinds of graduates. At the "traditional" end are the *deeni madaris,* religious schools affiliated with different mosques and sects, some of which trace their origins back hundreds of years (see chapter 5). Traditionally, most of their graduates became ulema. More recently, because of their expanded output, there has been a growth in store-front and tent mosques, as the madrassah graduates flock to the cities to earn a living.

Second, Pakistan has a few missionary and private schools that were established in the colonial years by Catholic and Protestant churches. These were nationalized by Bhutto in 1972. Most of their foreign faculty then departed and they went into decline. The second Nawaz government decided to denationalize missionary schools, but as of 2004, some remain under state control.[13] This group includes prestigious semiautonomous schools for the elite such as Aitchison, Lawrence, Forman Christian, and Kinnaird College (the latter a noted school for women). Some were established to educate the children of tribal and clan leaders, or to prepare them for service in the army. These are generally distinguished institutions but their output is tiny—they basically educate the children of the Establishment.

Third, Pakistan has a large number of government schools. These are found in the districts and major urban centers and are operated by the various provincial departments of education. Most of Pakistan's school-going children attend one of the 85,000 government primary schools, including 65,000 rural schools, and the system employs more than 186,000 teachers. According to one estimate, nearly one-quarter of these teachers are untrained, even though Pakistan does have training institutions for secondary and primary school teachers. However, faculty at these institutions are reportedly disillusioned, professionally inactive, and poorly paid.[14]

The scholar Hamid H. Kizilbash is not exaggerating when he concludes that Pakistan's primary rural schools "seem to be the last refuge of those who cannot find any other employment."[15] The condition of these schools can only be described as wretched: some lack water and others lack latrines (which makes it impossible for female students to attend).

The situation is all the more depressing because of their neglect by some of Pakistan's most noted politicians. Benazir Bhutto, for example, once boasted that under her administration Pakistan's rural schools were equipped with computers, but when challenged about the veracity of this statement, she blamed her successor for having looted the schools, the money, and the computers. In truth, there was no such program, and the money, if any, went in other directions. More recently, the Musharraf government has passed laws that require compulsory education for all children, *if* the provinces supply it, which they have not. The problem is especially acute in Baluchistan (the home province of the minister of education), rural Sindh, and southern Punjab.

There are important differences among the public schools, in the various provinces, and between those in rural and urban Pakistan, with the enrollment rate ranging from 18 percent for girls in Baluchistan to a high of 81 percent for boys in Punjab.[16] Nevertheless, some of the administrators of these schools soldier on and have a good understanding of the plight of Pakistan's primary and secondary educational institutions—they simply lack the resources to do much about it.[17]

There are also growing numbers of private schools, some of them established by nongovernmental organizations (NGOs), others run by for-profit institutions and catering to the rich. The fastest-growing such schools are the new madaris, at one end, and the private English-language schools, at the other. The patrons of these private schools can be quite varied. Pakistan almost had a chain of schools established by the radical al Qaeda, which had purchased land for at least one technical institution in Lahore, using an eminent Pakistani lawyer as a local partner.[18]

The products of Pakistan's schools differ enormously and appear to contribute to Pakistan's increasing polarization.[19] According to one analysis, carried out over several years, madrassah graduates think "so differently from the Westernized elite that they live in different worlds." Those coming from the private schools, especially the English-language institutions, are "alienated from Pakistani culture and full of contempt for their fellow citizens in the Urdu-medium schools and the madrassahs."[20] This suggestion is plausible, but not proven. That is why far more detailed work needs to be done on the impact of these different institutions, although it is clear that the English-language schools and some of the Urdu ones perpetuate Pakistan's rigid class structure; and only a few of the

NGO schools, and in some cases the many schools run by the Army Education Corps (AEC), attempt to inculcate a sense of social responsibility. A significant product of Pakistan's educational system is generation after generation of ill-trained and barely literate young men who head to the towns and cities where they find an expanding and tempting popular culture but no jobs; just as significant are the millions of young girls who do not receive *any* serious education, and who consequently tend to have many more children and are excluded from the formal workforce. Unlike Sri Lanka or Bangladesh, where thousands of young women have found employment in the textile sector and light manufacturing, Pakistan has an educational system, coupled with a traditional approach to the role of women, that rules out such activities, except for a tiny sector in Karachi and Lahore. These conditions are reflected in Pakistan television's Urdu-language TV dramas that are popular in India as well as Pakistan and compare favorably with the new wave of realist films being produced in Iran.

The system has had an impact—less than 25 percent of Pakistan's workforce is literate, which makes it difficult to train workers for any but the most menial tasks and discourages industry and foreign companies from investing in Pakistan. Pakistan's public education system has failed because it is not valued enough by the politically important components of the state's leadership. Pakistan's educational system is appropriate for a traditional hierarchical society that need not compete internationally with similar countries for markets, technology, and investment. If Pakistan were blessed with significant raw materials, oil, or some other source of energy, this situation might be tolerable, but it is not, and in the long term Pakistan's noncompetitive educational system will be one of the prime causes of economic stagnation and perhaps political turmoil.

Prospects for Change

Pakistan's overall economic growth was a respectable 6 percent for many years. Therefore resource shortage cannot be held responsible for the weakness in funding primary and secondary education. Low levels of priority and interest could provide more of an explanation. In the past, Pakistan's landed wealthy certainly had no interest in educating the masses and there was a large, educationally backward peasantry. Nor did religious figures see mass public education as beneficial; they could cater to the (then) tiny demand for religious scholars in the few madaris that produced the Ulema.[21] These were not highly regarded in terms of the quality of mathematics, science, or other subjects that might have been taught—except possibly for Arabic and Quranic studies (where Pakistan lagged behind the great seminaries of Iran and Egypt).

Pakistan's business community saw no need for an educated workforce that could adapt to changing production requirements since the companies had no such vision for themselves. In any case, an educated workforce would be more aware of its rights, raising problems of labor management. The army, of course, had its requirements taken care of by the Army Education Corps. For the politicians, many of them from a feudal background, mass education was a low priority compared with issues such as access to water, agricultural prices, ethnolinguistic demands, and in recent years, sectarian conflict. However, all these views were not peculiar to Pakistan; its literacy rate is low, but in the region so is that of India and Bangladesh; only Sri Lanka (and pockets of India) has achieved very high literacy (higher than 90 percent). Have these basic attitudes changed, and if not, can a reform-minded minister, backed by the present civilian-military combine, significantly improve Pakistan's educational structure?

They do have something to work with. There are, as noted, a few excellent private schools, and even some universities, and specialized institutions, although the Pakistan economy has trouble absorbing their products. There is also a vast military educational system run by the Army Education Corps. This is closed to the public but available to the children of officers and jawans. The AEC could theoretically form the core of an expanded Pakistan government initiative to improve primary and secondary education throughout the country.

A number of impressive community schemes, some run by NGOs, are also delivering high-quality education to a small clientele, especially in the cities. One is the Orangi Pilot Project (OPP), founded in April 1980 and based upon a model developed in the 1950s and applied to East Pakistan.[22] OPP operates in Karachi's largest *katchi abadi*, or urban slum, and addresses a large number of residents' needs, including water, sewage, health, family planning, and education. It is based on community participation and engagement, provides a large private sector in education, and has a high percentage of girls and women as students and teachers. In

Orangi, and in a few other places, the "virtuous" cycle of more educated girls producing more female teachers, which in turn leads to more schools, coeducation, and higher female literacy, has taken hold with collateral benefits for family planning and population control. Sindh and Baluchistan have significant NGO efforts under way to provide primary education, often with substantial international assistance, but these are the exception. More common is the vicious circle: few educated girls, few female teachers, fewer schools, no coeducation, and high female illiteracy.

With regard to the content of education, in the past three years the Musharraf government has announced a number of new programs, and it claims to be reexamining the contribution of such essentially peripheral subjects as Pakistan studies, a rigid and unimaginative rehash of the state's "official" version of Pakistan history, with stereotypes of the rest of the world thrown in for good measure.

The textbooks in the schools have been no better. As one distinguished Pakistani professor, Tariq Rahman, pointed out, the texts violate Jinnah's statement that the Pakistan state would not distinguish between citizens on the basis of their religion or sect. "The textbooks," Rahman says, "cannot mention Hindus without calling them 'cunning,' 'scheming,' 'deceptive,' or something equally insulting." The texts distort history badly, leaving the impression that Pakistan is co-terminus with the Islamic conquest of the subcontinent, ignoring Gandharan, Harappan, and other early civilizations, including Hindu and Buddhist empires that dominated the region before the Muslims came, except to put the Hindu predecessors in a negative, sometimes racist light.[23] Little had been done previously to review these texts, but in 2002 Pakistan undertook a major reform of textbook policy when Federal Education Minister Zubaida Jalal announced that history books from class six onward would be revised and would include fresh and more accurate accounts of the 1965 and 1971 wars.[24] In a refreshing departure from past government euphemisms and evasions, she was quoted as saying that "If we don't tell them the truth . . . and they find it out themselves, they would feel betrayed. They will accuse us, and even their parents, of telling them a lie."[25]

The Universities: Failing Grades

Pakistan's public universities and colleges, once quite promising, have fallen into such an abject state that some reputable scholars claim they are beyond redemption in their present form and should be transformed or abolished. Even numerically their output is minimal. Pakistan now has just over 100,000 students in tertiary institutions.[26] In contrast, Iran, with half of Pakistan's population, has over 700,000 students enrolled at this level, Bangladesh has approximately 878,537, Turkey 1,607,388, and India 9,404,460.[27]

The state of graduate programs throughout Pakistan has been described as decrepit. Faculties consist of bad teachers incapable of doing original research, science departments stake their reputation on plagiarized publications, and students gain entry with forged credentials. At one important Pakistani university, Islamabad's Quaid-i-Azam, eighteen of thirty graduate students admitted to the Pakistan Studies Department that they had counterfeit degrees.

This is not the worst case: some universities have long since become breeding grounds for political radicalism and violence, and peace is maintained on several major campuses only by the permanent posting of paramilitary forces. A few universities have military checkpoints, welcomed by students and faculty alike, in preference to the firefights formerly waged between student factions armed with automatic weapons. Pakistan's once-finest institution of higher learning, Punjab University, has long since become a training ground for the Jama'at-i-Islami, and its student group, the IJT, regularly terrorizes the campus, battling other groups (and sometimes the police), intimidating women, and turning the campus into a killing field complete with pistols, bombs, and AK-47s. (A number of senior JI leaders, including the amir, Qazi Hussein Ahmed, rose to power in the party exactly this way.)

At Karachi University, jawans practice their military drill on campus in the early mornings; then the officers take advantage of the posting by attending classes. In 2003, after three years of military rule, several of Karachi's universities and colleges were disrupted once again by pitched battles between the student wing of the Muttahida Quami Movement (MQM, then in power in Sindh province) and the Jama'at-i-Islami (then in control of Karachi's municipal government). Student unrest—usually fomented by the parties—continues even though several important universities have acquired retired generals as their vice chancellors. Rarely academically qualified, their concern has been to maintain law and order and beautify the campuses; while they have succeeded in the latter, they have failed in the former.

One notable development in recent years, in large part a response to the chronic violence on the government's own university campuses, has been the introduction of private institutions of higher education, particularly in the 1990s. Some, such as the Lahore University of Management Sciences (LUMS), are models of their type, with highly motivated students and faculty drawn from excellent Western institutions.[28] The same can be said of a few medical schools, notably the world-class Aga Khan University Hospital in Karachi, and technology universities such as the Ghulam Ishaq Institute of Engineering Sciences and Technology in the NWFP and the University of Engineering and Technology at Lahore. These draw a number of students from the Gulf and have little trouble placing their graduates with major companies, in good government posts, or institutions abroad for further education in the West. However, the output of these institutions cannot be dramatically increased since they charge very high tuition by Pakistani standards—and in any case the primary and secondary school systems do not produce enough adequately trained applicants for these elite institutions. Another problem is the lack of qualified faculty in the country. Government College Lahore, one of the subcontinent's premiere institutions, was deemed to be a university by the government, but despite its reputation, high-quality students, and prime location, it is short of qualified faculty to teach new graduate and postgraduate courses.

Pakistan does produce a few very good students, and under a 1980s scheme of the Ministry of Science and Technology, they were to be sent to foreign countries for Ph.D. degrees in various scientific and technical fields. Many of the nominees were already junior staff at various universities, but even they could not gain admission to second- and third-tier Western schools. Of the 171 selected for the United States, only 21 got their degrees, and only 7 of these finished in four years. The scheme was canceled.[29]

One prescription for the poor quality of higher education suggested a reduction in the number of universities and the consolidation of Pakistan's scarce educational resources into a few centers of excellence.[30] It also proposed a contract system for faculty members, and standardized admission tests (not degrees and grades, which can be forged and bought) for student selection. These recommendations were implemented in Punjab for medical schools while Shahbaz Sharif was chief minister, but not elsewhere. For political reasons, in a democracy (or even a quasi democracy such as Pakistan), academic institutions need to be widely distributed throughout the country. Further, any dramatic reform will be resisted by the entrenched teachers' unions as well as by the many unqualified aspirants to a place at a university.

The Musharraf government's scheme to rescue higher education concentrates on the production of 1,200 to 1,500 Ph.D.'s a year beginning in 2009. Announced in April 2003 by Attaur Rahman, chairman of the Higher Education Commission (a body separate from the Ministry of Education and accountable to the prime minister), it includes schemes to upgrade existing faculty. It will also send students out to a number of countries, including China, Germany, and Austria, and has provisions for recruiting qualified overseas Pakistanis to staff Pakistan's public and private universities and colleges. This scheme is in keeping with the technocratic vision of the military and bureaucracy and is viewed skeptically by some of Pakistan's leading educators and scientists as being overambitious and naive.[31]

The military services and some civilian institutions are forging ahead with their own tethered institutions, almost all of them technical in nature. The navy has founded Bahria University in Islamabad, the air force's Shaheen Foundation subsidizes the Air University, the Fauji Foundation the Foundation University, and the Pakistan Ordnance Factory has its own school. These are by and large subsidized institutions for service personnel and their dependents and fit the profile of an apolitical and technocratic educational system favored by the armed forces. None are in the first rank.

With the emphasis on scientific education, the liberal arts and humanities remain abysmally weak, and the generation of professors trained in the 1960s is not being replaced. Anecdotal reports indicate that the quality of basic university education is in steep decline, and that Pakistan is losing its cadre of teachers of literature, English, and the social sciences—the talents that set it apart from many other Muslim countries.[32]

A few Pakistani educators and businessmen are acutely aware that their country has let slip a golden opportunity, but key members of the elite, especially in the bureaucracy and army, let alone the conservative

Islamic parties, still regard public education at the elite or mass level as irrelevant or threatening. When, for example, a visitor to one of Pakistan's most important military training academies remarked that if only the facilities, dedication of the staff, and resources devoted to its students were available to Pakistan's university and college students, the angry reply was that "they would only waste it" and that the money was best spent on training the people who really made a difference to Pakistan, its soldiers and officers.[33]

Reform?

Can a few positive developments balance the historical trend in Pakistani education? It remains to be seen whether significant new resources devoted to education will make any difference without fundamental reforms in the entire educational structure itself. The most important scheme could be an investment in primary, secondary, and higher education under the rubric of Education Sector Reform Assistance (ESRA), which received significant American assistance.[34] This covers a small number of Pakistan's districts, primarily those located in Sindh and Baluchistan, and attempts to build administrative competence and public-private partnership.

In the case of educational reform, however, a skeptical attitude is warranted because of past performance, the limited technocratic vision of the senior leadership, a disdain for academic freedom and scholars, the absence of strong social pressures for better education from Pakistan's citizenry, and above all, a still-miniscule state budget for education. Foreign assistance for education makes up 76 percent of the government's educational expenditure, and Pakistan still ranks among the fifteen worst countries as far as education is concerned.[35]

The elite will manage for itself with a few choice institutions available to the wealthy and foreign education as an option. As for the ambitious lower-middle classes, the military schools and the burgeoning paramilitary forces and police provide an education and a career path:

> Instead of teaching people the skills they need for survival and success in their own fields of life or making them less fatalistic and superstitious, all that has been done is to equip them with substandard degrees after which they want middle-class jobs in the cities. . . . The state's agenda, which it carries out through history,

Pakistan Studies, and Language textbooks, is to create a nationalist Pakistani who will oppose ethnic identity and support militarism. The religious lobby has its own agenda of creating a theocracy and its madrassas operate with that in mind. The Westernized elite study the syllabi of the West in English so as to look down upon Pakistanis or leave this country forever.[36]

It is evident that Pakistanis crave education for their children—the streets of every major city are plastered with advertisements (often in English) for schools, technical training, and advanced study. There are also many trenchant and wise suggestions concerning education and reform.[37] However, close examination reveals that few of these schools provide a quality education, and many are simply money-making schemes. The military and other public institutions have long maintained separate school systems for their children, the wealthy can afford the few high-quality private schools, and the poor, if they are lucky, can get their children into a madrassah or a badly run government school. Pakistan's educational system is broken, perhaps beyond repair, and there appears to be little inclination (let alone the resources) to fix it.

Economic Prospects

Pakistan's much-studied economy is one of great contrasts. Until recently it could not manufacture a crankshaft. It has one antiquated and inefficient steel plant, and no chemical or plastics industry to speak of, but it fabricates nuclear weapons and missiles. On average, the economy has grown at a rate of 6 percent a year since 1950, a spectacular record. The Karachi Stock Exchange outperformed all other stock markets in Asia in 2001–03. Yet the country was so indebted that the Musharraf government had no choice but to cave in to every American demand regarding the war on terrorism lest Washington cut off donor aid and debt relief.[38] While the economy has done well recently in macro terms, with growth likely to again exceed 6 percent in 2004, Pakistan lacks any significant manufacturing capacity, is low on the list of states that can add value to goods—with the sole exception of its textile industry—and agriculture, its most important sector, is far behind exactly comparable regions in India.[39] Pakistan is also an energy-deficit state—its major import is petroleum. This burden could be lightened if it were to sell India some of its own unused gas and allow transshipment of gas and oil from Central Asia and Iran, but strained India-Pakistan relations (and American reluctance to include Iran in any pipeline scheme) have stymied such plans.

A number of factors have contributed to the mixed state of Pakistan's economy, including the lingering effects of Bhutto's nationalization of the 1970s, Zia's piling up of domestic debt in the 1980s, and a decade of widespread corruption and irresponsible spending in the decade of democracy through the 1990s. In addition, defense spending has always been high—although it has leveled off in the past few years as Pakistan was forced to comply with terms laid down by the International Monetary Fund (IMF) and other lenders. Pakistan's defense expenditure in 2003 stood at 54.5 percent of the budget, while developmental expenditures were around 35.5 percent.[40] Furthermore, there is a large unofficial economy, estimated to be 50 to 100 percent of the size of the regular economy; this makes it hard for the government to collect taxes and places a greater strain on civil servants and others who receive regular, documented salaries. Finally, the Pakistan economy is dependent on foreign capital.[41] The two most dramatic spurts in economic growth, during the Ayub and Zia years, were accompanied by high levels of aid from the United States, military grants from China, and subsidies from Saudi Arabia, augmented in the past twenty-five years by remittances sent home by 3 million Pakistani migrant workers in the Gulf. Foreign financial assistance to Pakistan once had a high ratio of grant to loan, nearly 80 percent in the first Five-Year Plan, but this dropped below 9 percent by 1998.[42]

Economic Reform: Past Efforts

The stabilization and rebuilding effort now underway goes back to the Zia years. One of Zia's first acts in office was to end state control over small firms (but not the bigger ones), ordering a series of deregulatory steps in an attempt to improve the investment climate in the country. Zia—or rather his financial adviser, Ghulam Ishaq Khan, who was to succeed him as president—removed price controls, cut and eliminated export duties, floated the exchange rate, rationalized tariffs, and encouraged investments and technology transfers. In 1984 a new industrial policy consolidated the gains of the post-Bhutto period, and by the mid- to late 1980s, the investment climate in Pakistan had improved. Even Zia, however, avoided land reform, failed to encourage investment in new advanced technology sectors, and left Pakistan's educational and technical infrastructure to stagnate.

Through the decade the economy grew at an average rate of 6.7 percent a year. Combined with the massive infusion of capital from foreign aid and remittances, investment activity picked up after it became clear that the Zia regime was indeed stable. The recovery of the 1980s was further energized by the economic reforms that were the brainchild of a noted economist, Mahbub ul-Haq.

Appointed finance minister in 1985 by Mohammed Khan Junejo, Mahbub ul-Haq had earlier been a planner and had worked at the World Bank.[43] He produced a program for the liberalization, privatization, deregulation, and globalization of the economy. He called for the collection of revenues through taxation, a chronic problem that had hobbled Pakistan's effort to generate economic growth from within the country. His revolutionary policies precipitated protest from many entrenched sectors: the bureaucracy, the landowners, and the business class all felt threatened by the reforms.

The protests led to Haq's removal as finance minister in January 1986, after less than a year in office. Despite his removal, the reform agenda remained. The multilateral agencies and the donor community held on to some of the key elements of the reform program even as their influence grew with the mounting fiscal, budget, and current account deficit.

As in the 1960s, the growth of the 1980s masked many problems. According to one Japanese study, Pakistan's high economic growth during the Zia years was "a house of cards built precariously upon external assistance" and workers' remittances.[44] Mahbub ul-Haq declared that Pakistan was "bankrupt" as fiscal deficits reached 7 to 8 percent of GDP every year, and overall debt, including domestic and external debt, increased to around 80 percent of GDP, while defense expenditure rose annually by 9.2 percent, with public spending on social development a mere 3.2 percent a year.[45]

Mahbub ul-Haq returned as finance minister in a caretaker government in May 1988. This time he launched an overhaul of the country's revenue system. Haq proposed to extend tax collection to sections of society that were not paying any taxes, especially the small traders, and he threatened evaders with tough punishment. He also declared that borrowers would have to repay their loans to state-owned banks on the penalty of foreclosure and imprisonment. This time Haq's policies were met with protests on the street. Factories and shops were shut, traders raised a hue and cry, and a political crisis erupted. Since then most elected governments have been wary of significant economic reform.

Zia's death in 1988 opened the door to democratization and more reform policies, which again were ignored. The decade of democratization turned into a period of ballooning debt. Following the withdrawal of the Soviet Union from Afghanistan, American aid to Pakistan was cut off after ten years of lavish support—it had amounted to nearly $6 billion in military and economic assistance, plus some concessional loans. The aid cuts coincided with reduced remittances from expatriates, the result of the recession in the Gulf in the late 1980s and the 1991 Gulf war. Though economic growth continued in the early years of the post-Zia democratic order, Benazir's shaky position in relation to Pakistan's Establishment meant that she could not raise tax revenues, leaving education and health care to suffer. The government's continuing inability to raise revenues would have serious effects on social investments in education and health care: eventually the gap would be filled by Islamic charities, many of them supported by the Saudis.

Nawaz Sharif's first government brought more dramatic changes in economic policy. He took Mahbub-ul Haq's reform program of liberalization, privatization, deregulation, and globalization seriously. Nawaz established a Privatization Commission to identify 100 state-owned enterprises that would be sold. He moved to privatize the Muslim Commercial Bank, one of the largest banks in the country. Nawaz also allowed some foreign exchange convertibility and moved to facilitate the transportation of goods and people. He announced a plan to build an expressway between Islamabad and Peshawar and introduced populist measures to alleviate urban unemployment, such as the Yellow Cab scheme allowing the duty-free import of cars. However, he too faced the wrath of the Establishment, which was by then heavily invested in the public sector. Nawaz was also accused of corruption in the privatization process. The military was particularly upset because its foundations were required to face private sector competition on a more level playing field.

In mid-1993, the ninety-day caretaker government of Moeen Qureshi, another former World Bank official, was finally able to implement the revenue augmentation policies required by the IMF, thereby averting economic collapse. Qureshi raised taxes, made the central bank autonomous, introduced an agricultural tax, and announced a tough regime for recovering debt. These measures were effective; but they also stirred opposition from entrenched sectors and raised the broader question of why elected democratic governments cannot carry out such reforms, which only seemed to be possible under conditions of benevolent autocracy in Pakistan.

Upon her return to power, Benazir tried to continue Nawaz's policy of privatization and signed a number of memoranda for foreign investment. But the charges of corruption only increased, notably with regard to the sale of twenty-eight state-owned companies between 1993 and 1995. Benazir's husband, Asif Zardari, previously known as Mr. Five Percent, acquired the nickname Mr. Ten Percent for the commission he reportedly asked for in return for government approval of industrial projects. Benazir imperiously dismissed such charges as "motivated by my enemies" and failed to take steps—such as appointing an independent observer to assess the detailed charges of corruption—that might have cleared the air. More critically, her government could not meet the financial targets set by the IMF for continued support, thus strengthening Pakistan's reputation as a "one-tranch country"—meaning one that often received the first payment, or tranch, in a loan, but could not meet the conditions for further installments. The multilateral agency withdrew, and Benazir in turn announced a year-long moratorium on further economic reforms, fearing they would cost her public support. In the end, however, she was forced to return to the IMF in much worse shape than before, and Pakistan's credit rating plummeted, increasing interest costs and making it more difficult to borrow money. Finally, in 1996, Benazir was dismissed again.

When Nawaz returned to office in 1997, he inherited an economically ungovernable country. The tit-for-tat nuclear tests in India and Pakistan in 1998 brought further economic sanctions from the United States, Japan, and other major donors. Nawaz's efforts for a strategic breakthrough with India failed; this might have undercut the army's dominant position, led to reduced military expenditure, and trimmed the deficits that plagued the economy. But the military resumed power in 1999, and Pakistan's economic problems again landed in the generals' laps. They inherited a state in which GDP growth had plummeted from 10 percent in 1980 to 3.6 percent in 1999.[46] It was a state in debt, most of it accumulated during Zia's last years and the subsequent decade of democracy:

over this period Pakistan's total debt had grown from $15 billion in 1986 to almost $34 billion in 1999.

Musharraf the Economist

In both public appearances and private conversations, President Musharraf likes to remind his listeners that he has made economic reform his number-one domestic priority, and that he has become something of an expert through his intense involvement in economic policymaking. One of his first decisions following the 1999 coup was to appoint Shaukat Aziz, a former Citibank executive, to be his financial adviser, and later his minister of finance, and in June 2004 his prime minister. Aziz and Musharraf introduced major economic reforms, including a much-opposed sales tax that resulted in an $800 million increase in tax collection in the fiscal year 2000–01, mostly from import duties. As part of these reforms, Pakistan's patronage-based industries came under serious threat and privatization was much discussed.

In 1998 economic growth had collapsed to 2.6 percent, barely enough to sustain the increase in population, but by 2000 it was back up to 4.3 percent, propelled by bumper crops of cotton and wheat. Despite growing energy costs, inflation dropped from 6 percent in 1998 to 3 percent in 2001. The budget deficit also declined, from 6 percent in 1999 to 5.2 percent in 2001.

In 2001, however, Pakistan's growth slowed to 2.6 percent and the deficit stood at $1.2 billion, made worse by $1.6 billion in interest payments. Despite the reforms, tax revenues that year were still less than 13 percent of GDP, as they had been in 1998, with less than 1.5 percent of the population filing tax returns of any kind. Furthermore, total external debt was still almost $32 billion, while foreign direct investment had fallen from $511 million in 1999 to $352 million in 2001. (In 2002, however, it more than doubled to $795 million, with most of the inflow presumably coming from resident Pakistanis moving funds from their overseas holdings.) A comparison of foreign direct investment (FDI) shows Pakistan's weak position despite its recent gains (table 7-3).

Aziz provided steady and consistent leadership that helped weather the fiscal slump in 2001, working around the economy's fundamental structural problems. Indirectly, the global war on terror also proved an economic boon for Pakistan as the United States, Japan, and international

Table 7-3. *Comparative Net Foreign Direct Investment*
Millions of U.S. dollars

Country	1990	2001	2002
Pakistan	243.3	352	795
China	2,656.9	3,7356.9	4,6789.5
India	237	3,636.8	2,577.3
Bangladesh	3.2	78.5	45.6
Indonesia	1092.9	–3,278	145
Turkey	700	2,768	861
Iran	–362	33	n.a.

Source: World Bank, *World Development Indicators (CDR)*, 2003, April 22, 2004.
n.a. Not available

financial institutions came to the rescue with new loans, debt relief, and in the case of Saudi Arabia, more than $600 million in oil concessions. Reserves in 2002 stood at $4.3 billion, almost four months of imports, up from $908 million in 2000, which was about one month of imports. Remittances also registered a huge growth—reaching $3.5 billion by 2002, which was more than twice the previous year—as overseas Pakistanis feared that their assets might be impounded by Washington and other Western governments. The turnaround in its foreign exchange keeps the Pakistan economy afloat even today, though the unofficial economy, healthier than ever, is doing its part as well.

Pakistan officials are justifiably pleased that their country is no longer seen as a state that could not consistently meet IMF and other international obligations.[47] Pakistan's growth hit 5.8 percent in 2002, it may be 6 percent in 2003–04, the country has one year's worth of foreign exchange reserves (about $10 billion), and the fiscal deficit has dropped from 6 to 4 percent of GDP. FDI hit $1 billion, although very little of this was American. Just as important, Finance Ministry officials claim a 15 percent increase in tax revenue due to new methods of taxation and increased efficiency. They also abolished the old assessment system, which was both costly to administer and susceptible to bribery. Since Pakistani industries did not develop behind a high tariff wall, as did India's, Pakistan has relatively low tariffs and may find it easier to meet World Trade Organization and other requirements.

Further heartening news is that the 2003 Transparency International Report charts upward movement as far as perceptions of corruption are concerned. Pakistan was ranked 93 in the world, below India (83), Iran (78), Egypt (70), and China (66), but ahead of all of the Central Asian republics, Indonesia (122), and the lowest-ranking state, Bangladesh (133).[48]

Defense spending continues to be a major factor in the economy. In 2002, $2.5 billion was budgeted for defense expenditure (actual spending was actually 9 percent higher than budgeted owing to a major crisis with India), and in 2003 it increased to $2.8 billion. Of the peer countries, Pakistan remained in the same bracket as those with a high defense burden, with about 3.9 percent of GDP going to defense expenditure. By comparison, India spent more than five times the amount but less than Pakistan as a percentage of GDP (2.7 percent). Indonesia spent 3.7 percent of GDP on defense, Turkey 5.1 percent, Bangladesh 1.4 percent, and Iran 4.6 percent.

The changes instituted by Musharraf, Aziz, and the Central Bank of Pakistan, along with those imposed by international financial institutions, have stopped the bleeding. The country's fiscal and monetary policies are skillfully managed, given the obvious constraints. Pakistan has met conditions attached to the IMF's $3 billion poverty reduction and growth facility, and to those imposed by the Asian Development Bank and World Bank. These conditions stress increasing tax revenue and privatization and improving Pakistan's social infrastructure. However, the lenders are still not satisfied with Pakistan's progress in reforming the vital power sector and spending on social services.[49]

Pakistan, like Iran, is also experimenting with new economic strategies and structures. One of these is "Islamic banking." The primary principle of Islamic banking is the prohibition of *Riba* (usury), which is believed to "be a means of exploitation of the masses."[50] The State Bank of Pakistan has sanctioned (and will supervise) one bank, owned by the NWFP, to allow one of its branches to convert to Islamic banking. At this stage, though, the process should be regarded more as a political gesture to the Islamists than as a transformation of banking procedures in Pakistan.

Despite the attempts at reform, problems remain:

—Pakistan has trouble persuading the public that short-term sacrifices may bring long-term gains. The reputation of politicians, bureaucrats, and increasingly the military for corruption is such that tax evasion and cheating are universal, and an attitude of cynicism pervades all discussion

---

Box 7-1. *Islamic Banking*

Islamic banking requires lenders to be more socially conscious and considerate of larger values than mere profit; disclosure standards are stringent, and Islamic banks are required to invest in identifiable and acceptable productive activities. Since the bank and its client share in losses and reputational risk, Islamic banks are theoretically more vigilant. Islamic banking began in Dubai and Jordan, and there were attempts to introduce it in Pakistan in the 1950s. In 1981, under Zia's Islamization program, all domestic commercial banks were permitted to accept deposits on the basis of profit-and-loss sharing (PLS). In 1985 new steps were introduced to formally transform the banking system to one not based on *Riba*. From 1985 no banks could accept any interest-bearing deposits, and all existing deposits became subject to PLS rules, although some operations were still allowed to continue on the old basis. Pakistan has maintained parallel banking systems, although the government formally remains committed to abolishing *Riba*. The government recently took a policy decision that will allow both conventional and Islamic bank systems to operate, with the choice left up to the consumer. The Islamic banks will license and regulate themselves, and the system is to be supervised by a *Shariat* board consisting of scholars, economists, accountants, and bankers.

---

of economic policy. The public economic debate is constricted—with the Islamists pushing a neopopulism and the remnants of the Bhutto regime criticizing from the old left. Pakistan's business community is still weak and of course always takes second place to the military.

—Oil imports make up one-quarter of Pakistan's total import bill, although this is softened by a subvention from Saudi Arabia.

—Consumer price inflation is expected to slip past 5 percent, which compares unfavorably to an all-Asian figure of less than 3 percent.[51]

On the other hand,

—Investments in Pakistan have grown in the past few years, especially from Europe and the Gulf, and the total may exceed $1 billion, with half of it directed to the financial business and oil sectors.[52]

—Privatization is moving ahead, with the prospective sale of the state oil company (the Habib) and Allied banks, two major gas companies, the Karachi Electric Supply Company, and Pakistan Steel, but not military and defense-related companies.

Despite its recent performance, Pakistan's economic recovery remains uncertain. Finance officials freely admit that there is "a long way to go." Although they dispute claims that poverty has increased in Pakistan, they acknowledge the weak system of data gathering and the long tradition of deceptive reporting. However, Pakistan has subscribed to various World Bank schemes for accurate data collection, and at the top, at least, there is a commitment to sustained and sober economic and fiscal management.[53]

President Musharraf's economic team freely acknowledges the errors of past policies. The president of the State Bank of Pakistan, Ishrat Husain, laid them out systematically before a conference on Islamizing the Pakistan economy in 2004.[54] He contrasted "what might have been" had Pakistan's economy been properly guided, its educational system well-funded, and human development attended to: with 100 percent literacy, Pakistan's per capita income would have doubled to $1,000; with technical skills of the labor force up to that of East Asia, Pakistan's exports would have been $100 billion instead of "a paltry" $12 billion; and with lower population growth, down to 2 or 3 percent, say, Pakistan's infrastructure would have been able to sustain higher health and educational levels.

What Husain did not mention was Pakistan's extraordinarily high defense burden and the distortion of Pakistani politics, social values, and the economy by the army's routine intervention. In short, what the Establishment fails to ask is *why* things went wrong for so many years. Ishrat and the rest of the Establishment find it easier to blame others for Pakistan's poor reputation than to address the central feature of the state for forty years: a military establishment that wants the facade but not the substance of a democracy. This inevitably puts some of Pakistan's finest civilians in a terrible position: to keep their position and to maintain "the system," they must defend what most know personally is indefensible.

This inherent flaw in the political system—the attempt to combine military rule with democracy—has extended to the economy. This cannot be sidestepped by appealing to things like Islamist principles—although these may be meritorious in their own right. The net effect on both growth and equitable distribution of this flawed system has been deleterious. Pakistan's economy continues to be at the service of the military, and quasi-military organizations have become an increasing factor in the economy. However, generals are not usually good financial managers, even if Pakistan is regarded as a less corrupt country—at least at the higher levels—than five years ago.

Structural Problems

Pakistan's economic difficulties stem in large part from a structure that is increasingly ill-suited to the modern world. Besides a very high defense burden, an unbalanced *land policy* remains at the core of Pakistan's social structure and influences its economic policy. The phenomenon of large landholders has had many detrimental consequences for Pakistan, not least of which has been the abysmal level of schooling provided to rural families, many of which are landless or tenant farmers. The slow pace of land reform and the lack of rural development have pushed more and more people into the cities in search of employment.

There have been three major attempts at land reform in the past, with a fourth now under way. The first, in 1959, focused on the abolition of revenue-free estates (the Jagirs), gave security to tenants, and imposed an ownership ceiling of 500 acres for irrigated land and 20,000 acres for unirrigated land. A second reform in 1972 reduced the size of holdings by 70 percent, and a third reform in 1977 lowered the ceiling on ownership to two-thirds of the 1972 levels. These reforms had a marked impact: one noted Sindhi feudal family, the Jatois, saw their original holdings shrink from 120,000 acres of prime farmland to 75,000 and then 30,000. However, this still makes the family the dominant economic and political force in an area northeast of Karachi, where they preside over hundreds of lesser landlords and maintain a private army of 1,200 "loyalists."[55]

Thus these reforms must be viewed with caution. Pakistan's weakened and corrupt bureaucracy will stymie land reform as there are innumerable ways to get around land ceilings. Furthermore, enforcement is often nonexistent as the politically powerful landowners can arrange for the transfer or punishment of offending officials (if bribery did not work).

More recently, a fourth round of reform, involving a constitutional amendment, is designed to *raise* the limits to thousands of acres to enable multinational corporations to invest in Pakistan's rural sector. Corporate farming will be new to Pakistan and could bring much-needed capital to the countryside, but it may also send even more people to the cities in search of jobs.

Besides land policy, another obstacle has been Pakistan's poor export performance. Efforts to increase *exports* have not taken off, with minor exceptions in the sporting goods, surgical instruments (manufactured in a factory started by American missionaries), and textiles sectors.

Box 7-2. *The Textile Industry*

Pakistan's export growth is based on textiles.* Pakistan's textile industry represents 46 percent of total manufacturing and provides 68 percent of Pakistan's export receipts. Four of Pakistan's five major exports are textile based, for an aggregate of about $5 billion. The fifth—rice—accounts for only $448 million. A few years ago there was some concern that Pakistan's textile industry might be overwhelmed by cheap Chinese goods once the Multi-Fiber Agreement on textiles expired in 2005, but a modernization program that poured billions of dollars into the industry eased these fears. Textile exports surged by 24 percent in 2003–04, owing to a more efficient sector; increased quotas agreed to by the United States, the European Union, and Turkey; and possibly because improved recordkeeping began including underinvoiced exports. The hope is that Pakistan's textiles will be competitive in American and other markets when quotas are eliminated.

*For background, see the Indian website BharatTextile.com at www.bharattextile. com/newsitems/1983268.

Unlike India, whose growth has partly been driven by exports of software and the products of it auto-parts industry (the largest in the world), Pakistan has no highly desirable product or service to spur its growth and inspire confidence that the country is a leader in some critical sector. Textiles, while a steady source of income, are a low-technology export, and Pakistan has been slow to become an innovator in the industry. Furthermore, with the widespread lack of education at all levels, it is unlikely that Pakistan will on its own become a powerhouse services provider in the global economy in the short to the medium term. Social policies, which tend to exclude women from public and economic life and which have downgraded education for many years, also restrict the range of economic opportunities open to Pakistan, and make a large percentage of the population unqualified to participate in a modern economy. Political conditions that restrict cooperation with India are also detrimental to Pakistan's economic growth.

A third structural flaw lies in the area of actual *tax collection,* which is believed to be almost half of what is held to be due. Much of the economy remains outside the government's reach, which gives the unofficial economy vigor but seriously hampers the government's ability to deliver services. Though Pakistan's official economy continually worsened through the 1990s, the unofficial economy showed much greater resiliency. The denationalization and the deregulation had led to charges of corruption, but they also opened the economy to entrepreneurial spirit. Whereas Pakistan's official per capita income is about $500, the unofficial economy is believed to be three times larger. Including the unofficial economy—though how that can be done is itself problematic—could take the figure of per capita income as high as $1,700.

Since Pakistan's official economy is unable to tap into this wealth that does exist in the country but is beyond its reach, revenue shortages and the balance of payments position remain a problem. Historically, foreign aid filled in on both these accounts, but when the aid pipeline dried up, the government found itself less and less able to govern.

As one observer notes, "while the establishment refused to cut huge government expenditures for defense or the civilian bureaucracy, the urban middle class, traders and industrialists avoided taxes by privately lobbying the government through a process of *sifaarish* (connections) to exempt them from the provision of tax laws, by hiding income and by publicly resisting any attempts to levy new taxes." [56] Many felt little obligation to pay taxes to a government that provided few services, especially when the government itself failed to tax the rural elite—part of its own support base. Moreover, any attempt by the government to raise taxes "resulted in protests, demonstration and strikes. In the absence of effective government, the urban middle class sought its own solutions through private rather than collective action. They created private educational facilities, private health care institutions and private protection forces. As Pakistanis withdrew into their own Leviathan, however, the society became increasingly fragmented on the basis of ethnic, sectarian and regional differences." [57]

The government's continued inability to raise the revenue to support the military and maintain high economic growth through investments in material and social infrastructure has been a major problem. Quite apart from the disrepair in the physical infrastructure, the government has had to curtail expenditure on education, health care, and even the police. This has created a vacuum that private interest groups such as Islamic radicals have entered to provide security and education, two of the most critical areas for long-term investment in any nation.

Perhaps most disturbing, the direct and the indirect hand of the military has had a deleterious impact on Pakistan's economy, with no sign of change. Not only have Pakistan's recent military leaders not understood economics—although a few have understood that they had an economic problem—the armed forces themselves have become entangled in the economy in a way that will be harmful to both economic growth and their professionalism.

While Pakistan has launched a program of privatization and divestment of inefficient state enterprises, it has expanded the economic role of the state in some sectors through the back door of quasi-public foundations and businesses linked to the military. The largest of these, the Fauji Foundation, was capitalized at the end of World War II with money set aside for demobilized soldiers, its purpose being to ease the transition of retired military personnel to civilian life.[58] Since then, the rise of military-business foundations has been nothing but spectacular. The Fauji Foundation's assets increased from Rs 152 million in 1970 to Rs 2.06 billion in 1982 and Rs 9.8 billion in 2000—and it is now one of the largest business conglomerates in the country.[59] It employs 45,000 former servicemen and between 6,000 and 7,000 active soldiers.

Three other service-specific foundations account for revenues of Rs 18 billion. These engage in activities ranging from the purely commercial to supplying the armed forces with goods and services. The Bahria Foundation, for instance, set up Pakistan's biggest paint factory in the hope that it would be able to supply the navy, its sponsor, with all its paint needs. Similarly, the air force's Shaheen Foundation runs Pakistan's biggest airport services, an airline, and after the Pressler Amendment cut off spare parts for Pakistan's F-16 fighters, it financed an aviation spare parts trading company.[60] The army's National Logistics Cell was established in the 1980s in response to a need to transport wheat during a food shortage; it was subsequently a prime mover in the provision of weapons and supplies to the mujahiddin in Afghanistan, but it is now Pakistan's largest freight company, competing with the state railways and private trucking companies.

These military-run businesses expanded not because they were profitable, but because they received government subsidies and preferential contracts. Pakistan's defense budget paid for part of their running expenses, especially the salaries of the serving officers and utilities, and the foundations flourished. There is some doubt about whether they even lived up to their initial objective of providing employment for retiring servicemen, but they certainly provide retired officers with the opportunity to supplement their pensions—and for the senior officers the chance to continue to receive perquisites such as housing and a car. However, they offer few opportunities for the junior and noncommissioned officers, who normally return to their villages upon retirement.

In several cases, these military-owned facilities have been the site of clashes between the services and those who earn their living from them, the most sensational being a year-long siege of the Okara Military Farm in Punjab. Farm tenants protested what they regarded as exploitive behavior, leading to paramilitary and army intervention and several deaths, witnessed by a number of journalists and other observers.[61]

Turning the Economic Corner?

As of 2004 the Pakistan economy seems to be in revival. Forecasts are generally cautiously optimistic for the next five years. One IMF official recently declared in Lahore that Pakistan may soon manage to attain 6 percent growth. However, the typical expectation is that real growth will continue at a steady but modest pace (over 5 percent), with modest inflation, a less promising agricultural future, and high import costs.[62] The forecasts remain cautious because Pakistan's economy is especially sensitive to changes in the weather, changes in foreign exchange remittances from overseas workers, and political tensions within the country and between Pakistan and India, which tend to frighten away new investment.

Despite the increase in foreign exchange holdings and a growth in exports and tax revenues, over the longer term the negatives are no less impressive. As of 2003 Pakistan's debt was still considerable—$33 billion—and this is projected to grow slowly over the next few years. Imports generally run a billion dollars or so more than exports, and the government's consolidated balance is about minus 4 percent of GDP. Pakistan's migrant workers abroad are at the bottom of the skill ladder; the expenditure on education, although increased, remains at 1.7 percent of GDP; and even that will be dependent on foreign assistance. The investment climate, for both foreign firms and Pakistanis, still remains unattractive, and situations such as those in the NWFP, where the provincial government stood by as street thugs tore down legally established signboards and harassed cinemas in the name of religious purity, only make it seem hostile. Political factors also inhibit the growth of a tourism industry in Pakistan (see box 7-3).

Thus, while Pakistan has avoided economic collapse, the future remains a question mark. The economy's best-case scenario assumes that Pakistan will remain at the center of international attention for the foreseeable future—providing the time and space for necessary structural changes and a steady flow of loans and assistance. The likelihood of either development, let alone both, is hard to predict. Pakistan's history with regard to reform is a monument to failure, but the country's Establishment had not earlier recognized the extent of the problem. The question is—does it now? By moving to a new constitutional arrangement, with the army directly involved in government policy, the country's political instability and uneven economic policies could be smoothed out—providing the army can manage the demands of the Islamists, those who want to restore full democracy, and those who advocate provincial autonomy. Further, Pakistan must continue to placate America, while avoiding provoking the Indians to the point where a war disrupts all plans for an economic reformation. Different possibilities are examined in chapter 8, and their policy implications in chapter 9, but for the moment Pakistan will be unable to move forward economically without skilled policies at home, a supportive America, and a tolerant India. The failure of any link in this chain could, at best, condemn Pakistan to stagnation or lead to one or more worst-case economic scenarios.

Constricted Opportunities

Pakistan's medium- and long-term futures will be hedged by certain demographic and economic trends:

—Pakistan's demographic future is unalterable, short of a major war, famine, or genocide. It will take an economic revolution, coupled with massive educational programs, to ensure that it does not become the world's fifth largest state by 2015.

—The population bulge, especially in the cities, is such that it will create fresh opportunities for political mobilization of the discontented and the unemployed. In the past, surplus males could go abroad or find a

Box 7-3. *Tourism*

In 2001 the United Nations suggested that Pakistan review its policy on tourism, which had the potential to bring in $500 million in foreign exchange over the next five years.* This had been a very undeveloped industry in Pakistan, compared with countries such as Turkey and Indonesia, let alone India and Sri Lanka.

Pakistan has considerable tourist potential. It has a long coastline, attractive and accessible deserts, and some of the world's highest mountains. It also has a number of Muslim, Sikh, Hindu, and Buddhist religious sites.

However, political and religious objections have stymied tourism. The Dalai Lama once expressed a desire to visit some of the Buddhist sites, but the invitation was vetoed by the government on the grounds that it might alienate the Chinese. Islamic leaders are uninterested in, even hostile to, the thought of allowing foreigners to visit non-Muslim sites.

In general, the Jama'at-i-Islami's attitude to foreigners is that those who want to visit Pakistan should adapt their lifestyle so as not to "offend" Pakistani sensibilities—which they would define themselves. Even Westernized Pakistanis find it increasingly difficult to holiday in Pakistan, where more and more hill stations and tourist sites are subjected to strict dress codes. Thus tourism has languished, and the few attempts over the years, such as overland trips to the northern areas or along the Karakoram highway, have been sharply reduced or abandoned. One of Pakistan's leading

position in the army and paramilitary forces, but will there be jobs for those without opportunity, or for those who do fill these positions and then retire, often at an early age?

—Pakistan's educational system, always marginal, is now increasingly divisive as the madaris churn out more and more poorly educated young Pakistani men. The Urdu-language schools are too few and too badly supported to keep up with the demand for education, and girls in particular do not have access to them.

—The elite missionary and private schools and the few excellent technology and management institutions serve the Establishment, and their graduates are increasingly looking abroad for their careers. This would be acceptable if they produced enough highly trained individuals to meet a growing domestic demand, and if expatriates saw their homeland as a good place to invest, but the trends are in the opposite direction.

hoteliers, the Avari chain, has long since given up trying to expand within Pakistan and has instead used its capital and trained staff to expand operations into Central Asia, the Middle East, and Africa. With hotel occupancy touching 20 percent at times, and tourism virtually nonexistent (excepting the flood of journalists who came to cover the Afghan war), Avari, run by an enterprising Parsi family, has diversified, opening a travel agency and moving into power generation.[†]

The costs to Pakistan of this decline in the tourist industry go beyond lost revenue. Pakistan is both increasingly isolated and seen as a backward-moving state by outsiders. One bright spot for tourism was the influx of several thousand Indians who came to observe the series of cricket test matches in April 2004. They were warmly greeted and filled the hotels of Lahore, Rawalpindi, and Karachi, if only for a few days. If India-Pakistan normalization proceeds, then India will be a source of tourist dollars, and the occasional visitor can be supplanted by Indian Punjabis who might use the new Lahore airport for international access.

[*]"United Nations Asks Pakistan to Revise Tourism Policy," *Dawn*, June 28, 2001.
[†]"Room for More," *Far Eastern Economic Review*, April 27, 1995.

—The economy is no longer characterized by great potential. Three squandered decades have ensured that Pakistan has fallen further behind other countries in terms of international competitiveness. Pakistan's economic performance, according to a Japanese analysis, is "shadowed by considerable uncertainty," and is highly dependent upon political and diplomatic developments.[63] The textiles sector, the one success story, will have to meet the challenge of cheap Chinese goods after 2005.

—If Pakistan's strategic importance declines and donors and international financial institutions are not as forthcoming in the future, Pakistan's approach to donors may subtly shift from one that invites growth to one that threatens failure.

With its thin natural resource base, high levels of corruption, dysfunctional bureaucracy, and political uncertainty at the best of times, Pakistan remains pretty far down the list for capital-seeking investment. However, the informal economy, a vast network of smuggling, trade, loans, and favors, thrives. If the Pakistan government could capture this sector's energy and dynamism, it might not only stimulate growth but be able to raise the revenue for vital social services, the police, education, and health and moderate the perception of its own citizens that their government is both rapacious and threatening.[64] In the meantime, Pakistan may miss some important opportunities. Though it is strategically important, its social and political indicators inhibit investment. Pakistan, alone of the South Asian states, completely fails to meet the complex criteria set forth by the U.S. Millennium Challenge Account (MCA).[65] According to a detailed study of the MCA, Pakistan fails on eleven of sixteen criteria: civil liberties, political rights, accountability, education spending, primary education completion rate, health spending, recent deficits, trade policy, regulatory quality, and the number of days it takes to start a business.[66]

Many of Pakistan's economic and social problems are, at their root, the product of a strategic elite that placed security interests ahead of economic ones.[67] In the past, not only did the military component of Pakistan's Establishment not allow democracy, it did not see that economic reform and social stability were also strategically important for Pakistan in the long run. Now that the long run is here, administrators find themselves running a country that, despite its potential, is decades behind its former peers, and very violent and corrupt. Pakistan's economy has crept forward slowly during Musharraf's spell as chief executive/president, but the gap between Pakistan and the modern world is growing, as is the distance between Pakistan and those states that it regards as peers and competitors.

CHAPTER EIGHT

PAKISTAN'S
FUTURES

Is Pakistan at a critical juncture? If so, it will not be the first time for a state that has had three wars and many minor military clashes with India, four coups, and a collapsed economy several times. Yet each time Pakistan has been declared a "failed state" it has come back from the grave—albeit with a weakened economy, a more-fragmented political order, less security in relation to its powerful neighbor, and disturbing demographic and educational trends.

Ian Talbot, the perceptive British Pakistan-watcher wrote a few years ago that "reports of Pakistan's death have been greatly exaggerated" and stressed the resilience of millions of Pakistanis living in thousands of towns and cities. [1] He suggested that analysis of Pakistan go beyond the cliché of the three "A's": Allah, the army, and America. However, it is hard to escape from the three A's with the army again in charge, America once again Pakistan's chief patron, and the Islamists governing in two provinces. Talbot's counsel of prudence and self-reliance, dignity and compassion, and the inclusion of marginalized groups such as women, minorities, and the rural and urban poor is wise but suggests a reform agenda that may be beyond the capacity of the present Establishment. Talbot is right, however, in his warning against predictions of the destruction or total failure of Pakistan. This is a state that is not likely to disappear soon. Parts of Pakistan may fail—some have—but it would be rash to predict an imminent "perfect storm" failure, meaning the conjunction, at the same moment, of failure in several sectors resulting in the collapse of both the state and the idea of Pakistan. The one scenario in which true catastrophe is now technically possible would be a nuclear exchange between Pakistan and India.

While Pakistan's elite may continue to pursue the present course, there are other potential futures. Some would be welcomed by the international community and most Pakistanis. Others are far more alarming and might turn Pakistan into a classic "rogue" state—one with a weak or malevolent government that supported terrorism and possessed weapons of mass destruction.

The stability and durability of Pakistan's present oligarchic-like order and alternatives that might emerge in the next five to ten years are the subject of this chapter. The present system is likely to continue, but certain events, trends, and policies might yet transform it. These include another war with India, the growth of radical Islamic groups, the loss of American and even Chinese support, the failure to come to grips with Pakistan's social and educational problems, a series of assassinations of senior Pakistani officials, or the revival of ethnic and regional separatism. Above all, and the hardest to detect, would be the continuing loss of confidence in the very idea of Pakistan—and confusion over what, if anything, Pakistan stood for.

Conversely, one can hypothesize the normalization of relations with India, the emergence of a benign and progressive leadership, continuing American and international support, perhaps the success of President Musharraf's version of "guided democracy," and the emergence of a Pakistani identity that did not rub up against India, Afghanistan, or other important states.[2] There are enough variables involved—called "drivers" in the literature—to make Pakistan's fate hard to predict with a high degree of certainty.

The future scenarios and subscenarios considered here are based on a perspective of five to eight years.[3] Some seem improbable, but the dramatic history of recent years—the fall of the Soviet Union, South Asia's nuclearization, the 9/11 terrorist attacks, the regime changes wrought by American power in Afghanistan and Iraq, and the frequent assassination attempts against Musharraf—must be kept in mind.

These scenarios include

—A straight-line projection of the present system
—The emergence of a moderate, democratic state

—The rise of authoritarianism
—The rise of an Islamist state
—Pakistan's possible breakup
—Pakistan after a major war with India.

In each case Pakistan's likely demographic, social, and economic trajectories cast a shadow. Other critical factors include the army's integrity and the debilitating rivalry with India. Each "future" has implications for Pakistan's security and nuclear policies, its domestic stability, support for terrorism, and relations with other major powers, notably India and the United States (the latter is considered in chapter 9).

The Present as the Future

It is reasonable to argue that in five years Pakistan will be pretty much what it is today. The legitimacy of overt army rule, the core foreign policies favored by the Establishment, and the basic social order may be challenged, but not the legitimacy of the state or the domination of what President Musharraf has frequently referred to as the "moderates of the center," which he has contrasted with the radical Islamic parties and the "liberals" of the left. Pakistan's present political and social order, dominated by an oligarchic-like Establishment with the military at its core and a center-right ideology that is strongly resistant to political or social change, could continue indefinitely.

A Permanent Establishment?

There are many arguments in favor of the possibility that an oligarchic-style system in Pakistan will continue. These also foresee little change in domestic or foreign policies.

First, the cost of defection from the elite consensus is substantial. Many members of the Pakistani elite, including academics and scientists, are state employees or have relatives in the employ of the state, and the threat of retribution is ever-present. Even if an individual finds himself or herself out of reach of the state apparatus, relatives and friends are vulnerable to police harassment, too-careful scrutiny of tax returns, and other threats. When the liberal wing of the Establishment does speak out, it is usually in English, and provocative thoughts that appear in the Urdu press are likely to result in sanctions.

Second, members of the Establishment have been cushioned from economic stagnation and the decay in public services that ravage Pakistan's poor and the lower-middle classes. This is especially true of the officer corps, which is rewarded for conformity in the form of retirement benefits, pensions, land grants, and civilian jobs. Pakistan's diplomats vie for similar postretirement positions or appointments to international agencies, but they have fewer domestic options, and many of them move overseas after retirement. Pakistan's business community is too weak to force a change in policy, and many businessmen have expanded their operations abroad, rather than in Pakistan. Knowing that their skills would be useful in any administration, technocratic and bureaucratic elites have a stake in the status quo as long as their prospects are unaffected. Recent revelations about the leakage of nuclear technology threatens some members of the nuclear weapons enclave, but a few scapegoats will likely be found and disciplined without any change in the overall political order, let alone the Islamist transformation of the state.[4]

Third, Pakistan has adapted to changing strategic circumstances by "renting" itself out to powerful states, notably the United States, but also Saudi Arabia and China. Occupying a piece of strategic territory, an inexhaustible resource, strengthens the central government and inhibits the prospect of genuine reform. Thus there is no urgent need to develop domestic capabilities, build human capital, or even look ahead to the day when the resource might be exhausted. The Establishment is prone to much wishful thinking that something or someone will always come to Pakistan's rescue because of its location; this also tends to dampen public and official debate over alternative strategies and link Pakistan's identity to seemingly immutable geography.

Fourth, Pakistan is a state that in the past propagandized its own people but does not command strong loyalty except in time of war and crisis. The Establishment presides over a state with a tradition of soft authoritarianism: it is capable of crudely shaping public opinion but susceptible to backlash from that very public.[5] If a foreign state that would like Pakistan to change its ways were to suggest a rapid or radical shift, the government would call it a threat to the ruling elite. Pakistan now negotiates with its allies and friends by pointing a gun to its own head.

The present army leadership, notably General Musharraf, will resist radical change in either foreign or domestic policy. Musharraf is himself replaceable; he has little standing beyond his official position as army chief, and were he to step down or be assassinated, his army replacement would be an officer who represents the army's wing of the Establishment consensus, perhaps with modest movement in one direction or another, and his civilian replacement as president would likely be the phlegmatic chairman of the Senate, Mohammedmian Somroo.

To summarize, there are good reasons to argue that Pakistan may not change very much. It has again become strategically important, the army's role seems unchallengeable, the Establishment is content and stable, and the opposition is divided. The latter, whether Islamists, liberals, or conservatives, can be fragmented or co-opted by a policy of divide and rule. Like the present Iranian regime, the Pakistani generals allow the political opposition to criticize, but not to organize. Defenders of the present system argue that Pakistan is *stable,* that any attempt to impose change on the country would only bring forth chaos, Islamic extremism, and Pakistan's withdrawal from the American-led war on terrorism. Pakistan will squeak by, if left alone; pressuring it will be counterproductive. This argument is most enthusiastically made by the Establishment itself, which points to its own weakness and the existence of domestic and foreign enemies as reason enough to support the system, forestalling something much worse. It just needs a minor tune-up, members of the Establishment claim, and then everything will work out fine. But many are privately worried and in increasing numbers seem to believe that their future—or that of their children—may be outside Pakistan.

A Failing Establishment?

Even if one concedes the inherent stability of Pakistan's oligarchic political and social order, a number of developments make it newly vulnerable. These come from within and without.

Domestically, there is no question that Pakistan is subject to unprecedented demographic pressures, exacerbated by the poor performance of the economy, an inadequate educational system, and a staggering rate of urbanization. Once a country of 32 million, Pakistan is now approaching 200 million, without an attendant increase in literacy or land reform, and with natural economic ties with India still thwarted. These developments will place increasing pressure on Pakistan's domestic institutions. It is anyone's guess whether they will bend or break, but it is certain that without massive investment, Pakistan will fall further and further behind as a "modern" state when compared with most of its peers.

Other factors may spell trouble for the Establishment in the short to medium term. One of these would be Pakistan's role in combating al Qaeda. Pakistan has turned over 500 Taliban and al Qaeda members to the United States over the past two years, but the overwhelming number of these were captured during and immediately after the American-led invasion of Afghanistan. Since then Pakistan has dribbled out al Qaeda leaders slowly, often when it is politically or strategically convenient to do so, and virtually no significant Taliban leaders have been produced.[6] Alas, there is not an inexhaustible supply of al Qaeda operatives standing by, waiting to be captured. In a few years Pakistan's role in tracking down and capturing al Qaeda cadres will end. When that happens, one claim on American resources will vanish. In the meantime, fresh revelations about Pakistan's role in supporting the Taliban, al Qaeda, and the sale of sensitive technology to other states badly damages the government's credibility.[7]

Another short-term challenge stems from Pakistan's place in a globalizing world. Pakistanis of all strata and regions are now awash in an expanding torrent of information via the Internet, new cable channels beamed in from abroad, new radio stations, and a profusion of vernacular papers.[8] This has already changed the way in which Pakistani politicians campaign and how the government deals with the people. Access to global television has seriously weakened the effectiveness of the state's propaganda apparatus; while the mistakes of 1965 and 1971 were concealed for years, the entire Kargil story is well known to informed Pakistanis who have access to cable television and Internet sources and are aware that their government was not only incompetent but lying to them. Even the tame Pakistan Legislative Assembly plans to investigate Kargil in late 2004, if the government permits it to do so.

To its further disadvantage, Pakistan has no highly desired product or service to offer except textiles. Even in this sector adequate performance is not assured if investments now being made in Pakistan's textile industry turn out to be too low to make the industry competitive in American and European markets. Pakistan's new geostrategic importance has brought it substantial economic aid, $7 billion from the United States alone—but will this do much to rebuild key social and political institutions? Pakistan will be hampered by maladministration, corruption, and a broken tax and revenue collection system unless the entire Establishment, not just a few high-profile officials, embraces fiscal and administrative discipline. Another uncertainty is whether Pakistan will alter its fundamental opposition to India and ease its obsession with Kashmir, thus paving the way for an atmosphere more conducive to economic growth. These issues go to the heart of the official identity of Pakistan, as promulgated by the army for over fifty years; it is questionable whether Pakistan can either be induced or pressured into changing these policies, despite some evidence of reconsideration in January 2004.

Pakistan's dependence upon its strategic location has created a policy community that thinks within very narrow parameters. Though sometimes tactically brilliant, regularly outperforming rival India, Pakistan's foreign service and army strategists focus entirely on the next step in what is seen as a chess game of infinite duration. Bhutto was an innovator in that he broadened Pakistan's support base beyond the United States to include China; Zia extended it to include the Arab states, notably Saudi Arabia. The bomb, seen as providing leverage over India, may deter an all-out war but also complicates Pakistan's identity problem, not to mention its debilitating rivalry with New Delhi. Privately, many senior Pakistani officials acknowledge the lack of long-range thinking and understand the critical nature of Pakistan's population explosion, the rise of Islamic radicalism, and economic stagnation. The costs of a prolonged, indefinite rivalry with a rising India are also clear to them. However, few members of Pakistan's Establishment dare group these together to challenge an adaptive status quo policy.

Transformation

It is very unlikely that General Musharraf will be able to transform the present oligarchy-Establishment, nor is this his major objective. He seems more at ease with international affairs than domestic ones. His bold but curiously indecisive leadership is characterized by dramatic statements, many policy initiatives, and little follow-up. He has the knack of agreeing with an interlocutor, be it a foreigner, an Islamist, a liberal, or an Indian official; his one guideline seems to be the "national interest," a term he uses incessantly, but there is no evidence of a vision beyond the army's traditional beliefs about the dangers of democracy, Indian arrogance and hostility, and America's unreliability as an ally. Musharraf's power ultimately rests upon the consent of a dozen or so generals, as did that of every Pakistani leader since the 1950s. He has the powerful TINA (There is No Alternative) force behind him, but this could change quickly in the face of a series of domestic, economic, or foreign policy crises.

Pakistan's army wants neither to govern directly nor to allow civilians to rule in their own right. Thus since the army itself is an inherently conservative institution (Musharraf's professed admiration for Ataturk is shared by few of his colleagues), radical change led by the military is unlikely.

It is also questionable that the army will conceive and implement a strategy of incremental change that would reform Pakistan's ailing civilian institutions. Overwhelming evidence suggests that the armed forces are quite comfortable—personally and professionally—with their central position in the management of state affairs, yet this is no substitute for strong civilian institutions and the rule of law. Pakistan's army is strong enough to prevent state failure, but not imaginative enough to impose the changes that might transform the state.

As for Pakistan's identity and what it means to be a Pakistani, the army is unlikely to be able to fabricate an identity compatible with Pakistan's multiethnic, multi-sectarian realities, as well as with Pakistan's environment, especially the still-contested relationship with New Delhi. Yet because of its dominant position, the army can block attempts to change the consensus concerning Pakistan's identity. The army is the key to changing Pakistan, but the army is itself slow to change, even if a few officers now worry about Pakistan's relative and absolute decline.

A further question is what conditions could prompt a transition from a soft autocracy or oligarchic system to a true democracy? Two states, Taiwan and South Korea, recently moved from authoritarianism to democracy after experiencing economic growth; the critical factor was not the *timing* of democratization, but the fact that the process took place beneath the protective umbrella of an American alliance. With security under control, autocratic governments could safely yield to a civilian democracy. In Pakistan's case, the army is unlikely to ever turn power over to civilians unless Pakistan's external security is assured. In the case of Taiwan and South Korea, the army had not penetrated deeply into the civilian economy, and economic growth was led by civilians. In Pakistan, the civilian

Box 8-1. *The Turkish Model*

Musharraf's admiration for Turkey has its antecedents in the Ayub years, when Pakistan, Turkey, and Iran, the three major non-Arab Muslim countries, had close strategic ties and a common link to the United States. Turkey was an approximation of what Pakistan would have liked to have become. It had one foot in Europe, close relations with the United States, and the army presided over a generally liberal and secular society. When he came to power, Pervez Musharraf openly praised Turkey—although this praise was subsequently muted out of fear of an Islamist backlash. Yet contemporary Turkey has itself changed, especially after the election to power of the Justice and Development Party (AKP), which despite its background has not pressed ahead with an Islamist agenda. Eager to join the European Union, the Turkish parliament has passed legislation that will curb the power of the army, weaken the authority of the National Security Council, and enhance freedom of expression. Turkey's minister for religious affairs, Mehmet Aydin, was caustically critical of Pakistan (and Iran and Saudi Arabia) for their un-Islamic treatment of women, asserting that all three had misinterpreted Islam and that none "can be considered religious states."* To drive home the point, he appointed a woman as *mufti*, deputy director for religious affairs, encouraged women to pray in any section of a mosque, and took other steps. Some of these reforms were mandated by the European Union; a comparable situation for Pakistan would be a similar offer of inducements for change in Pakistan—further removing the military from politics while shoring up civil liberties and freedom and backing off from an Islamist agenda in exchange for significant economic assistance and perhaps even greater American engagement in the Kashmir issue and other security-related issues.

*Leyla Boulton, "Islam Should Not Be Reason to Stop Turkey Joining EU, Says Minister," *Financial Times*, August 1, 2003; also editorial, "A Quiet Revolution," *Financial Times*, August 1, 2003.

sector is *losing* ground to the armed forces, and it may be that the latter will be reluctant to withdraw from power because of their institutional involvement in the economy and Pakistani society.

Implications

By definition, if the present Establishment-dominated system were to continue into the future, it would need to have at least mastered short-range challenges. The most important of these is the economy, where there are two possible safety valves. First, even without significant economic growth, Pakistan's geostrategic location will continue to make it important to other major powers, and thus the recipient of critical foreign and technical assistance. Second, to some degree the negative consequences of a stagnating economy for present-day Pakistan, such as more extensive internal migration, can be mitigated by tighter police control, a Chinese-style domestic passport system, and a further expansion of paramilitary forces. These, however, would be stopgap measures.

As for political unrest, an Establishment that was coping might continue to experiment with political and social reforms, and these in turn might enhance the possibility of a return to democracy. However, two "mights" in one sentence is a warning sign: Pakistan could just as easily regress in several areas, paving the way for more radical movements and the departure of more elites and their families, whose replacement might be less educated, less sophisticated, and less representative. This would make a return to liberal democracy more problematic, and it certainly would promote a narrower view of Pakistan's relations with the outside world.

Should the present system persist, there might also be little change in Pakistan's relations with its neighbors, notably India. This could mean the occasional crisis, or a fresh challenge to India, with the ever-present possibility of a war or a nuclear incident. Pakistan might also be able to again assert a strategic presence in the west or the north. As for the Islamists, this scenario also assumes that the Establishment will continue to use Islamist forces and outright terrorists as instruments of diplomacy in dealing with its neighbors, and even at home to balance liberal forces and perhaps divide the conservatives.

In short, Pakistan's political order of the past forty years depends on a balancing act organized by a small, tight-knit Establishment. It sits upon a huge and expanding society faced with many challenges, some beyond the reach of short-term fixes. The current system may continue if its leadership is able to do a few things reasonably well—such as repair the economy, contain the Islamist radicals, and maintain good relations with powerful states while avoiding a new major confrontation with India. This is not impossible, nor even improbable, but it is also unlikely. Under the pressures of globalization, which has brought the spread of mass communications and a globalized economy, the world is changing, and Pakistan with it, but not necessarily along the same path. The policies pursued by Musharraf (and his civilian predecessors) would indicate an uneven journey into the future.

Shaukat Aziz, President Musharraf's mid-2004 candidate for prime minister, brings special talents to that position. He is a widely regarded technocrat, having served for many years in high positions in an American bank and, since 1999, as Musharraf's finance adviser and then finance minister. Aziz gained the support of the army, international financial institutions, and major aid donors for his program of reform and economic restructuring.

Ironically, Shaukat Aziz may assume office shortly after another technocrat-economist, Manmohan Singh, becomes prime minister of India—but Singh has at his command a powerful political organization, the Congress Party, and a military establishment that is under firm political control. Aziz has never held any political position, and it is an open question whether his skills and his contacts will help him deal with Pakistan's spiraling sectarian and social violence, whether he will have any significant role in the ongoing negotiations with India, and whether he will acquire real control over Pakistan's nuclear program and its myriad intelligence services.

A Normal Democracy?

By most measures of freedom and democratization, Pakistan is far ahead of the Arab states, Indonesia, and even Malaysia, but well behind its South Asian counterparts: Sri Lanka, India, and even Bangladesh have true national political parties and competitive political systems, as well as higher literacy and participation rates.[9] Even the new democracies of Central Europe and the slightly older ones of East Asia have developed true, aggregative political parties that compete for power in a constitutional framework.

Pakistan has always been on the edge of democracy but it was surpassed by its East Asian counterparts, which moved quickly from economic growth to democratic development. The full restoration of democratic government and the rebuilding of the Pakistani state is a future that would have to fall on the side of the improbable rather than the likely.[10] Nevertheless, for a state that has been under military rule for more than half of its history and under corrupt or undemocratic civilian regimes for the rest, Pakistan has an astonishingly large number of citizens committed to democracy. It is rich in private organizations and replete with political parties, and even some of the Islamist parties have come to value democracy after being on the wrong end of an authoritarian state. These show a surprising resiliency and are bolstered by international pressure on Pakistan to hold elections. Pakistani politicians may not be able to make a democracy work, but they like to try.

There are also a large number of nongovernmental organizations (notably women's groups), an active peace movement, and thriving English-language and vernacular presses, supplemented recently by private television and radio stations. Pakistan has staggered along, decade after decade, with a revolving-door democracy.

Although many Pakistani civilian elites nominally favor democracy, they are uncomfortable with the idea of mass democratic politics. In Pakistan, democracy is still an avocation, more of a civic obligation than a career. To have a real democracy Pakistan must also have real political parties—not affinity groups of the rich and famous. Real political parties, unlike interest groups or NGOs, will aggregate diverse and even conflicting interests. Furthermore, key policy conflicts will generally be mediated at the party level. In Pakistan, however, it is easier to start a new political party than to keep the old one together (except in the case of certain regional parties and the PPP).

The army is unlikely to give up its claim to redirect Pakistan when it feels that the state is threatened, but neither is the army likely to stand in the way of a government formally run by civilians but under its supervision. For Pakistan to become a democracy, civilian leaders will be required to display a level of tact and competence that has not yet been evident. From the army's perspective, nominally civilian governments are merely an extension of the core civil-military alliance that has dominated Pakistan for forty years; for the military, a slight rebalancing of the civil-military relationship is adequate.

A full-blown democracy, in which the armed forces come under firm civilian control, will be impossible until Pakistan's strategic environment alters in such a way that the army retreats from its role as guardian of the state. Domestic politics in Pakistan is hostage to India-Pakistan relations; normalization with India is a necessary but insufficient condition for

Pakistan's redemocratization. Ironically, such a normalization process cannot be carried out by a civilian government alone. If India and Pakistan should reach agreement on Kashmir and their larger conflict, then the world will learn whether or not the army has reached the point at which its engagement with Pakistani society is so deep, and the benefits to its personnel are so strong, that it cannot withdraw.

If the army's involvement in domestic affairs is that deep, then any reduction in the army's *political* role will have to be accompanied by policies that place the army's *military* role on a new footing before Pakistan can emerge as a democracy. Two such policies suggest themselves. One would be the reorientation of the army toward international peacekeeping activities, with the retraining of the military for such roles. Another would be a deeper domestic economic and social role for the army by assigning it still more tasks such as the reconstruction of the Water and Power Development Authority, road building, transport, and construction. In the former case, however, Pakistan would be competing with other states for UN peacekeeping duties; in the latter it might entrench the army further in Pakistani politics. This might not be the cheapest way to carry out some vital tasks, and would further defer the development of civilian capabilities.

Twenty years ago I argued that the central issue of Pakistani politics was rebalancing the civil-military relationship, and that a gradual, staged retreat from politics by the army, coupled with a demonstration of increasing competence by the civilians, might lead to the restoration of full democratic rule in the country.[11] This not only underestimated the degree to which military rule in Pakistan is widely supported by people who nominally favor democracy, it also did not anticipate the severe economic and social problems exacerbated by ten years of *flawed* democracy that led many Pakistanis to welcome the army's 1999 political reentry or the difficulty of developing and maintaining true political parties that cut across regional, ethnic, and economic interests.

A democratic Pakistan would also have to reconcile democracy's procedural, human rights, and participatory dimensions with Pakistan's official status as an Islamic republic. Islam, like Judaism and Christianity, is not a "civilization" but a religion moving through a historical progression, adapting to circumstances and acquiring new characteristics over the years. The religion may shape the outlook of its adherents, but except in

> **Box 8-2.** *The Israeli and American Parallels*
>
> America and Israel compare with Pakistan in the latter's attempt to recon-
> cile democracy with its origins as a homeland for a threatened religious
> minority. Each was founded by such a minority, and all three subsequently
> had to determine how the state would relate to both the dominant and the
> minority religions. The early Americans first sought to establish a homeland
> where they could practice their religion unhindered by the state but then
> had to ensure that different religions would be able to live side by side; the
> solution was a secular state that favored no one religion. Territory and an
> acceptance of religious and ethnic diversity, rather than religious affilia-
> tion, became the foundation stone of national identity. Israel is more like
> Pakistan. Both originated in a diaspora located some distance from the
> eventual homeland; the diaspora mobilized popular and international sup-
> port for Israel and Pakistan, respectively. Both were based upon persecuted
> religious minorities, and both have been less than just toward their own sec-
> tarian and religious minorities. Both faced external threats and an identity
> crisis. In Israel's case, a minority of Palestinians—Christians and Muslims—
> could fit into Israeli politics without difficulty, and a number of Jewish
> laws (such as no public transportation on the Sabbath) were not a serious
> imposition on secular Israelis and non-Jews. However, once Israel acquired
> majority-Palestinian territories, the state's Jewish identity became linked to
> its foreign and security policy, and a debate arose between those who sought
> to define Israel in terms of territory and security and those who sought to
> fulfill a religious mandate. In Pakistan's case, non-Muslims could not hold
> certain offices, but Hindus and Christians were otherwise full citizens and
> well protected by the state. This was not true of minority sects, and Pak-
> istan's Islamic identity was defined in such a way as to make some of them
> (notably the Ahmediyyas) heretics, subject to criminal prosecution.

rare cases the religiously driven component of that outlook is subordinated to considerations of class, ethnicity, linguistic loyalties, and straightforward political ideologies and ambitions.

It is unimaginable that Pakistan would shed its religious identity and
become a formally secular state. If Pakistan becomes an established democracy, it will resemble Catholic Poland or Jewish Israel, or Buddhist Sri
Lanka and Thailand, with religion playing an ancillary but ultimately subordinate role. Pakistan has a greater chance of becoming a confessionally

hyphenated democracy than most of the Middle East states, but for it to move in this direction will require a more serious examination of its own complex identity. Is it a Muslim state, an Islamic state, or a democracy, or some combination of the three? As the American scholar Mahnaz Ispahani has written, the "muddle" in Pakistan has always been about its identity.[12] It is definitely not on the slippery slope of uncompromising Islamism, but it certainly is unclear about the degree to which it remains an ordinary country: that is to say, is it a homeland for its citizens, or an exceptional and ideologically driven Islamic state with a regional if not global mission?

The Indian and Bangladesh Models

Might Pakistan follow India's or Bangladesh's democratic path? For years comparison with India seemed to favor Pakistan. Its per capita income was higher, its army was the equal of India's, its air force was better, and it could draw upon the support of several great powers. Pakistanis got along very well with Westerners, particularly Americans, and had strategic links to the Islamic world, the West, and China, while the prickly Indians readily alienated would-be friends.

At a deeper level, however, the comparison also suggests that India's route to a more or less stable democratic order, with a reasonable degree of growth and political freedom, may be difficult for Pakistan. India had its political dynasties, but never an oligarchic Establishment, let alone one dominated by the army. India's economy is diverse and internationally competitive in many areas, and India's vast size and diversity actually protect it from sectarian and communal violence since the entire country is not likely to be agitated at the same time. The India model represents a road not taken, although it does remain a theoretical possibility.

One other democratic path for Pakistan might be that of its former East Wing. When Bangladesh became independent, it was governed for four years by the charismatic Sheikh Mujibur Rahman. After he was assassinated by a group of officers in 1975, the army ruled for fifteen years. Then in 1991, truly free elections brought a civilian government to power, and since then a two-party system has evolved, with the military back in the barracks. The leaders of these parties—Mujib's daughter and the widow of one of the generals—have no love for each other, and governance leaves much to be desired, but the country has achieved a degree of political stability that has escaped Pakistan. Its economy is growing at a respectable pace for such a poor country, it has done much to limit population growth (particularly by educating women), and its Islamic extremists are few in number and politically marginalized. Above all, while Bangladeshis are intensely suspicious of what they regard as an arrogant and insensitive New Delhi, the two states have no strategic conflict and are able to sort out their differences through normal means.

However, Bangladesh differs from Pakistan in four important respects: its army is now excluded from politics (after an extended period of military rule); there is an enormous international NGO economic presence in the country; Bangladesh is ethnically more homogenous than Pakistan, although it does have a substantially larger Hindu minority; and, of course, Pakistan is a nuclear weapons state that challenges a vital Indian interest (through its claim to Kashmir), whereas Bangladesh has grudgingly accepted Indian hegemony and does not believe that India poses an existential threat.

What conditions might turn Pakistan into "West Bangladesh"? The most important would be a strategic accommodation between India and Pakistan that transformed Pakistan into a status quo power. Assuming it retained its nuclear weapons, Pakistan could still stake a claim for middle-power status. These weapons would provide some insurance against a breakdown in any strategic accord reached with India. Although the major powers would exert pressure to reduce or eliminate them, a Pakistan at peace with its neighbors would not raise the kinds of fears that exist today. Should Pakistan reach such a strategic accommodation with India, it could afford to reduce its defense spending, and there would be some prospect of enhanced trade, a more influential South Asian Association for Regional Cooperation, and possibly a more influential "South Asian" voice at international forums.

The prospect of Pakistan becoming like Bangladesh is repugnant to the Pakistani leadership. Aside from being subordinate to India, Bangladesh is considered so aid-dependent that it has lost its sovereignty to a gaggle of NGOs and international organizations. The Islamists say Bangladesh is contaminated by Hindu influence, the strategists that it bowed to India because it was economically weak and dependent. Both assume that Pakistan's critical strategic location will make it important enough to always be supported, one way or another, by outside powers.

Some would ask whether a Bangladesh-like Pakistan would be strong enough to contain the still-powerful separatist movements. Would any weakening of the Establishment or any change in strategic policy of this magnitude be the prelude to a new partition of Pakistan? It is important to remember, others would add, that Bangladesh began as and remains a very poor country, whereas Pakistan had (and still has) a much higher per capita income. The comparison is cast into further doubt because Pakistan is unlikely to allow thousands of foreign NGOs to operate on its territory and will not grant them a de facto veto over key economic, social, and even foreign policy decisions, as it believes Bangladesh has done.

These are powerful arguments that probably foreclose a gradual or peaceful transformation of Pakistan into a status quo state of reduced ambition and reach. Nevertheless, a series of traumas to the state, on the one hand, or a lengthy spell of normal democracy, on the other, and an accommodation with India as a byproduct, might leave Pakistan resembling Bangladesh in some essential ways.

Implications

A democratic Pakistan would be applauded by some in the West, Pakistani liberals, and even many members of the Establishment. But could Pakistan withstand the learning process that would take place before its parties became true mediators between the people and the state?

Pakistan will never become a democracy if its political parties are prohibited from aggregating a broad range of social, economic, and ideological interests. Currently, they are highly personalized and must compete not only with the army but also with the many NGOs that serve narrow interests. To build the parties as institutions will require, first of all, that they be allowed to broaden their range and fill the political space occupied by the military and NGOs.

Pakistan's recent history and its underlying structural problems suggest that such a process may be difficult to sustain. The decade of democracy from the late 1980s to the late 1990s saw ruinous economic policies, a high level of corruption, the rise of Islamic extremism, and (in the case of the Nawaz government) abuses of human rights and civil liberties and a naked attack on major Pakistani institutions. Benazir was perhaps less ambitious, but her government was probably more corrupt. A new round of democratic government might arguably be more successful, as the "red lines" drawn by the military are clearer now, as are the perils of fiscal mismanagement. Today, on the other hand, Pakistan is a weaker state than in 1989 and the negative demographic and social indicators are more evident.

Would a democratic Pakistani government be able to take the necessarily tough steps to discipline the economy, reduce corruption, and send the army back to the barracks without the army's consent? For a time, a Pakistani democracy would have to be limited, essentially a civil-military coalition that had a timetable and an agreed-upon agenda for the restoration of full civilian government. This agenda would certainly have a foreign policy component that would provide the army with a veto over security policy.

Pakistan's fate as a democracy is likely to be that of some of the Greek city-states studied by Aristotle and described in *The Politics*. Most of these, according to Aristotle, were imperfect oligarchies that evolved into imperfect democracies, which in turn reverted to oligarchic states. Occasionally, one would become a tyranny. Rarely would they evolve into a "true" system, based on what Aristotle regarded as sound principles: governance by the few (or the many) in the interests of all. Under present conditions, a Pakistani democracy will face nearly insuperable problems in putting its economy in order, conducting a diplomacy within the parameters set by the army, and facing mounting social problems, while simultaneously developing a national identity that binds, rather than divides, its citizens.

Barring a cataclysm, however, Pakistan is also likely to retain many qualities *associated* with democratic government. Its elites value freedom of the press (within limits), and the Establishment wants to be seen as modern and progressive. It also wants to keep its links to the West and maintain some elements of a democracy. In this it has wide support. Practically speaking, however, moving from an oligarchy to a full-fledged democracy will be very difficult.

Authoritarian Pakistan

In 2000 a group of graduate students at Punjab University were asked to name their favorite Pakistani leader. All responded, "Jinnah," whose stern portrait looked down from the classroom wall. "Which present-day leader compares with Jinnah?" they were asked. Silence. "What about leaders of other states?" The class (composed equally of men and women) quickly agreed that Pakistan needed a Nelson Mandela—an incorruptible and visionary leader. A large number also praised Saddam Hussein for his defiance of the United States, and many praised Ayatollah Khomeini for his honesty, leadership skills, and, again, his willingness to stand up to America. Two years later, at the same university, another group of students gave similar answers, with the addition of "Lenin" as the choice of two angry and well-read young women. Can Pakistan produce a Mandela, a Lenin, a Khomeini, a Saddam, or another Jinnah? More modestly, could it produce another Ayub Khan (regarded at the time by Samuel Huntington as a latter-day Solon), or even another Zulfiqar Ali Bhutto? What circumstances would produce a leader who could govern Pakistan long enough to put his (or her) imprint upon the state? Is Pervez Musharraf a possible candidate for "great leader"?

Such a leader would require an institutional or organizational base, meaning the army and the political parties in this case. However, Pakistan is notable for lacking a party or movement that could sustain such a leader for very long, or that could evolve into a radical political organization. Pakistan had leftists but not a left political movement; the hostility of the landowners, the alliance with the United States, the dominance of the army, and the conservatism of most Pakistanis prevented that. The closest Pakistan came was the socialist-Islamic government of Zulfiqar Ali Bhutto, who believed that only a populist movement could counter the army's power.[13] This pattern could be repeated; the appetite for authoritarianism will increase if the present arrangement of a mixed military-civilian regime collapses, although the role of the military will still have to be factored in.

Pakistan does not yet have the social basis for *totalitarianism*—a form of government far more intrusive on the personal lives and beliefs of citizens than authoritarianism—because it is so fragmented and underdeveloped that the state cannot penetrate very deeply. It may even be able to sustain authoritarianism. Pakistan's countryside would require a revolution to remove the feudal aristocracy from its dominant position. The cities are also highly disorganized, with a huge influx of rural males whose orientation remains that of the countryside. Further, no political party or movement except the Jama'at among the Islamists seems capable of establishing a totalitarian party.

As for authoritarianism, Pakistan could yet be a state that did not attempt to mold the personalities and lives of its citizens as long as they remained politically and socially compliant. Such a Pakistan would require a movement and a leader whose appeal transcended regional and ideological lines. No such movement exists today, except for the PPP among the parties and the JI among the Islamists. There are no signs of a radical Baathist party, nor is Pakistan prone to authoritarianism except for short periods (the longest so far being that of Zia, 1977–85). Both the Establishment and the liberal community support at least the appearance of democracy. A brief glance at recent Pakistani leaders reinforces this judgment.

Benazir Bhutto was perhaps the most promising political leader in Pakistan's recent history, but she could not measure up to her father in ruthlessness, charisma, and experience. She did compare with him in her capacity for self-deception, however. Her friends more than her enemies were disillusioned by her tendency to see herself as more than she was. Had she commanded the army, had she been a man, this delusional streak could have turned her into a "great" leader—her father had these qualities and came upon the scene at a moment of political disorder. She very much resembled Indira Gandhi, but lacked Indira's intimate knowledge of her own country and had a much tougher set of enemies in the army.

Nawaz Sharif was not afraid to use extraconstitutional means and even plotted the removal of two army chiefs, but he badly overreached, bringing down the army's wrath upon himself. He was also widely regarded as constrained by his father, a pious man of limited vision. Prime Ministers Junejo and Jamali ruled by grace of the army, and Junejo was dismissed when he showed a flicker of independence, and Jamali for no reason.

As for the army, it seems to be an unlikely source for a "great" leader, even if some recent army chiefs, notably Musharraf, fancy themselves to be Pakistan's saviors. Musharraf thinks he could be a Sadat, a man with a liberal vision, boldness, and an opportunity to make history, but in his first few years he has turned out to be a Barak—the vision might have been there from time to time, but it was coupled with political ineptness. With luck, he could evolve into a Hosni Mubarak, or Hafez-al Asad, presiding over a failed state that was held together by a ruthless security apparatus, backed by the army, and as in Egypt's case, the recipient of lavish international support because of its strategic location.

Some of Musharraf's international backers see him as a wise and modern leader, a secular man who is not afraid to support the West or to offer peace to India, and a man who can hold back the onrush of demagogues and Islamic extremists. No serious Pakistani analyst sees Musharraf in these terms. If he resembles any past Pakistani leader, it is General Yahya Khan—also a well-intentioned general who did the United States a great favor (Pakistan then served as the facilitator of the opening to China), but was unable to cope with the competing demands of popular politicians. Musharraf solved that problem by forcing the leaders of Pakistan's two mainstream, centrist parties, Benazir Bhutto and Nawaz Sharif, out of the country.

Pakistan's army may have potentially "great men," but Musharraf, like Zia, has been astute enough to sidetrack potential rivals and promote officers with whom he has a personal link (many of the corps commanders are his former students or subordinates). This will not prevent one or more of them from stepping forward to demand Musharraf's removal should he become a liability to the army's institutional interests. If that happens, then the army's and the state's public relations apparatus will again produce the evidence to show that Musharraf's successor deserves the *gaddi* (throne), and that Musharraf, while well-meaning, was obviously incompetent, misguided, and led astray by his too-close relationship with the United States. The army does not produce individuals with the popular appeal and wide-ranging experience necessary to emerge as a credible national leader, but it can ex post facto manufacture them.

Outside of organized politics there is only limited scope for a major political career. Pakistan's greatest sports figure, the cricketer Imran Khan, added a new dimension to his already formidable public reputation after he became a crusader for a cancer hospital dedicated to his mother. However, this never morphed into political influence. He could not transfer his popularity because he never built a coherent organization. Imran's support came from a smattering of retired officials and bureaucrats who thought that his popularity, transparent sincerity, and freedom from any taint of corruption would translate into votes. It did not.

Pakistan's present political order might evolve into a dictatorship should the present civil-plus-army arrangement prove unable to cope with

Pakistan's critical economic, strategic, and political problems over the next five or six years. There are small signs that it is heading in this direction, including the 2003 arrests of several political leaders on the grounds that their criticism of the military constituted treason, the beating of a prominent Punjab provincial assembly opposition leader, and the increased surveillance of "suspect" liberal and mainstream journalists and scholars.

If one or more prime ministers, army chiefs, and presidents (or some combination thereof) were to fail, one could see Pakistan move further in the direction of authoritarianism. In the process a fresh face might appear, and if backed by the army and at least part of the Establishment, this could herald a new political order based upon a strong and ruthless leader with a touch of populism. Whether such an individual would do any better is a matter of conjecture, but it is probable that Pakistanis, like distraught citizens in any other country faced with several simultaneous crises, would welcome the change—for the moment. A soft authoritarian government is a more likely—but still improbable—alternative to the present Establishment system than a democratic Pakistan.

An Islamic State

Pakistan's Islamists hold out the prospect that a true revolution will transform the society. They were emboldened by the results of the 2002 elections through which they came to power in two provinces and became the leading opposition in the federal legislature. They have a program for change and international ties to other Islamist groups. Can Pakistan evolve into an Iran-like theocracy, or might it become "Talibanized" as radical Islamists expand their influence throughout the country?[14] These are valid, if premature concerns. An Iranian-style Islamic revolution is extremely unlikely within a five- or six-year time frame, and Pakistan is further away still from "Talibanization," that is, from falling under the influence of a simplistic Salafi-Wahabi Islamism.[15] Without a base in Afghanistan and unable to operate freely in Pakistan or India, Islamic radicalism of the Taliban kind will decline, although Pakistan will experience terrorist episodes. However, if Afghanistan were to again fall under the spell of a Taliban-like group, perhaps again backed by al Qaeda's money and technical assistance, then there would be some prospect for the Talibanization of parts of Pakistan.

As noted in chapter 5, Islamist forces are growing rapidly in Pakistan, in part because the state failed to deliver services and meet basic demands. Islamic sentiments are clearly on the rise, immensely strengthened by new perceived threats from the West, especially America. Pakistanis, as much as other Muslims, see in the West a threat to their honor, or *izzat*. These threats to Muslims are not merely spun out in Friday sermons but are widely discussed in Pakistan's middle and upper classes. Pakistan is rapidly acquiring an "Arab" view of the United States, which is being linked more and more to Jewish Israel and Hindu India as a civilizational threat to Muslim Pakistan. The recent warming of ties between Israel and India seems to confirm the existence of this axis and its supposedly anti-Pakistani premise.

Two "Islamist" scenarios are more likely than a revolution. One would be the gradual strengthening of Islamist parties to the point where they could stake a claim to power in a future government. Already, the MMA coalition governs the NWFP and holds power in a coalition government in Baluchistan; it has forced Musharraf to announce that he will step down as army chief, and to make other concessions. Within five years, Pakistan could be a more overtly Islamic state. If this happens, it will certainly be with the consent if not the connivance of the army. Those Islamists who have shown skill at parliamentary politics would be candidates for an army-supported government. A post-Musharraf army might be sympathetic to the Islamists, and in several years an outright army-Islamist coalition might emerge.

Before that could occur, the Islamist parties would have to grow rapidly in popularity. As of 2004, this is doubtful, even though the army and the intelligence services retain the option of playing one Islamic party off against another, and playing them all off against the mainstream parties. A major turning point might be an agreement among the Islamic parties to support a Kashmir compromise. This is an issue that already divides them—some are more concerned about Afghanistan than Kashmir. Should such a settlement be achieved, it is possible that the army would simply favor those Islamists who support the agreement and suppress those who oppose it.

A second and more likely scenario would see the return of a modified Ziaist regime. This would be a military-civilian coalition glued together by nominal adherence to Islamic doctrine, with the military as the senior partner. This scenario is highly unlikely in the next few years but becomes increasingly probable if the relatively secular leadership of Pervez Musharraf becomes discredited. In five years the bitter memories of the Zia years will have faded, but a soft Islamist regime would still be faced with the problem of governing Pakistan. Such a regime might initially impose martial law and would certainly defer the present nominal commitment to parliamentary democracy.

None of these medium-term scenarios resemble either Iran or Malaysia, two other states that have been held up as "Islamic" models for Pakistan. Iran's weakened army was swamped by a popular Islamist movement, aided by Islamist collaborators within the officer corps; there was strong popular opposition to the United States, and the Shah's regime was incapable of either liberalizing fast enough to accommodate new pressures or forcefully repressing the opposition. For this scenario to materialize in Pakistan, the army would have to be much weaker and itself more fully penetrated by Islamic revolutionaries, so that it would stand by and allow a true Islamic revolution to occur. Strategic factors also argue against such a development: a truly revolutionary Islamic Pakistan would be born with a ready-made rivalry with Shi'ia Iran and secular India. It might have the support of Saudi Arabia (whose own political stability is increasingly questioned), but it would also alarm China and the United States.

In the midterm, Malaysia would be a far more likely Islamic model for Pakistan than Iran, but important differences arise even here. Malaysia's leaders support many "Islamic" causes around the world and are quite critical of the American-led war on terrorism. Yet its large non-Muslim minorities are accommodated, and Malaysia's economy is closely tied to Japan and the West. Unlike Malaysia, Pakistan's domestic Islamist politics are tightly coupled to the politics of two of its neighbors, India and Afghanistan.

What if Pakistan acquired a more Islamic government? If the army remained the dominant political force, one could expect such a government to pursue somewhat tougher policies toward India and the West, and to be even more vocal in its denunciation of Israel, but it would also be constrained by the army's judgment about when harsher policies become counterproductive. Such a government might welcome an opportunity to proselytize in the armed forces, especially in the army, and a Ziaist military leadership would tolerate this. By 2006–07, if Pakistan seemed to be failing and the Islamists were the best-organized political force in the country, there would also be less resistance within the army to the more widespread imposition of Islamic practices, values, and strategies, and one could then imagine the army assuming a more ideological hue. At that point, present-day concerns about the army becoming Islamized might become reality.

State Breakup

The specter of separatism has haunted Pakistan since 1971. The causes of separatism in Pakistan are fairly clear: they include uneven development, inequitable distribution of resources, a lack of representative political institutions, and an oppressive state apparatus.[16] Balancing these are the enormous powers of the Pakistani state—linked directly to the armed forces and coupled with its ability to co-opt the leadership of separatist and autonomist groups. If Pakistan were to break up, though this seems unlikely in the next five years or so, it might occur in at least four ways.

First, the country might go the way of East Pakistan, Poland, or Lebanon. East Pakistan became Bangladesh, Poland was once partitioned out of existence, and Lebanon fell under Syrian and Israeli control. The basic cause of these breakups was a separatist movement combined with foreign support or a foreign takeover of component parts. In each case the national army was unable to hold the state together.

As discussed in chapter 6, this kind of a breakup could occur in Pakistan under several conditions. One would be the rise of a new Pashtun movement, egged on by Afghanistan and intent on NWFP separation. However, it is hard to imagine this happening without significant unrest elsewhere in Pakistan, notably in Sindh. Assuredly, India would again be involved in supporting or encouraging a new separatist movement in Pakistan, but so might other powers if they were concerned about the disposition of Pakistan's nuclear program and about terrorists residing within its borders.

Second, Pakistan might undergo a benign partition. There has been some discussion of a regional confederation, often in the context of achieving a settlement for Kashmir. If a South Asian confederation were to emerge, offering affiliate status to smaller regional entities, then a new international status in the form of membership in a confederation might enhance political autonomy and economic prosperity for Sindh and other provinces and thus induce changes in Pakistan's political order. The European Community's experiments with new and expanded forms of economic and political cooperation will be closely watched by some in South Asia for hints of how their region might adapt confederal mechanisms to long-standing regional political and economic problems. Conceivably, a settlement that gave Kashmir partial membership in a regional confederation might also be appealing to other provinces, and such a halfway house to independence could lead to another partition of Pakistan. However, this might also appeal to parts of India—which makes such a South Asian confederation very unlikely to begin with.

Soviet history suggests a third route to a reorganized Pakistan. The Soviet Union broke up largely because its dominant republic (Russia) calculated that it would do better without some of the non-European republics, and that Russia's future lay in becoming a modern European state. Could Pakistan evolve into a Punjabistan—a nuclear-armed, smaller, more efficient and generally secure state? This seems doubtful, but Punjab, like Russia, is the educationally and economically most advanced part of the country, and Punjabis regard themselves as culturally and civilizationally distinct, if not superior, to Sindhis, Baluch, and the tribals of NWFP.

Alternatively, might a new political order grow out of a civil war in Punjab fought along sectarian, geographical, or ideological lines? In this case, India and perhaps other states would be active on one (or more) sides in the conflict, if only because of their grave concern about the movement of refugees and the disposition of Pakistan's nuclear assets. In such a nightmare scenario, a divided army might split along unpredictable lines, taking different districts and provinces with them, depending on where army units were located as well as the links between different corps, divisional, or unit commanders and the kinds of arrangements they reached with local and regional power brokers.

The Army

These breakup scenarios lead back to the question of the army's integrity. What would lead to its fragmentation? The army appeared weak or vulnerable on four separate occasions. The first was very early in Pakistan's history, when young Pakistani officers—chafed at the conservatism of their British officers and a few leftist officers and aggravated by the stalemate in Kashmir—attempted a coup.[17] The second occurred immediately after the loss of East Pakistan, when the humiliated army was dependent upon Zulfiqar Ali Bhutto for the return of thousands of prisoners of war held by India. Several important developments followed in the 1990s: notably the puny "Islamic" coup attempt of General Abbasi, and Nawaz Sharif's effort to divide the senior army generals by playing favorites with the corps commanders and forcing one army chief (Karamat) to retire, while trying to fire another (Musharraf).

In every case the army stood united. Hence it is unlikely to buckle in a new crisis. At the same time, Pakistan is in many ways a weaker state now than it was ten, twenty, or thirty years ago, with perhaps its greatest vulnerability being a loss of confidence that it is on the right path.

A fresh challenge to the army's integrity could come from several directions. Pakistan's society may deteriorate to the point where violence, sectarianism, and economic stagnation began to affect the army (especially the officer corps) more directly. Second, the army's professional achievements might come under scrutiny. If, for example, there were full accountability for Kargil and other military misadventures or a fresh military humiliation, then the credibility of the senior leadership would be cast into doubt. Third, a division among the officer corps along ideological lines would hasten the fragmentation process. Such a split might stem from sectarianism (Sunni versus Shi'ia) but would more likely be due to Islamic versus secular differences among the dominant Punjabi element. These divisions would probably find expression in different army factions led by powerful personalities, who themselves would have strong links to politicians, bureaucrats, and business elites, each faction claiming to represent Pakistan's true national interest.

In most states with strong civilian institutions, a divided military is not a predictor of state failure. All failing states have weak armies, but not all weak armies are associated with failing states. If other institutions are powerful, if the economic, social or foreign policy challenges to the state are manageable because of strong civilian institutions, then a state may have a weak army and still thrive. But in Pakistan's case the army extracts whatever resources it requires, it is first in the queue for foreign exchange, it has a better educational and training system than any other public institution, and it is popular and socially influential. This strong army presides over an increasingly weakened state—an unsustainable situation. However, what if the army itself were divided on fundamental issues—the purpose and identity of Pakistan, relations with major outside powers, or the role of the army in correcting social and political problems? Then, all bets are off on the future of Pakistan.

Implications

In most of these breakup scenarios large numbers of minorities might be trapped on the wrong side of the new borders; even a voluntary dissolution of Pakistan could lead to bitter recriminations, a fresh slaughter of minorities, or their expulsion, with the New Punjab keeping only those vital to its own economy and security.

Security arrangements would be critical for a newly divided Pakistan.[18] While some provinces might accept Indian domination and even protection, would this be true of Pakistan's Punjabi heartland? It would still be armed with nuclear weapons, would have a large standing army and a powerful air force, and would certainly demand access to the sea and a major port. Indeed, an independent Punjab, with a dependent Sindh and pliable Karachi, would still be a formidable state. This state might seek new allies abroad, as would the other remnants of a broken-up Pakistan (unless this was accomplished by a reordering of South Asia). A new partition is very unlikely, for it could only occur after the army's cohesion was broken (or, as discussed shortly, a war broke out between India and Pakistan). But if it did take place, then Pakistan's remnants would certainly be drawn into various regional and global strategic relationships, further splintering South and Southwest Asia.

Postwar Pakistan

War between India and Pakistan is an ever-present possibility, even if the two sometimes appear to be on the road to a détente. The region has moved from limited, positional territorial wars fought with simple weapons to a situation where the next war could involve a nuclear exchange ranging from a few to a few dozen nuclear warheads. In five to ten years, it could be in the hundreds. The postwar scenario deserves special attention because of the possibility of a war going nuclear, and the importance of unexpected and unpredicted events in Pakistan's history.[19]

The timing, duration, and intensity of a future India-Pakistan war is impossible to predict, but some possible outcomes include the following:

—As in 1971, a less-than-total war might lead to the army's disgrace. This would provide an opportunity to reset Pakistan's political order. Whether or not this would happen would depend on the availability of responsible and experienced politicians; there might also be active foreign attempts to encourage the rise of moderate groups.

—A new war could lead to a limited or even major exchange of nuclear weapons. Japan's unconditional surrender and occupation is not a likely precedent, since Pakistan's own nuclear weapons would be available for retaliation. Unless a nuclear war was carefully limited—avoiding major urban areas and the production of large amounts of fallout—the devastation would be on the scale of World War II Japan or Germany, but without deep technical and administrative resources available for postwar reconstruction. In such an environment, the army would play an essential law-and-order role, but the reconstruction of Pakistan as a modern state, if attempted, could only be initiated from outside the country.

—A major war might cause a split in the army, with some factions wanting to fight on, others willing to sue for peace, and a few willing to bring down the enemy with a devastating city-busting nuclear strike. Such pro-war and anti-war factions might form along ethnic, sectarian, or even ideological lines, and a civil war flowing from an international war would be a distinct possibility.

—Pakistan is now *less* able to handle the consequences of a major war (or significant natural disaster) than it was ten or twenty years ago. The confidence of core elites in the future of Pakistan is reduced, the economic situation more uncertain, and Pakistan's military position, despite the bomb, is less secure than it was then. Further, many of Pakistan's institutions, including the army, are weaker now. In brief, the shock of even a limited war or other major disaster might be greater than it would have been ten years ago.

In the event of another conventional war, the nuclear threat would make Pakistan's escalation policy central to its survival. Military strategists seem to understand that a new round of war with India might, as in 1971, put their country at risk. Pakistan and India are engaged in a high-stakes game of puzzling out each other's nuclear and military policies. Given the mixed record of both states in managing earlier conflicts, there remains the small, but frightening possibility that they could stumble into a nuclear exchange, the result of which would be devastating for India, but probably terminal for Pakistan.

Which Path Forward?

Twenty years ago Pakistan was spoken of as the next major middle-income country. Recently it was thought to be on the verge of collapse or rogue status, although there are signs that the downward trend in some areas is halted. In the long run, the lack of economic opportunity, the booming birth rate, the youth bulge, intensive urbanization, a failed educational system, and a hostile regional environment could leave Pakistan with a large, young, and ill-educated population that has few prospects for economic advancement and could be politically mobilized.

For the near future, Pakistan will be a state-nation lodged between a weak democracy and a benevolent autocracy. Can it remain in this uneasy position indefinitely? Table 8-1 summarizes Pakistan's probable and less-probable futures.

Barring a cataclysmic event (a nuclear war) or a conjunction of major crises such as a military defeat, a serious economic crisis, *and* extended political turmoil, the failure of Pakistan as a state can be ruled out. However, failure can still take place slowly or in parts. Pakistan may be unable to maintain minimal standards of "stateness": its taxes could go uncollected and its borders undefended; health, education, and nutrition could suffer; and decent government could be notable by its absence. Many of these trends can be reversed with concerted and effective policies. On the other hand, the possibility of more extreme scenarios—civil war, separatism, authoritarianism, or the triumph of Islamic radicalism—should not be discounted. Pakistan's own history provides grim evidence that its government can make fundamentally wrong choices.

Failure can also be defined in terms of aspirations and expectations. In Pakistan's case, these hopes relate to a particular *idea*, which has met with at least partial failure. It took a leap of faith to create Pakistan: a state without a shared historical experience, divided along many ethnic and linguistic lines, and split geographically by a thousand-mile expanse. The failure lay with a lack of imagination in expecting the two wings, united only by opposition to India, to remain together without Indian cooperation. That cooperation was not forthcoming. Indians, including the liberal, secular Nehru and most of his successors, fully expected Pakistan to fail,

Table 8-1. Pakistan's Possible Futures

Scenario	Time frame and probability	Political, strategic impact
Continuation of Establishment-dominated oligarchic system	Over the next five or six years: do not underestimate the capability of a small elite to manage a big country, but do not exaggerate their ability to work together and avert disaster.	Pakistan manipulates terrorist threat, Establishment searches for external alliances, little movement in relation to India, nuclear and missile production continues despite weak economy.
Liberal, secular democracy	Democracy could happen, but likely to be unstable; more likely to revert to military rule, or to Islamist or personalistic system.	Possible clampdown on sectarian terrorism, fresh effort at accord with India, somewhat more accommodating policy on nuclear weapons, but no disarmament.
Soft authoritarianism	Emergence of an authoritarian party, probably led by a charismatic leader, civilian or military; not likely to be sustainable.	Likely to remain in conflict with neighbors, greater human rights violations, possible rise of Islamist or democratic revolutionary forces, unstable.
Islamist state	Soft: Malaysia. Hard: postrevolutionary Iran. More likely would be a modified Ziaist regime, a military-civilian coalition glued together by Islamic doctrine, with the military as the senior partner; possible end of commitment to parliamentary democracy, probable imposition of martial law.	More open support of "freedom fighters," in name of Islamic causes; more visible and threatening use of nuclear weapons; possible strategic alliance with Saudi Arabia, and Pakistani military presence in Gulf.
Divided Pakistan	Could come about through several routes, but all now seem unlikely.	Great danger of loose nukes, balkanization of rump Pakistan, intervention of foreign governments.
Postwar Pakistan	Could theoretically happen by accident or design, given the nascent state of Indian and Pakistani nuclear programs, or might come about through an escalation process; the odds of a major war are in inverse proportion to the stability of the leadership in *both* India and Pakistan, and the willingness of outsiders to manage regional conflict situations.	A nuclear exchange could end the modern state of Pakistan in minutes, a long, drawn-out war might also ruin it; because both India and Pakistan have a modest second-strike capability, deterrence is in effect; the rest of the world would be traumatized by any use of nuclear weapons and would certainly intervene if possible.

and when it did not, they blamed the West for Pakistan's success. Obsessed with and angry at Pakistan, some Indians wanted Pakistan to fail more than they wanted India to succeed and were willing to accept the costs of competing with Pakistan even if that competition hurt India. This approach was replicated in Pakistan, where it is most evident in the army, the Pakistani institution with the longest memory but least foresight.

Perhaps the most interesting debate now raging in Pakistan is that between competing ideas of Pakistan, with the Quaid's original vision pitted against Islamist conceptions. With the rise of Islamism and a new Islamic sensibility, this debate, once a sideshow of interest only to academics and theologians, has moved to center stage. Without meaningful democratization, political accountability, equitable economic development, and in recent years, growth, the ruling Establishment finds it increasingly difficult to neutralize the demands of the fundamentalists. Rather than reorient the society by returning to Jinnah's secular vision, or emulating the Turkish or even the privately admired Israeli model, Pakistan's Establishment bought time by co-opting the Islamists' agenda.

Without question, Pakistan must transform the "Islamic" component of its identity and bring the idea of Pakistan into alignment with twenty-first-century realities. This does not mean abandoning cherished principles, but it does mean adjusting them to the modern world. In the words of one distinguished Urdu journalist-commentator, Mahmood Mirza, Islam needs a reformation—and Pakistani Islam in particular needs to be reconciled with the modern world. "Unless there is a movement such as Martin Luther's and a reinterpretation of Islam," he adds, "Muslim societies will remain backward and continue to create problems for themselves and others."[20] Pakistan needs its own modern Islamic university and access to modern Islamic education in such countries as Malaysia and Tunisia. Mirza (and others) also notes that Pakistan needs civilian governments that can tackle the religious extremists, not by supporting or tolerating them, but neither by suppressing nor eliminating them. The need for reform was eloquently articulated by one of Pakistan's most brilliant journalists, who had begun his career as a militant leader in the JI's student wing and then served in three different governments:

> As a younger man, I was attracted to the notion of Pakistan as an ideological state. But over the years I have seen the failure of ideologues

to practically define Pakistani ideology and witnessed the debilitating consequences of enforcing ideological paradigms on an unwilling Pakistani populace. Islam is important to Pakistanis but they are exhausted by the efforts of some to experiment with different notions of an Islamic state."[21]

Given the omnipresence of the military, moreover, Pakistan will likely remain a national security state, driven by security objectives to the neglect of development and accountability and unable to change direction because of a lack of imagination and legitimacy. The performance of Pervez Musharraf as both army chief and president over a four-year period has left much to be desired. It is hard to see how five more years of Musharraf's leadership will dramatically change Pakistan's future—but then it is hard to envision any other leader doing much better.

Balancing this, Pakistan has a number of assets. Its size, its Islamic ties, its nuclear capabilities, and its location make it important to many powers. When approaching other governments for assistance Pakistani governments invariably cite one or more of these qualities: in recent years they have also argued that the failure of Pakistan would be a multidimensional geostrategic calamity, generating enormous uncertainties in a world that craves order and predictability. Thus Pakistan, like Egypt, may fail to meet the needs of its citizens, but it could be propped up indefinitely by others.

Further, Pakistan does not lack for ability and expertise. Even though its educational system is crumbling, it has produced trained professionals, administrators, scholars, thinkers, and religious leaders of a very high order. Though prevented from practicing their profession, many of its politicians are highly qualified. Even Pakistan's generals, some badly misinformed about the modern world and their own country, are widely regarded as competent—their special problem is that they have wandered into the minefield of politics without proper training or equipment. In summary, the human material is there to turn Pakistan into a modern state, but it has been systematically squandered for three generations by an elite persuaded that Pakistan's critical strategic location would be enough to get it through difficult times. Now, the distant future has arrived, with Pakistan unequipped to face a fast-changing world while coping with new and mounting domestic problems.

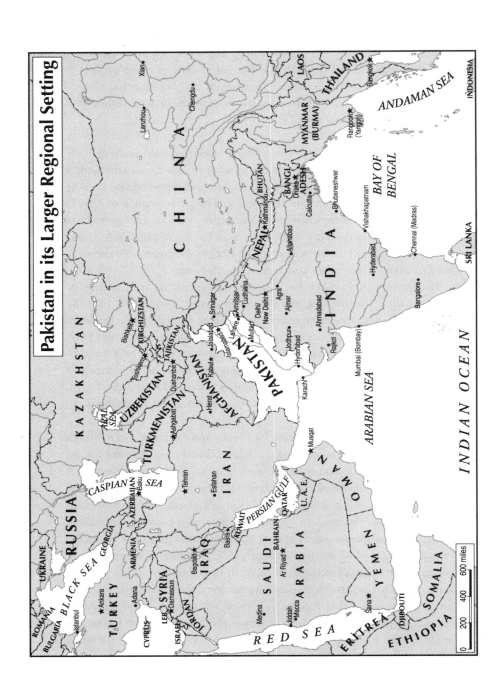

Pakistan in its Larger Regional Setting

CHAPTER NINE

AMERICAN
OPTIONS

The attacks on the Pentagon and World Trade Center again transformed the U.S.-Pakistan relationship. Once buried under three layers of sanctions, Pakistan became a vital strategic partner whose head of state would spend a day at Camp David in June 2003. Only three years earlier, candidate George W. Bush could not name Pakistan's leader, General Pervez Musharraf (nor, for that matter, India's prime minister, Atal Behari Vajpayee).

Pakistan is situated at the crossroads of many American concerns. These include terrorism, nuclear proliferation, democratization, and relations with the Islamic world and other important Asian states. There is no question that Washington will pay close attention to Pakistan in the short run, and the aid package announced at the Camp David meeting confirms this interest.

For obvious reasons, U.S.-Pakistan relations merit close attention. The spotlight here is on the central American interests in Pakistan and policies that might advance them. The most important and difficult policy issue is whether Washington should address Pakistan's deeper problems and prepare for the eventuality that Pakistan may become a failed or rogue state. In the past, short-term gains always had priority over long-term concerns, but the analysis in this book suggests that ignoring the long term could have grave consequences.

America and Pakistan

Over the years, America's relationship with Pakistan has been one of engagement and withdrawal. At one time, Pakistan was "the most allied" of American allies.[1] Washington turned to Pakistan in the early 1950s when India chose nonalignment, and Pakistan, desperate for outside support, eagerly reciprocated. Islam was assumed to confer a natural immunity to communism; Pakistan was at once both explicitly Muslim and near the world's two great communist powers. By joining the Central Treaty Organization (CENTO) and the Southeast Asia Treaty Organization (SEATO), it acquired military power that allowed it to maintain balance with India. As a democratic ally, Pakistan was often held up by the United States as a "model" for the Islamic world, although no other Muslim state regarded it as such.[2]

In the early 1960s, the U.S.-Pakistan alliance frayed when Pakistan turned to China for assistance while America backed India in its war with that country. After a failed American effort to mediate the Kashmir dispute, the alliance became dormant, only to be revived briefly in 1970–71 when Washington wanted to show its gratitude to Islamabad for facilitating the opening to Beijing. Afterward, the two countries went their separate ways, and the alliance quickly gave way to indifference, bolstered only by very small economic and military training programs.

With the loss of the East Wing and subsequent development of a Pakistani nuclear program, the Carter administration introduced sanctions. Two years after Zia's 1977 coup, relations reached their lowest imaginable point when mobs burned the U.S. Embassy and several information centers while the Pakistan government stood by. Pakistan's image as a friend of the United States and a staunch anti-communist member of the "free world" was in shreds. However, American policy did a complete about-face when Islamabad provided essential support for the anti-Soviet operations in Afghanistan. A second U.S.-Pakistan alliance now took shape.

At this time, American ambassadors in Islamabad liked to check off the many important interests they were attempting to advance, such as supporting the Afghan mujahiddin, containing the Pakistani nuclear program, edging Pakistan toward a more democratic political order, averting an India-Pakistan crisis, and slowing the flow of narcotics. When difficult decisions had to be made, the first interest—sustaining Pakistan's cooperation in the war against the Soviet Union—trumped all others. Washington was mild in its language regarding democratization, it underestimated the risks of an India-Pakistan war, and it averted its eyes from the Pakistani nuclear program. About the only successful policy (other than containing the Soviets) was curbing the drug trade.

However, a second checklist can be drawn up. This would include trends that were ignored by the Reagan administration and some of its successors, such as Pakistan's uneven economic development, its crumbling educational system, and the growth of Islamic radicalism. Only the nuclear program received sustained high-level American attention until the linkage between Pakistan, the Taliban, and Osama bin Laden's al Qaeda became evident in 1996.

These lists show not only that the urgent often drives out the important but also that the choice of what is "important" is often very subjective. The Reagan administration was uninterested in the consequences of supporting radical Islamists because they were thought to be the best anti-Soviet fighters, and their religious fervor appealed to some American officials and politicians.[3] A few years later, the Clinton administration was heavily focused on nuclear issues and the Taliban–Osama bin Laden nexus in Afghanistan—two urgent problems. *No* American administration thought it important to ask why Pakistan's educational system was collapsing and why Islamic schools were replacing them. The latter were considered "soft" issues, but are now correctly seen as critical ones.

In 1988 Americans were guardedly hopeful about Pakistan's future.[4] It appeared to be entering an era of democracy, was free of major conflicts with its neighbors, and was well situated to take advantage of changes in the global economy since it had begun to liberalize its economy well before India. Except for the nuclear issue, American policy toward Pakistan (and India, for that matter) was one of disinterest, diverted by the fall of the Berlin Wall, the breakup of the Soviet Union, and (in 1991) the first war with Iraq.

During the decade of democracy, Pakistan's institutions continued to deteriorate. A huge debt was accumulated and official cultivation of radical Islamic groups continued. Nevertheless, the nuclear issue continued to shape American judgments. During the last two years of Clinton's final term and in the first year of the new Bush administration, Pakistan was more or less ignored in favor of the emerging India, and the prevailing

American view of Pakistan, when it was thought of at all, was that it was an irritation.

The 9/11 attacks led to a third U.S.-Pakistan alliance as the Bush administration replayed Jimmy Carter's policy of lifting sanctions and providing aid in exchange for Pakistani cooperation in a war in Afghanistan. Pakistan again served as a support base for a war in Afghanistan, and then as a partner in tracking down al Qaeda and Taliban leaders who had fled to Pakistan. By mid-2003 economic and military aid was flowing in large quantities; Washington wrote off $1 billion of Pakistani debt in 2001–02 and offered a $3.2 billion, five-year economic and military aid package in June 2003, to begin in 2004.[5] The package, which will roll over into another administration, may contain provisions regarding issues of nuclear proliferation, democratization, and cooperation on terrorism that Pakistan may not accept. This history illustrates two important features of the U.S.-Pakistan relationship.

First, it has been episodic and discontinuous, driven on the American side entirely by larger strategic calculations during the cold war and later by the need for military allies in the war against terrorism. On the Pakistani side, of course, the purpose of the alliances was to acquire resources and political support for Pakistan's contest with India.

Second, although American aid strengthened the hand of the army, the on-again, off-again quality of the relationship made the army itself wary of America. The military training programs familiarized Pakistan army officers with America and American strategic policies and fostered a better understanding of American society, but they did not create a cadre of "pro-American" generals. Meanwhile, anti-Americanism grew among Pakistani civilians who saw the U.S. alliances as perpetuating the army's role.

The economic consequences of the U.S. relationship were equally ambiguous. While Pakistan did receive a lot of aid and most of its economic growth took place during the periods of highest aid flows, the new assistance was to be conditioned on economic and social reform.

American Interests

With this history in mind, one can now ask what Pakistan-related concerns are important for the United States today? *Terrorism* has certainly zoomed to the top of the American agenda, although it has different sources: notably al Qaeda and to a lesser degree the Taliban; Pakistan's homegrown terrorists; and non-Pakistani terrorists residing in its territory. Thus "terrorism" as an issue has a short-term alliance-like quality about it, but also a long-term preventative quality. Washington must work with Islamabad over the next few years to round up or neutralize al Qaeda operatives, but it must also view Pakistan as a potential problem. Twice Pakistan almost made it to the list of "terrorist-sponsoring" states, and a truly failed Pakistan could be a terrorist production factory.[6]

Islamabad's *nuclear program* is another leading concern, one of long standing but continued importance, especially in view of recent revelations about the movement of nuclear and missile technology to and from Pakistan. While Pakistan may (or may not) manage its nuclear arms race with India, leakage of its nuclear expertise is a potentially destabilizing factor in other regions, notably Northeast Asia (via ties to North Korea), the Persian Gulf area (via Saudi Arabia and Iran), and even the Middle East (via Libya, and perhaps other countries).

The *democratization* of Pakistan also remains an American interest, although in a different way than in the 1980s. Then, democratization was seen as a threat to the military regime led by President Zia, who was only lightly pressed to civilianize his government. Today, the Musharraf government and its American supporters argue that democratization could bring incompetent politicians or radical Islamists to power. In the long term, a democratic Pakistan is desirable, but getting there might disrupt the state in the short term, with worse consequences than the continuation of a military-led Establishment.

Pakistan's *hostile relationship with India* is also on the list because it impinges on both short- and long-term American interests. Besides having a desire to prevent another India-Pakistan war, Washington wants to maintain its excellent relations with India and has high hopes for wider strategic cooperation and stronger economic ties. The Bush administration skillfully preserved these ties even as it restored close relations with Islamabad. For the first time in decades, America has good relations with both South Asian states, but can this continue indefinitely? In other regions, the United States has had good relations with rivals (for example, Greece and Turkey), but usually when they were each part of a larger alliance framework, did not have nuclear weapons, and had not fought a war with each other for many decades. There is no overarching strategic framework for South Asia—and being against "terrorism" does not provide one.

Yet another concern is that Pakistan's identity as a *moderate Islamic* or Muslim state is being challenged by Pakistan's own Islamists. They are stronger than ever before after ten years of foreign support from Saudi Arabia, al Qaeda, and other Islamist groups and thirty years of patronage by Pakistan's intelligence services. They oppose President Musharraf's cooperation with the United States and the American presence in Pakistan and Afghanistan, which have led some radical Islamists, notably the al Qaeda leadership, to call for Musharraf's assassination and an Islamic revolution in Pakistan. How long can it remain a "moderate" state under Islamist attack and domestic political disorder, and will these forces eventually sever the present relationship with Washington?

One long-term concern is that Pakistan might become a *rogue state,* meaning one that seeks weapons of mass destruction and supports terrorism. To the degree that they subscribe to their own rhetoric, American policymakers must look beyond al Qaeda to troubling developments *within* Pakistan and consider the possibility that Pakistan, an ally, might become a major threat to a number of American interests. The 2003 aid package nominally addresses domestic stability, but it is not large enough or structured in such a way as to demonstrate a long-term American commitment to a domestically stable and progressive Pakistan. Policymakers in Islamabad, let alone many members of the Establishment, are wary that their country might become America's next target when the current partnership ends.[7]

Policy Alternatives

With America again assuming the role of Pakistan's chief external supporter, there is an opportunity to correct old mistakes. Getting the new relationship right might just bring Pakistan into the category of stable and relatively free states. Getting Pakistan wrong could accelerate movement toward authoritarianism, radical Islam, regional separatism, renewed war with India, or state failure. The ideal, of course, would be some low-cost, easy-to-implement strategy that would turn Pakistan into a reasonably democratic state enjoying good relations with its neighbors. However, there is no magic policy bullet, and the United States must balance competing interests, take account of the long and the short run, and recognize the difficulty of fostering change in another state's fundamental institutions, all the while preparing for worst-case futures.

Pakistan's possible failure along one or more dimensions is a prospect that should sharpen American interest and focus efforts on prevention. This would mean moving beyond the headline issues of capturing Osama bin Laden, rounding up the al Qaeda dregs, and chastising Pakistan for its nuclear leakage and the growth of the madaris. These are urgent concerns, but the long-term problem is the domestic timebomb ticking away in Pakistan society. Achieving short-term objectives, though important, will mean little if Pakistan were to evolve into a truly dangerous state or come apart, spewing nuclear technology and terrorists in every direction. The recommendations offered below parallel, but go beyond, those suggested in the final report of the National Commission on Terrorist Attacks upon the United States (the "9/11 Commission"), issued in July 2004.

What possible policy alternatives can ensure that these long- and short-term interests will be maximized? Right now the United States is not inclined to pursue a broad policy of *alliance*, such as that followed from 1954 to 1962 and during the 1980s. Such a policy implies a tight linkage between the two countries, with Pakistan offering itself as a strategic asset for a larger American policy and, in turn, finding itself the recipient of significant economic and military aid.[8]

The current relationship is best described as a *partnership* of uncertain duration, implying a joint objective, presumably the roundup of al Qaeda and Taliban cadres, without the legal and strategic implications of an alliance. If the partnership remains limited, the exchange will be simple and straightforward: Pakistani cooperation in intelligence and military operations against terrorists would bring a quantity of economic and perhaps military assistance. A broader partnership would be similar to what the British journalist Anatol Lieven terms a "management" strategy, in which Washington works with and through Pakistani governments in whatever form they take, seeking to shape their domestic as well as their foreign policies.[9] Lieven argues that the United States cannot contemplate using force against Pakistan, nor can it escape the fact that Islamabad is central to the war against terrorism, so it must work with whatever Pakistani government comes to power.[10]

Most Pakistanis and some Americans believe that the present policy of partnership and engagement will give way to the historic default option: *ignoring* Pakistan. For part of the 1960s, much of the 1970s, and the first half of the 1990s, Washington had no Pakistan policy to speak of, either ignoring the country or focusing on a single issue, nuclear proliferation.

One could imagine several reasons for returning to such a policy: the war on terrorism may go well, and Pakistan's assistance may not be required; Washington's attention may be diverted elsewhere, as a result of new crises or opportunities, relegating Pakistan to a second- or third-tier level of interest; or the United States may not be able to agree upon a consistent policy toward Pakistan; or Congress may not be willing to vote for the $3.2 billion aid package, or might place such conditions on the aid that Pakistan will decide not to accept it. Some or all of these things *could* happen. Even so, it seems unlikely that America will soon lose interest in Pakistan.

One could also foresee a policy of *opposing* Pakistan, to the point of forcing a regime change by diplomatic and economic pressure or even invasion. Although, as Lieven and others have noted, a nuclear-armed Pakistan would be a dangerous country to take action against, there might be circumstances—such as a civil war, or the existence of loose nuclear weapons—in which active opposition was the lesser danger. Other scenarios can also be envisioned: an Indian decision to achieve the military defeat of Pakistan might tempt an American government to side with India to keep the war short and to prevent the use of nuclear weapons or their transfer to terrorists and other nonstate groups.

While governments often seek simple and uncomplicated policies, this is not possible in Pakistan's case. A policy of uncritical alliance, or one of outright hostility, does not do justice to the range of important American interests embedded in the relationship. Further, some of these interests are of a short-term nature, or have a clear timeline (such as antiterrorist operations), while others (such as preserving Pakistan's status as a relatively moderate state) are long-term projects.

Some policies can be ruled out in the short run. Currently, a sanction-oriented policy, in which economic and military aid was terminated and sanctions were imposed on Pakistan in order to punish it for its nuclear program, or its ambivalent policies regarding terrorism, would be counterproductive to the extent that it would strengthen radical forces in the country.[11] But such policies might make sense in the future, perhaps as contingencies should Pakistan's behavior threaten to damage vital American interests. The "default" policy of ignoring Pakistan also seems unwise at this moment, and one of Pakistan's greatest bargaining chips is the threat that it might just become a rogue state if its friends do not help it. This strategy—the suicide gambit—exaggerates both the vulnerability of Pakistan's moderate leadership and the danger of growing Islamic radicalism.

This suggests that American policy, the policies of other important states, and of Pakistan itself, need to seize the opportunity to do more than provide short-term assistance. A strategy that purchases insurance against the more frightening long-term scenarios discussed in chapter 8 should be part of any American approach to Pakistan. Given the range of possible futures set forth in that chapter, which policies will advance American interests, those of Pakistan, and other concerned states?

The Short Run versus the Long Run

At the June 2003 Camp David summit, President George W. Bush set out three major goals of American policy toward Pakistan: keeping it as a partner in the war against terrorism, constraining the spread of nuclear weapons, and democratization.[12] The first two are urgent policy priorities, the third a hope.

In the past, the urgent need for an ally caused long-term interests to be sacrificed in the pursuit of short-term gains. This was especially true in the 1980s when the United States accommodated Pakistan's nuclear program and left to successor administrations the problem of not only a nuclear Pakistan but its export of nuclear technology to North Korea and several other states. At that time officials refused to link the aid package with Pakistani nuclear restraint. Similarly, there was no effective restraint on the way Pakistanis distributed weapons to various mujahiddin groups, selecting the most radical and anti-American for support, while shutting out the more moderate factions. Furthermore, American economic aid to Pakistan during this period was unaccountable, with much of it winding up in the hands of a thriving class of middlemen, who invested it abroad or spent it in ways that effectively subsidized Pakistan's defense budget.

Therefore, while American policy must be effective in the short term, it needs to be in harmony with important medium- and long-term goals. The following list of American policy options is presented in order of short-run to long-run application, but *all are important and should receive close attention by American policymakers.* The first group focuses on Pakistan itself; the second, on Pakistan's environment.

Terrorism

The new relationship with Pakistan derives primarily from its importance in combating terrorism aimed explicitly at America by al Qaeda and (to a lesser extent) the Taliban. The Taliban were accessories, in that they permitted Afghanistan to be used by al Qaeda as a safe haven in which training and planning took place, and from which cadres were sent on terror missions. American and Pakistani interests diverged on the Taliban regime, Pakistan seeing it as the first friendly Afghan government in recent history. Pakistan has been cooperative in rounding up foreign al Qaeda cadres, but less enthusiastic about targeting the Taliban, which still receive significant support from Pakistani Pashtuns, some of the Islamist parties, and Pakistan's intelligence agencies. Beyond this shared policy, however, lurk two other terrorism concerns.

One is Pakistan's direct and indirect support for Kashmiri-related groups that have attacked innocent civilians. Some of these groups now seem intent on precipitating a war between Delhi and Islamabad and oppose the latter because it abandoned the Taliban and reversed course on Afghanistan.[13] To compound the problem, terrorism has a domestic face in Pakistan. Many of its sectarian terrorist groups have factions operating in Kashmir/India and Afghanistan, and a number of them have ties to various Pakistani parties, Islamabad's intelligence services, or the army.

Should American policymakers ignore terrorism directed against India or Pakistan itself and focus only on U.S.-related groups? Obviously, such a policy is intellectually and morally unsustainable. All three types of terrorism are of grave concern, and in many cases the groups are linked. Since compelling American interests are involved, Washington should focus on three strategies.

First, since the army remains at the center of political power in Pakistan, Washington should link the quantity and quality of *military assistance* to good performance in countering all three kinds of terrorist groups, beginning, obviously, with the first category, but eventually including the second and third. Many possible steps have been discussed between American and Pakistani officials in this regard, including greater control over the madaris, closer surveillance of suspect groups, the closing of terrorist training camps, improved surveillance along the LOC, and efforts to counter extremist propaganda. If Pakistan demonstrates vigor and competence in such matters, military aid and cooperation could be *increased* from the modest levels now planned.

Second, there should be continued support to improve the professionalism of Pakistan's police forces, which are notorious for their capricious abuse of power. The police are seen as predators, not protectors, and support for terrorist groups is partly a byproduct of alienation from the Pakistani state. For its part, the Pakistan government should ensure that the police receive salaries and support commensurate with their grave responsibilities; in the long run this is more important for the security and stability of Pakistan than money spent on advanced weapons and military hardware.

Third, Pakistan's movement against terrorists operating in Kashmir will have to be linked to progress in a peace process (see the next section) since Pakistan will not want to unilaterally strip itself of a key policy instrument. To summarize, nothing will happen if America demands merely an end to Pakistani support for terrorist groups without offering positive inducements in the form of aid and active support for a dialogue with India.

Retrograde Islamism

Washington must be careful not to interfere, or even appear to be interfering, in Pakistan's religious institutions and its religious parties. However, it cannot let pass the vicious anti-Americanism that is cultivated by many groups in Pakistan, often in the name of protecting Islam and frequently with funding from Saudi Arabia and the United Arab Emirates. America must attempt to meet this challenge in the realm of ideas and thought, just as it met the challenge of Nazism and communism with a vigorous defense of its own principles and values via the press, academic exchanges, public information programs, and a willingness to debate hostile Islamists on their own turf.

The United States should address directly the civilizational arguments propounded by the same radical Islamists; Islam has not had a reformation, but most Pakistani thinkers do not subscribe to al Qaeda's view that Islam is in danger and that the West, plus its Jewish and Hindu allies, have targeted Islam and Pakistan. In the days of the cold war, the U.S. Information Service reprinted and commissioned numerous books on the ideological dimension of that conflict. Today, however, balanced views of

America and the Islamic world are difficult to find, especially in the vernacular press. As in the case of public education, the cost of a few high-technology weapons would more than pay for such an information program and would do more to protect American interests, lives, and property.

As for the Islamic parties that seek power through peaceful means, Pakistan should be encouraged to let them meet an electoral test in a free and fair contest; they are far weaker than the centrist mainstream parties, and their victory in two provinces did not represent a national trend—except to the degree they were strengthened by anti-American feelings prevalent throughout Pakistan and weakened by the actions of the security forces and Musharraf's manipulation of the electoral process.

American officials have been either disingenuous or badly informed in their assessment of Pakistan's madaris, especially the radical ones. One senior Bush administration official noted that of the $3 billion "planned" for Pakistan over a five-year period, $100 million would go toward education, and this would be used in the 1,200 madaris that had registered with the Pakistan government and receive some government support. Aside from the fact that this represents only 1 to 3 percent of the madaris, and there is no reliable assessment of the success of the government's program (most private observers dismiss it), the vast number of madaris are independent, with many receiving support from Wahabi ideologues.

Washington should not attack the madaris, or demand that the government of Pakistan close them down; neither should it count on any effort to "reform" them. As one Pakistani official who has studied the madaris noted, "If you give them access to the Internet, they'll only surf the radical websites." The strategy should be to support the kind of education that will contribute to a broader view of the world and prepare graduates for real-world employment. As for the mullahs, again the strategy (in the words of a Punjabi Nazim concerned about their growth) should be to strengthen the moderates and the state system of education, not to "go after [the Islamists] hard, which would only make them martyrs."[14]

The Economy

After the 1999 coup, General Musharraf turned to Shaukat Aziz to rescue Pakistan's economy. With international assistance, close monitoring of expenditures, and a consistent policy over a three-year period, Pakistan showed signs of economic growth, and in 2002 Musharraf insisted that Aziz be taken on as finance minister by the new civilian government. Aziz's policy has moved Pakistan away from bankruptcy, with foreign exchange holdings at $8 billion in 2002, according to the World Bank, and $12.5 billion by mid-2004, according to Pakistani officials. The international debt is still large, and unemployment and underemployment remain high.[15] America should continue to support the economy with macro-level assistance, but continued (and even expanded) economic aid should be linked to several key policy changes.

To begin with, the Pakistani people must see tangible evidence that the government's tilt in favor of the United States brings significant benefits to all socioeconomic strata. Most aid is invisible to the average Pakistani, who cares little about debt relief or balance of payment problems. Without being obtrusive or boastful, the message should be that America is vitally concerned about Pakistani economic progress and wants to see Pakistan's economy adapt to a fast-changing world. Specific projects in the arena of high technology, improving indigenous manufacturing, and research and development capabilities would demonstrate that a globally competitive Pakistan is in America's interest.[16]

Next, Washington should vigorously pursue the initiative announced by President Bush at the 2003 Summit: one by which American companies would be encouraged to invest in Pakistan. They are likely to be wary of establishing a presence in Pakistan itself, given the security problems, but it is important that American companies invest in areas important for balanced Pakistani growth, not merely the source of extraordinary profits for a few American companies (President Musharraf has complained that some foreign firms have reaped profits of up to 40 percent from their Pakistani operations.)[17]

Then, Japan should be closely consulted on economic matters regarding Pakistan. It is the country's largest foreign investor and aid donor, and it has major economic investments in India and other regional states.

In addition, aid accountability is vital. Pakistan must agree to benchmarks and guidelines to ensure that economic assistance is not wasted, stolen, or diverted. Until recently, Pakistan was consistently one of the worst performers on Transparency International's corruption list. The United States and other donors have every right to link economic assistance to evidence that the money is being properly spent.[18] The essential principle for American aid administrators to keep in mind is that aid is not merely a payoff to a regime; its purpose, in this case, is to help the regime make the structural changes that will prevent Pakistan from evolving into a dangerous state. An important warning sign would be Pakistan's refusal to accept accountability for the significant amounts of aid headed in its direction. Regrettably, the plan devised by the U.S. Agency for International Development (USAID) is weak when it comes to holding Pakistan to high standards of performance: it does not provide much money for Pakistan's economic and social development, and it fails to target the most immediate social and political problem.[19] This is *not* illiteracy in the countryside—bad enough as that is—but the disenchantment and potential radicalization of Pakistan's middle classes and elite, especially the many college and university students who constitute a fertile recruiting ground for a Pakistani version of al Qaeda.

Education

Both the American and Pakistani governments are aware of the collapse of Pakistan's educational system, but they tend to look at different dimensions of the problem. Washington has focused on the madaris, seeing them as schools for terrorism, and President Bush asked Musharraf about progress in this area (his answer was: not as good as we would like). The new U.S. aid package includes a multiyear $100 million educational program, to be managed by a North Carolina firm.[20] As of 2003, only $21.5 million of American aid was directed at primary education and literacy, about half the cost of an F-16. Even then, aid experts note, a large percentage of this will be swallowed up by administrative costs.

Meanwhile, Islamabad would prefer to emphasize the importance of improving advanced technical education and has started another training scheme for scientists and technicians. Pakistan's leadership sees the problem in technocratic terms: they would like to educate scientists and engineers who are politically apathetic but technically adept, who could help Pakistan compete with India and other rivals. Their model is the huge military-educational-industrial complex already in place, with a series of technical institutions feeding workers and scientists into the weapons programs. This is an educational vision appropriate for a totalitarian state, not for one that aspires to be a free society.

Given the failure of the Pakistani state to invest in education, this sector (like those of family planning and health care, which suffer because of a similar failure to invest in them) should be opened to international nongovernmental organizations (NGOs). This approach has worked with some success for Bangladesh. Following liberation in 1971, Bangladesh was one of the poorest countries in the world, significantly more so than Pakistan. But Dhaka was able to make significant progress on basic quality-of-life measures, including education and population control, by allowing foreign NGOs to operate freely within the country. The problem in Pakistan has been that many NGOs were Islamic charities, tainted by fundamentalism and Wahabi militancy. The stranglehold of such groups over Pakistan's privatized services must be loosened.

At the graduate and postgraduate levels, American educational assistance should focus on restoring the private institutions that once thrived in Pakistan, including church-related schools, and on restoring Pakistan's liberal arts, humanities, and social science expertise that is so necessary for the establishment of an informed citizenry. Where will Pakistan train these individuals? A massive expansion of the Fulbright program and an emergency training program for Pakistani educational administrators and faculty members are in order. However, Pakistan should follow the lead of Bangladesh and many other states and send some advanced students to India and other comparable states for technical and nontechnical training. These programs might well be sponsored by the South Asian Association for Regional Cooperation (SAARC), which may make them politically more palatable to all parties and also strengthen this regional organization.

At the lower levels—elementary and secondary education—aid must be highly conditional upon actual achievement in literacy levels and teacher training. Indeed, the problem of teacher training is so great that Pakistan should be encouraged to bring in teachers from India and other countries, who will not only provide high levels of technical skill but will also help break down the cultural isolation of many Pakistanis.

Perhaps the most important condition on aid for the educational sector should be that the Pakistan government itself assume increasing responsibility for its funding and administration. The governmental share spent on education, especially primary education, should increase, and if it is cut, then Pakistan should pay the price in terms of reduced military aid.

Any educational aid program must calibrate the amount of aid in relation to the sector's absorptive capacity. Nothing contributes more to corruption than the feeling that money must be spent, even if there are no good projects to spend it on. Thus educational aid programs should be treated as a very long-term project, with measured increases as Pakistan's absorptive capacity grows. To reiterate, the essential principle to bear in mind is that this aid is not being given for its own sake, but to achieve permanent and positive change in Pakistan.

Administrative Reform

As in the case of its police and educational system, Pakistan once had a highly respected civil service and judiciary. Both have been eroded over the years because of corruption and politicization under military and civilian governments. Washington should assist Pakistan in rebuilding these institutions, where possible, not only by the usual visits to America (and visits by American experts to Pakistan), but by encouraging Pakistanis to visit states with similar social, political, and economic systems that have developed innovative solutions to the tasks of providing professional and efficient administration and running an impartial judicial system.

Asia's newly industrialized countries, for example, were once behind Pakistan in most social and economic indicators, but with the help of a relatively strong civil service were able to achieve rapid growth and economic success. Of this group, Malaysia and Indonesia are also largely Muslim countries, with Thailand being another state that has moved forward. Malaysia and Thailand also have a high percentage of English language speakers.

Democratization

Democratization is one of the three benchmarks in Washington's aid package. Washington should press hard on this benchmark and frame a timetable for the gradual restoration of democracy—even if Musharraf rejected the idea during his 2003 visit to the United States. This is an important goal, and the size and schedule of the package should be linked to Pakistani progress toward it.

It will be difficult to persuade the present Pakistan government that real democratization is in its own interest. A return to complete civilian government, the military fears, would generate policies inimicable to the army's conception of "the national interest" because civilians simply do not understand what that interest is. The army's hostility toward politicians cannot be erased overnight, yet there needs to be a "staged" withdrawal of the army from politics, staged in both meanings of the word.[21] Ironically, the chief obstacle to democracy—the army—is also the principal barrier to political extremism. The army should be encouraged to develop a timetable and stick to it. This timetable may stretch over several years, but there is no better opportunity than now to restore the civil-military balance in Pakistan to something resembling normalcy.

While democracy in Pakistan may be problematic, the best way for the United States to forestall the rise of radical Islam, safeguard a modicum of civil liberties, and preempt separatist movements, is to insist as a condition of aid that the Pakistan government allow the mainstream political parties (such as Pakistan People's Party and the Pakistan Muslim League) to function freely. The goal should be a spectrum of moderate parties, Islamic and secular, that are willing to operate within a parliamentary and peaceful context, and are tolerant of sectarian and other minorities. The Pakistan government must be accountable for its toleration of radical Islamist groups, parties, and leaders that have practiced and preached violence within Pakistan and across its borders in India and Afghanistan. Here, the army's historic linkages with extremist Ulema parties is incompatible with democratic norms, and the army should begin its retreat from politics by severing these ties. Any moderate Islamic state must be built on the foundation of Pakistan's mainstream parties.

The United States need not fear democracy in Pakistan. The centrist "mainstream" parties still have an overwhelming capacity to win votes, but the political system has not operated in a normal fashion. Those in the West who argue against democracy for Pakistan end up placing their bets on the army and a group of Islamic parties. Yet the former cannot effectively govern Pakistan, the latter may see democracy as a shortcut to absolute power, and in any case their capacity to govern is questionable while their antagonism to the West is tangible. The army uses the threat of radical Islam to alarm its Western supporters, while the Islamists bide their time as they burrow into many Pakistani institutions and gradually build their own infrastructure, including new madaris throughout the country. If present-day trends continue, there is some chance that a coalition of the army and the Islamist forces will eventually dominate Pakistan.

Military Training Programs

The United States should be unambiguously supportive of military training programs that bring officers to the United States and send Americans to Pakistan. To the degree that the senior ranks of the Pakistan army used to have a liberal, secular outlook, this was strongly reinforced by their contacts with American (and British) officers in various overseas training programs and joint exercises. These programs were among the first to disappear when sanctions were imposed in 1990 because of Pakistan's nuclear program. They were restored after 9/11. As of 2004, approximately 200 Pakistani officers are receiving training in the United States under the auspices of the Pentagon's International Military Education and Training (IMET) program, and another hundred or so under a program dealing with counterterrorism. These programs should be maintained indefinitely, insulated from future cutbacks.

The cost of these programs runs to about $1 million a year. Should Islamabad pursue policies inimicable to the United States, Washington might want to reduce or eliminate military and even economic aid, but the training programs provide a channel to Pakistan's most important institution, and no administration (or Congress) should touch them. They are not a reward for good behavior; they provide unique access to the Pakistan army. Terminating them would hurt America more than Pakistan. Washington should not limit these programs to military subjects; they can be expanded to include fellowships for Pakistani officers to join American universities and research centers, as was done during the Zia years.

Might the United States be creating a new "generation" of Pakistani army officers via this training program? It is hard to tell at this point what the impact of training, studying, and working alongside Americans will be, but this generation could be pivotal in helping Pakistan move from a stagnant oligarchy to a more innovative state. Certainly, if the American contact is broken off by a new round of sanctions, this group will react negatively and might support a more efficient Pakistani autocracy; however, it could also be an agent of change in the direction of openness and democracy if the U.S. connection is maintained along with continuing American assistance to the social sector. In any case, these young officers will be closely watched by other Pakistanis and foreign governments.

Shaping the Environment: India

Pakistan's future will depend in large part on its relations with its neighbors, especially India and Afghanistan. The conflict with India places the army front and center domestically and allows national security issues to cast a disproportionately large shadow over Pakistan's economy, politics, and society. Nevertheless, despite high defense spending for years and two major wars, Pakistan is less secure today than it was fifty years ago—and the same can be said of India. Jinnah's original optimism regarding normalization has long-since proven naive and been replaced by narratives of nuclear holocaust, civilizational war, and terrorism.

Pakistanis came to view Indian society as the cause of their insecurity, thereby implying war would be permanent and Indians always impossible to trust. Latterly, Pakistanis have conjured up a grand alliance of Hindu and Western civilizations, bent upon destroying Muslim power by first attacking the strongest and most modern Islamic states, including Pakistan itself. This apocalyptic vision includes the belief that betrayal justifies revenge, that alien cultures have robbed Pakistanis of their identities, and that false friends (like America) placed tyrannical leaders in power and exploited Pakistan's wealth and geostrategic position. A state that has been wronged so much by others need not abide by ordinary standards. Like extreme Wahabism, the view is growing among the Pakistani elite that all Muslims everywhere are victims and that the only response is to hit back ruthlessly. This theme of betrayal is echoed in India by Hindu nationalists who seem bent upon turning their country into a Hindu Pakistan, and by "secular" Indians who believe the two states have incompatible identities and thus cannot live in peace as neighbors.

It is true that Pakistan's identity as a homeland for the oppressed was hijacked: instead of building a state, Pakistan's Establishment sought to build a nation by acquiring allies, developing nuclear and conventional weapons, and manufacturing myths, all in the service of balancing out a more powerful and seemingly implacable India. However, the changed international order has made such a strategy impractical for Pakistan, not to mention highly dangerous for India. What both states have in common now is their ability to destroy each other, and neither has yet begun to absorb the implications of how their new strategic relationship matches up with their identity wars.

Pakistan's relations with India have been deteriorating for many reasons, a primary one being their pathological nature: each side feels threatened and insecure. Also important is the disparity between their nuclear power, which brings the region notoriety, not peace; the rise of groups beyond state control, including separatists and radical Islamic (and Hindu) movements; and the lack of interest among outside powers, especially the United States, in long-term solutions.[22] If these issues cannot be addressed comprehensively, the army is unlikely to yield power, Pakistan will not concentrate on the business of growing economically and achieving domestic tranquility, and the odds in favor of some future cataclysmic crisis will rise.

What can the United States do to reduce these obstacles to a more normal India-Pakistan relationship? For a start, it should recognize the importance of indirect steps, for it actually has meager influence on the psychological cold war between India and Pakistan. Washington should continue to encourage unofficial dialogues (funded heavily in the 1990s, but with nuclear proliferation being the chief issue) on Kashmir, nuclear issues, and areas of cooperation and conflict management. Private foundations should be encouraged to promote such programs, to arrange meetings of parliamentarians, and to support educational endeavors that bring younger Indians and Pakistanis together. A step in this direction would be to expand the summer and winter schools for the "next generation" of Indian and Pakistani journalists, academics, and young officials and encourage them to discuss regional security issues, including nonmilitary sources of conflict.[23]

The disparity in power between India and Pakistan *is* something that the United States can influence. Washington is again in the position of having its finger on the scales via its sale of military equipment and technology to both India and Pakistan. Pakistan should not be provided with military assistance under the assumption that making it more powerful is more likely to bring India to the negotiating table. Rather, such aid should be a way of assuring Pakistan that if it does make concessions to India it will be better able to safeguard its own security. Above all, military and dual-use assistance must not trigger a regional arms race. To this end, it is essential to have an objective assessment of the actual conventional and nuclear balances, edging India and Pakistan toward some kind of understanding of the parameters of military acquisition.[24] In this way the region may be encouraged to move to a defensive-oriented military structure, acquire systems that are less provocative, and thus enhance stability and reliability in the nuclear area.

It would be the height of folly to introduce antiballistic missile systems into South Asia without a careful examination of their impact on the regional nuclear balance. It *does* make sense to encourage India and Pakistan to acquire them if it could be ensured that the strategic balance did not tilt too sharply in either direction *and* if they could achieve nuclear stability at lower rather than higher levels, with the region moving to a strategic regime that emphasized defense rather than offense.

The conventional balance must be complemented by policies that will help India and Pakistan manage their nuclear weapons in a safe and secure fashion, without persuading them to go to more and more advanced systems. Indian Muslims do not, as Jinnah once assumed, regard themselves as hostages to good treatment of Hindus resident in Pakistan. They have ironically become hostages to a nuclear Pakistan that threatens them with annihilation. The risks of nuclear theft and seizure in Pakistan have been exaggerated, for the army is unlikely to lose its coherence and control over the country's nuclear assets; however, Pakistan has allowed its nuclear scientists to roam the world, and any military aid should be tightly linked to the utmost nuclear restraint. Indeed, the issue is so important that Washington should consider the most devastating sanction of all—indicating that should Pakistan continue to leak technology to states hostile to Washington, then it would face the prospect of direct American action or a strengthening of India's strategic and nuclear capacities.

Another point to remember is that radical ethnic and confessional groups have followed parallel trajectories in India and Pakistan, and that extremist Hindu and Muslim groups have interacted with each other for over seventy years. With the mass media recording their provocations, the extremists in green are virtually indistinguishable from those in saffron. There is little that Washington can do directly regarding such groups, but its officials must speak out against outrages, and American private foundations and think tanks should monitor the excesses of these groups. In fact, many India and Pakistan groups are already doing this, and they deserve outside support and encouragement.

Above all, the United States must go beyond mere lip service and more actively promote the peace process between the two countries, perhaps in partnership with like-minded states.[25] Although the Bush administration loathes the idea of "mediation," India and Pakistan have clearly reached the point where they will find it harder to move forward without outside assistance, and they stand a good chance of stumbling into still another crisis or war. American officials now seem to accept "facilitation" as a legitimate and useful role.[26] Ambassador Robert Blackwill insisted on Indian television that the United States would facilitate two-party talks between India and Pakistan, but that it would not provide substance, a road map, or a blueprint.[27] A task force sponsored by two important American foreign policy institutions subsequently recommended (in September 2003) that the administration appoint a high-level official to aid and abet the India-Pakistan dialogue, especially on Kashmir, and assume a more "forward-leaning" posture in attempting to deal with India-Pakistan crises before they start.[28] After completing its deliberations, the task force shared its recommendations with the Bush administration, and fortuitously or otherwise, Secretary of State Colin Powell encouraged India and Pakistan to resume their dialogue at the January 2004 SAARC meeting.[29]

American support for such a process—no matter what it was called—would do much to undercut the Islamic extremists on the Kashmir issue, would make the army less central to Pakistan's future, and, in the long run, would be in India's interest too. If India and Pakistan are to be believed, any concessions would bring out the radicals (both Hindu and Muslim), so the other side must take the first step. This is negotiating with a grenade in one's own hand: make concessions or I will destroy us both. Sustaining this process should be a major American activity. Although disputes over Kashmir, Cyprus, Palestine-Israel, and other such issues are considered intractable and beyond a definitive solution, in short, "conflicts unending," the formula to deal with them is not to wait until they are "ripe" for resolution, or to turn away, or to search for a definitive solution when none is available. Rather, the answer is management.[30] The goal should be slow movement toward a stable relationship. It takes a very long journey and patient nurturing to resolve these conflicts. Furthermore, it must be seen as a bipartisan, multiadministration task. A Kashmir solution should evolve in a region-centered process of negotiation, with Washington encouraging both sides to think through the implications of various solutions without endorsing any until an agreement is near, and perhaps linking enhanced aid and political support to positive movement in the process.

A peace process between India and Pakistan should attempt to redefine the issue from its fossilized debate over sovereignty, law, and constitutional rights, which leads nowhere, to a search for an improvement in the lives of Kashmiris—Hindu, Muslim, and Buddhist. It should be framed not in terms of "majority" and "plebiscite," but in terms of actually improving the lives of those most affected by Pakistani-supported terrorists and Indian police and military operations. An emphasis on human rights puts the right kind of pressure on India, while allowing Pakistan to save face after fifty-five years of irredentist policies. Needless to say, it also addresses the major concerns of most Kashmiris and removes one of the "causes" of radical Islamists. A solution to, or amelioration of, the Kashmir problem will be difficult to achieve, but its long-term resolution should be an American goal.

If the United States were to commit itself to a normalization process, would India and Pakistan respond? Although Pakistanis now openly call for a peace process, New Delhi actually has a greater stake in the peaceful settlement of outstanding disputes with Pakistan and the normalization of the Pakistani state. From Delhi's perspective, Pakistan could be a Canada, but it could also be more threatening than a nuclear-armed Cuba: a radical, armed state, bent on fostering an Islamic revolution in India. New Delhi can do more than any other state to steer Pakistan in one direction or another. While it seems willing to take the rhetorical first step, it is historically reluctant to take the substantive second step—in the present case, to make the kind of concessions that Musharraf can use to get the military and others to "bite the bitter pill" of a status quo settlement for Kashmir.

Shaping the Environment: Afghanistan

Any comprehensive policy toward Pakistan must also address Pakistan's relationship with Afghanistan. The two states have a long-standing and complex relationship, which took an astonishing turn when American forces removed the Taliban government with Pakistan's reluctant assistance. While the United States, Afghanistan, and Pakistan now have a tripartite security committee to monitor the progress against al Qaeda and Taliban, and on paper Pakistani statements regarding Afghanistan are reassuring, many in Islamabad still regard Afghanistan as a potential client state. Given the opportunity, some Pakistanis would again interfere in Afghan affairs. Islamabad has legitimate interests in Afghanistan that include the desire to prevent the expansion of Indian power into Afghanistan in order to prevent India from encircling it (another concern is Iran's presence there). Further, the fear is that the Pakhtoonistan movement could be revived on either side of the Durand Line. Radical Islamic groups in the NWFP are especially attuned to developments there.

The best American policy is prevention, to ensure that Afghanistan does not collapse into chaos and that Pakistan remains supportive of the Karzai regime, or something like it, and allows the formal and effective neutralization of Afghanistan. The process of nation and state building must continue in Afghanistan and be seen to be continuing with American and international support. Afghanistan needs substantial and long-term outside assistance to help manage its own security, and Washington should actively support the process in the knowledge that the greatest danger of an Afghan collapse might be the radicalization of large parts of Pakistan, along with the re-Talibanization of Afghanistan.

Danger Signs

As this book is being completed, two earlier alliances seem to be in rerun: according to "pragmatic" and "realistic" assessments of Pakistan, the man in power is America's best bet. Experts in the West, such as Robert Kaplan and former officials such as General Anthony C. Zinni, agree that Musharraf's importance lies not so much in his personal qualities but in the belief that "what would come after him would be a disaster."[31] On the contrary, the potential for a radical leadership in the next four or five years, Islamic or otherwise, is low. Pakistan has a grace period of several years, perhaps more. What is undeniable is that radical forces, especially among the Islamists, are growing, that social chaos and demographic pressures are mounting, and that many of Pakistan's liberals (or "mainstream" thinkers) are frustrated and may turn to radical Islam, as Marxism is no longer an option. Any change in the army's cohesion—unlikely, but not impossible—could bring forth a radical Pakistan.

Therefore an optimal American policy would be to support the present regime, whether or not Musharraf heads it, but press Pakistan very hard for the political, economic, and even ideological changes discussed above, including a new approach to India. During this period the United States should watch for several danger signs. If they appear, then it should start reconsidering the policy of helping Pakistan through a difficult time and look at other, more drastic options, such as allying with India and other states to contain a Pakistan that seems to be unable or unwilling to reform itself. Over the next few years, the following will be some of the danger signs:

—*Failing to adopt a political timetable.* In early 2004, President Musharraf claimed that he would give up his army position by the end of the year, but he could easily defer this step. There remains a danger that Musharraf will, like Ayub Khan and Zia ul-Haq, slip into personalized rule and not know when or how to give up power. He is not a truly exceptional person, and the best service he could do for his country would be to allow a system of constitutional checks and balances to emerge and to give up his official positions to qualified successors. Otherwise, Washington will be in the position of supporting an individual, when what Pakistan needs is to build institutional capabilities.

—*Political repression and a new spell of martial law.* Blocking secular, provincial, and ethnic channels of expression by a fresh ban on political activities would pry open the door for radical Islamists, who are adept at using the mosques and madaris for recruitment and mobilization.

—*A lack of accountability regarding the significant amounts of aid now in the pipeline and planned for the future.*

—*No significant progress in educational reform.* Without a transformed school system, the madaris will continue to expand, spreading hatred of India, Israel, and the United States and miseducating their students.

—*An inability to confront* domestic *sectarian terrorist groups.* This is in Pakistan's vital interest and is a goal often proclaimed by the Pakistani leadership; if Pakistan is incapable of bringing these groups under control, then that is a particularly grim indicator that the Establishment is losing ground.

—*Popular anger at Musharraf and the United States.* The continuation of anti-Americanism in Pakistan for a few more years would be a sign that aid and the new political relationship with Pakistan are not working. The next generation of officers, frustrated with Musharraf's secularism, somewhat more Islamized, and even more adamantly opposed to the United States, could produce an army chief who would play Islamic and anti-American cards.

—*Another major conflict with India.* This could strengthen the hand of radical forces in Pakistan and might further weaken the army's now-challenged reputation, and of course, would compel a fresh round of American intervention to prevent escalation to the nuclear level.

—*No progress in Afghanistan.* The war in Afghanistan was a major reason for the Muttahida Majlis-e-Amal's success in Baluchistan and NWFP. A continuing U.S. presence without tangible positive results for the Afghan people, or a civil war, will further intensify Pakistani grievances and fuel discontent with Washington and any government that supported it. Of special concern would be an alignment of Pashtun nationalism with radical Islamism.

For the United States, Pakistan is part problem and part solution. An ally in the war against terrorism, it is also a potential source of Islamic radicalism, nuclear proliferation, terrorism, and even a participant in a nuclear war. Washington has no option but to work with Pakistan in the short run, cajoling Islamabad to adopt policies that go beyond its short-term cooperation in the war against terrorism. However, America should be concerned about the deeper causes of Pakistan's malaise, lest the country become the kind of nuclear-armed monster state that its critics already think it is.

In summary, American policy must go beyond a policy of cooperation and encompass a strong dose of prevention. The cost of such a policy would be minimal but would have to go beyond the supply of limited amounts of military equipment and an aid package that does not address Pakistan's underlying weaknesses. Debt relief is important but only buys time before the reckoning. An effective policy will require sustained attention, include assistance to Pakistan's weakened civilian institutions, especially education, and revive technical and other assistance schemes that helped Pakistan become a candidate-member for middle-income status fifteen years ago. A policy of prevention will involve working closely with other states and would be welcomed by those Indians who also see a reasonably liberal, moderate Pakistan to be in India's interests. This policy would also mean engagement with the idea of Pakistan; Washington has, once again, come to view Pakistan as a "moderate Muslim state" and a role model for other Muslim states. But the idea of a "moderate Muslim state" must have content. If the end goal is a liberal modern state, functioning in the global system, at peace with its neighbors, then there is a very long road ahead, with no assurance that either the Pakistani state or the Pakistani nation is willing and able to travel it.

Pakistani Perspectives

For *any* policy to succeed, the American policy community will also have to understand Pakistani views toward America. These include a belief that America is a fickle and unreliable state. Washington, many Pakistanis say, likes to use their country like a condom, throwing it away when no longer needed. They also fear that Washington will choose New Delhi over Islamabad. Pakistan's Establishment is confident that it can play on short American memories and a relative lack of knowledge about South Asia, keeping Washington thinking that "we are your best chance" for stability and strategic cooperation. Islamabad now raises the bogey of Islamic radicalism, as it once talked about the international communist threat or the danger of expansionist Hindu India.

Pakistanis are expert at deciphering American interests and appealing to short-term American fears in the hope of establishing a relationship of mutual dependency in which Pakistani obligations are minimal while American ones are substantial. In the words of a young Pakistani woman, "Pakistani officials, like Pakistani beggars, become alert when they see Americans approaching." In dealing with Pakistan, the United States must also recognize that Islamabad may complain about being constrained by public opinion, but the government is what shaped that opinion over the years.[32]

American officials must also remember that the elite public in Pakistan is deeply skeptical of the United States. Some of its Islamists are ideologically opposed to the United States, the left complains that America supports the Establishment, and the Establishment itself has long ceased to trust Washington. Post-9/11 harassment and assaults on Pakistanis in the

United States are widely publicized and discussed in Pakistan, and the Islamists cite them as incontrovertible evidence of American hostility.[33] Almost all Pakistanis are deeply troubled by what they see as an American tilt toward Israel in the Middle East (which they compare with America's perceived tilt toward India against Pakistan), and regard the U.S. invasion of Iraq as an anti-Muslim act, and potentially a model for an American attack on Pakistan itself.[34]

As for knowledge about the United States, there are no functioning American Centers in Pakistan (there used to be seven, but well before 9/11 these were reduced in size and number). With travel warnings to that country having been in effect for years and terrorists having singled out Americans over the past decade, actual exposure to Americans is minimal.

Americans must remember that although Pakistan will pursue its own vital interests as it sees them, an opportunity may exist to incrementally shape Pakistan's future in a direction that is compatible with important American (and Pakistani) interests. Pakistan has demonstrated an ability to resist America in the case of its nuclear program, its provocative policy in Kashmir, its tolerance of domestic extremists, and its support for the Taliban. In each case Washington was unable to persuade Pakistan that these policies threatened vital Pakistani interests, as well as American ones. Before writing Pakistan off as the hopelessly failed state that its critics believe it to be, Washington may have one last opportunity to ensure that this troubled state will not become America's biggest foreign policy problem in the last half of this decade.

NOTES

Introduction

1. Pakistan's performance as a frontline state is hard to measure. A few months after the invasion of Afghanistan, it was widely reported that Pakistan had assisted in the capture of or had directly captured 500 top al Qaeda and Taliban leaders; two years later, that figure had risen to only 550, which suggests the rate of capture has been very slow, perhaps one or two a month at best, with no independent verification of whether those captured, except in a few known and important cases, are really high-level individuals.

2. For an excellent history of Pakistan by a British scholar, see Ian Talbot, *Pakistan, A Modern History* (New York: St. Martin's Press, 1998); also Lawrence Ziring, *Pakistan at the Crossroads of History* (Oxford: Oneworld, 2003). For a contemporary account by an informed British correspondent, see Owen Bennett-Jones, *Pakistan: Eye of the Storm* (Yale University Press, 2002); and for a brief, bitter evaluation of Pakistan by a former *New York Times* correspondent, see Barry Bearak, "Pakistan Is . . . : A Journey through a State of Disequilibrium, *New York Times Magazine,* December 7, 2003.

3. Pakistan's structural weaknesses are said to be so advanced that it "could well become the world's newest failed state—a failed state with nuclear weapons." See Mary Anne Weaver, *Pakistan: In the Shadow of Jihad and Afghanistan* (New York: Farrar, Straus and Giroux, 2002), p. 10.

4. Cited in a review of recent books on Pakistan by Mahnaz Ispahani, "The Cauldron," *New Republic,* June 16, 2003, p. 31.

5. Remarks of Foreign Secretary Kanwal Sibal, at the Indian government website, www.meadev.nic.in/speeches/id-uspart.htm. Singh made this comment to Strobe Talbott, deputy secretary of state, during their long dialogues after the 1998 Indian nuclear tests. See Strobe Talbott, *Engaging India: Diplomacy, Democracy and the Bomb: A Memoir* (Brookings, 2004).

329

6. For example, National Security Adviser Condoleezza Rice praised Pakistan and President Pervez Musharraf after the public disclosure of Pakistan's secret nuclear technology sale program to Libya, Iran, North Korea, and perhaps other states. Salamder Davoudi and Guy Dimore, "US Cements Pakistan Links Despite Fear of Nuclear Deals," *Financial Times* (London), February 12, 2004, p. 11.

7. Stephen P. Cohen, *The Pakistan Army* (University of California Press, 1985; reprinted and expanded, Oxford University Press, 1988 and 1998; Urdu edition, 2003; pirate Chinese edition, 1997).

8. Ibid., p. 133.

9. For a broad perspective on failure from a cultural and comparative perspective, see Joseph A. Tainter, *The Collapse of Complex Societies* (Cambridge University Press, 1988). He notes (p. 4) that "collapse" is manifest in many ways, and that collapsing societies may not collapse in every dimension.

10. Iranian intellectuals joke about the "Pakistan syndrome," meaning a state that has failed along many dimensions but can still do one thing well—build a nuclear bomb.

11. On Pakistani political history, see Talbot, *Pakistan, A Modern History;* and Ziring, *Pakistan at the Crossroads.* Also the web-based timeline produced by a Pakistani software company, Jin Technologies (Karachi and Islamabad), *The Story of Pakistan* (www.storyofpakistan.com [last accessed June 26, 2004]).

12. For a comprehensive overview of this program, as well as a history of the U.S.-Pakistan-Afghan relationship, see Steve Coll, *Ghost Wars* (New York: Penguin Press, 2004).

Chapter One

1. Early travelers are covered by Sanjay Subrahmanyam, *The Portuguese Empire in Asia, 1500–1700: A Political and Economic History* (New York: Addison-Wesley Longman, 1993); the history of the "discoveries" is still evident in many monuments in Lisbon and Goa, the largest former Portuguese colony in India.

2. On the geostrategy and decline of the Mughals, see John Richards, *The Mughal Empire* (Oxford University Press, 1993).

3. See Richard M. Eaton, "Temple Desecration and Indo-Muslim States," in *Beyond Turk and Hindu: Rethinking Religious Identities in Islamicate South Asia,* edited by David Gilmartin and Bruce B. Lawrence (New Delhi: India Research Press, 2002).

4. *Alberuni's India*, edited and translated by Edward C. Sachau, 2 vols. (New Delhi: Low Price, 1991; originally published 1910), p. 22. Alberuni, born in A.D. 973, was taken prisoner by Mahmud of Ghazni in Khiva and accompanied him to India as a court historian; his full name was Abu-Raihan Muhammed Ibn Ahmad al Beruni.

5. For an overview, see Aziz Ahmad, *Studies in Islamic Culture in the Indian Environment* (Oxford University Press, 1964), pp. 81–86.

6. See Peter Hardy, "Modern European and Muslim Explanations of Conversion to Islam in South Asia: A Preliminary Survey of the Literature," in *Conversion to Islam,* edited by Nehemia Levtizion (New York: Holmes and Meier, 1979).

7. Ibid.

8. See Ahmad, *Studies in Islamic Culture,* p. 81, noting that Islam spread particularly quickly in the northwest and east, where Buddhism had been strong and Brahminical Hinduism relatively weak.

9. Conversion in east Bengal is detailed in Richard M. Eaton, *The Rise of Islam and the Bengal Frontier, 1204–1760* (University of California Press, 1993).

10. Ṣufism, or *tasawwuf* in Arabic, is generally understood to be the inner, mystical, or psychospiritual dimension of Islam, although some contemporary Islamists regard it as un-Islamic.

11. See Hardy, "Modern European and Muslim Explanations of Conversion," p. 91, summarizing the work of Ishtiaq Husain Qureshi: "Adherents often made their way to membership of the Muslim community by many bypaths, and more as the eventual outcome of a process, perhaps extending over several generations, which began as a loosening, rather than an abandoning, of old religious and social ties and an immediate entering into new ones with a known and established Muslim community."

12. Ibid., p. 86.

13. Eaton, *The Rise of Islam and the Bengal Frontier,* presents various retrospective theories of conversion, including the view that many Hindus were drawn to the more egalitarian Islam, were coerced or bribed into conversion, or forced to do so by economic and environmental circumstances. Islam, he argues, was a better-organized religion for the exploitation of resources in certain regions of India, notably Bengal.

14. On the controversy, see Eaton, "Temple Desecration and Indo-Muslim States," pp. 246–81.

15. Christians have been the target of Hindu extremists in India and Islamic ones in Pakistan.

16. This inscription, and many other relics of the Raj inscribed on statues and buildings throughout India, reflect John Stuart Mill's idea that until nations achieve a certain level of development, they need a benign emperor/guide. Toward the end of the nineteenth century, this view displaced the easygoing social and cultural integration of the early Raj, when the British and Indian populace intermingled and intermarried. The process in the princely state of Hyderabad is described by William Dalrymple, *The White Mughals* (London: HarperCollins, 2002).

17. Eaton, "Temple Desecration," pp. 246–47.

18. Akbar S. Ahmed, *Jinnah, Pakistan and Islamic Identity* (Oxford University Press, 1997), p. 43.

19. Ibid.

20. Hamza Alavi argues that the Pakistan movement was based in what he terms the Muslim "salariat," a middle class that had grown up under the British,

especially in the non-Muslim majority regions of British India. See "Pakistan and Islam: Ethnicity and Ideology," in *State and Ideology in the Middle East and Pakistan,* edited by Hamza Alavi and Fred Halliday (New York: Monthly Review Press, 1988).

21. However, see Ahmed, *Jinnah, Pakistan and Islamic Identity,* p. 110, who notes that while many scholars trace the idea of the "two-nation theory" to Sir Syed, the stirrings of a Muslim nationalist movement were anticipated in the first half of the nineteenth century in both Bengal and North India, areas with a strong Muslim peasantry.

22. The lists, or schedules, of these castes gave rise to the appellation "schedule caste," now termed "Dalits." Similarly, it has long been a common practice at the provincial and local levels in South Asia to reserve seats for women and other "weaker" elements of society.

23. The Khilafat movement and Gandhi's role in keeping it nonviolent are discussed by Ian Talbot, *India and Pakistan* (Oxford University Press, 2000), pp. 64–67.

24. Hamza Alavi, "Parting of the Ways," in *The South Asian Century: 1900–1999,* edited by Zubeida Mustafa (Oxford University Press, 2000), p. 16. See also Asma Yaqoob, *Muslims as an Identity Group in South Asia* (Islamabad: Institute for Regional Studies, 2003).

25. Hardy, "Modern European and Muslim Explanations of Conversion," p. 69.

26. See Mohd Aslam Khan, Rahmat Ali, Sheikh Moh'd Sadiq, and Inayat Ullah Khan, *Now or Never: Are We to Live or Perish Forever?* (www.mediamonitors. net/noworever.html [January 1933]). Rahmat Ali was, by the 1940s, extremely critical of Jinnah for seeking a Pakistan that only included East Bengal, Sindh, Baluchistan, and West Bengal, and his latter-day views were presented in a large and often fantastical history of Pakistan written and published in the 1930s. See Choudhary Rahmat Ali, *Pakistan: The Fatherland of the Pak Nation* (Lahore: Book Traders, 1978; 1st ed. 1935). For a graphic presentation of the different concepts of Pakistan, see Joseph E. Schwartzberg and others, *A Historical Atlas of South Asia,* rev. ed. (Oxford University Press, 1992), plate VIII.C.4, p. 72.

27. For two sympathetic accounts of Jinnah's career, see Stanley Wolpert, *Jinnah of Pakistan* (Oxford University Press, 1984); and Ahmed, *Jinnah, Pakistan and Islamic Identity.*

28. Quoted in Latif Ahmed Sherwani, *Partition Schemes Leading to the Pakistan Resolution* (Islamabad: Quaid-i-Azam Academy, 1990), p. 10.

29. Azad's life is still the subject of controversy, and not all of his papers and correspondence have been released; for a study of the historiography of this complex man, see Ayesha Jalal's review of the "complete" version of Azad's autobiography, *India Wins Freedom,* and a biography of Azad. Ayesha Jalal, "Azad, Jinnah and the Partition," *Economic and Political Weekly,* May 27, 1989.

30. Talbot, *India and Pakistan,* p. 54.

31 B. R. Ambedkar, *Pakistan, or the Partition of India* (Bombay: Thacker, 1945), p. 236.

32. This remains the case today, and in contemporary Gujarat the Brahmin-dominated Bharatiya Janata Party has attempted to recruit Dalits into an anti-Muslim coalition, using them as shock troops in the recent anti-Muslim riots in that state. Elsewhere, Dalits and Muslims often form a political coalition against upper-caste Hindus.

33. Presidential address to the Allahabad Session of the All-Indian Muslim League, December 29, 1930.

34. Shaukatullah Ansari, *Pakistan: The Problem of India* (Lahore: Minerva Book Shop, 1944), p. 105.

35. Ambedkar, *Pakistan, or the Partition of India*, pp. 85–87.

36. The Muslim League won in Bengal and Sindh but did not achieve a majority in Punjab. Schwartzberg and others, *A Historical Atlas of South Asia*, p. 222.

37. Shahid Javed Burki, *Pakistan: The Continuing Search for Nationhood*, 2nd ed. rev. (Boulder, Colo.: Westview Press, 1991), pp. 22–23.

38. For the major collection of documents, see the twelve-volume series edited by Nicholas Mansergh, E. W. R. Lumby, and Penderel Moon, *The Transfer of Power, 1942–47* (London: Her Majesty's Stationery Office, 1970–83); a shorter collection is in C. H. Philips and M. D. Wainwright, eds., *The Partition of India: Policies and Perspectives 1935—47* (London: Allen and Unwin, 1970). New archival material appears regularly as British military documents of the period are declassified.

39. See Ainslie T. Embree, *Imagining India: Essays on Indian History* (Oxford University Press, 1989), esp. chap. 3, "An Outsider's View: Al-Biruni."

40. Pakistan does not have a "right-of-return" policy. Indian Muslims were allowed to migrate to Pakistan for about ten years after partition; afterward they were required to have a visa and were regarded as Indian citizens. After the loss of East Pakistan, there was a flood of migrants from that province, but most were non-Bengalis who had supported the west in the civil war. Chapter 6 examines the role of these "Biharis" in Pakistan's ethnolinguistic brew. See also Ishtiaq Ahmed, "Pakistan and South Asian Muslims," *Daily Times* (Lahore), November 2, 2003 (www.dailytimes.com.pk/default.asp?page=story_2-11-2003_pg3_3 [last accessed June 26, 2004]).

41. For a comprehensive cultural-historical explanation of Indian insecurity and expansionist tendencies, see Javed Hassan, *India: A Study in Profile* (Rawalpindi: Army Book Service, 1990), written while the author was a colonel attached to the Staff College in Quetta. It became the standard Pakistan army text on India. Hassan was a key figure in the Kargil War, having commanded the Northern Light Infantry; by 2004 he had become a corps commander.

42. For a discussion of the role of *Izzat*, see Akbar S. Ahmed, *Islam under Siege: Living Dangerously in a Post-Honor World* (Oxford, U.K.: Polity Press, 2003).

43. Mohammed Ali Jinnah, speech at Lahore, March 22, 1940, at the historic

session of the Muslim League at which a resolution demanding the creation of Pakistan was passed.

44. The sentiment was echoed some forty years later by a major-general of the Pakistan army who told me that personally he had no grievances against Indians, and that "Indians and Pakistanis are brothers; but if my brother has a gun and I do not, I feel a little—perhaps—unsure of him."

Chapter Two

1. Pashtun is also spelled Pathan or Pakhtoon. I use the latter only when referring to Pakhtoonistan, the putative homeland that would include Pashtuns living on both sides of the Durand Line between Afghanistan and Pakistan.

2. For a summary of the public services in the early years, see Keith Callard, *Pakistan: A Political Study* (London: George Allen and Unwin, 1957), pp. 284–301.

3. This is the man portrayed in the controversial film *Jinnah:* in several scenes he is shown to be deeply upset by the chaos and killing of partition; however, some of those associated with Jinnah (notably S. S. Pirzada) reject the film's interpretation of him.

4. *Quaid-i-Azam Speaks: Speeches of Quaid-i-Azam Mohammad Ali Jinnah* (Karachi: Ministry of Information and Broadcasting, 1950). Also quoted in Ardeshir Cowasjee, "Sole Statesman-2," *Dawn* (Karachi), June 2, 2000 (www.dawn.com/weekly/cowas/20000625.htm [last accessed on June 26, 2004]).

5. Exact figures are hard to come by, but the total number of migrants to India and Pakistan is variously estimated at between 10 million and 15 million people, approximately 3 percent of India's total pre-partition population.

6. Shahid Javed Burki, *Pakistan: The Continuing Search for Nationhood,* 2nd ed. rev. (Boulder, Colo.: Westview Press, 1991), pp. 40–41.

7. Jinnah, in response to a question from a German journalist, *Dawn* (Karachi), March 12, 1948. Dawn News Service week ending August 5, 2000. Archived at http://64.233.161.104/search?q=cache:C7-AraRrjXQJ:www.lib.virginia.edu/area-studies/SouthAsia/SAserials/Dawn/2000/aug05.html+jinnah+german+journalist+dawn&hl=en (last accessed June 26, 2004).

8. Jinnah was himself a Shi'ia, and some of his bitterest critics were Deobandi Sunni ideologues who warned against Pakistan being ruled by a *kaffir*—unbeliever. After partition, some Islamic sects were declared heretical, and some of Pakistan's most distinguished scientists and public servants, were they alive today, would be suspect on the grounds of religious deviance. See chapter 5 for a further discussion of sectarianism.

9. See Hasan Askari Rizvi, "In Search of the Real Jinnah," *Business Recorder* (Karachi), December 25, 2003.

10. This migration was overshadowed at the time by the better-publicized movement of millions to India and the migration of Jewish survivors to Israel.

Only recently has there been a serious examination of the cultural and psychological impact of partition. For a representative example of the new scholarship, see Saros Cowasjee and K. S. Duggal, eds., *Orphans of the Storm: Stories on the Partition of India* (Delhi: UBSPD, 1995); Mushirul Hasan, *India Partitioned: The Other Face of Freedom* (Delhi: Roli Books, 1995); and Hasan, "Partition: The Human Cost," *History Today,* September 1997.

11. In Punjab, for instance, the Muslim League had little initial support, and politics was dominated by the Unionist Party, an alliance of Muslim, Sikh, and Hindu feudal landlords who were more interested in preserving their power than providing support for the mass politics of the Congress or the Muslim League.

12. United Nations Development Program (UNDP), *Pakistan: National Human Development Report, 2003* (Islamabad, 2003), p. 49. The author, Akmal Hussain, is a leading Pakistani economist.

13. According to 1951 census data, migrants were particularly numerous in West Pakistan, where they constituted 57 percent of the population of Karachi, Pakistan's largest city, and 65 percent of Hyderabad. Most of these were Mohajirs, from the Urdu-speaking regions of North India. The migrants from east Punjab were better integrated into Pakistan's Punjab.

14. It is estimated that 2 million Hindus, Sikhs, and Muslims died as a result of partition. One who came to Pakistan was the young Zia-ul-Haq, subsequently the general most enthusiastic about Islamizing Pakistan; one who left was L. K. Advani, who was to become the most hardline member of the Vajpayee cabinet from 1998 onward, ascending to the post of deputy prime minster in 2002.

15. See Akbar S. Ahmed, *Islam under Siege: Living Dangerously in a Post-Honor World* (Oxford, U.K.: Polity Press, 2003).

16. The following discussion is taken primarily from Stanley A. Kochanek, *Interest Groups and Development: Business and Politics in Pakistan* (Oxford University Press, 1983).

17. Ibid., pp. 21–22.

18. Shahid ur-Rahman, *Who Owns Pakistan?* (Islamabad: Aelia Printing Communication, 1998), p. 139.

19. Kochanek, *Interest Groups and Development,* p. 21.

20. There could be no plebiscite, the Indians argued, until all forces were removed from the state, including Pakistani ones. There the dispute has remained for fifty-plus years, now the oldest dispute ever brought to the United Nations (by India). For an overview of Kashmir, see Stephen Philip Cohen, *India: Emerging Power* (Brookings, 2001); also Sumit Ganguly, *The Crisis in Kashmir: Portents of War and Hopes of Peace* (Cambridge University Press, 1997). There is no comprehensive Pakistani statement of the Kashmir issue.

21. Zulfiqar Ali Bhutto, The *Myth of Independence* (Oxford University Press, 1969), pp. 179–80.

22. For a family portrait by his daughter, see Sara Suleri Goodyear, *Meatless Days* (University of Chicago Press, 1989).

23. Interview with Z. A. Suleri, Lahore, March 1990.

24. In the west, water was linked to Kashmir, because India controlled the sources of the Indus in the state.

25. In 1942 landlords formed the largest single group in the Muslim League Council, accounting for 163 of the total of 503 members. The largest single provincial representation was Punjab, with 51 members. For details, see Khalid Bin Sayeed, *Pakistan: The Formative Phase* (Karachi: Pakistan Publishing House, 1950), p. 244; and Mushtaq Ahmed, *Government and Politics in Pakistan* (Karachi: Pakistan Publishing House, 1959), p. 91.

26. For a survey, see S. M. Zafar, "Constitutional Development," in *Pakistan: Founder's Aspirations and Today's Realities,* edited by Hafeez Malik (Oxford University Press, 2001).

27. Ibid., pp. 31–32.

28. This history is concisely surveyed in Javed Iqbal, "The Judiciary and Constitutional Crises in Pakistan," in *Pakistan,* edited by Malik. Iqbal, the son of poet-politician Mohammed Iqbal, was a Supreme Court justice and now heads the Iqbal Institute. For a full-length discussion of his views, see Javed Iqbal, *Islam and Pakistan's Identity* (Lahore: Vanguard Books, 2003).

29. See Zulfiqar Khalid Maluka, *The Myth of Constitutionalism in Pakistan* (Oxford University Press, 1997). Several of Pakistan's civilian prime ministers, notably Zulfiqar Ali Bhutto and Nawaz Sharif, also manipulated the constitution and courts.

30. In 2002 Lahori lawyers assembled in collective protest against both the army's extraconstitutional Legal Framework Order program and the Supreme Court judges who agreed to stay on past their retirement date, which had been extended by such an order. They were vindicated when, as part of the resulting compromise between Musharraf's government and opposition parties, these judges resigned at the very end of 2003, to be replaced by a new set of justices.

31. For a comprehensive account, see Allen McGrath, *The Destruction of Pakistan's Democracy* (Oxford University Press, 1996).

32. Ibid., pp. 230 ff.

33. One man who stood and fought the new order was Nawabzada Nasrullah Khan, who opposed Ayub and helped form the Democratic Action Committee, the first of many alliances of democratic parties to oppose military rule. He had been an ardent supporter of Pakistan before partition and sought to establish a liberal democracy informed by Islamic practices—more or less what Jinnah would have wanted. His death in 2003 caused widespread melancholy among Pakistan's political classes as much for their failure as for his passing. See David Rhode, "In One Man's Life, a Glimpse of Democracy's Agony," *New York Times Week in Review,* October 5, 2003, p. 5.

34. Mohammed Ayub Khan, *Friends Not Masters* (Oxford University Press, 1967), p. 172.

35. Ibid., p. 115.

36. Ibid., p. 47.

37. Ibid., p. 126.

38. Ibid., p. 127.

39. Samuel P. Huntington, *Political Order in Changing Societies* (Yale University Press, 1969), pp. 250–51, cited in Ian Talbot, *Pakistan, A Modern History* (Oxford University Press, 1998). Though Yahya was not in power long enough to earn such fulsome praise, Musharraf has received it from contemporary observers. See, for example, Fareed Zakaria, *The Future of Freedom: Illiberal Democracy at Home and Abroad* (New York: Norton, 2003), pp. 100–01, 146.

40. Herbert Feldman, *Revolution in Pakistan: A Study of the Martial Law Administration* (Oxford University Press, 1967) p. 208.

41. Kochanek, *Interest Groups and Development*, p. 89.

42. Ibid.

43. Ayesha Siddiqa-Agha, "Power, Perks, Prestige, and Privileges: Military's Economic Activities in Pakistan," paper presented at the International Conference on Soldiers in Business: Military as an Economic Actor, Jakarta, October 17–19, 2000.

44. Shahid Javed Burki, *Social Groups and Development: A Case Study of Pakistan* (Harvard University Center for International Affairs, 1971), pp. 18–21.

45. Kochanek, *Interest Groups and Development*, pp. 92–93.

46. For the classic discussion of the importance of education in maintaining a state's political orientation, see the last quarter of Aristotle's *Politics*.

47. Ian Talbot, *India and Pakistan: Inventing the Nation* (London: Arnold, 2000), p. 201.

48. K. K. Aziz, *The Murder of History: A Critique of History Textbooks used in Pakistan* (Lahore: Vanguard Books, 1993).

49. For example, *The Pakistan Army* was praised by Zia, who nevertheless thought that it dealt with too many "sensitive" issues, i.e. Islam and the Pakistan-Israel comparison, and that "our people are very emotional about such things" [conversation with the author, 1988]. He nevertheless "allowed" it to be published shortly before his death; similarly, authors of other books were asked to alter some passages before a Pakistan edition was published, and most Pakistanis simply did not write about subjects that ran against the official ideology.

50. Three of these would be the difficulty of launching a real national debate on Kashmir, the phony national discussion over the Comprehensive Test-Ban Treaty (CTBT), which was shot down by the government's own subsidized think tanks, and most recently, the wary response to Musharraf's suggestion that Pakistan might consider recognizing the state of Israel.

51. For the classical writings on oligarchies, see Aristotle, *The Politics*, edited and translated by Ernest Barker (Oxford: Clarendon Press, 1952); Gaetano Mosca, *The Ruling Class*, edited by Arthur Livingston (New York: McGraw-Hill, 1939); C. Wright Mills, *The Power Elite* (Oxford University Press, 1956); and Robert Michels, *Political Parties* (New York: Free Press, 1966).

52. One contemporary chronicler of the Establishment is Syed Mushahid Husain, who became a senator in 2000; he is a sometime member of the Establishment, having served as minister of information for Nawaz Sharif and as editor of several very influential papers. He first wrote about the Establishment in *The Nation* (Lahore), on November 3, 1996, and returned to the subject in another *Nation* column on June 18, 2002, after serving a year's house arrest after Musharraf's coup.

53. Some American ambassadors in Islamabad have been very close to governing regimes; others have found themselves part of the political process even if they wanted to keep their distance, as Pakistanis regard the U.S. ambassador (and the embassy) as critical players in their political system.

54. Pirzada is regarded with mixed feelings by his fellow lawyers. Some claim that he has served each government faithfully by helping them to suborn the constitution so that he "can make money," a charge that he staunchly denies.

55. General Musharraf's former minister of information has written on the "media war" being waged against Pakistan in 2004 and the need for Pakistanis to avoid providing grounds for its critics. He urges Pakistani academics, columnists, and think tank members to mind their language, especially when dealing with the foreign press, and praises Musharraf as a "valuable yet inadequate counterweight to the imbalance of the media forces aligned against us." See Javed Jabbar, "Facing a Media World War," *Dawn* (Karachi), March 22, 2004 (www.dawn.com/2004/03/22/fea.htm [last accessed June 26, 2004]). Journalists have been harassed, even beaten, after writing too many critical op-ed pieces, or speaking about Pakistan in critical terms—especially to foreign audiences—under both civilian and military regimes. In 2004 one parliamentary opposition party leader was convicted of treason in an unpersuasive case involving a letter from a disgruntled officer.

56. The original Lahore declaration, successfully opposed by Jinnah, talked of states, not one state.

57. Nevertheless, Indian strategists do. Like most elites, they are sensitive to their own traumas, such as the 1962 war with China, and insensitive to those of other states, notably those of Pakistan. ·

58. M. H. Askari, "The Trauma of 1971 and After," *Dawn* (Karachi), December 19, 2003 (www.dawn.com/2003/12/19/op.htm [last accessed June 26, 2004]).

59. For an early and comprehensive Bangladeshi version, see Rounaq Jehan, *Pakistan: Failure in National Integration* (Columbia University Press, 1972). For an American overview of the 1971 war, including the diplomacy that preceded it, see Leo E. Rose and Richard Sisson, *War and Secession: Pakistan, India and the Creation of Bangladesh* (University of California Press, 1990). For a one-year retrospective of Musharraf's visit, see Moonis Ahmar, "A Year after Musharraf's BD Visit," *The News,* July 29, 2003 (www.asianscholarship.org/publications/papers/.doc [last accessed July 6, 2004]).

60. *Frontline* (Chennai), August 17–30, 2002.

61. War Inquiry Commission Report (www.bangla2000.com/Bangladesh/Independence-War/Report-Hamoodur-Rahman/chapter5.shtm [2002]).

62. See Bhutto's famous declaration, often repeated, that the Hindu, Jewish, and Christian civilizations had their bombs, so the Islamic world had to have one also. Zulfiqar Ali Bhutto, *If I Am Assassinated . . .* (New Delhi: Vikas, 1979), p. 138.

63. See Zulfikar Ali Bhutto, *Bilateralism: New Directions* (Islamabad: Ministry of Information and Broadcasting, n.d., probably 1977). This document contains a number of Bhutto's earlier memoranda addressed to Ayub Khan.

64. Stanley A. Kochanek, "Interest Groups and the New Economic Policy in Pakistan," paper presented at the Twenty-Sixth Annual Conference on South Asia at the University of Wisconsin, Madison, October 16–19, 1997.

65. A. R. Kemal, "Industrial Development in Pakistan," *Pakistan Journal of Applied Economics* 14, no. 1–2 (1998): 108–09.

66. Interview with a Karachi businessman, April 1997.

67. Personal interviews, Islamabad, 1977.

68. "The [economic] policies of Z. A. Bhutto were anti-imperialist based on state socialism following the mould of other Third World leaders such as Gamal Abdel Nasser of Egypt, Ahmad Soekarno of Indonesia, and his own contemporary Salvador Allende of Chile who was elected, overthrown and assassinated during the same period." PPP website (www.ppp.org.pk/history.html [last accessed June 26, 2004]).

69. Hasan-Askari Rizvi, cited in Talbot, *India and Pakistan,* p. 201.

70. Talbot, *India and Pakistan,* p. 201.

71. Brigadier Siddiq Salik, Zia's public relations adviser, wrote an Urdu novel, *Pressure Cooker,* lampooning these efforts.

72. Chiniot is a town of less than 250,000 on the banks of the Chenab in Jhang District, Southwest Punjab. Many Chiniotis have set up businesses throughout Pakistan and even the subcontinent; several thousand remain in India, and the community is close-knit, very much like India's Marwaris. The Sharif family was not Chinioti, having come originally from Kashmir, but its community and Punjab business prospered enormously during Nawaz Sharif's prime ministership.

73. Iqbal, *Islam and Pakistan's Identity,* pp. 372–73.

74. Personal interview, Lahore, August 2003.

75. Owen Bennett-Jones, *Pakistan: Eye of the Storm* (Yale University Press, 2002), p. 230; Raja Asghar, "Low Turnout, Mixed Trend," *Dawn* (Karachi), October 11, 2002 (www.dawn.com/2002/10/11/top2.htm [last accessed June 26, 2004]).

76. The commission's website stresses its independence, but no close observer of Pakistan agrees—the intelligence services, both national and provincial, have influenced outcomes in many cases, with the commission, Chicago-like, ratifying the results. See Pakistan's Election Commission (www.ecp.gov.pk/Intro.asp [last accessed on June 26, 2004]).

77. Andrew Bolger, "Terror Map Shows States at Risk of Attack," *Financial Times,* May 9, 2003, p. 8. The story is based on work done by Aon, a leading insurance broker.

78. Human Rights Commission of Pakistan, "State of Human Rights in 2002" (www.hrcp-web.org/book1.cfm [last accessed June 26, 2004]).

79. Ibid.

80. "Kidnapped HRCP Activist Freed," *Dawn* (Karachi), March 27, 2003 (www.dawn.com/2003/03/27/top5.htm [last accessed June 26, 2004]).

81. U.S. Department of State, Bureau of Democracy, Human Rights, and Labor, *Pakistan: Country Report on Human Rights Practices, 2003* (February 25, 2004).

82. Transparency International (www.transparency.org/cpi/1997/cpi1997.pdf [last accessed June 26, 2004]).

83. Cited in ibid.

84. "State Should Decide on Meeting People's Needs," *Dawn* (Karachi), May 1, 2003 (www.dawn.com/2003/05/01/top7.htm [last accessed June 26, 2004]).

85. The outflow of Shi'as, an especially educated sector of Pakistan's middle and upper class, was alarming; Shi'ia doctors, for example, were targeted by radical Sunni assassination squads. This trend continues today, and senior police officials have acknowledged that terrorists can strike at any place and any time they want in Pakistan despite a heavy police presence. *The Nation,* March 21, 2002.

86. For an authorized English translation, see President Pervez Musharraf's address, January 12, 2002 (www.infopak.gov.pk/President_addresses/prsidential_addresses_index.htm [last accessed June 26, 2004]).

87. In the past fifteen years Pakistan has acquired a number of very effective human rights groups, and human rights violations are more carefully and thoroughly documented now than ever before. Amnesty International and Human Rights Watch issue detailed reports on Pakistan's human rights situation, and the Pakistan Human Rights Commission is bravely active; its leadership is widely recognized as effective and responsible.

88. The numbers are derived from Freedom House's coverage over a thirty-year period, during which they classified states as free, partly free, and not free on the basis of several criteria, including civil liberties and political freedom. See Freedom House Scores (www.freedomhouse.org/ratings/allscore04.xls [last accessed July 6, 2004]).

89. Pakistan's two spells of "not free" correlate with the military rule of Zia and Musharraf and reflect the absence of political rights; civil rights, according to Freedom House, varied somewhat, clustering around 4 on a scale of 1 (high) to 7 (lowest).

90. For a discussion of the methodology, see Freedom House, *Countries at the Crossroads: A Survey of Democratic Governance,* 2004 (www.freedomhouse.org/research/crossroads/cac.htm [last accessed June 26, 2004]).

91. UNDP, Pakistan, *Pakistan: National Human Development Report, 2003* (Islamabad, 2003), p. viii.

92. Chief among these is the *Jang* group's GEO, the television station broadcasting from Dubai, which has such programs as "Live and Let Live" that raise questions and discuss important issues of politics, religion, and economics.

93. For one international response to the Pakistan government's threats to the editor of a Lahore weekly, see the letter of the Committee to Protect Journalists to President Musharraf, March 13, 2002 at www.cpj.org.

Chapter Three

1. For comprehensive surveys of the origins and views of the Pakistan army, see Stephen Philip Cohen, *The Pakistan Army*, 2nd ed. (Oxford University Press, 1998); and Brian Cloughley, *A History of the Pakistan Army: Wars and Insurrections*, 2nd ed. (Oxford University Press, 2000).

2. For an overview of the army's structure see "Pakistan Army Command and Structure," http://pakistanidefence.com/PakArmy/CommandStructure.htm

3. Stephen P. Cohen, *The Indian Army*, rev. 2nd paperback edition (Oxford University Press, 1999), chap. 5, "The Professional Officer in India."

4. Muslim officers from the areas that were to become Pakistan were not given the option of choosing service in the Indian army, although Muslims from what was to be independent India were. The Indian army thus inherited a number of Muslim officers and has had a small (and declining) Muslim presence in the officer corps, as well as the other ranks, ever since.

5. On the INA, see Cohen, *The Indian Army*, pp. 147–63. On the Rawalpindi Conspiracy, see "What Was the Rawalpindi Conspiracy Case?" *Outlook* (Karachi), November 11, 1972; and "Was the Rawalpindi Conspiracy a Myth?" *Outlook* (Karachi), January 13, 1973. A comprehensive overview of the conspiracy is in Hasan Zaheer, *The Times and Trial of the Rawalpindi Conspiracy, 1951: The First Coup Attempt in Pakistan* (Oxford University Press, 1998).

6. See Akbar Khan, *Raiders in Kashmir*, 2nd ed. (Islamabad: National Book Foundation, 1975).

7. Those sent abroad are usually the best and most impressive soldier-scholars the army can muster, and they have consistently done well at foreign military schools, especially in the United States.

8. See *1905–1980: Command and Staff College, Quetta*, edited and compiled by Command and Staff College (Quetta, Pakistan: Command and Staff College Press, September 1980), p. 79.

9. Cohen, *The Pakistan Army*, pp. 152–58, 177.

10. For an extended discussion, see ibid., throughout.

11. The army's emphasis on the martial qualities of the Pakistani soldier ran aground on Pakistan's own ethnic mix: Bengalis, Sindhis, and other ethnolinguistic groups were "nonmartial" and still underrepresented in the Pakistan military.

12. For a comprehensive discussion of the army's internal and external propaganda operations by a former director of army public relations see Brigadier (ret.)

A. R. Siddiqi, *The Military in Pakistan: Image and Reality* (Lahore: Vanguard, 1996).

13. For three representative articles, see Major S. A. El-Edroos (Frontier Forces Regiment), "A Plea for a People's Army," *Pakistan Army Journal* 4 (June 1962): 19–25; El-Edroos, "Afro Asian Revolutionary Warfare and Our Military Thought," *Pakistan Army Journal* 4 (December 1962): 35–41; and Major Mohammed Shafi, "The Effectiveness of Guerilla War," *Pakistan Army Journal* 5 (June 1963): 4–11.

14. Shafi, "Guerilla War," p. 11. In addition, the increasing American interest in India after the development of Sino-Indian conflict (culminating in a war in 1962) led many Pakistanis to search for an "equalizer" between their own forces and an expanded Indian military. The latter received American, British, and Soviet support after 1962, whereas the American arms program to Pakistan was virtually completed by 1959.

15. Ironically, several Bengali officers who had been in Pakistan's special forces took the lead in organizing guerrilla units in what was to become Bangladesh, often fighting those special forces officers with whom they had earlier served.

16. One of these episodes is described by Salmaan Taseer, once a close confidant of Bhutto: "Suddenly the atmosphere [at a meeting in which a senior general was trying to explain the events surrounding the 1971 disaster] had become defiant and rebellious. The air was thick with cigarette smoke, and it was beginning to look more and more like a 'people's court' during the French Revolution. Overt respect for senior rank had vanished. The younger officers were shouting 'Bastards!', 'Drunkards!', 'Disgraceful!', and 'Shame!'" Taseer, *Bhutto: A Political Biography* (London: Ithaca Press, 1979), p. 130.

17. Bhutto discussed this at length in his death-cell testament, *If I Am Assassinated . . .* (New Delhi: Vikas, 1979). In it he argued that the military, especially Zia, had been "soft" on India and incompetent to boot. The *Defense White Paper* (see chapter 5) clearly bears his hand; what the authorities resented were his attempts to attack the reputation of Ayub Khan and some other generals.

18. Usually the United States, Great Britain, and a few other Commonwealth countries also send officers.

19. For an influential and comprehensive attempt to analyze India see Javed Hassan, *India: A Study in Profile* (Rawalpindi: Army Education Press, GHQ, 1990).

20. For a sample, which reads very much like his never-given coup speech, see the article Abbasi wrote for the Staff College's professional journal: "The Quranic Concept of Leadership: Its Adoption and Application in the Pakistan Army," *Citadel*, no. 1 (1992): 35–51. For a good overview of the "coup," see Zafar Abbas, "The Coup That Wasn't," *Herald*, November 1995. The coup was fully reported by the authoritative *Defence Journal*, which contains extracts of the speech that Abbasi was to deliver as well as extracts from doctrinaire Islamic articles that appeared in the army's own weekly, *Hilal*, and a speech by Benazir Bhutto. Her speech to PMA graduates encouraged the new officers to "make themselves ready

for jihad." Benazir was here following a strategy developed by her father of being more "Islamic" than the mullahs (*Defence Journal*, vol. 21 [April-May 1996]).

21. One such "bearded" officer, Lieutenant General Javed Nasir, led the ISI from March 1992 to May 1993, reporting to Prime Minister Nawaz Sharif. He has boasted that he was "a true practicing Muslim" and was the first officer with a full beard promoted to the rank of major general in 1983, thus breaking "the Taboo and tradition of clean shaven generals only." Deposition before the Anti-Terrorist Court, Lahore, October 23, 2002 (www.satribune.com/archives'dec23_02/msr_case05.jpg).

22. Hasan-Askari Rizvi, "Rumblings in the Army," *Daily Times*, September 8, 2003.

23. Hasan-Askari Rizvi, *Military, State and Society in Pakistan* (New York: St. Martin's Press, 2000), p. 243.

24. Ibid., pp. 208–10.

25. In past years, statements by a former army chief, General Aslam Beg, and the former ISI chief, Hamid Gul, have emphasized these themes. More recently, a speech by General Aziz Khan, the chairman of the Joint Chiefs of Staff (and one of the key people involved in the coup that brought Musharraf to power in 1999) has been highlighted. One such speech, delivered in Azad Kashmir while Musharraf was in the United States, was especially embarrassing. See *Nawa-i-Waqt*, June 24, 2003.

26. Wm. Theodore de Bary and others, comp., *Sources of Indian Tradition* (Columbia University Press, 1958), p. 722.

27. The Turkish model (a state with a predominantly Muslim population, governed by a secular political authority), later favored by some Pakistani officers including Musharraf, was explicitly rejected by Iqbal as un-Islamic. The Turks had rejected both the concept of Islamic rule and pan-Islamism and were thus doubly in error. Aziz Ahmad, *Islamic Modernism in India and Pakistan, 1857–1964* (Oxford University Press, 1967), p. 140.

28. Address to two antiaircraft regiments on February 21, 1948, reprinted in *Quaid-i-Azam Mohammad Ali Jinnah, Speeches, 1947–1948* (Islamabad: Ministry of Information and Broadcasting, n.d.), p. 63. There had been a more careful analysis of strategic problems, as discussed later in this chapter and in chapter 6.

29. Ibid., p. 154. In an important speech to the officers of the Staff College, Quetta, just before he died, Jinnah noted that "every officer and soldier, no matter what the race or community to which he belongs, is working as a true Pakistani," and he made similar references on other occasions.

30. Interview with Zia ul-Haq, June 1988, Islamabad.

31. B. Raman, a former senior Indian intelligence official, "After Musharraf, What?" South Asia Analysis Group (www.saag.org/papers9/papers870html [December 25, 2003]).

32. M. Attiqur Rahman, *Our Defence Cause* (White Lion Publishers, 1976), p. 187.

33. *On Striving to Be a Muslim* (Lahore: Islamic Book Center, 1978). In his range of scholarship and his approach to the linking of Islam and career, Qayyum most clearly resembles Iqbal.

34. Ibid.

35. Because of accusations that the army was becoming a hotbed of Islamic extremism, the military high command recently opened up some of its training facilities to visitors. For a snapshot of current trends, see John Lancaster, "Pakistan Struggles to Put Army on Moderate Course," *Washington Post*, April 45, 2004.

36. Hasan-Askari Rizvi, "The Military," in *Power and Civil Society in Pakistan*, edited by Anita M. Weiss and S. Zulfiqar Gilani (Oxford University Press, 2001), p. 208.

37. Rizvi, "Rumblings in the Army," *Daily Times*, September 9, 2003.

38. These resemble the Samurai tradition of Japan, the Prussian code of honor, and the martial traditions of India's Rajputs and Nepal's Gurkhas—which also emphasize the importance of preserving honor.

39. For a discussion, see Cohen, *The Pakistan Army*, pp. 98–104.

40. Brig. S. K. Malik, *Quranic Concept of War* (Lahore: Wajidalis, 1979), p. 59.

41. Ibid., p. 57.

42. Hasim Amir-Ali, *The Message of the Qur'an* (Tokyo: Charles E. Tuttle, 1974).

43. Ibid., p. 60.

44. This includes statements by the present foreign minister, Kamal Kharzai, and President Khatami (www.president.ir/cronicnews/1382/8207/820729/index-e.htm). How serious they are in making this argument is another matter; apparently there is a deep division within Iran about the ethical as well a strategic justification for an Iranian bomb.

45. *Encyclopedia Britannica,* quoted by "Rangrut" (Major General M. Akbar Khan), *The Islamic Pattern of War—Planning and Training*, vol. 1: *Theory*, rev. ed. (Karachi: Islamic Military Science Association, 1968), p. 118.

46. Malik, *Quranic Concept of War*, p. ii. This closely follows the argument and tone of several earlier Indian Muslim thinkers, including Sir Syed Ahmed Khan and the Islamic socialist Ubayd-Allah Sindhi. See Aziz Ahmed, *Islamic Modernism*, pp. 50, 195.

47. Rangrut, *Islamic Pattern of War*, p. 118.

48. The various confidence-building and arms-control proposals developed over the past fifty years are evidence that a practical solution to both states' strategic concerns is at hand, but they remain largely irrelevant as long as the more fundamental problem of a clash of identities—now seen as a clash of civilizations in some quarters—remains alive.

49. For an early discussion of military thinking along these lines, see Cohen, *The Pakistan Army*, p. 153.

50. Field Marshal Ayub Khan, *Friends Not Masters* (Oxford University Press, 1967). Many Pakistanis paraphrased the title as "Friends Not, Masters."

51. Rizvi, *Military, State and Society*, p. 101.

52. Interview, January 2001.

53. For a rare attempt to compare Pakistan's economic performance under military and civilian regimes, see "Ravian," "Who Best Serves the National Economic Interest?" *Daily Times,* February 13, 2004. The author concludes that there is no significant pattern one way or the other. As for corruption, many more cases of military corruption have come to light since Musharraf's coup, but it is not clear whether this is due to an increase in corruption, better press coverage, or more rigorous application of the law.

54. Musharraf has stated that two areas are "vital" to Pakistan: Kashmir and the nuclear program, but it is hard to tell whether this is a deeply held conviction or a spur-of-the-moment remark.

Chapter Four

1. Bhutto was also wary of the links between the NWFP's Pushtoon-dominated National Awami Party and Kabul; he used a political assassination as an occasion to dismiss NAP governments in NWFP and Baluchistan.

2. For an excellent overview of Pakistani parties and various coalitions over the years, see Ian Talbot, *Pakistan, A Modern History* (New York: St. Martin's Press, 1998), app. C, "Pakistan Political Parties and Organisations."

3. Indian and Pakistani leaders have learned from each other about manipulative politics; it was Indira Gandhi who had perfected this strategy in India.

4. "Unified PML to Boost Progress, Hopes Musharraf," *Dawn* (Karachi), May 18, 2004 (www.dawn.com/2004/05/18/top1.htm [last accessed June 27, 2004]).

5. Bhutto was prolific during these years, producing a number of important pamphlets and books with his views on Pakistan, South Asia, and world politics. See especially *The Myth of Independence* (Oxford University Press, 1969).

6. For accounts of the first years of the PPP, see Mubashir Hasan, *The Mirage of Power: An Inquiry into the Bhutto years, 1971–77* (Oxford University Press, 2002).

7. The PPP website offers a history of Bhutto's thoughts at www.ppp.org.pk.

8. Hasan, *Mirage of Power,* pp. 29–30. Pakistan never had a truly "left" political movement; the hostility of the landowners, the alliance with the United States, the dominance of the army, and the conservatism of most Pakistanis helped eliminate a communist movement and enfeeble the political left.

9. Bhutto had refused to allow East Pakistan's Sheikh Mujibur Rahman to ascend to the prime ministership and had backed the army's crackdown in the East Wing, defending it before the United Nations.

10. Sir Morrice James, *Pakistan Chronicle* (Oxford University Press, 1993), p. 17. This view is confirmed by many of Bhutto's supporters, including those who broke with him over the years.

11. At that time it was widely rumored that Zia was a reluctant coup-maker and had been egged on by some of his corps commanders. For a spirited defense

of his own position, see Lieutenant General. (ret.) Faiz Ali Chishti, *Betrayals of Another Kind* (Rawalpindi: PCL Publishing House, 1989); for an account by Zia's closest military adviser, see General (ret.) K. M. Arif, *Working with Zia* (Oxford University Press, 1995).

12. For a survey of these measures, see Stephen P. Cohen, *The Pakistan Army* (University of California Press, 1985), p. 125.

13. Hasan, *Mirage of Power*, p. 213.

14. As early as 1965, Bhutto was concerned about the Indian nuclear program; see George Perkovich, *India's Nuclear Bomb* (University of California Press, 1999), p. 108. Also "The Brown Bomb," *Manchester Guardian*, March 11, 1965, p. 10.

15. Ironically, Pakistan's success at acquiring arms in the late 1970s and early 1980s led the Indians into a major dependency on the Soviet Union.

16. Bhutto, *Myth*, chap. 6, p. 79.

17. While prime minister, Bhutto released a number of documents—including transcripts of conversations between Ayub and the British high commissioner during the height of the 1965 war—in an attempt to expose Ayub's dependency on the West and his incorrect obsession with communism. These are gathered in *White Paper on the Jammu and Kashmir Dispute* (Islamabad: Ministry of Foreign Affairs, 1977).

18. Bhutto, *Myth*, p. 102.

19. See Zulfikar Ali Bhutto, *Bilateralism: New Directions* (Islamabad: Ministry of Information and Broadcasting, n.d., probably 1977). This document contains a number of Bhutto's earlier memoranda addressed to Ayub Khan.

20. Bhutto, *Myth*, p. 11.

21. Interview with Benazir Bhutto, "Benazir Admits That Proxy War Was a Conscious Decision," *Hindustan Times,* December 13, 2003 (www.hindustan-times.com/2003/Dec/13/181_494939,001300680000.htm [last accessed June 28, 2004]). In the interview she claimed that her party reviewed Pakistan's confrontational policy in her second term and decided to return to a policy of dialogue.

22. The slippage in Pakistan's position as a liberal or "moderate" and tolerant Muslim state is reflected in the increasingly anguished columns by several of its noted Parsis, especially M. P. Bhandara and Ardeshir Cowasjee.

23. For a discussion, see Ejaz Haider, "NGOs and Depoliticization," *Friday Times* (Lahore), May 25–31, 2003.

24. This charge comes not only from Islamists but also from some hypernationalist academics who deride the foreign support of such organizations as the Sustainable Development Policy Institute. See the remarks of Dushka Syed, "SECOND OPINION: The Real Problem with Textbooks—Khaled Ahmed's TV Review," *Daily Times* (Lahore), April 20, 2004 (www.dailytimes.com.pk/default.asp?page=story_20-4-2004_pg3_6 [last accessed June 27, 2004]).

25. For details of the Haider episode, see George Lardner Jr., "Brookings Scholar Is Detained by INS; Registration Rule Snags Pakistani Editor," *Washington Post,*

January 30, 2003, p. A1. Haider had been invited on several occasions to address seminars organized by the Department of State, which was deeply angered by his arrest.

26. Interview with Sharif colleague, 2003.

27. The charge of attempted murder was based on the possibility that Musharraf's civilian flight from Sri Lanka, diverted from Pakistan, might have run out of fuel, killing all aboard.

28. For a perceptive Indian overview of Jamali's first months in office, see B. Muralidhar Reddy, "Survival Strategies," *Frontline*, vol. 20, issue 2, January 18–31, 2003 (www.frontlineonnet.com/fl2002/stories/20030131001305700.htm [last accessed June 27, 2004]).

29. See the NAB's website at www.nab.gov.pk/.

30. In three years the NAB has entered into 181 plea-bargain cases through accepted court process and recovered an amount of US$36 million.

31. The NRB's charter and activities are described on its website (www. nrb.gov.pk/), which is far more comprehensive and informative than the NAB's.

32. One newspaper labeled the bureaucracy, particularly Pakistan's elite District Management Group, "bleeding victims" of the devolution scheme, while some senior officials argue that the real goal of the Musharraf government is to weaken the provincial governments, further turning Pakistan into a unitary state directed from Islamabad. *The News* (Lahore), August 14, 2003 (www.jang.com.pk/thenews/aug2003-daily/14-08-2003/main/index.shtml [last accessed June 27, 2004]).

33. Interview with a Lahore Nazim, August 2003.

34. Farhan Bokhari, "Guards Get the Blues as Pakistan Cleans Up Security; Protection Services: Tighter Rules Are Coming to a Sector That Has to Offer More than Gunmen," *Financial Times*, May 6, 2003, Features, p. 9.

35. The annual UN World Crime Survey has not included data for Pakistan since 1980. Overall, data on crime are scarce: Bangladesh has only reported for the period 1980–86. China reports total recorded crimes but does not provide breakdowns. Data on India are not available for 1984–86, and data after 2000 are still being analyzed. Data are missing for other countries too, including Iran. The Pakistan Federal Bureau of Statistics provides a 1994–2001 breakdown of various crimes. Since there is no way to check the accuracy of that information against other sources, it has limited use for analysis. The biggest category of crimes, for instance, is listed as "others." Serious crime does not include gender crimes such as rape.

36. For an astute analysis, see I. M. Mohsin (a former secretary in the Interior Ministry), "Police Reforms Delayed," *Daily Times* (Karachi), March 31, 2003 (www.dailytimes.com.pk/default.asp?page=story_31-3-2003_pg3_4 [last accessed June 27, 2004]). The operation of the Karachi Public Safety Commission is discussed in *Herald* (Karachi), June 2003, pp. 48–49.

37. By mid-2004 Musharraf had backed away from this pledge, and in any case there is no constitutional or political way to ensure that he will keep it. The same

uncertainty surrounds his statement that Parliament would, for the first time in Pakistan's history, complete its five-year term.

38. This quotation comes from one of Musharraf's strong supporters. See Masood Anwar, "Domestic Political Scene," *Defence Journal* (Karachi), August 2003 (www.paksearch.com/dj/2003/Aug/opi-f.htm [last accessed June 27, 2004]).

39. The heading of this section is from the title of a thoughtful essay by one of Pakistan's leading young scholars. See Aqil Shah, "Pakistan's Armored Democracy," *Journal of Democracy* 14 (October 2003).

40. See Ahmed Aamir Khan, *Herald* (Karachi), March 2001, p. 77 (www.dawn.com/herald/mar01.htm [last accessed June 27, 2004]): "I think we need to be very clear about what we want from the COAS." This was Karamat's first public interview after resigning as chief in 1999.

Chapter Five

1. Pakistan's most "Islamic" ruler, President Zia, believed this and often drew the comparison for visitors. For a study of the similarity between Pakistan and Israel, see P. R. Kumaraswamy, "The Strangely Parallel Careers of Israel and Pakistan," *Middle East Quarterly*, June 1997, pp. 31–39.

2. For an overview of the origins and Indian, British, and Bangladeshi activities of the TJ, see Yoginder Sikand, *The Origins and Development of the Tablighi-Jama'at 1920–2000* (Hyderabad [India]: Orient Longman, 2002).

3. Seyyed Vali Reza Nasr, *The Vanguard of the Islamic Revolution: The Jama'at-i-Islami of Pakistan* (London: I. B. Taurus, 1994), p. 10. This is the authoritative English-language account of the Jama'at. For a comprehensive biography of Mawdudi, see Seyyed Vali Reza Nasr, *Mawdudi and the Making of Islamic Revivalism* (Oxford University Press, 1966).

4. Nasr, *Vanguard*, p. 109. This contact was analogous to that of many other Indian figures: a key event that shaped a worldview, a career, and perhaps the future of a state. Gandhi was thrown off a train in South Africa, Nehru's father was denied entry into a British club, and Subhas Bose was refused admission to a military training class at Oxford.

5. Ibid, p. 21.

6. Ibid.

7. Today, there are eight Jama'at-i-Islami organizations: one each in Pakistan, India, Pakistan's Azad Kashmir, India's Kashmir province, Sri Lanka, Bangladesh (created after the breakup of Pakistan in 1971), Great Britain, and the Jama'at-linked Islamic Circle of North America (ICNA). Nasr, *Vanguard*, p. 78. See also the ICNA website, www.ICNA.com. The Jama'at also controls a major publishing house and several think tanks, including the Institute of Policy Studies (IPS), Islamabad; IPS's board has a number of members in common with the Foundation for Research on International Environment, National Development and Security, and "FRIENDS," the vehicle for retired General Aslam Beg (www.friends.org.pk).

8. The high point—or perhaps low point—in this campaign was the attempt to prohibit kite flying in Pakistan, which the religious parties considered a "Hindu" execrence, being associated with Basant, the springtime festival. The success of this movement can be seen in any Pakistani city during Basant, as the skies are filled with colorful, combative kites, in open defiance of the mullahs. See Khaled Ahmed, "Will Qazi Hussain Ahmed Stop Basant Next Year?" *Friday Times* (Lahore), March 7–13, 2003.

9. Jamal Malik, *Colonialization of Islam: Dissolution of Traditional Institutions in Pakistan* (New Delhi: Manohar, 1996).

10. Ibid., p. 302.

11. Constitutionally, Pakistan is an Islamic state. Its legislative foundation is supposedly based on the Hanafi interpretation of Islam, itself divided between Deobandis and Barelvis, but the colonial legal system is still widely applicable. Besides these systems, both officially recognized since 1977, customary law (*'urf*) is popular in most areas of Pakistan, with wide regional variations. Ibid., p. 4.

12. Mawdudi had to be persuaded to support a woman as a candidate; as the Quaid's sister and a Mohajir (still a high percentage of the Jama'at's political base), she was acceptable. Nasr, *Vanguard*, p. 155.

13. Mohammed Ayub Khan, *Friends Not Masters* (Oxford University Press, 1967), p. 196.

14. In Islam the Arabic word *Sunnah* has come to denote the way the Prophet lived his life and is the second source of Islamic jurisprudence after the Quran. The *Hadith* are sayings of the Prophet, as opposed to the manner of his life itself.

15. For a thoughtful survey of Bhutto's ideas in relationship to Pakistan's evolving political culture, see Anwar H. Syed, *The Discourse and Politics of Zulfikar Ali Bhutto* (London: Macmillan, 1992).

16. UGC directive, quoted in Azhar Hamid and others, *Mutalliyah-i-Pakistan* (Islamabad: Allama Iqbal Open University, 1983), p. xi. For a full discussion of the process, see Pervaiz Amirali Hoodbhoy and Abdul Hameed Nayyar, "Rewriting the History of Pakistan," in *The Pakistan Experience: State and Religion*, edited by Mohammad Asghar Khan (Lahore: Vanguard, 1985), pp. 164–77. For a recent discussion on rewriting Pakistani history, see Aliya Inam, "Telling It Like It Wasn't," *Friday Times* (Lahore), March 19–25, 1992, p. 8.

17. A comprehensive overview of Pakistan's textbooks is in K. K. Aziz, *The Murder of History: A Critique of History Textbooks Used in Pakistan* (Lahore: Vanguard Books, 1993).

18. Brigadier Dr. Allah Bukhsh (Pakistan army), "The Dynamics of National Will to Fight: A Psychological Re-interpretation," *Defence Journal* 15, no. 12 (1989): 13–18.

19. Barrister Sameen Khan, "Defense: The Jihad Syndrome," *Defence Journal* 16, no. 1 & 2 (1990): 29, with a reserved introduction by the editor, A. R. Siddiqui.

20. Ibid.

21. Zahid Malik, *Dr. Abdul Qadeer Khan and the Islamic Bomb* (Islamabad: Hurmat, 1992), p. 70.

22. For an overview, see the foundation's website (www.paks.net/edhi-foundation/).

23. A hapless Tablighi was captured in Afghanistan and sent to Guantanamo Bay as a suspected member of the Taliban/al Qaeda but was freed after a year's imprisonment. He is quoted as saying: "I'm not a jihadi, we went to spread Islam, but not to fight on behalf of someone." See Iqbal Khattak, "Freed Pakistani Demands Compensation," *Daily Times* (Lahore), November 5, 2002 (www.dailytimes.com.pk/default.asp?page=story_5-11-2002_pg1_7 [last accessed June 27, 2004]).

24. Khaled Ahmed, "The Grand Tableeghi Congregation," *Friday Times* (Lahore), November 7, 2002.

25. Pakistan's radical Islamic groups are defined here as organizations that favored major change in the Pakistani political and social order *and* would approve of violence to achieve those changes. They also include ones that have used violence against India in Kashmir or have supported such transnational terrorist groups as al Qaeda.

26. Ispahani in a review essay, "The Cauldron," *New Republic,* June 16, 2003, p. 31.

27. Some Jama'at leaders share Zia's private admiration for Israel because its state is also based upon religious affinity.

28. The meeting took place on March 3, 2003; for an account, see "UN Envoy meets JI Ameer" (www.jamaat.org/news/pr030303.html [last accessed June 27, 2004]).

29. Nasr, *Vanguard*, p. 66.

30. Ibid, p. 67.

31. HUM, reportedly founded in 1989 at the behest of Pakistan's ISI, is the largest militant outfit operating in Kashmir, with cadres drawn from both sides of the cease-fire line, Pakistan, and perhaps other sources. It favors the absorption of Kashmir into Pakistan. Indian reports indicate that it is responsible for only about 10 to 20 percent of all terrorist strikes; Pakistani reports estimate that it controls about 60 percent of terrorists operating in the state. In 2002 it made a conditional cease-fire offer, the second instance in which a militant outfit in Kashmir has declared a cease-fire. For an Indian source, see South Asia Terrorism Portal (www.satp.org/satporgtp/countries/india/states/jandk/terrorist_outfits/hizbul_muja hideen.htm).

32. The JI's leader has denied a link between al Qaeda and JI. When asked whether the JI regards al Qaeda members as "heroes," Qazi Hussain Ahmed evaded the question, replying that Osama and al Qaeda have become a symbol of anti-Americanism, and Osama "will be considered a hero by people around the world, irrespective of whether we agree with him or not." E-mail interview with Qazi Hussein, *Newsline,* March 2003 (www.newsline.com.pk/NewsMar2003/editornotemar2003.htm).

33. The secular Pakistani press gave this linkage considerable coverage. See editorial, "Jamaat Must Explain Links with al Qaeda," *Daily Times* (Lahore), March 6, 2003 (www.dailytimes.com.pk/default.asp?page=story_6-3-2003_pg3_1 [last accessed June 27, 2004]).

34. Rabbani even named his group the Jama'at-i-Islami Afghanistan. The Hekmatyar-JI relationship developed when the present amir of the Jama'at, Qazi Hussein, led the JI in NWFP. Bhutto's government used the JI to funnel aid and equipment to Hekmatyar's forces, and the relationship has been maintained since then. JI students who went to Afghanistan were trained in Hekmatyar's camps.

35. Steve Coll, *Ghost Wars* (New York: Penguin Press), p. 291.

36. See "In Response to Allegations," by Qazi Hussain Ahmad, *Dawn* (Karachi), June 10, 2004 (www.dawn.com [accessed June 11, 2004]) and Pervez Hoodbhoy, "Pluralism and Qazi Hussain," *Dawn, Encounter Section,* June 19, 2004 (www.dawn.com [accessed June 19, 2004]), in which the Amir's commitment to pluralism as expressed in a talk given at the Brookings Institution in 2001 was contrasted with his *Dawn* article. According to one report, the Netherlands denied the Amir a visa because of his attacks on the Aga Khan Foundation. See Muhammad Shehzad, "Qazi Sahib is hoist by his own petard," *Friday Times* (Lahore), June 3, 2004, p. 3.

37. For expressions of these positions, see Fareed Zakaria, *The Future of Freedom: Illiberal Democracy at Home and Abroad* (New York: W. W. Norton, 2003); and the review by Robert Kagan, "The Ungreat Washed: Why Democracy Must Remain America's Goal Abroad," *New Republic Online,* July 7, 2003.

38. The name derives from the North Indian town of Bareilly, where the movement was founded. Khaled Ahmed, "The Power of the Ahle Hadith," *Friday Times* (Lahore), July 15, 2002.

39. For a reasonably accurate Indian account of these groups, see the weekly postings of the Institute of Conflict Management, South Asia Terrorism Portal (www.satp.org/satporgtp/countries/Pakistan/terroristoutfits/index.html [last accessed June 27, 2004]). The institute's leading member, K. P. S. Gill, was responsible for the strategy that eventually defeated the Khalistan movement in India's Punjab state.

40. Around this time, there was speculation that a "grand bargain" might be at hand, with Pakistan pursuing a more moderate policy in Kashmir in exchange for a rebalancing of politics in Afghanistan, and the Pashtuns in the form of the "moderate" Taliban playing some role in the government of Hamid Karzai.

41. Mandavi Mehta and Ambassador Teresita C. Schaffer, *Islam in Pakistan: Unity and Contradictions* (Washington: Center for Strategic and International Studies Project on Pakistan's Future and U.S. Policy Options, October 7, 2002).

42. Ibid., p. 11. As of August 2003, the case had been postponed six times.

43. Ibid.

44. Ahmed, "Power of Ahle Hadith."

45. Hassan Abbas, "Rent-a-Son Agencies," *News* (Lahore), November 28, 2001, reprinted in *Tufts Journal,* February 2002. Abbas is a Pakistan government official and the author of a major study of the growth of madaris in Pakistan, especially south Punjab. One well-informed Pakistani scholar who has studied their growth puts the number at 10,000 or more, with a sharp increase beginning with Zia's and Saudi patronage in the 1980s. The Pakistan government estimates the total number of students in these seminaries to be 800,000–1,000,000. For an American study, see P. W. Singer, "Pakistan's Madrassahs: Ensuring a System of Education Not Jihad," *Brookings Project on U.S. Policy Toward the Islamic World,* Analysis Paper 14 (Brookings, November 2001). A sympathetic analysis of the madaris can be found in Institute of Policy Studies, *Pakistan: Religious Education Institutions: An Overview* (Islamabad, 2002). For a firsthand account by a Punjab province official, see Syed Tauqir Shah, "A Case Study of Madrassahs: Ahmadpur East," unpublished manuscript, 1994 (http://tuftsjournal.tufts.edu/ archive/2002/february/oped/index.shtml [last accessed June 27, 2004]).

46. Singer, "Pakistan's Madrassahs," p. 2.

47. Malik, *Colonization of Islam,* p. 304.

48. Ibid., p. 305.

49. Tariq Rehman, "Tolerance and Militancy among Schoolchildren," *Dawn* (Karachi), February 23, 2003. Also, see Khaled Ahmed, "Our Madrasas and Our World View," *Friday Times* (Lahore), March 14–20, 2003 (www.eduvision.edu. pk/clip_feb03.html [last accessed June 27, 2004]).

50. Rahman, cited in Ahmed, "Our Madrasas."

51. Ibid.

52. For a survey, see the Institute for Religion and Public Policy, Washington, Press Release, February 4, 2003.

53. The JI's think tank, the Institute for Policy Studies (Islamabad), headed by Professor Kurshid Ahmed, issues a number of publications in English and Urdu; these are not regarded highly for their serious analysis of economic and social issues and merely repeat the JI's stated positions on political and strategic ones. See the IPS website, www.ips.org.pk/.

54. For an outstanding history of Islam and science, and the distortions of "Islamic" science in Pakistan, see Pervez Hoodbhoy, *Islam and Science: Religious Orthodoxy and the Battle for Rationality* (London: Zed Books, 1991).

55. Lashkar-e-Jhangvi was originally a jihadi group that targeted Shi'ia; it was born in 1996 and has mutated into a terrorist group that specializes in suicide missions—rare for Pakistan. It is regarded as out of the control of ISI, and the Pakistan government has banned it. For an overview, see Nasra Hassan, "Al Qaeda's Understudy," *Atlantic Monthly,* June 2004.

56. For an overview, see Khaled Ahmed, "Was Pakistan Being Talibanised?" *Friday Times* (Lahore), December 9, 2001.

57. For an excellent overview of the founding of al Qaeda and its relations with various Afghan and Pakistani factions, as well as connection with the intelligence services of several countries, see Coll, *Ghost Wars.*

58. Gilles Kepel, *Jihad: The Trial of Political Islam* (Harvard University Press, 2002).

59. For a detailed account of the Taliban-Pakistan-U.S. relationship, see Coll, *Ghost Wars*.

60. For a former school friend's revealing account of Omar's transformation, see Mohamed Ahmed Khan, "A Pakistani Gora in Lahore," *Herald* (Karachi), August 2002. Omar's life parallels the story of the radicalized British-Pakistani youth in the film *My Son the Fanatic* (2001).

61. The Indian film about the Tamil separatist movement, *The Terrorist,* superbly describes how individuals are recruited to the cause and sent to their death. It reinforces the notion that terrorist organizations are carefully constructed bureaucracies, highly differentiated in their operations.

62. John Ward Anderson, "Extremist Groups Renew Activity in Pakistan," *Washington Post,* February 8, 2003, p. A1.

63. Pakistan has followed the same pattern regarding its pledges to end certain practices with regard to its nuclear and missile programs. In both cases the private rationalization is that in matters of vital national interest the threatened Pakistan is justified in deceiving outsiders, including the United States.

64. The most comprehensive account of the shadowy ties between Pakistan, Afghan fighters, Arab volunteers, and the United States is in Coll, *Ghost Wars*.

65. For a discussion, see Stephen Philip Cohen, *The Pakistan Army,* 2nd ed. (Oxford University Press, 1998), esp. the 1998 postscript; and Hasan Askari Rizvi, *Military, State and Society in Pakistan* (New York: St. Martin's Press, 2000), pp. 245 ff., "Islam and the Military."

66. See chapter 3 for a discussion of Major General Zahir ul Islam Abbasi.

67. This is the view of a study by the International Crisis Group, "Pakistan: The Dangers of Conventional Wisdom," March 12, 2002 (www.crisisweb.org/home/index.cfm?id=1818&l=1 [last accessed June 27, 2004]).

68. Nasr, *Vanguard,* pp. 219–20.

Chapter Six

1. In Pakistan's case, the Pakistan Oppressed Nations Movement, wielding Soviet-era rhetoric, calls for the liberation of all nationalities in Pakistan and recognition of their rights. The movement is discussed later in the chapter.

2. Kashmiris were a sixth group but were not technically part of Pakistan since Kashmir's accession was yet to be decided; later, after the loss of East Pakistan, the symbol of Pakistan displayed on billboards on independence day (August 14) became four arms, each holding another's wrist.

3. The term Mohajir is derived from the Arabic *Hijra,* traveler or "breaking of relations," and is related to *hegira,* which refers to the Prophet's departure for Medina, and in Islamic tradition means "companions of the Prophet." In India and in parts of Pakistan, notably Sindh, it is used derogatively.

4. *Pathan* is a term developed by the British; the official Pakistan government spelling is Pashtun. Another common usage is Pashtoon, and the language is spelled both Pashto and Pakhto.

5. Quoted in Akbar S. Ahmed, *Jinnah, Pakistan and Islamic Identity: The Search for Saladin* (London: Routledge, 1997), p. 236.

6. Owen Bennett-Jones, *Pakistan: Eye of the* Storm (Yale University Press, 2002), p. 110.

7. Ibid.

8. This would make Karachi a home for the entrepreneurial Urdu-speaking community, just as Singapore became a home for Malaysia's unwanted minority Chinese.

9. Pakistan's leading monthly magazine, *Herald,* is based in the city and has given it extremely good coverage. See, for example, *City of Death,* the 1995 annual issue, and the subsequent series of articles a few years later, *City of Life,* the 2000 annual issue.

10. According to the Pakistan Medical Association, of the sixty-four doctors murdered in Karachi from 1995 to 2001, fifty-nine were killed merely because they happened to be Shi'a. See Ardeshir Cowasjee, "Twenty Years to Zero," *Dawn* (Karachi), July 8, 2001 (www.dawn.com/weekly/cowas/20010708.htm [last accessed June 28, 2004]).

11. This is apocryphal, appearing first in a *Punch* cartoon a year after the event.

12. For an overview, see Anil Seal, *The Emergence of Indian Nationalism: Competition and Collaboration in the Later Nineteenth Century* (Cambridge University Press, 1971), p. 68; and Adeel Khan, "Pakistan's Sindhi Ethnic Nationalism: Migration, Marginalization and the Threat of 'Indianization,'" *Asian Survey* 52 (March–April 2002): 213–29.

13. Ayesha Jalal, *The Sole Spokesman: Jinnah, the Muslim League and the Demand for Pakistan* (Lahore: Sang-e-Meel Publications, 1992), p. 110.

14. Feroz Ahmed, *Ethnicity and Politics in Pakistan* (Oxford University Press, 1998), pp. 44–45.

15. For an elaboration see Bennett-Jones, *Pakistan,* pp. 115–17.

16. Ahmed, *Ethnicity,* p. 71.

17. Water rights and the abuses of the Punjab have been one of the main issues of the World Sindhi Institute, based in Washington, D.C. See various issues of *Sindh Watch* (Washington) and the institute's website, www.worldsindhi.org. A British-based group, the World Sindhi Congress, holds similar views (worldsindhicongress.org). Both groups include Indian Sindhis, although they focus on Pakistan Sindh.

18. Charles Kennedy, *The Politics of Ethnicity,* p. 946, cited in Khan, "Pakistan's Sindhi Ethnic Nartionalism," p. 224; and Kennedy, "Pakistan: Ethnic Diversity and Colonial Legacy," in *The Territorial Management of Ethnic Conflict,* edited by John Coakley (London: Frank Cass, 2003).

19. Khan, "Pakistan's Sindhi Ethnic Nationalism," p. 223.

20. Rodney Jones, "The Prospects for State Failure in Pakistan: Ethnic Regional and Sectarian Fissures," paper presented to a seminar on the Future of Pakistan, Lawrence Livermore National Laboratory, May 1, 2001, available at the website of Policy Architects International (www.policyarchitects.org/pdf/pak_statefailure-exsumm.pdf).

21. In 1992 substantial evidence appeared to confirm these suspicions. After the army was ordered into Sindh to crack down on terrorists, especially those drawn from the Mohajir community, it was revealed that the MQM—the largest and clearly neo-Fascist party of the Mohajirs—had run its own interrogation centers in Sindh and Karachi, and subsequently that operational support had come from the ISI.

22. Sindhis once faced a threat from a different kind of Punjab; according to its maps, the Sikh separatist Khalistan movement would have carved out a chunk of Sindh to provide its would-be state with access to the Arabian Sea.

23. Mohammed Waseem, *Politics and the State in Pakistan* (Lahore: Progressive Publishers, 1989), p. 109. I have drawn heavily on this and other works by Waseem in this discussion.

24. Ekram Kabir, "The Leftovers of History: Bihari Muslims in Bangladesh," *Asian Affairs,* November 2002 (www.asianaffairs.com/nov2002/exclusive_the_leftovers.htm).

25. The party's original name was Mohajir Quami Movement.

26. Bennett-Jones, *Pakistan,* p. 138.

27. Rodney Jones, "The Prospects for State Failure," p. 3.

28. For an account, see Robert G. Wirsing, *The Baluchis and Pathans* (London: Minority Rights Group, 1979).

29. For different estimates, see Asad Rahman, "Origins of Quetta Violence," *News* (Pakistan), July 29, 2000; and Selig S. Harrison, *In Afghanistan's Shadow: Baluch Nationalism and Soviet Temptations* (Washington: Carnegie Endowment for International Peace, 1981).

30. One of these grievances is that the federal government intends to create a new province or directly administered zone along the Makran coast and populate it with Mohajirs and Punjabis.

31. William S. Richter, "Regionalism in Central Pakistan: The Bahawalpur Suba and Siraiki Movements," paper delivered to the 1980 meeting of the Association for Asian Studies, March 23, 1980, p. 9.

32. Another movement in the 1960s looked to create a separate province based on Bahawalpur, roughly following the contours of the former princely state. It was supported by Sheikh Mujibur Rahman, the leader of the Awami League, and if the results of the 1970 election had been allowed to stand, a separate Bahawalpur province (and other new provinces) might well have been created by an Awami League government of Pakistan. Under Bhutto's inducements and punishments, the Bahawalpur agitation merged into the larger Siraiki movement.

33. For an account, see M. Ilyas Khan, "Disagree and Be Damned," *Herald* (Karachi), December 2000.

34. The group's website characterizes the Balawaristanis as "innocent and simpleton people" (www.balawaristan.net/english.htm); for an interview with Hamid Khan, chairman of the Balawaristan National Front, see the Indian magazine *Outlook* (www.balawaristan.net/outlook.htm [June 28, 2002]).

35. Justice (ret'd.) Hamoodur Rahman, "Ideology of Pakistan: The Raison d'Etre of Our Country," *Pakistan Army Journal*, June 1978, p. 9.

36. For an extended study of ethnicity and the Pakistan army, see Stephen Philip Cohen, *The Pakistan Army*, 2nd ed. (Oxford University Press, 1998). For estimated figures of ethnic representation, see Ahmed, *Ethnicity and Politics in Pakistan*, p. 252.

37. Waseem, *Politics and the State in Pakistan*, p. 20.

Chapter Seven

1. United Nations, *World Urbanization Prospects. The 1994 Revision—Estimates and Projections of Urban and Rural Populations and of Urban Agglomerations* (New York, 1995), pp. 4–5. Reprinted with the permission of the UN Department of Public Information.

2. Imtiazuddin Husain and Tanvir Kiyani, "On the Industrialization of Small Towns in Pakistan," *Asia-Pacific Population Journal* 5, no. 3 (1990): 51–62 (www.unescap.org/esid/psis/population/journal/1990/v05n3a3.pdf [last accessed June 27, 2004]). Pakistan has eight cities of 1 million or more; the other four are Peshawar, Rawalpindi, Multan, and Hyderabad.

3. For a discussion of the urbanization process, see Husain and Kiyani, "On the Industrialization of Small Towns in Pakistan"; Population Census Organization website (www.statpak.gov.pk/depts/pco/statistics/demographic_indicators98/demographic_indicators.html); and UNDP, *Pakistan: National Human Development Report, 2003* (Islamabad, 2003), p. 99 (www.un.org.pk/nhdr/nhdr-pak-2003.pdf [last accessed on June 27, 2004]).

4. UNESCAP Population Data Sheet, 2004 (www.unescap.org/esid/psis/population/database/data_sheet/2004/display.asp?step=3 [accessed July 2004]).

5. See Population Research Center (www.prcdc.org/summaries/pakistan/pakistan.html [last accessed June 27, 2004]).

6. Graham E. Fuller, "The Youth Factor: The New Demographics of the Middle East and Implications for U.S. Policy," Brookings Project on U.S. Policy Toward the Islamic World, Analysis Paper 3 (July 2003), p. 4.

7. Shahid Javed Burki, "Population as an Asset," *Dawn* (Karachi), July 31, 2001.

8. There are periodic suggestions that Pakistan might play a larger role in stabilizing the Persian Gulf, and at one time the Pakistan army did briefly station a

brigade in Saudi Arabia, under the command of the future army chief, Jehangir Karamat. In the 1980s, as the U.S. entered a new alliance with Pakistan, Francis Fukuyama proposed a Pakistani force for the Middle East and suggested that Washington should agree to protect Pakistan from the consequences of such a decision. See "The Security of Pakistan: A Trip Report," Rand Note N-1584-RC (Santa Monica, Calif.: September 1980), p. 4. The idea was raised again in 2003, but Pakistan countered by saying that its India front had to be stabilized before it could sends forces to Iraq. The Indian rejection of the role came as a relief to the Pakistanis, who feared domestic opposition to such a force.

9. Nasir Jalil, "Pakistan's Education—The First Decade," in *Education and the State: Fifty Years of Pakistan,* edited by Pervez Hoodbhoy (Oxford University Press, 1998), p. 42. For a careful overview of Pakistan's official textbooks and curricula from a liberal perspective, see A. H. Nayyar and Ahmad Salim, *The Subtle Subversion: The State of Curricula and Textbooks in Pakistan* (Islamabad: Sustainable Development Policy Institute, 2004), online at www.sdpi.org.

10. The ghost schools were often the product of a corrupt agreement between school authorities and teachers, whereby the teachers returned a percentage of their salary to the officials, who in turn never checked to see whether the teacher actually taught, or whether there was even a school.

11. Cited in Mahnaz Ispahani, "The Cauldron," *New Republic,* June 16, 2003, p. 31.

12. "Tawana Pakistan Working in 650 Girl Schools," *Dawn* (Karachi), January 20, 2004 (www.dawn.com/2004/01/20/nat24.htm [last accessed June 27, 2004]).

13. One such school, Forman Christian College (FCC), is the alma mater of President Musharraf, a few of his close civilian advisers, and two prime ministers, India's Inder K. Gujral and Pakistan's Zafarullah Khan Jamali. More than 139 years old, FCC was reopened by the Presbyterian Church, with an American principal, in 2003 but was immediately shut down by non-FCC students, notably the Islamist student wing of the Jama'at-i-Islami. The school has reopened under heavy police protection. Fasih Ahmed, "I Will Not Live in Fear," *Friday Times* (Lahore), April 11–17, 2003.

14. Hamid H. Kizilbash, "Teaching Teachers to Teach," in *Education and the State,* edited by Hoodbhoy, p. 104.

15. Ibid., pp. 115–16.

16. Shahid Kardar, "The Economics of Education," in *Education and the State,* edited by Hoodbhoy, p. 44.

17. As an example of excellence, the Punjab provincial educational department has undertaken careful studies of the achievements of its students and has documented these. See the publications of the National Education Management Information System, Islamabad, and the Punjab EMIS Centre, especially *Education in Punjab.*

18. Amir Rana, "Al-Qaeda Planned to Open Varsity," *Friday Times* (Lahore), April 11–17, 2003.

19. See Tariq Rahman, *Language, Ideology and Power* (Oxford University Press, 2002); and his "Tolerance and Militancy among Schoolchildren," *Dawn* (Karachi), February 23, 2003.

20. Rahman, "Tolerance."

21. Of the religious parties, only the JI has placed great stress on education, and it runs a chain of schools throughout Pakistan emphasizing the education of girls.

22. See Akhtar Hameed Khan, "Community-Based Schools and the Orangi Project," in *Education and the State,* edited by Hoodbhoy. Another important effort is the Citizens Foundation (TCF) founded in 1995, a nonprofit educational NGO that runs over a hundred primary and secondary schools throughout Pakistan. This is a drop in the bucket but indicates that there is an unmet need. See Mehvish Hussein, "First Chance," *Herald* (Karachi), April 2003.

23. For a major study by another Pakistani scholar, see K. K. Aziz, *The Murder of History: A Critique of History Textbooks Used in Pakistan* (Lahore: Vanguard Books, 1993). An Indian scholar who compared Pakistani and Indian textbooks came to the same conclusion, finding the Pakistani books marginally worse than the Indian ones. Swarna Rajagopalan, *State and Nation in South Asia* (Boulder, Colo.: Lynne Rienner, 2001), pp. 116–23.

24. Musharraf's minister of education, Zubaida Jalal, is a well-intentioned former secondary school teacher who "hopes" for incremental and gradual change, reform of the madaris, and "more" women's education, but she lacks administrative experience, a strategic view of Pakistan's educational problems, and most fundamentally, the resources to implement even the modest plans that she has drawn up with the assistance of an understaffed and inexperienced Ministry of Education.

25. Quoted in "Textbook Changes Overdue in India-Pak: Teaching Mutual Hate," *Milli Gazette,* September 1–15, 2002 (www.milligazette.com/Archives/01092002/0109200272.htm [last accessed June 27, 2004].

26. Hoodbhoy, *Education and the State,* p. 260.

27. UNESCO Education Database, http://portal.unesco.org/uis.

28. LUMS, which claims it is one of the top twenty Asian business schools, has recently received applications from five prospective students from India, but the Government of Pakistan has not been able to decide whether they should be granted student visas. Hameedullah Abid, "Indian Students Wait for Pakistani Visa decision," *Daily Times* (Lahore), August 16, 2003 (www.dailytimes.com.pk/default.asp?page=story_16-8-2003_pg7_32 [last accessed June 27, 2004]).

29. In another instance, in the 1980s, 120 students from all over Pakistan took a standardized five-hour test designed to test competence in physics, with a scholarship to MIT as the reward for the best students. Not one student passed the exam, and the results were suppressed by the educational authorities. Pervez Hoodbhoy, "Pakistani Universities," in *Education and the State,* edited by Hoodbhoy, p. 265.

30. Ibid.

31. For a lengthy interview with Dr. Rahman, see *Dawn* (Karachi), June 20, 2004 (http://dawn.com [accessed June 27, 2004].

32. Some of Pakistan's elite universities have had to appeal directly to the armed forces for assistance, as their training of army officers (in such fields as security policy) will go into even steeper decline in the next few years, and the army itself has no capacity to offer broadly based education in such fields.

33. This conversation took place shortly after the military was assigned to track down the ghost schools.

34. See further discussion in chapter 9. A major contract to improve Pakistan's primary schools given to a North Carolina company, RTI International, provided $60 million over a four- year period. RTI will lead an international consortium to improve policy, teacher training, literacy, and public-private partnerships. "RTI to Improve Education in Pakistan under USAID Grant," press release (www.rti.org/page.cfm?objectid=BF8B11E2-95CD-449F-8191E96718719003 [posted January 30, 2003].

35. Aileen Qaiser, "Reviving the Half-Dead Schools," *Dawn* (Karachi), March 22, 2004 (www.dawn.com/2004/03/22/fea.htm [last accessed June 27, 2004]).

36. Tariq Rahman, *Unpleasant Essays: Education and Politics in Pakistan* (Lahore: Vanguard Books, 2000), p. 19.

37. For an especially poignant comment by one of Pakistan's most erudite lawyer/scholars, see F. S. Aijazuddin, "The Cost of Ignorance," *Dawn* (Karachi), February 9, 2004.

38. Pakistan had over US$25 billion in foreign debt by the time Musharraf took over in 1999; in contrast to this profligacy, its foreign debt was just US$3 billion between 1947 and 1970, and the country was often cited as a model in its use of foreign developmental loans. At the time of Zia's death the figure stood at $13 billion, so ten years of democracy doubled Pakistan's debt, placing the country in a perilous economic position without much to show in terms of growth or development. All in all, between 1988 and 1999 Pakistan borrowed, and failed to repay, $13 billion. Owen Bennett-Jones, *Pakistan: Eye of the Storm* (Yale University Press, 2002), p. 232.

39. The differences are painfully visible when crossing from India to Pakistan. The latter's once-vaunted agricultural colleges and universities created in the 1950s and 1960s are in shambles, the agricultural extension systems barely operate, and salinity, water logging, and mismanagement characterize the vast irrigation system that dates back to the Mughals. Improving these is the objective of a major IMF loan.

40. Based on Pakistan Ministry of Finance figures submitted to the International Monetary Fund. See Khaliq Kiani, "Defence Outpaces Development Spending: Report," *Dawn* (Karachi), March 1, 2004 (www.dawn.com/2004/03/01/top1.htm [last accessed June 27, 2004]). Shortly afterward the government announced a 50,000-man *reduction* in the size of the army, largely through the elimination of personal aides to officers, the first such reduction in the history of Pakistan.

41. Numerous economists and political scientists have made this point. For a

recent summary and analysis of the argument, see M. Tariq Yousuf Khan and Komei Sasaki, "Roles of Public Capital in Pakistan's Economy: Productivity, Investment and Growth Analysis," *Review of Urban and Regional Development Studies* 13, no. 2 (2001): 143–45.

42. Institute of Developing Economies (IDE), Spot Survey, *Crisis of Statehood? Afghanistan and Pakistan* (Tokyo, 2002), p. 19.

43. Mahbub ul-Haq's key writings include *The Poverty Curtain* (Columbia University Press, 1976) and *First Things First* (Washington: World Bank, 1982). For a collection of his articles on Pakistan's economy, see *A National Agenda: Critical Choices for Pakistan's Future* (Islamabad: Mr. Books, 1993).

44. IDE, *Crisis of Statehood?* p. 19.

45. IDE, *Pakistan's Crisis, Political and Economic Analysis* (Tokyo, 2000), p. 10.

46. These and the following figures are drawn from the Pakistan Finance Ministry and the World Bank's *World Development Indicators* (Washington: World Bank, 2003).

47. For a current overview of Pakistan's economy, as presented by the government, see the Ministry of Finance website, "Economic Survey, 2003" (www.finance.gov.pk/).

48. See Transparency International Corruption Perceptions Index, 2003 (www.transparency.org/cpi/2003/cpi2003.en.html).

49. The Economist Intelligence Unit (EIU), *Pakistan Country Report, January 2004* (London, 2004), p. 5.

50. Ishrat Husein, president, State Bank of Pakistan, keynote address at the Conference on Islamization and the Pakistani Economy, Woodrow Wilson Center, Washington, January 27, 2004.

51. EIU, *Pakistan Country Report, January 2003* (London, 2003), p. 12.

52. According to Ministry of Finance officials interviewed in Washington, D.C., in 2004.

53. One noted journalist-economist, Sultan Ahmed, acknowledges Aziz's considerable accomplishments but offers a nuanced and comprehensive critique of Pakistan's fiscal and economic policies in "Focus on the Bright Side," *Dawn* (Karachi), April 22, 2004 (www.dawn.com/2004/04/22/op.htm [last accessed June 27, 2004]).

54. Keynote address at the Conference on Islamization and the Pakistani Economy, Woodrow Wilson Center, Washington, January 27, 2004.

55. John Lancaster, "Pakistan's Modern Feudal Lords," *Washington Post,* April 8, 2003, p. A29. For an entertaining study of feudal Pakistan, see Tehmina Durrani, *My Feudal Lord* (London: Corgi Books, 1994). Durrani was the eighth wife of Mustafa Khar, a feudal associate of Zulfiqar Ali Bhutto and a former governor of Punjab.

56. Stanley A. Kochanek, "Interest Groups and the New Economic Policy in Pakistan," paper presented at the Twenty-Sixth Annual Conference on South Asia at the University of Wisconsin, Madison, October 16–19, 1997, p. 14.

57. Ibid.

58. Stephen Philip Cohen, *The Pakistan Army,* 2nd ed. (Oxford University Press, 1998), p. 121.

59. Ayesha Siddiqa-Agha, "Power, Perks, Prestige and Privileges: Military's Economic Activities in Pakistan," paper presented at the International Conference on Soldiers as an Economic Actor, Jakarta, October 17–19, 2000 (www.bicc.de/budget/events/milbus/confpapers/siddiqa-agha.pdf).

60. Ibid. Also, the Frontier Works Organization, which was originally established for road building in the frontier areas and is now engaged in for-profit construction activity.

61. "Qabza, Military Style," *Herald* (Karachi), June 2003.

62. See, for example, projections through 2005 in Economist Intelligence Unit, *Pakistan Country Report, January 2004,* p. 6.

63. IDE, *Crisis of Statehood?* p. 19.

64. An unremarkable headline in a pro-government newspaper, *Nation,* was "Police Abetting in Increasing Poverty," followed by a story of police theft from needy individuals in Islamabad, August 12, 2003.

65. Pakistan is not eligible for the Department of State's Middle East Partnership Initiative (MEPI), a $130 million program designed to assist Arabs develop their political, economic, and social institutions and to facilitate their transition to democracy. There is also talk of a "Greater Middle East Initiative," which may include Pakistan, but even this has been reduced from earlier plans. Guy Dinmore and Roula Khalaf, "US Offers Scaled-Back Version of Mideast Initiative," *Financial Times,* April 26, 2004.

66. Sri Lanka and Bhutan qualify, Nepal comes close to qualifying, Bangladesh qualifies except for corruption, and India misses by one indicator. See Lael Brainard, Carol Graham, Nigel Purvis, Steven Radelet, and Gayle E. Smith, *The Other War: Global Poverty and the Millennium Challenge Account* (Brookings, 2003), pp. 64–65, 73.

67. The civilian government installed by the military after the 2002 elections was afraid to even debate the defense budget in parliament, claiming that the tradition of keeping defense expenditures immune to debate in parliament "was in vogue" all over the world. Statement of the Federal Information Minister, "Rollback of Nuclear Plan Ruled Out," *Dawn Weekly,* June 14, 2003 (www.dawn. com/2003/06/14/top5.htm [accessed on June 27, 2004]).

Chapter Eight

1. Ian Talbot, *Pakistan, A Modern History* (New York: St. Martin's Press, 1998), p. 372.

2. For wide-ranging American and Indian attempts to look at Pakistan's future, see National Intelligence Council, *Global Trends 2015: A Dialogue about the Future with Nongovernmental Experts* (Washington, 2002) (www.cia.gov /nic/pubs/index.htm); and International Centre for Peace Initiatives, Strategic Foresight Group, *The Future of Pakistan* (Mumbai, 2002). For a recent American

study of Pakistan's futures, see Teresita C. Schaffer, *Pakistan's Futures and U.S. Policy Options* (Washington: Center for Strategic and International Studies, March 2004).

3. For discussions about the methodology of prediction, see Craig L. Denny, "Long-Range Signposts: Assessing Their Role in Strategic Warning, Analysis, and Planning," *Futures Research Quarterly*, vol. 15, no. 2 (Summer 1999). Also Peter Schwartz, *The Art of the Long View* (New York: Doubleday Currency, 1991); Pierre Wack, *Scenarios: The Gentle Art of Reperceiving* (Harvard College, 1984); and Jay Ogilvy, "Future Studies and the Human Sciences: The Case for Normative Scenarios," *Futures Research Quarterly*, vol. 8, no. 3 (Fall 1993): pp. 41–46.

4. The motives of the nuclear evangelists and the Pakistan governments that allowed them to roam abroad were mixed. Some were Islamists, others may have sought personal profit, and for the government there was probably a strategic calculation—defying America by creating new nuclear weapons states.

5. Three important examples are the difficulty of initiating a real debate over Kashmir, over the Comprehensive Test-Ban Treaty, and recently over Pakistan's relations with Israel. Though the government may have wanted a debate to proceed in each case, its own propaganda organs, often in the form of captive think tanks, argued against a policy change and in favor of orthodoxy.

6. This has been much criticized by Islamists in Pakistan, who term the deportation of Pakistanis and non-Pakistanis illegal. For a summary, see Valentinas Mite, "Pakistan: Hunt for Taliban, Al-Qaeda Fugitives Find Little Local Support," Radio Free Europe/Radio Liberty, March 2003 (www.rferl.org/features/2003/03/12032003173300.asp [last accessed on June 27, 2004]).

7. A comprehensive account of the role of Pakistani scientists in spreading nuclear weapons technology is in David E. Sanger and William J. Broad, "From Rogue Nuclear Programs, Web of Trails Leads to Pakistan," *New York Times*, January 4, 2004, p. 1.

8. Electronic media are coming to dominate Pakistan, as the combined circulation of all newspapers in Pakistan in every region and every language is less than that of the sale of newspapers in New Delhi alone. For an overview by a distinguished Pakistani columnist, see Irfan Husain, "Switching Channels," *Dawn* (Karachi), January 24, 2004 (www.dawn.com/weekly/mazdak/20040124.htm [last accessed June 27, 2004]).

9. The Pakistan Institute for Legislative Development and Transparency (PILDAT), funded by a German foundation, produces quarterly reports of very high quality on the state of democracy in Pakistan (www.pildat.org/). For an excellent balance sheet of Musharraf's performance, see Mushahid Hussein, "Three Years After," *Nation*, October 12, 2003.

10. For an international and an American perspective on Pakistan's possible transition to democracy, see International Crisis Group, *Pakistan: Transition to Democracy*, Asia Report 40 (Islamabad/Brussels, October 2002); and National Democratic Institute for International Affairs, *The State of Democracy in Pakistan: A Survey Mission Report, June 4–14, 2002* (Washington, 2002).

11. In Stephen Philip Cohen, *The Pakistan Army* (University of California Press, 1985), pp. 107–08.

12. Mahnaz Ispahani, "The Cauldron," *New Republic,* June 16, 2003, p. 31.

13. And, one might add, a nuclear weapon. Bhutto started the Pakistani nuclear weapons program in part to counter the army's claim that it was responsible for the defense of the state. In the end the army gained control over the nuclear program and hanged Bhutto.

14. This scenario is discussed by India's Strategic Foresight Group, *The Future of Pakistan* (Mumbai: International Centre for Peace Initiatives, 2002).

15. Also, the recent shock to Saudi Arabia, as a result of the terror attacks of May 2003, make outside support and money even less likely than before.

16. Kavita Khory, "The Ideology of the Nation-State and Nationalism," in *State, Society and Democratic Change in Pakistan,* edited by Rasul Bakhsh Rais (Oxford University Press, 1997), p. 131.

17. This was one reason why the British commander in chief of the army decided to leave, and to move more quickly to the "Pakistanization" of the army than originally planned.

18. Especially if the restructuring of Pakistan left nuclear weapons in several provinces, for example, Sindh and Baluchistan, as well as in Punjab.

19. Three should be noted: in 1979 false rumors of an attack on the Grand Mosque in Jerusalem incited attacks on American facilities in Pakistan and reinforced the fear that Zia's still-insecure regime might be toppled; in 1988 Zia and several senior leaders were killed in a still-mysterious plane crash, which was followed by the restoration of civilian rule; and the 2001 attack on the World Trade Center and Pentagon transformed Pakistani foreign policy, revived the American alliance, brought in massive economic assistance, and strengthened General Musharraf.

20. Interview with Iskander Mirza, Lahore, 2003. He writes on political economy in the leading Urdu dailies, including *Nawa-i-Waqt, Jang,* and *Pakistan.* For a similar view, see the writings of Ishtiaq Ahmed, a Pakistani academic resident in Europe. For a straightforward argument in favor of a reformation, see Ahmed, "Waiting for an Islamic Revolution," *Daily Times* (Lahore), September 14, 2003 (www.dailytimes.com.pk/default.asp?page=story_14-9-2003_pg3_3 [last accessed June 27, 2004]); and his *The Concept of an Islamic State in Pakistan* (Lahore: Vanguard Books, 1991).

21. Husain Haqqani, a former member of the Jama'at-i-Islami student wing, sometimes government official, ambassador, and journalist, now resident in the United States. *Nation,* July 23, 2003.

Chapter Nine

1. For an overview of U.S.-Pakistan relations, see Dennis Kux, *The United States and Pakistan: Disenchanted Allies* (Johns Hopkins University Press, 2000); and for a review of the first twenty-five years, see Robert J. McMahon, *The Cold*

War on the Periphery: The United States, India and Pakistan (Columbia University Press, 1994).

2. In its dealings with the Islamic world, Pakistan did not claim to be such a model but emphasized its Islamic origins and its anti-Israeli credentials. The Arab states and Iran look down on Pakistan, and Afghans are too wary of Pakistan to regard it as a model. Furthermore, when Pakistan tried to advance itself into Central Asia, the Muslim states there rebuffed it.

3. For a perspective on this issue by one of the leading supporters of the mujahiddin, Representative Charlie Wilson, see George Crile, *Charlie Wilson's War* (New York: Atlantic Monthly Press, 2003).

4. Several contemporary U.S.-Pakistani dialogues reflect the perceptions, hopes, and concerns of both sides. See Leo E. Rose and Noor A. Husain, eds., *United States-Pakistan Relations* (Berkeley, Calif.: Institute of East Asian Studies, 1985); and Noor A. Husain and Leo E. Rose, eds., *Pakistan-U.S. Relations: Social, Political and Economic Factors* (Berkeley, Calif.: Institute of East Asian Studies, 1988).

5. In the twenty-one months since 9/11, the United States provided Pakistan with $600 million in cash, $350 million in military aid, and $3.6 billion in U.S. and IMF credits. It also allowed Pakistan to postpone payments of $12.5 billion in Pakistani debt to a U.S.-led consortium of aid donors. See Selig S. Harrison, "Bush Needs to Attach Strings to Pakistan Aid," *USA Today,* June 24, 2003, p. 13A. The Camp David package came to $3.2 billion in economic and military aid over a five-year period. Most American editorials that discussed the subject agreed with conditionality or "strings" on the aid. See Harrison, "Bush Needs to Attach Strings"; and "Pakistan's Reward—Half Now . . . ," *New York Post,* June 29, 2003, p. 24.

6. Officials note that there are no hard and fast criteria for being included on the list; Pakistan's support for various terrorist groups was evident in the 1990s, but it was not put on the list for fear of further strengthening the hands of extremists and weakening those of the civilian government of Nawaz Sharif.

7. As a leading British paper put it, behind the bravado lurks a worry that Washington's interest in its traditional regional ally is starting to wane. "Musharraf Stands Up and Hopes to Be Counted," *Financial Times,* June 19, 2003, p. 10.

8. During both periods, Washington was politically supportive of Pakistan, although it never endorsed Pakistan's Kashmir policy. The Ayub years saw massive economic assistance flow to Pakistan, with major investments in education and social infrastructure; the Zia years brought considerable economic aid, but much of that was siphoned off by defense and nuclear programs, and little or no pressure was applied to Zia to change domestic social and economic priorities.

9. Anatol Lieven, "Managing Pakistan," in *The State of Pakistan* (Washington: School of Advanced International Studies, South Asia Program, 2003), p. 19.

10. Lieven notes that Pakistan's nuclear deterrent is so dangerous that any use

of force to compel change in the Pakistani government, or to strip it of its nuclear assets, could lead to catastrophe: "In South Asia the melancholy fact is that whatever the ties of sentiment linking the US and India, it is the Pakistani state which is the vital ally in the war against terrorism, because the threats to the US (and to the US position in Afghanistan) stem from Pakistani society, which only a Pakistani state can control." Ibid., p. 25.

11. America did pursue a policy of imposing sanctions and ignoring Pakistan in response to its nuclear program. This brought no change in Pakistan's nuclear program, but it did cut off American contacts with the Pakistan military, removing an important channel of influence with Pakistan's key institution.

12. For the text of remarks at the June 24, 2003, summit, see http://164.109.48.86/topical/pol/conflict/03062402.htm; and for a postsummit briefing that elaborated American policy, see Background Briefing, http://164.109.48.86/topical/pol/conflict/03062403.htm (June 24, 2003).

13. These Kashmir-specific groups may have a wider reach; a group in northern Virginia was charged with being part of a Lashkar-e-Toiba cell and accused of plotting attacks on a "friendly country," that is, India. At least two of the eight arrested were Pakistani nationals, and others were born in Pakistan. "Two Pakistanis among Eight Indicted in US: Kashmir Freedom Struggle," *Dawn* (Karachi), June 28, 2003 (http://www.dawn.com/2003/06/28/top13.htm (last accessed June 27, 2004).

14. Interview with a Nazim, Lahore, August, 2002.

15. For an assessment of prospects, see Daniel Bogler, "Pakistan Plans Dollars 500m Return to Bond Market," *Financial Times* (London), June 20, 2003, p. 13.

16. For studies of Pakistan's economic plight, with a discussion of American policy options, see Teresita C. Schaffer, "Reviving Pakistan's Economy: A Report from the CSIS Project" (Washington: Center for Strategic and International Studies, January 2002).

17. One group of companies to focus on would be those already invested in South Asia: General Electric, Microsoft, and Boeing already have experience in the region, and their products might help break the trade barriers erected by India and Pakistan. This is also the case for other multinationals or companies possibly using a base in one South Asian state to sell their products in the other. Beyond this, there is some prospect of a pipeline going through Pakistan and linking India with Central Asian gas reserves.

18. Pakistan does not now qualify for the Millennium Challenge Account (MCA), but some social sectors may qualify, and in that case the MCA legislation, now being developed, should allow for assistance to these.

19. See "USAID/Pakistan Interim Strategic Plan, May 2003–September 2006" (Islamabad, Pakistan, May 2003).

20. An overview of the AID program is in ibid. See also "Fact Sheet: Additional U.S. Aid to Pakistan Proposed," White House Fact Sheet (http://usinfo.state.gov/regional/nea/sasia/text/0214pkaid.htm [February 13, 2002]).

21. For a discussion of such a process, originally published in 1985, see Stephen P. Cohen, *The Pakistan Army,* 2nd ed. (Oxford University Press, 1998), pp. 131–32.

22. For an extended discussion, see Stephen Philip Cohen, *India: Emerging Power* (Brookings, 2001), chap. 7, "India and Pakistan."

23. For a discussion, see Stephen Philip Cohen, "Track II and Unofficial India-Pakistan Diplomacy: Building Peace or Wasting Time?" forthcoming in *Essays in Honor of Dr. K. Subrahmanyam,* edited by P. R. Kumaraswamy (New Delhi: Sage, 2004).

24. There is no such objective assessment, but policy is driven by hunches and often uninformed guesses about what might be stabilizing or destabilizing, and certainly there has been no effort to coordinate American arms sales with allies and other states that are major arms suppliers to India and Pakistan.

25. Japan should be closely associated with America's policies in Pakistan, and it is remarkable that no recent administration has taken steps to do so. Japan is Pakistan's largest aid donor. It is very much concerned about the proliferation of nuclear weapons, and there are no cultural or political obstacles to a more important Japanese role in Pakistan—or, for that matter, India. Indeed, Japan should be associated with any attempt to sustain a peace process between India and Pakistan, and Japanese officials are very likely to join in, if asked.

26. American officials have been willing to intervene in South Asia at the last minute, in an effort to either avert an impending war or to end an ongoing one. Deputy Secretary of State Richard Armitage's visits to India and Pakistan during the 2002 buildup of forces on both sides made it easier for both to back down; in this regard, it resembled the intervention of Robert Gates, then deputy national security adviser and director during the 1990 crisis. In 1999 American diplomacy during the Kargil crisis may have provided the key to bringing that miniwar to a close. Inadvertently, it contributed to Nawaz Sharif's removal from power, although it certainly shored up U.S.-Indian relations.

27. Press Trust of India, June 28, 2003.

28. Nicholas Platt and Frank Wisner, *Chairmen's Report of the Independent Task Force on India and South Asia,* cosponsored by the Council on Foreign Relations and the Asia Society, New York, November 2003.

29. Powell claimed that his intervention was resposible for what was regarded as a successful summit. This claim was immediately dismissed by India's Ministry of External Affairs. If Powell was correct, he should not have trumpeted the summit outcome as a product of American diplomacy.

30. Ibid.

31. Robert Kaplan, "A Nuclear Yugoslavia," *New York Times Book Review,* November 3, 2002, p. 13. Kaplan was reviewing Mary Anne Weaver, *Pakistan: In the Shadow of Jihad and Afghanistan* (New York: Farrar, Straus and Giroux, 2002), and Owen Bennett-Jones, *Pakistan: Eye of the Storm* (Yale University Press, 2002).

32. When the government wants to, it can repress public statements of anger, as it did after several Pakistani soldiers were accidentally killed by American forces when both were operating along the Afghan-Pakistan border in August 2003.

33. See Khalid Hasan, "Pakistanis Bear Brunt of Immigration Swoop," *Daily Times* (Lahore), July 29, 2003 (http://www.dailytimes.com.pk/default.asp?page=story_29-7-2003_pg1_10 [last accessed June 27, 2004]). Shahzeb Jillani, "Big Trouble in Little Pakistan," BBC News, July 10, 2003. The most heartbreaking case was that of the family members of a Pakistani murdered shortly after 9/11. They were threatened with deportation because they no longer met "green card" requirements. Such events are widely reported in the Pakistani press, often with imaginative embellishments. Without an information program, Washington has no way of presenting its side of the story.

34. For a summary of Pakistani anger at the American war in Iraq, see Ayaz Amir, "The New Ugly American," *Dawn* (Karachi), April 23, 2004 (www.dawn.com/weekly/ayaz/20040423.htm [last accessed June 27, 2004]): "This may not be worse than Vietnam but it is more significant than Vietnam. In Vietnam the US was at its innocent best, convinced it was stemming the tide of communist expansion. . . . Iraq, by contrast, was mischief and unholy motives writ large on America's heart from the start. . . . Where Vietnam was about moral certainty, Iraq was about imperial hegemony, oil and Israel. . . . If I were younger, or possessed of more spirit, I would leave my desk and, without caring two hoots for Osama bin Laden, go and fight in Iraq."

INDEX

Abbasi, Zahir ul Islam, 108, 113, 293
Abdullah, Sheikh, 217
Adamjee family, 50
Administrative reform, 273, 316
Advani, L. K., 18
Afghanistan: and future of U.S.-Pakistan relations, 304, 323–24; and Islamization in Pakistan, 116, 190, 196; Pakistan aiding U.S. against Soviets in, 86, 105, 108, 121, 170, 302–03; U.S. success in reconstructing, 326; young Pakistanis as jihadis in, 235. *See also* Taliban
Aga Khan, 11, 222
Aga Khan Foundation, 11, 174, 180
Aga Khan University Hospital, 245
Ahle Hadith movement, 181
Ahmed, Akbar S., 23, 47
Ahmed, Qazi Hussein, 176, 177, 180, 244
Ahmediyyas, 11, 44, 93
Air University, 246
Alberuni, 18, 28, 34
Alcohol policy, 114, 170
Ali, Choudhary Rahmat, 26, 52
Aligarh Muslim University, 25, 48

All India Muslim League, 133
al Qaeda: background, 191–92, 196; influences on, 164; Jama'at links to, 179; Pakistan aiding U.S. against, 1, 304, 307; Pakistani support for, 70, 192; and Pakistan's image, 272. *See also* Afghanistan
Ambedkar, B. R., 30, 32, 121
Amin, Hafizullah, 218
Ansari, Shaukatullah, 31
Army, 97–130; alcohol policy, 114; American generation, 102–10; anti-U.S. sentiments, 105–06, 117, 144, 304, 326; under Ayub Khan, 71; under (Benazir) Bhutto, 146; under (Z. A.) Bhutto, 106–07, 138, 139–40; British generation, 99–102; civilian interactions, 110, 127, 278–79; and Code of Honor, 118; distrust of India, 101; foundations linked to, 261; and future of Pakistan, 128–30; history under Britain, 21, 22; and Islam, 71, 108, 110–20, 129, 172, 198–99; and Maoist military doctrine, 104; Military Academy graduates, 97–98;

369